Challenges of Active Ageing

Simonetta Manfredi • Lucy Vickers
Editors

Challenges of Active Ageing

Equality Law and the Workplace

Editors
Simonetta Manfredi
Oxford Brookes University
Oxford, United Kingdom

Lucy Vickers
Oxford Brookes University
Oxford, United Kingdom

ISBN 978-1-137-53249-7   ISBN 978-1-137-53251-0   (eBook)
DOI 10.1057/978-1-137-53251-0

Library of Congress Control Number: 2016943536

Printed on acid-free paper

This Palgrave Macmillan imprint is published by Springer Nature
The registered company is Macmillan Publishers Ltd. London.

*To our children
Wishing them happy ageing*

Foreword

When discrimination on the grounds of age was identified as a protected characteristic by Directive 2000/78, the EU Member States were forced to address some difficult issues. As a society, we are highly age-conscious. Newspapers print contributors' ages ('Mary, 56, says ...') but never a person's sexual orientation, colour or religion, unless of relevance to the story. A large number of rules are (still) age-dependent (individuals need to be 16 to marry, 17 to drive, 18 to vote and 65 to receive a state pension, 75 to get a free TV licence and 100 to receive a letter from the Queen). Some of these rules reflect the fact that with age comes experience, and a number of employment practices are premised on this basis. Long(er) service may bring with it greater pay and benefits and increasing protection by employment law. The prohibition against age discrimination has perturbed the established order.

Age is different for another reason. Age, unlike sex and race, is constantly changing. I am younger today than I will be tomorrow. Age is thus on a continuum—the old, by definition, were once young and the young hope to grow old. This raises the question whether older workers should be able to demand all the opportunities available to the young (and vice versa). Or is this the wrong question? Should age, in fact, not be a relevant factor in any decision-making? What happens when age and infirmity become aligned? Does an ageing workforce also raise issues of gender and disability discrimination? These issues come to a head over the vexed issue of retirement age. For some, individuals should be defined by what they are (their capacities) and not by how old they are (their chronological age). For others, a mandatory retirement age is necessary to ensure younger workers have access to opportunities enjoyed by their older colleagues.

The prohibition against age discrimination thus forces governments, employers and courts to engage with difficult questions of law and policy. Some of these questions raise familiar legal issues in a new context (who is the appropriate comparator in an age discrimination context, to what extent should employers be able to justify discrimination?). But others are more profound and require decision-makers to grapple with difficult issues concerning our ageing society. For example, how can the circle be squared between the desire of some individuals to carry on working later into their lives, the need of states for all individuals to continue working for more years to reduce the pressure on welfare budgets, and the need of young people to have employment and promotion opportunities.

This book considers some of these more challenging legal and social questions in the context of the active ageing agenda. With a strong focus on case studies and learning from a number of European jurisdictions, the book provides valuable insights as to how to manage the largest demographic challenge facing the European Union: active ageing.

Trinity College   Professor Catherine Barnard,
Cambridge, UK   October 2015

Preface

Demographic change and a changed legal environment have created multiple challenges for those seeking to manage age diversity in the workplace. Demographic and labour market trends showing an ageing population have led to a desire to encourage greater participation by older people in the workplace and to promote active ageing. This is in part a response to evidence of discrimination against older workers, but it is also a response to economic challenges caused by the economic costs of increased life expectancy. At the same time, concerns are often raised about high unemployment among young people, with consequent pressures on older workers to retire. This has been referred to as the 'double bind' in age discrimination[1].

In the midst of this complex policy area can be found the Equal Treatment Directive 2000/78/EC, adopted as part of enhanced equality protection in Europe. It introduced the prohibition on discrimination on the grounds of age in employment and training, which has been implemented across the EU. Despite the aim of addressing age discrimination, mandatory retirement, a practice which is clearly based on age, has continued in many Member States. This practice can be justified under the Directive if pursues it a legitimate aim of employment policy and is deemed to be a proportionate means to achieve that aim. The Court of

---

[1] F Hendrickx (2012) 'Age and European Employment Discrimination Law' in F Hendrickx (ed) *Active Ageing and Labour Law*, (Cambridge: Intersentia).

Justice of the European Union (CJEU) has accepted reasons such as the need to enable younger workers to have access to work and employment opportunities as valid. The acceptance of retirement practices within a framework that tackles age discrimination reflects very clearly the tension between the age equality agenda of the Directive and its implementation in practice in the context of retirement.

This book draws on papers presented at a two-day interdisciplinary symposium held by the Centre for Diversity Policy Research and Practice at Oxford Brookes University in June 2014 attended by lawyers, human resources practitioners, trade unionists, academics and policy makers. The book takes a multi-disciplinary approach to consider the double bind of age discrimination, and to explore and debate the challenges of the active ageing agenda for equality law and management practice.

Our aim is to enable readers to consider the implications of active ageing for the law, the workplace and working lives from a holistic perspective. To this end, the book brings together academics from different disciplines, including law, industrial relations, human resource management and occupational psychology, to explore and debate the challenges of the active ageing agenda for equality law and management practice. It also takes an innovative approach to multi-disciplinary research by including shorter contributions from practitioners from various fields such as law, human resource management, business, the public sector and trade unions in order to fully reflect how active ageing with reference to extending working lives is affecting practice.

Part I discusses the development of the law at the EU level. The CJEU jurisprudence on age discrimination in employment is examined by two authors. The first, Frank Hendrickx, focuses on how the CJEU is addressing the double bind in age discrimination law and its struggle to reconcile the interplay between individual and collective approaches to retirement and age equality. In the second chapter, Alvaro Oliveira addresses the fact that the case law of the CJEU is not yet settled and considers how the law may evolve in future.

Part II focuses on the issue of retirement. First, in Chapter 3, Jo Grady questions the narrative of a pension crisis, which is largely driving the extended working lives agenda, and asks whether an end to retirement is necessary on this basis. In Chapter 4, Simonetta Manfredi and Lucy Vickers then assess the approach to retirement in the UK and query whether the abolition of mandatory retirement can meet the challenges of the active ageing agenda.

Part III considers the challenges of extending work lives from a range of disciplinary perspectives. First, in Chapter 5, Jenny Julén Votinius examines the intersection between age and gender, using Sweden as an example. Second, in Chapter 6, Luciana Guaglianone and Fabio Ravelli use a case study of the Italian experience to consider the strategic challenges for the social partners in extending working lives. Third, in chapter 7, Nicola Johnson and Simonetta Manfredi consider the implications of extending working lives in the context of the National Health Service (NHS) in the UK. They highlight the importance of involving trade unions, NHS employers and health department representatives in striking a balance between the needs of the service and the needs of individual workers. Fourth, in Chapter 8, Alysia Blackham uses an innovative research methodology to develop and test a range of suggested options for legal and policy responses to facilitate extended working lives.

Part IV considers the perspectives of workers themselves and explores how the wishes of older workers may inform organisational responses to developing policies for extending working lives. In Chapter 9, Wendy Loretto explores the question of what older workers want from their later careers, while in Chapter 10 Karen Handley and Birgit den Outer use a narrative approach to identify the concerns and aspirations of older workers. In Chapter 11, Leena Pundt, Jugen Deller, Kenneth Shultz and Ulrike Fasbender then explore how differences in former professional jobs can affect post-retirement activities among retirees. These chapters identify a number of matters that may influence older workers when deciding whether to retire or continue work, matters such as levels of stress, desire for reduced or flexible work schedules and a desire in later career stages to 'reinvent' oneself.

Part V includes contributions from a range of senior practitioners and organisations bringing the perspective from practice to the discussion of the challenges of active ageing. The perspective of the Trade Union Congress (TUC) is presented by Sally Brett in Chapter 15, and that of a practising lawyer by Saphieh Ashtiany in Chapter 14. Three case studies are provided: Oxford City Council (Bob Price), the army (Vincent Connelly) and BMW (Martin Hall and Andrea Rathbone).

A number of common themes emerge from the multi-disciplinary approach taken in this collection. First is the heterogeneity of responses to retirement. Some will choose to retire as they wish to enjoy a more leisured and less pressured life, and they have the savings or pension income to do so. Others wish to remain at work, in some cases to maintain sufficient income in older age. It is clear from a number of contributions (Handley and den Outer and Pundt et al.) that decisions to retire can depend on a range of factors, and responses can be very varied. Some may choose 'cliff edge' retirement where they stop work completely in one go. Others wish to continue to be productive in alternative forms of work, and an increasing number of options are being developed to enable people to choose ways to continue to find fulfilment in some form of work: paid or unpaid; drawing on existing skills or 'reinventing' oneself into a new area of interest; reduced responsibility or expert consultancy work; flexible hours, part-time or fixed-term work. Both Loretto and Julén Votinius explore the ways in which gender may interact with these choices, introducing yet more variables into the responses to retirement. The variations are endless, and the examples explored in this collection demonstrate emphatically that retirement is not a 'one size fits all' concept. Indeed, the heterogeneity of people's needs and desires suggests that retirement is perhaps not a helpful concept at all. Instead, managing the working lives of older workers requires creative and imaginative responses, responses that are explored throughout the collection.

A second linked theme that emerges from the chapters is that of choice, or perhaps more accurately lack of choice. Since the introduction of age discrimination laws, the questions of whether and when to retire is often presented as a matter of personal choice. However, in reality this choice may be more apparent than real. First, it becomes clear from both Brett and Loretto that the choice to retire is not evenly available. For lower-paid older workers (particularly women), there may be less choice about when to retire than the rhetoric suggests. Thus, the choice is less about whether or how to engage in reinvention, but more one of economic necessity, under new pension provisions, to work. The notion of choice goes beyond different financial circumstances where only some can afford to retire. The idea of choice is also challenged because the sort of flexible work that many identify as ideal (unstressed, very flexible hours, pald, etc.) does not exist, or certainly does not exist in the quantities that would be needed to meet demand. Brett identifies increased work intensification as a barrier to continued working for those who can afford to retire; and Pundt et al. also identify how much retirees value additional time and flexibility. Concerns about work intensification and the need for greater flexibility also emerge from Johnson and Manfredi's research in the context of the NHS. These factors suggest that unless more flexible ways of working can be developed, even those workers faced with an economically unconstrained choice may well chose not to continue working into older age. Furthermore, although a move towards self-employment might be suggested as a way to increase flexibility of hours, this may prove illusory as a mechanism to meet the needs of older workers. Whist high-skill freelance consultancy work may be empowering in its flexibility, in practice self-employment often occurs in lower-skill work such as cleaning and caring, where the self-employment label can mask what is in reality very precarious work.

Even the narrative of a pension crisis can be understood in terms of choice. Often framed as a matter of the demographic time bomb, which can only be resolved by requiring workers to work for longer, in fact, the narrative of a crisis may be chosen. Grady suggests that this narrative is more a matter of political rhetoric than economic inevitability. This again points towards a response to the 'problems' of an ageing population based on creative management of older workers' careers, rather than forcing workers to work longer than they wish.

Another theme developed through the book is the need for solidarity between the generations. As Hendrickx notes, the CJEU and other areas of European social policy[2] refer to the concept of 'solidarity between generations'. He also notes that this involves a need to balance the interests of older workers against those of younger workers and may also require older workers to work for longer to maintain economic welfare. One benefit of the use of the concept of solidarity in this context is that it

---

[2] See Towards a Europe for All Ages—Promoting Prosperity and Intergenerational Solidarity (COM 1999) 221, Renewed Social Agenda: Opportunities, Access and Solidarity (COM 2008) 421 accessed on 21/9/2012 at http://eur-lex.europa.eu/LexUriServ.do?uri=COM:2008:0412; and C Barnard 2010 'Solidarity and the Commission's "Renewed Social Agenda"' in M Ross and Y Borgmann-Prebil (eds) *Promoting Solidarity in the European Union*, (Oxford OUP), 94–97.

can avoid the danger of setting one generation against another. To set older workers against younger workers, assuming that the disadvantage falls according to this binary divide, is clearly wrong once it is accepted that retirement is not a realistic choice for many people; it is not the case that older workers can be assumed to be advantaged and younger workers disadvantaged. This becomes even clearer once the interconnections between age and gender are taken into account (Julén Votinius), as well as due to the fact that many lower-paid workers are not retiring on generous pensions. The need for solidarity as a concept underpinning the social policy response to age equality is also demonstrated by the interconnectedness of the generations as illustrated by Loretto who notes that many older workers undertake care work for their children, providing child care so as to enable young parents to enter the workforce. Thus, instead of seeing retirement in terms of intergenerational rivalry, 'solidarity' allows for better relations between the generations to be maintained by taking into account the socio-economic impact of active ageing policies on individuals.

The final theme that is addressed across the collection is the more practical question of how to move towards meeting the challenges of the active ageing agenda in the workplace. To this end, Ashtiany, a lawyer with many years' experience in the area of anti-discrimination legislation, reflects on the challenges and benefits of adopting an Employer Justified Retirement Age (EJRA) in the context of the UK where mandatory retirement has been removed. She considers how in practice employers may retain an EJRA or adopt other practices including an increased use of fixed-term contracts in order to maintain a balance between older and younger employees, especially in senior posts where the turnover tends to be low. To illustrate some of these points, she uses the examples of a few higher education institutions which have chosen to adopt an EJRA. Other contributions from practice can serve as case studies for good practice, which could be adopted more widely, including adapting working time, work space, equipment, tasks and helping workers with the transition into new careers and job opportunities (Price, Hall and Rathbone, and Connelly). Such practices enable workers to remain productive at work for longer, with consequent economic benefits both to the individual worker who works for longer, as well as to the broader economy in terms of delayed pension provision. These practices also share the benefits with other workers too, such as where ergonomic design reduces the physical strains of jobs for all workers, or where flexible working can benefit parents, carers and older workers together.

Beyond the practical suggestions of how to develop creative and imaginative responses to managing age equality in individual workplaces, the collection also addresses the broader question of how to move things forward and who is best placed to do this. Local-level arrangements are explored in the case studies, but change will also be needed at other levels. For example, the social partners have potential to play a significant role in developing sectoral responses to the active ageing agenda, and the approach of social partners in Italy explored by Guaglianone and Ravelli may be compared to that in the UK, as outlined by Brett, where some significant work has been undertaken. In addition, national legislative and judicial responses are also needed. Oliveira and Hendrickx both point out that national legislatures have taken a fairly light touch approach to their interpretation of the EU level protection, with national practices which justify mandatory retirement in many workplaces tending to be upheld by the CJEU. While this is perhaps understandable as society adjusts to the new age equality framework, it may well be that a stronger standard setting role will be needed at national and EU level to tackle age discrimination in the workplace in future. The contributions from this collection taken together suggest that the way forward must involve all three levels if the active ageing agenda is to be met. Legislative protection is in place but needs clear enforcement at national and EU level. At the same time, at local level, good practice needs to be extended beyond the pockets where it already exists, and social partners may well have a key role to play here, to press for all employers to meet the standards of the best. This three-pronged approach involving the legal process, individual employers and the social partners may help to meet the economic and social challenges of managing age diversity in the work place in a way that benefits all.

Oxford Brookes University   Simonetta Manfredi
Oxford, UK   Lucy Vickers

Acknowledgements

This volume was conceived as a result of the conference held at the Centre for Diversity Policy Research and Practice, Oxford Brookes University, in June 2014. The editors are indebted to all who contributed to that conference by presenting papers, chairing panels or participating as attendees. Those contributions created energy to produce the current volume. We would like to thank Oxford Brookes University for both funding and hosting the conference, and Kate Clayton-Hathway and Emma Meats for their unstinting support in facilitating the two-day event and enabling it to take place. We are grateful to those who have contributed to this volume and whose work is represented in the chapters which follow. There are many silent contributors to a work such as this and we acknowledge the contributions of all who have shaped our thinking. We acknowledge too the enriching contribution of anonymous participants in studies referred to in respective chapters. We would particularly like to thank BMW, Oxford City Council, the TUC and the Ministry of Defence for allowing contributions which give insight into practices within their organizations. We are grateful too to Sarah Hayes who has proofread this volume and supported us in our editing of it.

Contents

Part I   The Development of the Law at EU Level   1

1   Setting the Scene: Development of the CJEU
    Jurisprudence on Age Discrimination in Employment   3
    Frank Hendrickx

2   A Freedom Under Supervision: The EU Court
    and Mandatory Retirement Age   29
    Alvaro Oliveira

Part II   The Issue of Retirement   47

3   Retirement and the Pension Crisis   49
    Jo Grady

4   The Challenges of Active Ageing in the UK:
    A Case Study of the Approach to Retirement in the UK   71
    Simonetta Manfredi and Lucy Vickers

Part III   The Challenges of Extending Working Lives   93

5   Intersectionality as a Tool for Analysing Age and Gender
    in Labour Law   95
    Jenny Julén Votinius

6   Active Ageing in Italy: Labour Market Perspectives
    and Access to Welfare   117
    Luciana Guaglianone and Fabio Ravelli

7   Older Workers in the Nursing and Midwifery
    Profession: Will They Stay or Will They Go?   139
    Nicola Johnson and Simonetta Manfredi

8   Emerging Options for Extending Working Lives:
    Results of a Delphi Study   159
    Alysia Blackham

Part IV   The Perspectives of Workers   185

9   Extended Working Lives: What Do Older Employees
    Want?   187
    Wendy Loretto

10 Work and Careers: Narratives from Knowledge
    Workers Aged 48–58   209
    Karen Handley and Birgit den Outer

11 Function, Flexibility, and Responsibility: Differences
    Between the Former Professional Job and
    Post-retirement Activities   231
    *Leena Pundt, Jürgen Deller, Kenneth S. Shultz,
    and Ulrike Fasbender*

Part V   The Perspective from Practice   255

12   BMW Group Case Study: Help a Workforce to Age   257
     Martin Hall and Andrea Rathbone

13   Managing Older Workers in a Local Authority:
     The Case of Oxford City Council   263
     Councillor Bob Price

14   What Scope for an Employer Justified Retirement Age?
     A View from Practice   269
     Saphieh Ashtiany

15   Extending Working Lives: A Trade Union Perspective   277
     Sally Brett

16   'Changing Step': The Transition from the Regular
     Army to Civilian Life and Work   287
     Vincent Connelly

Bibliography   299

Index   333

Notes on Contributors

Saphieh Ashtiany is Principal of Ashtiany Associates and Visiting Professorial Fellow, Queen Mary University of London.

Dr. Alysia Blackham is a senior lecturer at Melbourne Law School at the University of Melbourne in Australia, and an affiliated lecturer at the Faculty of Law, University of Cambridge in the UK.

Sally Brett is a Senior Policy Officer in the Economic and Social Affairs Department of the Trades Union Congress in the UK.

Vincent Connelly is Professor of Psychology and Programme Lead for Psychology at Oxford Brookes University. Vince has worked with the Army on developing various personnel policies in recent years.

Jürgen Deller is Professor of Business Psychology and speaker at the Institute for Strategic Human Resource Management Research and Development at Leuphana University of Lüneburg in Germany.

Dr. Ulrike Fasbender is Lecturer in Human Resources Management (Equality & Diversity) at Oxford Brookes University in the UK.

Dr. Jo Grady is Lecturer in HRM and Industrial Relations in the School of Management at the University of Leicester in the UK.

Luciana Guaglianone is Associate Professor of Labour Law and Industrial Relations at University of Brescia in Italy.

Martin Hall is a Senior Human Resources Manager at the BMW Group MINI Plant in Swindon.

Dr. Karen Handley is Reader in Work and Organisations in the Department of Business and Management at Oxford Brookes University.

Frank Hendrickx is Professor of Labour Law at the Law Faculty of the University of Leuven (Belgium).

Nicola Johnson is a qualified and Chartered HR professional who worked for 15 years in the NHS. She now works as an HR Partner at the University of Reading.

Wendy Loretto is Deputy Dean & Professor of Organisational Behaviour at the University of Edinburgh Business School.

Simonetta Manfredi is Professor of Equality and Diversity Management and Director of the Centre for Diversity Policy Research and Practice at Oxford Brookes University in the UK.

Álvaro Oliveira is Legal Officer at the European Commission, in the unit D1, dealing with Equality Legislation, within the Directorate-General for Justice and Consumers.

Birgit den Outer is a researcher at the ASKe Pedagogy Research Centre in the Department of Business and Management at Oxford Brookes University.

Bob Price is the Leader of Oxford City Council.

Leena Pundt is Professor of Human Resource Management at the SiB School of International Business, Hochschule Bremen University of Applied Sciences in Germany.

Dr. Fabio Ravelli is Lecturer of Labour Law at the University of Brescia.

Kenneth S. Shultz is Professor of Industrial/Organizational Psychology at the California State University in the USA.

Lucy Vickers is Professor of Law in the School of Law, and Assistant Director of the Centre for Diversity Policy Research and Practice at Oxford Brookes University.

Jenny Julén Votinius is Associate Professor of Private Law at the Faculty of Law, Lund University in Sweden.

List of Figures

Fig. 8.1   The Delphi process   163
Fig. 8.2   Relationship between Round 1 and Round 2 Delphi
             survey instruments   165
Fig. 9.1   Most popular reinvention activities among women   193
Fig. 9.2   Most popular reinvention activities among men   194
Fig. 9.3   Most popular reasons for reinvention among women   195
Fig. 9.4   Most popular reasons for reinvention among men   195
Fig. 9.5   Barriers to reinvention   196

List of Tables

Table 8.1   Response rate for Delphi method by survey round   165
Table 8.2   Results for Round 1 of the Delphi survey   173
Table 8.3   Results for reworded scenarios, Round 2 of the
             Delphi survey   175
Table 8.4   Results for repeated scenarios, Round 2 of the
             Delphi survey   176
Table 8.5   Results for new scenarios, Round 2 of the Delphi
             survey   177
Table 8.6   Results for age management implementation scenarios,
             Round 2 of the Delphi survey   178
Table 8.7   Results for information and guidance implementation
             scenarios, Round 2 of the Delphi survey   179
Table 9.1   Percentage of men and women in employment, by
             age, 2004–2013   191
Table 9.2   Retirement expectations of men and women
             (numbers and percentages)   192
Table 10.1   Demographic profile of participants   214
Table 10.2   Dominant narratives in our sample, shown alongside
             profile of participants   216
Table 11.1   Differences in activity before and after retirement   243
Table 11.2   Item statistics comparison, former and today   245
Table 11.3   Item wording and distributions for person-related
             variables   246

Table 11.4   Correlations among study variables   248
Table 11.5   Factor analysis of differences between activity
             before and after retirement and with person related
             variables   249
Table 11.6   Correlations of person-related variables with
             job-related factor scores   249

Part I

The Development of the Law at EU Level

1

Setting the Scene: Development of the CJEU Jurisprudence on Age Discrimination in Employment

Frank Hendrickx

1 Introduction

Age discrimination law in the European Union can be understood only if the case law of the Court of Justice of the European Union (CJEU) is taken into account. Since the adoption of Directive 2000/78, many cases relating to age have come up. However, a proper understanding of age discrimination case law is not self-evident. The case law of the CJEU is quite dynamic and shows a high degree of flexibility, which leaves it difficult to predict.

This chapter draws on earlier work on the CJEU's case law,[1] which proposed that there is a 'double bind' in age discrimination law. On the one hand, there is an aim to establish a strong principle of non-discrimination on the basis of age, based on a fundamental rights approach to the equal treatment principle. On the other hand, the role of age in our societies and the relationship between age and ageing and the labour market, as well as the traditions and compromises made in Member States' systems, are

---

[1] F Hendrickx (2012) 'Age and European employment discrimination law' in F. Hendrickx (ed.) *Active ageing and labour law. Contributions in honour of Professor Roger Blanpain* in *Social Europe Series 3* (Intersentia) 3–30.

© The Editor(s) (if applicable) and The Author(s) 2016
S. Manfredi, L. Vickers (eds.), *Challenges of Active Ageing*,
DOI 10.1057/978-1-137-53251-0_1

3

also reflected in age discrimination case law. This reflects the difficult balance which needs to be made between an individual and rights-based approach of age discrimination law on the one hand and a collective and interest-based approach on the other.[2]

The purpose of this contribution is to foster further discussion based on a case law analysis and to explore new avenues which may explain or frame the case law of the CJEU in age discrimination.

This dual aspect of age discrimination law may bring the analysis and discussion to two normative perspectives. The first could be derived from the CJEU's perspective offered in *Hörnfeldt*,[3] where the Court used a right to work approach and referred to an inclusion strategy for older workers on the labour market. In particular, the CJEU stated that 'the prohibition of discrimination on grounds of age set out in Directive 2000/78 must be read in the light of the right to engage in work recognised in Article 15(1) of the Charter of Fundamental Rights of the European Union'. It also referred to the participation of older workers in the labour force, and thus in economic, cultural and social life, and mentioned the potential and the quality of life of the workers concerned.[4] This normative perspective offered by the Court operates quite closely to a fundamental rights discourse which pays attention to the perspective of an individual worker potentially subject to discrimination.

The second normative perspective is related to perspectives offered in labour market and employment policy. Age discrimination case law cannot neglect the socio-economic role and impact of the age factor. The age structure of the European population is projected to change dramatically, as life expectancy at birth is anticipated to increase significantly in the next decades.[5] This will have an impact on not only the labour market in the strict sense, but will also involve issues of financing of social welfare systems and solidarity between generations in terms of both work and social benefits.

---

[2] Henrickx 'Age and European employment'.
[3] CJEU C-141/11 *Torsten Hörnfeldt v Posten Meddelande AB (Hörnfeldt')* judgment 5 July 2012.
[4] Para 37 *Hörnfeldt.*
[5] The 2012 ageing report, Economic and budgetary projections for the 27 EU Member States (2010–2060), *Joint Report prepared by the European Commission (DG ECFIN) and the Economic Policy Committee (AWG)*, European Economy 2, 2012, 25–26.

The 'active ageing' agenda of the European Union also shows this duality. For the European Union, 'active ageing means growing old in good health and as a full member of society, feeling more fulfilled in our jobs, more independent in our daily lives and more involved as citizens'.[6] This is a quite inclusive approach for older workers. However, it is clear that active ageing strategies also imply the reconciliation of various interests and perspectives—for example, in terms of intergenerational solidarity or in terms of the socio-economic impact of ageing.[7] The economic contribution to be made through ageing policies is also clear in the EU's actual definition: 'active ageing means helping people stay in charge of their own lives for as long as possible as they age and, where possible, to contribute to the economy and society'.[8]

The two mentioned normative perspectives are relevant and valid. However, the question is which deeper layers or ideas concerning age discrimination law are determining them. In this chapter, the characteristics and underlying considerations of the age discrimination concept are examined, as they influence the balancing between the two normative perspectives. They need to be made explicit, not only to understand the case law but also to provide and build up a proper synthesis. In short, it aims to take the 'double bind' one step further.

This chapter contains two main sections. Firstly, an overview and analysis of the case law will be provided, focusing on the cases which may be seen to be key in the development of age discrimination law in the EU and to be relevant to the normative perspectives mentioned above. Taking into account reasons of limitation, the selection is limited to retirement and pay cases. Secondly, and on the basis of this overview and analysis, a critical discussion will be undertaken whereby characteristics of the age discrimination concept and underlying considerations will be discovered. For the purposes of embedding the case law, a brief overview of the legislative provisions at EU level is provided.

---

[6] *Cf.* European Year for Active Ageing website: http://europa.eu/ey2012/ey2012main.jsp?catId=971 (accessed 11 September 2012).

[7] The WHO speaks about 'good economic reasons' referring to cost in pensions and health care as well as intergenerational solidarity: World Health Organization (April 2002) *Active Ageing: a Policy Framework, A contribution of the World Health Organization to the Second United Nations World Assembly on Ageing*, (Madrid, Spain) 17.

[8] See: http://ec.europa.eu/social/main.jsp?catId=1062&langId=en (accessed 15 June 2015).

2   European Age Discrimination Legislation

The principles governing age discrimination in Directive 2000/78[9] show a strong connection with the context and functioning of labour markets and employment policies, although the emphasis on the fundamental right to equal treatment is not overlooked.

2.1   The Preamble

The Preamble of Directive 2000/78 starts with a reference to fundamental rights but, subsequently, also refers to the employment policy objectives laid down in the European Union since the beginning of the twenty-first century.

It is provided, for example, that the European Union 'includes among its objectives the promotion of coordination between employment policies of the Member States. To this end, a new employment chapter was incorporated in the European Commission Treaty as a means of developing a coordinated European strategy for employment to promote a skilled, trained and adaptable workforce'.[10] The Preamble also states that 'the Employment Guidelines for 2000 … emphasize the need to pay particular attention to supporting older workers, in order to increase their participation in the labour force'.[11]

The Preamble also seems to nuance, or stress the specificity of, the prohibition of age discrimination. It is provided that 'the prohibition of age discrimination is an essential part of meeting the aims set out in the Employment Guidelines and encouraging diversity in the workforce. However, differences in treatment in connection with age may be justified under certain circumstances and therefore require specific provisions which may vary in accordance with the situation in Member States. It is therefore essential to distinguish between differences in treatment which are justified, in particular by legitimate employment policy,

---

[9] Council Directive 2000/78/EC of 27 November 2000, establishing a general framework for equal treatment in employment and occupation, *OJ* 2 December 2000, no. L 303.

[10] Directive 2000/78, Preamble 7.

[11] Directive 2000/78, Preamble 8.

labour market and vocational training objectives, and discrimination which must be prohibited.'[12]

The difficult tensions underlying this approach to age discrimination are reinforced by the connection between the right to equal treatment and the right to work. This connection is supported by the Preamble of Directive 2000/78: 'Employment and occupation are key elements in guaranteeing equal opportunities for all and contribute strongly to the full participation of citizens in economic, cultural and social life and to realising their potential.'[13]

2.2   The Provisions

The special position of age discrimination is also reflected in the provisions of Directive 2000/78.

According to Article 1 of Directive 2000/78, its purpose is to lay down a general framework for combating discrimination on the grounds of religion or belief, disability, age or sexual orientation as regards employment and occupation, with a view to putting into effect in the Member States the principle of equal treatment.[14]

The directive provides protection against direct and indirect discrimination. According to the directive, there is *direct* discrimination where one person in a comparable situation is, has been or would be treated less favourably than another. There is *indirect* discrimination where an apparently neutral provision, criterion or practice would put persons having a particular religion or belief, a particular disability, a particular age or a particular sexual orientation at a particular disadvantage in comparison to other persons.

The directive provides that differential treatment can be justified and will not amount to discrimination, under certain conditions. In principle, the possibility for differential treatment is wider for indirect than for direct discrimination. In case of *indirect* discrimination, a 'provision, criterion or practice is objectively justified by a legitimate aim and the means of achieving that aim are appropriate and necessary'.[15] In case of direct

---

[12] Directive 2000/78, Preamble 25.
[13] Directive 2000/78, Preamble 9.
[14] *Cf.* article 1 Directive 2000/78.
[15] Article 1, b, i Directive 2000/78.

discrimination, the directive accepts that specific 'occupational requirements' may form an exception to the principle of non-discrimination. According to the directive, Member States may provide that a difference of treatment which is based on a characteristic related to any of the grounds referred to in the directive shall not constitute discrimination where, by reason of the nature of the particular occupational activities concerned or of the context in which they are carried out, such a characteristic constitutes a genuine and determining occupational requirement, provided that the objective is legitimate and the requirement is proportionate.[16] This concerns normally a strict category of exceptions.

However, *direct* age discrimination is subject to an exceptional regime. For direct discrimination based on age, an additional and wider possibility for justification is provided in Article 6 of Directive 2000/78. Member states may provide that differences of treatment on grounds of age shall not constitute discrimination if, within the context of national law, they are objectively and reasonably justified by a legitimate aim, including legitimate employment policy, labour market and vocational training objectives, and if the means of achieving that aim are appropriate and necessary.[17] This standard of justification is not as restrictive as the one provided for the other grounds of discrimination protected in the directive. On the contrary, the standard of justification of *direct* age discrimination resembles the directive's standard of *indirect* discrimination. In other words, age discrimination can be objectively and reasonably justified by a legitimate aim, and if the means of achieving that aim are appropriate and necessary.

Article 6 of the directive explicitly gives a particular category of justification which may be accepted under this regime. It provides that differences of treatment may include, among others:

(a) the setting of special conditions on access to employment and vocational training, employment and occupation, including dismissal and remuneration conditions, for young people, older workers and persons with caring responsibilities in order to promote their vocational integration or ensure their protection;

---

[16] Article 4, 1 Directive 2000/78.
[17] Article 6, 1 Directive 2000/78.

(b) the fixing of minimum conditions of age, professional experience or seniority in service for access to employment or to certain advantages linked to employment;
(c) the fixing of a maximum age for recruitment which is based on the training requirements of the post in question or the need for a reasonable period of employment before retirement.

It is thus clear that the directive accommodates a wish to take into account a wide range of considerations concerning the functioning of external or internal labour markets. However, due to the fact that it concerns an example of justification grounds, the exceptions under Article 6 of the directive would not necessarily need to remain limited to that. This open character of the justification of *direct* age discrimination shows the special position of, and the apparent need for flexibility in the approach of, age discrimination in the directive.

Furthermore, Directive 2000/78 states that Member States may provide that the fixing for occupational social security schemes of ages for admission or entitlement to retirement or invalidity benefits, including the fixing under those schemes of different ages for employees or groups or categories of employees, and the use, in the context of such schemes, of age criteria in actuarial calculations, does not constitute discrimination on the grounds of age, provided this does not result in discrimination on the grounds of sex.[18]

3 Development Through the Case Law of the CJEU

3.1 A Strong Principle in *Mangold*

The CJEU was invited to set the tone for the approach of age discrimination in the case of *Mangold*.[19] The Court dealt with German legislation allowing for the conclusion of fixed-term contracts of

---

[18] Article 6, 2 Directive 2000/78.
[19] CJEU C-144/04 *Werner Mangold v Rüdiger Helm* ('*Mangold*') judgment 22 November 2005.

employment once a worker reached the age of 52. The assessment was made under Article 6 of Directive 2000/78, as labour market and employment policy considerations were underlying the national measure. The Court pointed out that the purpose of the legislation was to promote the vocational integration of unemployed older workers, in so far as they encounter considerable difficulties in finding work, which was to be accepted as a legitimate objective.[20] In the light of this, the Court accepted those policy aims as justifying 'objectively and reasonably' a difference of treatment on grounds of age.[21] The Court, furthermore, found that 'the member states unarguably enjoy broad discretion in their choice of the measures capable of attaining their objectives in the field of social and employment policy'.[22] However, the Court followed that the application of the national legislation concerned led to a situation in which all workers who reached the age of 52, without distinction, whether or not they were unemployed before the contract was concluded and whatever the duration of any period of unemployment, could lawfully be offered fixed-term contracts of employment repetitively. The Court reasoned that a significant body of workers, determined solely on the basis of age, was in danger, during a substantial part of its members' working life, of being excluded from the benefit of stable employment, which constitutes a major element in the protection of workers.[23] The Court thus stressed the importance of the non-discrimination principle and the perspective of the individual rights of the disadvantaged older workers. The Member States' defence under Article 6 of Directive 2000/78 was thus severely scrutinised. Moreover, the Court held that the principle of non-discrimination on grounds of age must be regarded as a general principle of Union law.[24]

---

[20] Para. 60, *Mangold.*
[21] Para. 61, *Mangold.*
[22] Para. 63, *Mangold.*
[23] Para. 64, *Mangold.*
[24] Para. 75, *Mangold.*

3.2 Approval of Compulsory Retirement In *Palacios*

When the case of *Palacios de la Villa*[25] was submitted to the CJEU, the question was how the Court would deal with a system of compulsory retirement, which was the major point of discussion.

When Mr. Palacios de la Villa, an organisational manager, reached the age of 65, he was informed by his employer that his contract had terminated automatically, as he had reached the compulsory retirement age provided for in the applicable collective agreement. Mr. Palacios de la Villa had completed the periods of employment necessary to draw a retirement pension under the social security scheme amounting to 100% of his contribution. He nevertheless claimed that his right not to be discriminated against on the ground of age was violated.

The CJEU took the opportunity to nuance Recital 14 of Directive 2000/78, and held that it merely states that the directive does not affect the competence of the Member States to determine a retirement age, but does not in any way preclude the application of the directive to national measures governing the conditions for termination of employment contracts where the retirement age, thus established, has been reached.[26] However, looking at the justification of the compulsory retirement system, in the light of Article 6 of Directive 2000/78, the Court found that Spain introduced it against an economic background characterised by high unemployment in order to create opportunities for job seekers.[27] The Court considered this to be a legitimate aim of public interest as 'employment policy and labour market trends are among the objectives expressly laid down in the first subparagraph of Article 6(1) of Directive 2000/78'.[28] The Court then had to assess whether the measure was appropriate and necessary. It referred to a, until then, perhaps underestimated line in the *Mangold* decision,[29] namely that the Member States and, where appropriate, the social partners at national level, enjoy broad

---

[25] CJEU Félix *Palacios de la Villa v Cortefiel Servicios SA* judgment 16 October 2007.

[26] Para. 44, *Palacios.*

[27] Para. 58, *Palacios.*

[28] Para. 64, *Palacios.*

[29] Para. 63, *Mangold.*

discretion in their choice not only to pursue a particular aim in the field of social and employment policy, but also in the definition of measures capable of achieving it.[30] Taking into account this national margin of discretion, the Court did not find a violation of the prohibition of discrimination based on age.

The impressions after the *Palacios* case remain mixed. The approval by the Court of a compulsory retirement system could be seen in relation to the retirement benefits that Mr. Palacios de la Villa received and which were understood to be decent. That would imply an approach of balancing the work-related rights of younger workers with the rights of older people related to social security benefits. It would anyway nuance the judgment, as only a system of compulsory retirement would be approved for workers who are able to obtain a decent income and standard of living after retirement.[31] However, it would seem that this is not the Court's approach, or at least, not completely.

3.3   A Cold Shower? *Rosenbladt*

After *Palacios*, the question remained whether the CJEU would scrutinise deeply rooted compulsory retirement systems. The widespread mechanism, often supported by legislation or collective agreements in European states, whereby the employment contract is terminated upon the employee reaching the applicable retirement age, came under attack. The Court was invited to assess the German law on this point in the case of *Rosenbladt*.[32]

Mrs. Rosenbladt, a part-time employee of a cleaning firm, intended to continue working beyond 65, but her contract ended when she reached the retirement age. Her statutory old age pension amounted to 228.26 euro net per month. Dealing with the justification under Article 6 of Directive 2000/78, the CJEU reminded the parties that, in Europe, this

---

[30] Para. 68, *Palacios*.
[31] This point is elaborated in M. Schlachter (2011) 'Mandatory Retirement and Age Discrimination under EU Law', *Int J Comp LLIR* Vol. 27(3), 290.
[32] CJEU 12 October 2010, C-45/09, *Rosenbladt v Oellerking Gebäudereinigungsges.*

practice is 'widely used in employment relationships'.[33] It was seen to be 'based on the balance to be struck between political, economic, social, demographic and/or budgetary considerations and the choice to be made between prolonging people's working lives or, conversely, providing for early retirement'.[34]

The German government defended the system of automatic termination of the employment contract on the basis of the notion of sharing employment between the generations. It also pointed at the advantage of not requiring employers to dismiss employees on the ground that they are no longer capable of working, which may be humiliating for those who have reached an advanced age.[35]

The Court accepted these objectives, such as the better distribution of work between the generations, as legitimate and found that the system was not unreasonable 'in the context of national employment policy'.[36] The Court's proposition that Mrs. Rosenbladt, after automatic termination of her employment contract, could not be refused new employment either by her former employer or another, on a ground related to her age, remains solely theoretical.[37]

3.4   Right to Work? *Georgiev, Fuchs* and *Hörnfeldt*

In three subsequent cases, compulsory retirement systems were found to be in conformity with the age discrimination provisions, although the individual perspective of the (old aged) workers came under the CJEU's scrutiny more explicitly. It allowed the Court to use language proper to a right to work approach.

In *Georgiev*,[38] the Bulgarian system of compulsory retirement of university professors at the age of 68 was challenged. The Court held that

---

[33] *Pro memorie*, the governments of Denmark, Italy, Ireland and the United Kingdom intervened in the case.

[34] Para. 44, *Rosenbladt*.

[35] Para. 43, *Rosenbladt*.

[36] Para. 51 and 62, *Rosenbladt*.

[37] Para. 74, *Rosenbladt*.

[38] CJEU Joint cases C-250/09 and C-268/09, *Vasil Ivanov Georgiev v Tehnicheski universitet—Sofia, filial Plovdiv* judgment 18 November 2010.

the encouragement of recruitment in higher education by means of the offer of professorial posts to younger people may constitute a legitimate aim.[39] A mix of different generations of teaching staff and researchers was seen to promote an exchange of experiences and innovation, and thereby the development of the quality of teaching and research at universities.[40] In the light of Article 6 of Directive 2000/78, the Court tried to strike a balance between various concerns. As university professors were offered the opportunity to work until 68, the measure could not be regarded, in the view of the Court, as unduly prejudicing the legitimate claims of older workers. The Court also pointed at the financial compensation by way of a retirement pension.[41] The relation with employment termination inspired by concerns about individual performance was already anticipated by the Court in *Rosenbladt*, where it was held that employment termination should not be 'humiliating for those who have reached an advanced age'.[42] The employee's individual perspective obviously has a legal foundation, as it is related to the right to work.

In *Fuchs*,[43] the CJEU was confronted with a German system of compulsory retirement of civil servants, in particular of prosecutors, at the age at which they were entitled to a full pension. There was a possibility that the persons concerned could continue to work, if it was in the interests of the service, until the maximum age of 68. The Court allowed this system, with various considerations, such as the aim of establishing a balanced age structure in order to encourage the recruitment and promotion of young people, or to improve personnel management and thereby prevent possible disputes concerning employees' fitness to work beyond a certain age.[44]

A right to work approach became very explicit in the *Hörnfeldt* case. It concerned the Swedish '67-year rule' under which employees enjoy an unconditional right to work until the last day of the month of their 67th birthday, on which date the employment contract may be terminated

---

[39] Para. 45, *Georgiev.*
[40] Para. 46, *Georgiev.*
[41] Para. 54, *Georgiev.*
[42] *Cf.* para. 43, *Rosenbladt.*
[43] CJEU, C-159/10 and C-160/10, *Gerard Fuchs en Peter Köhler v Land Hessen* judgment 21 July 2011.
[44] Para. 50 and 68, *Fuchs.*

without dismissal. The Court took into account the various arguments of the Swedish government, including the avoidance of situations which are humiliating for workers and the opportunities for young people to enter the labour market, but also the establishment of a right (and not an obligation) to work until the age of 67.[45] The Court was sensitive to the connection between the non-discrimination principle and the right to work and stated that the prohibition of discrimination on grounds of age must be read in the light of the right to engage in work recognised in the Charter of Fundamental Rights of the European Union. Nevertheless, the Court ruled in favour of the automatic termination of the employment contracts, reasoning that account must be taken both of the hardship that it may cause to the persons concerned and of the benefits derived from it by society in general and by the individuals who make up society.[46]

3.5 Age-Related Pay or Employment Rights and Seniority: *Kücükdeveci* and *Hennigs*

After the introduction of Directive 2000/78, the expectation grew that age-related pay structures, such as 'wage classifications', as found in various collective bargaining systems in Europe, would be challenged before the Court. Likewise, other age-related working conditions and employment rights were expected to come under the Court's review. A problematic issue would be the widespread use of seniority-related pay, about which the Court had been able to make a series of rulings before in the context of gender discrimination.[47]

The question is whether seniority-related pay amounts to direct or indirect discrimination based on age. Furthermore, there is question of whether it can be justified in the light of Article 6 of Directive 2000/78.

---

[45] CJEU, C-141/11, *Torsten Hörnfeldt v Posten Meddelande AB*, para. 26 judgment 5 July 2012.
[46] Para. 38, *Hörnfeldt*.
[47] Cf. CJEU C-109/88 *Handels- og Kontorfunktionærernes Forbund I Danmark v Dansk Arbejdsgiverforening, acting on behalf of Danfoss* ('*Danfoss*') judgment 17 October 1989; CJEU C-184/89 *Helga Nimz v Freie und Hansestadt Hamburg* ('*Nimz*') judgment 7 February 1991; C-127/92 *Dr. Pamela Mary Enderby v Frenchay Health Authority and Secretary of State for Health* ('*Enderby*') judgment 27 October 1993; CJEU C-17/05 *B F Cadman v Health & Safety Executive* ('*Cadman*') judgment 3 October 2006.

The Court's principle of *Cadman*,[48] formulated in the gender discrimination context, still stands. The Court held that, as a general rule, recourse to the criterion of length of service is appropriate to attain the legitimate objective of rewarding experience acquired which enables the worker to perform his duties better. The employer does not have to establish specifically that recourse to that criterion is appropriate to attain that objective as regards a particular job, unless the worker provides evidence capable of raising serious doubts in that regard.

This case law seems to be transplanted to the age discrimination field. In the *Kücükdeveci* case,[49] the Court referred to the principle of non-discrimination on grounds of age as a general principle of Union law and its protection as a fundamental right.[50] But in *Hennigs*,[51] the *Cadman* approach became clear. Assessing age-related wage classifications, the Court took the seniority rule seriously and found that taking account of the employees' professional experience must in principle be regarded as 'objectively and reasonably' justifying a difference of treatment on grounds of age.[52] Nevertheless, the fact that the German collective bargaining provisions under scrutiny related to age instead of seniority made them inappropriate and unacceptable under the age discrimination provisions.

4   Discussion

The overall outlook of the age discrimination case law of the CJEU is mixed. The Court does not neglect an individual rights perspective of age discrimination, but the public interest dimension may ultimately take precedence. In *Mangold*, the Court held that the principle of non-discrimination on grounds of age is to be regarded as a general principle

---

[48] *Cadman.*

[49] *Cf.* C W G Rayer (2010) note on 'European Court of Justice, 19 January 2010, C-555/07', *ELLJ* Vol. 1 (2), 264–268; D Schiek, (2010) 'Constitutional principles and horizontal effect: *Kücükdeveci* revisited', *ELLJ* Vol. 1(2), 368–379.

[50] CJEU, C-555/07 *Seda Kücükdeveci v Swedex GmbH & Co. KG*, para. 22 judgment 19 January 2010.

[51] CJEU C-297/10 and 298/10, *Sabine Hennigs v Eisenbahn-Bundesamt & Land Berlin v Alexander Mai* ('Hennigs') judgment 8 September 2011.

[52] Para. 72 *Hennigs.*

of Union law. It therefore stressed the importance of the general principle. But in subsequent cases, such as *Palacios* and *Rosenbladt*, the Court showed itself to be equally concerned with the exceptions, giving broad leeway to Member States to justify deviations from the general principle. The Court also seems to take a different view depending on whether a case concerns compulsory retirement or pay. In contrast with compulsory retirement, age-related pay structures cannot count on mercy by the Court. Seniority pay schemes, though, are in principle approved by the Court.

The complexity of the age discrimination issue is undeniable. However, some characteristics of age discrimination law, or considerations underlying the concept, could be selected to explain and facilitate an understanding of the case law of the CJEU. In addition to being explanatory, the characteristics identified may together form a platform from which the complexities can be unravelled, and so provide a basis on which to found a correct understanding. They could at least provide avenues for further debate.

4.1   The Relative Importance of Age Discrimination Law

A first area of debate is concerned with the concept and importance of age discrimination. Should age not be as equally protected as other grounds of discrimination?[53] Age discrimination seems to be only 'relatively' important. This is due to the fact that 'age' seems to have a specific position in anti-discrimination law.[54] It may be argued that, compared to other grounds, such as race or sex, age represents a more dynamic factor. In sex discrimination law, different sexes can be compared, but people will, except for transsexualism, remain in the same sex category during their whole life. In age discrimination, most of the time young versus old age are compared, but most people will transfer from young age to old age during the course of their lives. This life-cycle argument may

---

[53] For a negative answer: E Howard (2006) 'The case for a considered hierarchy of discrimination ground in EU law', *MJ* Vol. 13(4), 445–470.

[54] M Sargeant (2006) *Age Discrimination in Employment*, (Aldershot, Gower) 4; J. Macnicol (2006) *Age discrimination: an historical and contemporary analysis*, (Cambridge, Cambridge University Press) 24–25.

imply that the disadvantages incurred by a person at a certain age may be compensated with advantages at another age of this same person.[55] On this ground, it may be argued that it is not unfair for older people to make room for younger people on the labour market when the first group has had its turn, chance or opportunity.[56] Furthermore, compared to other grounds of discrimination, such as race or sex, the age factor is often viewed as more neutral, or as less suspicious. A suspicious ground of discrimination is one which is considered to have no link with someone's ability to contribute to society.[57] Furthermore, there is the context of ageing and employment policy, referred to above, with which the issue of age discrimination is closely connected.

The 'double bind' mentioned above seems to give age discrimination a special position in European Union anti-discrimination law. Age is a factor which is widely used and 'deeply rooted' in the industrial relations traditions and social welfare systems of European states. This is clearly taken into account in both the European legislation (Directive 2000/78) as well as in the case law of the CJEU. It might look as if age would be more neutral than other grounds of discrimination, but that impression should be countered, as equality law may precisely have to do away with historical, social and political choices and cultural attitudes. Age factors on the labour market are often based on false presumptions and stereotypes.[58]

4.2   The Subsidiarity and Proportionality of Age Discrimination Law

According to Article 5 of the EU Treaty, the use of Union competences is governed by the principle of subsidiarity and proportionality.[59] This could play a role in debating the age discrimination provisions under

---

[55] M H S Gijzen (2006) *Selected Issues in Equal Treatment Law: A multi-layered comparison of European English and Dutch law*, (Antwerp, Intersentia) 436.

[56] *Cf.* S Fredman in S Spencer (2003) *Age as an equality issue*, (Oxford, Hart Publishing) 47.

[57] M Bell and L Waddington (2003) 'Reflecting on Inequalities in European Equality Law', *E.L.Rev.* Vol. 28(3), 359.

[58] Cf. K Riach (2007)' 'Othering' older worker identity in recruitment', *Human Relations*, Vol. 60(11), 1719.

[59] Further elaborated in Protocol No 2 on the application of the principles of subsidiarity and proportionality, *OJ* C83, Vol. 53, 30 March 2010.

Directive 2000/78. The potential issue with the EU's mandate in this field has been signalled by O'Cinneide[60] when referring to the Advocate General's Opinion in *Palacios*: '*it would... be very problematic to have this Sword of Damocles hanging over all national provisions laying down retirement ages, especially as retirement ages are closely linked with areas like social and employment policies where the primary powers remain with the Member States*'.[61] Read together with the employment policy exception provided for in Article 6 of Directive 2000/78, it can be interpreted to mean that the European Union was not intending to interfere too much with the Member States' own labour market policies. Put otherwise, in this respect, age discrimination provisions should be 'proportionate' to their impact on national systems; and, therefore, major policy choices should lie with Member States. While this respect for national policy choices must be recognised, it cannot be decisive in determining outcomes. The EU's respect for national Member State employment policies is also visible in the set-up of the EU's competences under the TFEU's Employment Title. There, the EU coordinates through recommendations and guidelines, while Member States remain fully competent in their national employment policies. Nevertheless, this respect for Member State autonomy is clearly only relative and not unconditional, and leaves an uncertain and ambiguous outlook. The same ambiguity can be seen with regard to age discrimination. Directive 2000/78 promotes a non-discrimination principle on the ground of age, but it does not aim to interfere too much in Member States' labour market policies and social welfare systems. Preamble 25 of Directive 2000/78 proposes 'to distinguish between differences in treatment which are justified, in particular by legitimate employment policy, labour market and vocational training objectives, and discrimination which must be prohibited'. It is furthermore provided that what the directive does is without prejudice to retirement ages or social benefits.[62] In sum, it may explain why the Court accepted 'that the complexity of the policy issues which surround the difficult issue of retirement age justified granting states a relatively

---

[60] C O'Cinneide (2009–2010) 'Age discrimination and the European Court of Justice: EU equality law comes of age', *R.A.E.—L.E.A.* 2009–2010/2, 265.

[61] Para. 63–65 *Palacios*.

[62] See Preambles 13 and 14 of Directive 2000/78.

wide margin of discretion in this area of employment policy'.[63] It seems to be a reason for a cautious approach, where the Court realises that age discrimination law does not only grant individual rights but is also concerned with 'political, economic, social, demographic and/or budgetary considerations'.[64]

The context of this discussion may also explain why the Court is, as it seems to be, strict with regard to *internal* labour market justifications. In most instances, for example in the Preamble of Directive 2000/78, the references concern broad employment policy goals and *external* labour market concerns. The margin between what is internal and what is external may not be wide. In the *Wolf* case,[65] the Court took the fire service's *internal* labour market considerations into account, not only including manpower planning but also questions of budgetary sustainability. In *Age Concern*,[66] however, the Court was rather clear in pointing at the fact that 'by their public interest nature, those legitimate aims are distinguishable from purely individual reasons particular to the employer's situation, such as cost reduction or improving competitiveness', although, according to the Court, 'it cannot be ruled out that a national rule may recognise, in the pursuit of those legitimate aims, a certain degree of flexibility for employers.'[67] In putting limits to the Member States' margin of discretion, but at the same time showing the ambiguity of this approach, the Court added that 'mere generalizations concerning the capacity of a specific measure to contribute to employment policy, labour market or vocational training objectives are not enough'.[68] It is, in sum, doubtful whether the Court would approve an age discrimination claim which would put welfare systems under severe pressure.[69]

---

[63] C O'Cinneide 266.

[64] Para. 28, *Hörnfeldt*.

[65] CJEU C-229/08, *Colin Wolf v. Stadt Frankfurt am Main* judgment 12 January 2010.

[66] CJEU 5 March 2009, C-388/07, *The Incorporated Trustees of the National Council on Ageing (Age Concern England) v. Secretary of State for Business, Enterprise and Regulatory Reform* ('*Age Concern*').

[67] Para. 46 *Age Concern*.

[68] Para. 51 *Age Concern*.

[69] *Cf.* W Swinnen (2010) 'The economic perspective in the reasoning of the ECJ in age discrimination cases', *ELLJ* Vol. 1(2) 261.

4.3   The Interdisciplinarity of Age Discrimination law

The case law of the CJEU has proven that age discrimination law is an interdisciplinary subject. In its case law, the Court has proven that implicit theories are used to understand how the labour market works or labour relations function. They have not been made explicit, as the Court uses them rather as assumptions. If explicit references were to be made, then most likely economical, sociological or psychological sciences would become involved.

One theory of the labour market is that flexibility in labour law may increase job opportunities. Making employment protection less rigid would help outsiders and vulnerable groups to get more easily into employment,[70] and rigid rules may thus contribute to the segmentation of the labour market.[71] This is sometimes known as 'easy out, easy in'. This theory is, self-evidently, more nuanced and, already in 2004, the OECD reported that strategies to introduce temporary jobs would not necessarily lead to more stable jobs and may clash with other employment policy goals such as investment in skills and development.[72] The discussion seems to give a useful context for the CJEU's approach in *Mangold*, where it responded to the underlying assumptions of the German legislation which aimed to make employment for older workers more flexible. The Court seemed, at least implicitly, to be aware of the fact that unilateral flexibility measures did not necessarily work in practice and would lead to older workers being 'excluded from the benefit of stable employment which constitutes a major element in the protection of workers'.[73]

---

[70] T Andersen, J H Haahr, M E Hansen and M Holm-Pedersen (2008) *Job mobility in the European Union: optimising its social and economic benefits*, Final Report, prepared under contract to the European Commission, Directorate General for Employment, Social Affairs and Equal Opportunities in response to tender no. (VT/2006/043 (Danish Technological Institute, Centre Policy and Business Analysis) 5–6.

[71] S Nickell and R Layard (1999) 'Labor market institutions and economic performance' in O Ashenfelter and D Card (eds.), *Handbook of labor economics*, III (Amsterdam, Elsevier Science) 3062–3063; P Skedinger (2010) *Employment protection legislation. Evolution, effects, winners and losers* (Cheltenham, Edward Elgar), 57–65.

[72] OECD, Employment Outlook, 2004, 98–99 (available at www.oecd.org).

[73] Para. 64, *Mangold*.

In *Palacios*, the Court seemed to believe in the assumed labour market hypothesis that if older workers leave the labour market, there will be more opportunities for younger people to enter the labour market. In *Rosenbladt*, the Court assumed that a dismissal on the ground that the worker is no longer capable of working may be humiliating for those who have reached an advanced age. Just like in the case of an 'easy in' labour market policy, it could be argued that these assumptions may be true in certain circumstances but cannot be unilaterally applied or accepted. Nevertheless, contrary to its rejection of unilateral measures in *Mangold*, the Court saw the assumptions to be valid. This raises questions with regard to the role of normative or explicit assumptions stemming from other scientific disciplines in age discrimination case law. It shows at least that the age discrimination discussion should engage in a dialogue with those disciplines.

The CJEU has also expressed itself on the relation between age and pay. With the case of *Hennigs*,[74] the Court refers back to seniority pay. Referring to its case law on sex discrimination, the Court accepts the relationship between length of service and performance. It can be agreed with the Court that rewarding experience may be a legitimate tool of personnel and wage policy. However, the question is whether this is to be seen 'as a general rule'.[75] That question, again, does not appear to be of a purely legal nature. Pay structures oriented to economic value may also produce undesired results, but high wages for older workers work to their disadvantage.[76] Self-evidently, the Court accepts that seniority pay is only conditionally valid. It may be that circumstances point to a different relationship.

4.4   The Dilemmatic Nature of Age Discrimination Law

This case law shows that age discrimination law is full of dilemmas. It proposes an individual rights approach to the non-discrimination principle versus a collective and public interest approach, whereby labour market

---

[74] CJEU C-297/10 and 298/10, *Hennigs* 8 September 2011.

[75] Para. 72, *Hennigs*.

[76] *Cf.* H Meenan (2007) 'Age discrimination in the EU and the framework directive' in M. Sargeant (ed.), *The law on age discrimination*, (Alphen aan den Rijn, Kluwer Law International) 26.

and societal considerations are taken into account. In various cases, it also requires the weighing of rights and interests of older workers against those of younger workers, implying the age discrimination principle to be an instrument of intergenerational solidarity.

The problem is that the dilemmatic nature of age discrimination causes the CJEU to engage in a balancing exercise. In weighing rights and interests, the Court makes wide use of the proportionality principle but, in reality, it is conducting a balancing act. In most cases, the test of justifying age discrimination with a legitimate aim is rather easily passed. The crucial assessment lies in the test of appropriateness and reasonableness of the measure—in other words, the proportionality of a measure. In applying this proportionality test, the Court's outcome becomes quite unpredictable.

An example is the compulsory retirement case of *Palacios*, in which the Court states that it is necessary to 'find the right balance between the different interests involved'.[77] The Court then reasons that 'it does not appear unreasonable for the authorities of a Member State to take the view that a measure such as that at issue in the main proceedings may be appropriate and necessary'.[78] The Court states that 'the measure cannot be regarded as unduly prejudicing the legitimate claims of workers subject to compulsory retirement.'[79] It is reasonable to propose that in balancing these arguments, the Court could go either way. Put otherwise, the outcome of the case could have been different with the same arguments at stake. It would therefore seem that the Court uses a reasonableness standard which may be distinct from a means–ends test proper to proportionality reasoning.[80]

4.5   The Collective Nature of Age Discrimination Law

The case law may lead to an opinion that a more collectively oriented view on age discrimination law takes precedence. An individual right of older workers not to be retired (compared with termination based on

---

[77] Para. 71, *Palacios*.

[78] Para. 72, *Palacios*.

[79] Para 73, *Palacios*.

[80] T I Harbo (March 2010) 'The Function of the Proportionality Principle in EU Law', *European Law Journal*, Vol. 16(2) 185.

retirement age) is not yet actually granted. The right to work of older people remains only a right to continue to work after the collectively determined retirement age. It could be questioned whether this fits into an 'active ageing' context in which societies are increasingly challenged to keep older workers on the labour market. Furthermore, it shows that the collective interest concept needs further development and that a view is needed on how this collective interest relates to the individual right.[81]

However, it is clear that the discussion is more complex than that. In another view of the case law, the Court is confronted with the opposition of two equally weighted rights: the right to work of both older and younger workers. In the retirement cases, the Court pays attention to the benefits for younger workers and calls on the concept of intergenerational solidarity. Similarly, the European Union declared the year 2012 as the European year for active ageing *and* 'solidarity between generations'. However, solidarity may go in different directions. It may imply the promotion of job opportunities for younger people, sometimes at the expense of the older person's security of employment. It may also require older workers to stay motivated and to remain in the labour market in order to ensure the sustainability of economies, social welfare and social security systems.

4.6   The Economic Paradigm of Age Discrimination Law

A final aspect of the debate concerns what could be called the 'economic paradigm' behind age discrimination law. Age discrimination law is connected with how work should be viewed, appreciated or rewarded. The fact that the CJEU is rather lenient towards automatic or default retirement rules and is willing to accept seniority pay schemes seems to stand in contrast with the rather progressive case law that the Court developed in sex/gender discrimination law.

It should be considered what norms would come into place when automatic retirement or default retirement schemes were to be removed. As employment protection will not be able to rely on an age-related

---

[81] *Cf.* L Rodgers (2011) 'Labour law and the "public interest": discrimination and beyond', *ELLJ* Vol. 2 (4) 302–322.

criterion, the right to remain in employment will most likely be associated with business-related norms relating to productivity, which are often determined by, or are within the control of, the employer.[82] The question is, of course, why employment protection of older workers could not rest on dismissal law, a legal context which also applies to younger workers. If this is taken from the perspective of the productive older worker, it is indeed 'unconvincing that someone should suddenly lack the capacity to do a cleaning job just as a result of reaching the age of 65'.[83] The question is, however, at what exact point a cleaner will no longer provide additional value to an employer compared with his or her salary. Many restructuring scenarios in Europe show that it is not assured that this will be after the age of 65. In many cases, people become 'too expensive' earlier in their career stage. Abolishing compulsory retirement might decrease *de facto* a worker's employment protection well before the retirement age is reached[84] as the 'implicit' or 'psychological' contract could change. Nevertheless, early retirement schemes already prove at this moment that even with a compulsory retirement rule, there is a problem with older workers' job security.

This issue shows that compulsory retirement and seniority pay are connected. The alternative for seniority is obviously performance-related pay. Pay would then rely more on the economic strength or capacity of the worker. Although this may seem objective, it might also lead to a more subjective, meritocratic view of work. This model could pose the danger of imposing a new pay gap. The assessment of qualities and performances of older workers might be controlled by stereotypes rather than objective standards. If performance criteria are applied generally or 'neutrally' across different age groups, older workers might have to fit the mould of the average, less aged, worker and suffer from particular disadvantages. At the other end of the spectrum, rewarding seniority is seen as a

---

[82] S Manfredi & L Vickers (2013) 'Meeting the challenges of active ageing in the workplace: is the abolition of retirement the answer?', *ELLJ* Vol. 4, 271: 'left to be determined by market forces and by employer's business needs'.

[83] M Schlachter (2011) 'Mandatory retirement and age discrimination under EU law', *Int. J. Comp. L.L. and I.R.* Vol. 27(3) 294.

[84] A Numhauser-Henning (2013) 'Labour law in a greying labour market—in need of a reconceptualisation of work and pension norms', *ELLJ* Vol. 4 94.

positive discrimination strategy, to the extent that it 'can help to increase the social status and associated well-being of older employees' and put emphasis on 'socioemotional skills' in measuring performance.[85]

5   Conclusions

In age discrimination law, it seems almost inevitable to take into account the context of an ageing society and the impact of age policies on employment and labour markets. The European cases give the impression that the European Court has been more involved in construing exceptions to the principle of equal treatment related to age instead of construing and polishing the principle in terms of individual protection. Anyhow, it affirms the special position of age in anti-discrimination law.

The 'double bind' mentioned at the outset is clearly present, but is complex and does not seem to be purely 'binary'. It may well be that the CJEU's case law may be seen as developing on the basis of a case-by-case approach and not necessarily through a deliberate strategy. However, in making the sum of the cases, various characteristics and considerations can be pointed out which are underlying or proper to the concept of age discrimination and which, either implicitly or explicitly, influence the case law.

The CJEU can be understood as being in favour of a 'traditional' view of the labour market, including consensus-building, strong replacement ratios of older workers by younger workers and the avoidance of the negative side effects of performance measurement. The question is whether another view is possible or desirable. It would make sense to use the active ageing policy concept in this context. If the discourse is pointing towards 'activation' of older workers and longer working lives, the question is how this can be reconciled with compulsory retirement schemes. It seems contradictory to place a duty on the workforce to work longer without giving them the right to work longer. Furthermore, seniority pay drives older workers out of the market and puts high pressure on their employment security.

---

[85] R Fischer (2008) 'Rewarding seniority: exploring cultural and organisational predictors of seniority allocations', *The Journal of Social Psychology* Vol. 148(2) 181; See also: B Barrett & M Sargeant (2015) 'Working in the UK without a default retirement age: health, safety, and the oldest workers', *ILJ* Vol. 44(1) 97.

Thus, a shift to new paradigms seems inevitable. A longer and continuing active career also challenges the role of non-discrimination provisions. The age factor challenges discrimination law from more than one perspective. The 'ageing' context is prevalent in age discrimination, but a too one-sided view of the age discrimination problem must be avoided and the position of both young and mid-aged workers should be taken into account. Even in the old age debate, the young age perspective seems inevitably involved, since intergenerational solidarity is an undeniable issue. Furthermore, policies directed at 'working longer' require updated views on careers. If careers are extended, then employability of workers should also mean that work can be adapted according to age. Only in this manner can active ageing policies be seen as inclusion strategies. This may also require new duties requiring employers to contribute to 'workable' work training opportunities, work-life balance and end-career scenarios. The concept of reasonable accommodation may also receive a meaning in age discrimination law as a translation of a wider notion of accommodation in workplaces. All this makes clear that the age discrimination debate is multi-perspective and requires responses which cannot be other than holistic.

2

A Freedom Under Supervision: The EU Court and Mandatory Retirement Age

Alvaro Oliveira

This chapter analyses how the Court of Justice of the European Union ('the EU Court', or 'the Court')[1] deals with national provisions on mandatory retirement age.[2]

At first sight, the case law of the Court in this respect is simple and clear. The Court regularly recognises that Member States have broad discretion in defining their employment and social policies. This applies also to national provisions defining a compulsory retirement age when

---

[1] PhD in law from the European University Institute, Florence. Currently working for an EU institution. I would like to thank Professors Simonetta Manfredi and Lucy Vickers for their precious assistance in the drafting of this paper, as well as Declan O'Dempsey and Alison Fraser for fruitful discussions. The opinions expressed are those of the author only.

[2] For an interesting analysis see Elaine Dewhurst (2013) 'Intergenerational Balance, Mandatory Retirement and Age Discrimination in Europe: How can the ECJ better support National Courts in Finding a Balance between the Generations?', *Common Market Law Review* 50(5), 1333. For an analysis of the European case law in connection with the Seldon case in the UK, see Lucy Vickers and Simonetta Manfredi (2013) 'Age Equality and Retirement: Squaring the Circle', *Industrial Law Journal* 42(1), 61.

© The Editor(s) (if applicable) and The Author(s) 2016
S. Manfredi, L. Vickers (eds.), *Challenges of Active Ageing*,
DOI 10.1057/978-1-137-53251-0_2

they are analysed under Directive 2000/78,[3] which prohibits discrimination based on age. In most cases, the EU Court has either ruled such provisions compatible with the Directive, or has opened the way for national courts to do so.

Out of the nine judgments on this matter, the Court has struck down rules on mandatory retirement age in only two cases, and they concerned very specific situations. The position of the Court is based fundamentally on the argument that 'solidarity between generations' in the distribution of employment opportunities makes a compulsory retirement age acceptable as social and employment policy. Even if it is open to question and has been criticised both by economists and lawyers, this position seems to be quite clear.

However, looked at more closely, the case law of the Court is more complex. There are reasons indicating that the Court's stance is not absolute and may evolve over time. On the one hand, there are the exceptions to the general trend: that is, the judgments in which the Court, after very careful consideration, rejects the compatibility of national provisions with the Directive. On the other hand, even in cases where the Court does not find the national provisions incompatible with Directive 2000/78, it often scrutinises their justification very closely. Both aspects indicate that the Court is not willing to give Member States complete discretion. The Court seems ready to use its powers fully to interpret EU law in order to protect the equal treatment objective of the Directive.

This chapter starts by making a summary of the case law of the Court in this area and by explaining why it is more complex than first meets the eye. Judgments striking down and allowing national rules will be considered. Subsequently, it is suggested that the Court's case law will probably be under pressure to evolve with time, notably in line with the reality of an ageing population and the evolution of national employment policies confronting it.

The previous chapter of this book provides a detailed explanation of the provisions of Directive 2000/78 on age discrimination, and it will not be repeated here. However, the analysis in this chapter is somewhat different from that of the previous chapter, which examines the relationship between

---

[3] Council Directive 2000/78/EC of 27 November 2000 establishing a general framework for equal treatment in employment and occupation, (2000) OJ L303/16 ('Directive on Equality in Employment'). This Directive also prohibits discrimination based on religion or belief, disability and sexual orientation.

the individual/fundamental rights and the collective/social policy aspects of the age discrimination law (the 'double bind') in the context of the case law on age discrimination in general. In contrast, the present chapter focuses on cases dealing with mandatory retirement age only and, in particular, on analysing how much the Court has been, and may in future be, willing to scrutinise national provisions on mandatory retirement age.

1   The Judgments on Mandatory Retirement Age

Out of all of the judgments of the Court which concern the two anti-discrimination Directives,[4] the majority concern discrimination based on age (from a total of 46 judgments, 30 concern age). In turn, amongst the judgments concerning age discrimination, nine alone concern provisions on a mandatory retirement age. This probably makes this substantive issue the most frequently examined by the Court in discrimination cases, other than sex.

We may compare the outcome of age discrimination cases from the perspective of the plaintiff, or of the employees directly affected by the national provisions in question. There is a remarkable difference between cases concerning mandatory retirement age, on the one hand, and all other age discrimination cases, on the other hand. In cases on mandatory retirement age the worker concerned has hardly ever won. As mentioned above, out of the nine cases the Court has struck down national provisions only twice,[5] whilst accepting or opening the door for accepting such provisions in seven cases.[6] However, the situation is different

[4] Council Directive 2000/43/EC of 29 June 2000 on Racial Equality and Council Directive 2000/78/EC of 27 November 2000 on Equality in Employment.

[5] Cases C-447/09 *Reinhard Prigge and Others v. Deutsche Lufthansa AG 2011 I-08003*, judgment of 13 September 2011 ('*Prigge*'); and C-286/12 *Commission v. Hungary*, judgment of 6 November 2012 ('*Commission v. Hungary*').

[6] Cases C-411/05 *Palacios de la Villa v. Cortefiel Servicios SA* [2007] ECR I 8531 ('*Palacios de la Villa*'); C-388/07 *The Queen, on the application of The Incorporated Trustees of the National Council for Ageing (Age Concern England) v. Secretary of State for Business, Enterprise and Regulatory Reform* [2009] ECR I 1569 ('*Age Concern*'); C-341/08 *Domnica Petersen v. Berufungsausschuss für Zahnärzte für den Bezirk Westfalen-Lippe* [2010] ECR I-47 ('*Petersen*'); C-45/09 *Gisela Rosenbladt v. Oellerking Gebäudereinigungsges* judgment of 12 October 2010 (*Rosenbladt*); C-250/09 & C-268/09 *Vasil Ivanov Georgiev v. Tehnicheski universitet - Sofia, filial Plovdiv* [2010] ECR I-11869 ('*Georgiev*');

concerning other age discrimination cases. Out of the 21 other cases, the outcome was favourable to the concerned employee in seven cases[7] and unfavourable in ten cases,[8] while it was mixed or left open for the national court to decide in four cases[9]—which is a more balanced result. Therefore, at first glance at least, the case law of the Court appears to be quite clear on mandatory retirement age. One might gain the impression that the Court is quite flexible with Member States and is normally ready to accept national provisions on mandatory retirement age. In principle, a claim of discrimination in this respect seems doomed to failure.

However, such an impression would be misleading. On the contrary, it is argued that there are reasons to believe that the Court may be more demanding in the future in its analysis of the justification for national rules. This argument is based on two main factors. The first is internal to the Court: important aspects of its case law show that it is ready to intervene when it deems it to be necessary. The second is external to the Court and

---

C-159/10 & 160/10 *Gerhard Fuchs (C-159/10) and Peter Köhler (C-160/10) v. Land Hessen* judgment of 21 July 2011 ('*Fuchs and Kohler*'); and C-141/11 *Torsten Hörnfeldt v. Posten Meddelande AB* judgment of 5 July 2012 ('*Hörnfeldt*').

[7] Cases: C-144/04 *Werner Mangold v. Rüdiger Helm* [2005] I-09981 ('*Mangold*'); C-88/08 *David Hütter v. Technische Universität Graz* [2009] I-05325; C-555/07 *Seda Kücükdeveci v. Swedex GmbH & Co. KG* [2010] I-00365; C-499/08 *Ingeniørforeningen i Danmark v. Region Syddanmark* judgment 12 October 2010 ('*Andersen*'); C-546/11 *Dansk Jurist- og Økonomforbund, acting on behalf of Erik Toftgaard v. Indenrigs-og Sundhedsministeriet* Judgment of the Court 26 September 2013 (*Toftgaard*); C-416/13 *Mario Vital Pérez v. Ayuntamiento de Oviedo* judgment of the court 13 November 2014; and C-530/13 *Leopold Schmitzer v. Bundesministerin für Inneres* judgment of the court 11 November 2014.

[8] Case C-427/06 *Birgit Bartsch v. Bosch und Siemens Hausgeräte (BSH) Altersfürsorge GmbH [2008] I-07245*, C-229/08 *Colin Wolf v. Stadt Frankfurt am Main [2010] I-00001* ('*Wolf*'); C-246/09 *Susanne Bulicke v. Deutsche Büro Service GmbH [2010] I-07003*; C-297/10 & C-298/10 *Sabine Hennigs (C-297/10) v. Eisenbahn-Bundesamt and Land Berlin (C-298/10) v. Alexander Mai [2011] I-07965;* C-415/10 Galina Meister v. Speech Design Carrier Systems GmbH Judgment of the court (second chamber) 19 April 2012; C-132/11 *Tyrolean Airways Tiroler Luftfahrt Gesellschaft mbH v. Betriebsrat Bord der Tyrolean Airways Tiroler Luftfahrt Gesellschaft mbH* Judgment of 7 June 2012; C-476/11 HK Danmark, acting on behalf of Glennie Kristensen, v. Experian A/S,intervener: Beskæftigelsesministeriet judgment of 26 September 2013; C-429/12 *Siegfried Pohl v. ÖBB Infrastruktur AG judgment of 16 January 2014;* C-529/13 *Siegfried Pohl v. ÖBB Infrastruktur AG* judgment of 21 January 2015;and C-262/14 *Sindicatul Cadrelor Militare Disponibilizate în rezervă și în retragere (SCMD) v. Ministerul Finanțelor Publice judgment of 21 May 2015.*

[9] Cases: C-152/11*Johann Odar v. Baxter Deutschland GmbH reported 6 December 2012; Thomas Specht (C-501/12), Jens Schombera (C-502/12), Alexander Wieland (C-503/12), Uwe Schönefeld (C-504/12), Antje Wilke (C-505/12) and Gerd Schini (C-506/12) v. Land Berlin and Rena Schmeel (C-540/12) and Ralf Schuster (C-541/12) v. Bundesrepublik Deutschland* reported 19 June 2014; C-417/13, *ÖBB Personenverkehr AG v. Gotthard Starjakob reported 28 January 2015;* and C-515/13 *Ingeniørforeningen i Danmark v. Tekniq* reported 26 February 2015 ('Landin').

relates to the evolution of the underlying reality of the ageing population and national social policies to address it. Arguably, their likely evolution in the future runs in favour of a more strict scrutiny of the justification of provisions on mandatory retirement age. This section examines the internal factor: the case law of the Court.

1.1   Judgments Rejecting National Measures

Naturally, the two exceptions to the general trend, the two judgments in which the Court rejected the compatibility of national provisions with the Directive, show very clearly the extent to which the Court is willing to closely examine national provisions.

The case **Commission v. Hungary** is a particularly important example in this regard. [10] The case related to the rules of the new Hungarian Basic Law. They provided for the sudden lowering of the compulsory retirement age of judges, prosecutors and notaries from 70 years to 62 years within a period of one year. The Court considered the measure not necessary for one of the alleged aims: the equalisation of retirement ages within the civil service, since there was no evidence that a less abrupt transition could not achieve such an aim. Moreover, while the rule in question was applied within the period of one year only, the government had enacted legislation raising the retirement age for civil servants in general from 62 years to 65 years over a period of eight years.[11]

The Hungarian government also claimed that dismissing older judges allowed it to establish a more balanced age structure in the judicial system and to facilitate the access of young lawyers. The Court had accepted this basic argument before. It had considered that establishing an age structure balancing young and older workers in order, *inter alia*, to encourage the recruitment and promotion of young people, to improve personnel

---

[10]Case C-286/12, *Commission v. Hungary* (see fn 5). See Uladzislau Belavusau (2013) 'On age discrimination and beating dead dogs: Commission v. Hungary', *Common Market Law Review* 1145; also Tamás Gyulavári and Nikolett Hős (2013) 'Retirement of Hungarian Judges, Age Discrimination and Judicial Independence: A Tale of Two Courts', *Industrial Law Journal* 42(3) 289.
[11]Case C-286/12 *Commission v. Hungary*, paras 69–74.

management and to provide a high-quality service, could constitute a legitimate aim of employment and labour market policy.[12]

The depth of the analysis of the national legislation made by the Court in this respect is particularly striking. The Court accepted that the objective of the Hungarian government was a legitimate aim but, in a somewhat surprising move, ruled that the reduction of the retirement age in question was not appropriate to achieve that aim and, therefore, not compatible with Article 6(1) of Directive 2000/78. To justify this assertion, the Court engaged in an analysis of the long-term effects of the national law In the short term, the sudden reduction of the retirement age from 70 to 62 years made available many judicial posts for young lawyers. However, in the medium and long term, since the new judges were admitted in one go only, in comparison it decreased the chances of young lawyers getting jobs as judges in the near future.[13]

Admittedly, the circumstances of this case were peculiar. The national legislation was not really based on established social policy resulting from a national consensus, but may rather be explained by strictly political reasons.[14] Most of the judges forced to retire were high-rank judges (who were usually the older judges) and the new judges to fill the vacant posts were to be appointed by people close to the government party.[15] In any event, the fact that the Court was ready to engage in an analysis of the

---

[12] Cases C-159/10 and C-160/10 *Fuchs and Köhler*, para 50, repeated in essence in Case C-286/12, *Commission v. Hungary*, paras 62–63.

[13] Case C-286/12, *Commission v. Hungary* paras 76–79. As explained by Advocate General Kokott, a 'fair balance between the various generations of lawyers' would serve to distribute the posts made vacant by reducing the age-limit as evenly as possible among future age groups. The best way of achieving that balance would be to reduce the age-limit progressively to 65, which is the age-limit ultimately sought [by the social security legislation in force] in any event', para 73 of her Opinion.

[14] It seemed to pursue the political objective of the Fidesz party to take control of the various state institutions. The Fidesz party had won the elections in 2010, electing more than two-thirds of the members of the Hungarian Parliament, which allowed it to change the Constitution by itself, without having to obtain the agreement of any other party. For a succinct but rather comprehensive description of the situation regarding the judicial system, what the authors calls the 'Belarus-ization of Budapest', see Belavusau cited in fn 10, 1150–1154.

[15] For a detailed analysis of the overall situation, see the European Parliament Report of 25 June 2013 on the situation of fundamental rights: standards and practices in Hungary, drafted by Rui Tavares on behalf of the Committee on Civil Liberties, Justice and Home Affairs, doc. ref. PE 508.211v04-00. Accessible at: http://www.europarl.europa.eu/sides/getDoc.do?pubRef=-//EP//NONSGML+REPORT+A7-2013-0229+0+DOC+PDF+V0//EN. Accessed 24 September 2015].

long-term effects of the national legislation shows its willingness to intervene. This was the only occasion where the Court directly struck down national legislation on mandatory retirement age.

Prigge is the other case in which rules on mandatory retirement were rejected by the Court. In contrast to the case mentioned above, this case did not concern national legislation on age retirement, but a collective agreement authorised under national law. It concerned the collective agreement of Lufthansa, which set the retirement age of airline pilots at 60 years instead of 65 years, as required by national and international law. The Court considered that ensuring air traffic safety could not justify a different treatment based on age under Article 6(1). Instead, that objective could be considered under the concept of 'public security', according to the derogation clause provided by Article 2(5) of the Directive.[16] Moreover, the Court also accepted that physical capabilities diminish with age and that possessing particular physical capabilities could be a genuine and determining occupational requirement for airline pilots under Article 4(1) of the Directive.[17]

However, as exceptions to the principle of equality, both Article 2(5) and Article 4(1) should be interpreted narrowly.[18] The Court noted that no reason had been put forward justifying why the retirement age of airline pilots should be 60 years for Lufthansa pilots, instead of 65 years, according to national and international law. Therefore, the Court ruled that such a requirement was incompatible with the Directive.[19]

---

[16] Case C-447/09, *Prigge*, paras 58 and 82. Article 2(5) of Directive 2000/78/EC provides that 'This Directive shall be without prejudice to measures laid down by national law which, in a democratic society, are necessary for public security, for the maintenance of public order and the prevention of criminal offences, for the protection of health and for the protection of the rights and freedoms of others.'

[17] Article 4(1) of Directive 2000/78/EC allows Member States to 'provide that a difference of treatment which is based on a characteristic related to any of the grounds referred to in Article 1 shall not constitute discrimination where, by reason of the nature of the particular occupational activities concerned or of the context in which they are carried out, such a characteristic constitutes a genuine and determining occupational requirement, provided that the objective is legitimate and the requirement is proportionate.'

[18] Case C-447/09, *Prigge*, paras 56 and 72. See also *Petersen*, para 60.

[19] Case C-447/09, *Prigge*, paras 63 and 75. The Court ruled it was not necessary to ensure public security under Article 2(5) and it was disproportionate within the meaning of Article 4(1).

What is interesting in this case is that the EU Court does not leave it to the national court to further examine the factual situation, in order to establish whether or not there was any reason justifying a special treatment of the Lufthansa pilots. The EU Court was satisfied with the evidence it had before it. Together with *Palacios de la Villa* and *Rosenbladt*, analysed below, this is one of the few cases where, in a preliminary ruling procedure,[20] the EU Court took a categorical position on national provisions on mandatory retirement age.

1.2   Judgments accepting or Opening the Way to Accept National Provisions

Even in cases where the Court does not find national provisions on mandatory retirement age to be incompatible with Directive 2000/78, it appears willing to closely scrutinise these national provisions and, in particular, their justification.

Palacios de la Villa was the first case in which the Court dealt with national provisions imposing a mandatory retirement age.[21] It concerned a collective agreement applicable to the textile trade sector in the 'Autonomous Community' of Madrid. In conformity with an authorisation provided for by the applicable Spanish law, it allowed for an employment contract to be automatically terminated once the worker reached the age of 65. This was the normal retirement age in Spain at the time.

The Court immediately showed its willingness to keep an eye on national provisions. A fundamental preliminary issue had to be decided: whether or not provisions on mandatory retirement age were covered at all by Directive 2000//8. Recital 14 of that Directive states that it is 'without prejudice to national provisions laying down retirement ages', which, on the face of it, leaves the issue wide open. However, the Court recalled that Article 3(1) (c) of the Directive, on its material scope, prohibits discrimination 'in relation to employment and working conditions, including dismissal and pay'. For the Court, Recital 14 meant

---

[20] *Commission v. Hungary* was an action brought by the Commission against Hungary for infringement of Directive 2000/78.

[21] Case C-411/05, *Palacios de la Villa*. See Felipe Temming (2007) 'The Palacios case: turning point in age discrimination law?' *European Law Reporter* 382.

only that the Directive did not limit the competence of Member States to define the retirement age of their workers. However, the Directive did apply to rules providing for the termination of employment contracts once that retirement age was reached.[22] In this way, the Court conveniently distinguished the definition of retirement age for the purposes of being entitled to a pension, which concerns social security law and is a national competence,[23] from the termination of a contract of employment, which is covered by the scope of the Directive. This ruling was of course essential to assert the jurisdiction of the Court in this matter.

On substance, the Court pointed out that the objective of the national provision was to reduce unemployment and to promote better access to employment.[24] Moreover, it had been included in the legislation at the instigation of social partners, in the context of high unemployment in Spain.

The Court recalled the general principles: Member States (as well as social partners, when they have regulatory powers) enjoy broad discretion in their social and employment policies regarding both the aims to be pursued and the measures to achieve them. In this context, the choices made at the national level may be based on 'political, economic, social, demographic and/or budgetary considerations and having regard to the actual situation in the labour market'. Accordingly, Member States may decide, for example, either 'to prolong people's working life or provide for early retirement'.[25]

In the case, the Court ruled that the provision in question could be considered objectively and reasonably justified within the meaning of Article 6(1) of Directive 2000/78. The Court underlined that the termination of the employment contract was possible only if the worker qualified for a normal (contributory) retirement pension. Otherwise, if the worker had not completed the necessary period of pension contributions, the termination of the contract was not possible.

This judgment is best seen in context. It followed *Mangold*, the first case on Directive 2000/78, which was decided in 2005 and had created

---

[22] Case C-411/05, *Palacios de la Villa*, para 42–47.

[23] Article 3(3) of *Directive 2000/78/EC* excludes from its scope 'payments of any kind made by state schemes or similar, including state social security or social protection schemes'. See also fn 16.

[24] Case C-411/05, *Palacios de la Villa*, paras 53 and 62.

[25] C-411/05, *Palacios de la Villa*, paras 68 and 69. The latter remark was later repeated in Cases C-45/09, *Rosenbladt*, para 44; and C-141/11, *Hörnfeldt*, para 28.

considerable controversy. There the Court struck down a provision of a German law of 2002 allowing for the conclusion of fixed-term contracts with workers over 52 years old, ruling it contrary to Article 6(1) of Directive 2000/78.

The problem was that the case concerned an employment relation between private parties, which took effect in July 2003, when Directive 2000/78 had not yet been transposed in Germany. Normally, the Court considers that EU Directives as such do not produce effects between private parties.[26] However, the Court recalled its doctrine that, while a Directive has not yet been transposed, Member States must refrain from adopting measures that compromise its objectives.[27] Moreover, the Court ruled that the principle of non-discrimination on grounds of age is a general principle of European Union (EU) law. This principle should be applied to the legislation in question because it fell within the scope of EU law, since it implemented Directive 1999/70 on fixed-term work. Finally, the Court concluded that the national court, in order to ensure the legal protection deriving from EU law rules (such as the principle of equality on the grounds of age), was responsible for setting aside any provision of national law conflicting with EU law, such as the German law in question.[28]

This conclusion, and the reasoning of the Court in *Mangold*, created a huge debate.[29] In contrast, the specific facts of *Palacios de la Villa* gave the Court all the reasons to show a different face, one more accommodating to Member States. For example, in *Mangold* the Court complained that the German rule applied 'regardless of any other consideration linked to the structure of the labour market in question or the personal situation of the person concerned'. But *Palacios de la Villa* concerned a collective

---

[26] They produce effects between them when they are transposed into national law. See Case C-91/92 *Paola Faccini Dori v. Recreb Srl*, [1994] ECR I-3325, para 24.

[27] Case C-144/04 *Mangold* [2005] ECR I-9981, paras 66–68.

[28] *Mangold*, paras 74–78.

[29] See, for example, Jan H. Jans (2007) 'The Effect in National Legal Systems of the Prohibition of Discrimination on Grounds of Age as a General Principle of Community Law', *Legal Issues of European Integration* 34(1) 53 and, more recently, Ján Mazák and Martin Moser (2013) 'Adjudication by Reference to General Principles of EU Law: A Second Look at the Mangold Case Law' in Maurice Adams and others (eds), *The Legitimacy of the Case Law of the European Court of Justice* (Hart Publishing) 61.

agreement (thus concluded with trade union representatives') covering only one economic sector in one Autonomous Community in Spain. Moreover, the interests of the worker were taken into consideration, at least to a certain extent, since he could be dismissed only if he was entitled to a retirement pension. The facts justified a different ruling, but the timing was also appropriate to show the critics of *Mangold* that the Court respected Member States' choices of social policy.

Age Concern[30] was the next judgment of the Court on the mandatory retirement age. The case examined the legislation transposing Directive 2000/78 in the United Kingdom, which provided that employees reaching the normal retirement age or, in its absence, the age of 65, could be dismissed by reason of retirement. A specific procedure had to be followed which, *inter alia*, obliged the employer to give the worker a notice of his dismissal of at least six months and allowed the worker to request not to be dismissed—a request that the employer had the duty to consider, but not the obligation to accept.[31] The UK legislation itself did not set a mandatory retirement age, but allowed employers to dismiss a worker because he had reached retirement age. Age Concern, a non-governmental organisation (NGO) concerned with the needs and interests of older people, argued that the legislation was incompatible with Article 6(1) of Directive 2000/78 and the principle of proportionality.

The UK legislation did not state the aims of the provision that allowed for dismissal at 65 years, but the Court did not consider that indispensable, on condition that the general context of the measure allows for those aims to be identified. The Court pointed out that 'legitimate aims' within the meaning of Article 6(1) of the Directive have to be social policy objectives 'of a public interest nature' and not 'purely individual reasons specific to the employer's situation, such as cost reduction or improving competitiveness'. Yet, in the pursuit of those legitimate aims, the national law may recognise 'a certain degree of flexibility for employers'.[32]

---

[30] Case C-388/07, *Age Concern England* [2009] ECR I-1569.

[31] In the hearing of the case, the rapporteur of the case, Judge Pernilla Lindh, seemed surprised and upset when she was told that, provided that the procedure was followed, the concerned worker could be dismissed without difficulty.

[32] Case C-388/07, *Age Concern*, para 46.

Moreover, a simple reference to a legitimate aim is not sufficient to prove the means chosen are suitable for achieving that aim.[33]

In any case, after so much guidance, the EU Court left it for the UK to examine whether the national legislation could be deemed justified by a legitimate aim and whether the means chosen were appropriate and necessary to achieve it. It was as if the EU Court had decided not to decide the case, but nevertheless wanted to establish strict boundaries to the assessment to be made by the national court.

The outcome of the case at the national level is interesting. The High Court of England and Wales did not find the national legislation incompatible with Directive 2000/78. It stated that the decision to allow the legislation in force was based on the circumstances and evidence available when it was introduced. Meanwhile, the government had decided to bring forward a review of the legislation from 2011 to 2010, to consider whether it was still 'appropriate and necessary'. The High Court stated that its decision could have been different if the government had not announced this review and indicated that it could not foresee that 65 years would still be the selected age afterwards. Eventually, in April 2011, the legislation ceased to be in force.

The judgment of the EU Court in 2009 did not have immediate effect. Neither the EU Court nor the UK court struck down the legislation. However, it may be argued that close analysis of the national provisions made by the EU Court and its detailed instructions to the national court made a decisive contribution to the legislative change a few years later, in 2011.

In *Petersen*, the Court dealt with a German provision setting a maximum age of 68 years for practice as 'panel dentists', those whose work can be reimbursed by the social security system. Several objectives were alleged in favour of the provision. The Court accepted that the protection of patients' health, related to the competence of doctors, or the financial balance of the public health care system could be accepted as objectives covered by Article 2(5). It left the national court to decide whether the provision was necessary to ensure the financial balance of the health care system. Meanwhile, the EU Court ruled that, because dentists could work in private practice beyond the age of 68 years, the provision

---

[33] *Age Concern.*

was not necessary to protect the health of patients. [34] This was the first case on the mandatory retirement age where the Court stated that in order for a legislative provision to be deemed 'appropriate for ensuring attainment of the objective pursued' it must 'genuinely reflect a concern to attain it in a consistent and systematic manner'.[35]

The argument that mandatory retirement age led to 'sharing out employment opportunities among generations' was analysed by the Court in the light of Article 6(1) of the Directive. In the line of *Palacios de la Villa*, the Court accepted it as a legitimate aim as such and examined whether the provision was appropriate and necessary. The German government had invoked its discretion to take measures to avoid the existence of an excessive number of dentists. Imposing a maximum age facilitated the entry into the labour market of younger dentists. While recognising Member States' discretion, the Court stated that the provision would neither be appropriate nor necessary for achieving that purpose if the number of dentists was not excessive in relation to the needs of the patients. However, it also pointed out that the German government had underlined, for example, that the age limit did not apply to regions where there was a shortage of dentists. Therefore, it left the national court to establish whether there was a risk of an excessive number of dentists.[36]

Again, the EU Court makes a very close examination of the national provision, including its various exceptions, and of their possible justification. It discards the protection of patients' health as a justification and leaves the national court to examine whether or not the provision is necessary for the financial balance of the public health care system, or to avoid having an excessive number of dentists working, which could make it more difficult for young dentists to enter the market. Therefore, although the Court accepted many of the arguments in favour of the provision, the judgement is quite balanced on the whole.

By contrast, in **Rosenbladt** the Court took a clear position in favour of the mandatory retirement age. Its lawfulness was seen as founded on a long-lasting political and social consensus, based primarily on the notion

---

[34] Case 341/08, *Petersen* [2010] ECR I-47, para 53.
[35] *Petersen* paras 62–64.
[36] *Petersen*, paras 68–76.

of sharing employment between the generations, which benefits both younger and older workers. It facilitates younger workers in finding work, while older workers avoid the humiliation of being dismissed because they are no longer capable of working.[37] The fact that the plaintiff, a part-time cleaner, would be obliged to retire at 65 under the applicable collective agreement and would have a pension of 228 euro only was not an obstacle to the Grand Chamber of the Court in reaching this verdict.

In *Georgiev,* the Court came back to a more balanced approach. It analysed legislation in Bulgaria which provided that, from the age of 65, university professors would only have one-year fixed-term contracts and, in any event, they would be obliged to retire at the age of 68. The Court accepted again that the alleged objective of encouraging the recruitment of young people could be a legitimate aim under Directive 2000/78. However, the plaintiff argued that such an aim was only an abstract assertion and that the legislation was not in line with the labour market reality, because young people were not interested in careers as university professors.

Surprisingly, the Court did not reject this argument, in spite of its being contrary to the Court's previous case law based on the idea of solidarity between generations. Instead, it left the Bulgarian court to examine whether the aims alleged by the public authorities (the university and the Bulgarian government) did actually 'correspond to the facts'.[38] Furthermore, regarding the proportionality of the provision, the national court should also examine whether it pursued the alleged aim in a consistent and systematic manner and, in particular, the allegation of the plaintiff that the legislation made a distinction between lecturers, university professors and other university teaching staff.[39]

Fuchs concerned a situation regarding two prosecutors and the legal requirement that civil servants of the German land of Hessen retire in principle at 65. They could continue to work until 68, but only if that was deemed to be in the civil service's interest. The Court accepted that the retirement age had the legitimate aim, *inter alia*, of establishing a balanced age structure in the civil service. As to proportionality, the

---

[37] Case C-45/09, *Rosenbladt*, paras 43–45.
[38] Joined Cases C-250/09 and C-268/09, *Georgiev*, paras 47, 48 and 53.
[39] Joined Cases C-250/09 and C-268/09, *Georgiev*, para 56.

Court underlined that prosecutors retire at the age of 65 with a full pension equivalent to about 72% of their final salary. Therefore, the measure took into account their legitimate interests. Finally, the Court ruled that, in order to examine whether a measure was appropriate and necessary, it 'must be supported by evidence, the probative value of which is for the national court to access'.

Finally, in **Hörnfeldt,** the Court basically applied its ruling in *Rosenbladt,* this time to the Swedish legislation providing for the automatic termination of the employment contract when workers reach the age of 67 (two years later than in *Rosenbladt*). The case concerned also a part-time worker. He received a retirement pension equivalent to approximately 230 euro at the time of the ruling, although apparently he could also obtain housing benefit and/or old age benefit in case of need. The Court considered that the measure was, in principle, appropriate and necessary to promote the access of young people to employment. Still, in the present case the EU Court left it to the national court to make the final decision in that respect.

As a final comment, it is important to note that, often, the Court does not itself declare whether national provisions are compatible with a correct interpretation of the Directive but leaves it to the national court to decide the case.[40] The EU Court gives guidance on what can be considered a legitimate aim and on how to determine if the provisions are appropriate and necessary to achieve that aim. Such guidance can be detailed and is often quite finely balanced. It is then for national courts to ultimately decide the case based on the facts in question. In practice, the EU Court invites them to closely scrutinise the justification of national provisions.

Under the technical justification of not interfering with the examination of facts, effectively the EU Court shares its political responsibility with the national courts and empowers them to make a demanding analysis of national legislation. Even when this does result in immediate changes, it introduces a dynamic of close examination of the need for the specific provisions at stake. For example, in *Age Concern*, neither the EU Court declared the legislation incompatible with Directive 2000/78/EC nor the

---

[40] Except in *Palacios de la Villa* and *Rosenbladt.*

UK court struck it down, but the UK legislator ended up changing it in the aftermath of their judgments.

2   External Factors: 'The World Out There'

In principle, time runs in favour of older workers. [41] It is estimated that between 2005 and 2030, the total working population in the EU will fall by 20.8 million. Meanwhile, between 2010 and 2030, the number of people aged 55 and over will grow by 15.5%.[42] Keeping more people at work when they are older and for a longer period of time will be crucial to avoid economic decline and to ensure sustainable social protection systems.[43] This need may increase the pressure for a closer scrutiny of the justification of national rules on the mandatory retirement age.

It is also important to realise that the use of mandatory retirement age is already declining in the developed world[44] and also throughout Europe. At the present moment, only a minority of EU Member States (eight) have a mandatory retirement age that applies generally, across all occupations. Meanwhile, 13 Member States apply it to some professions only, such as police officers, judges or pilots; for example, 10 Member States have a mandatory retirement age for civil servants in general. [45]

In the future, the overall trend will probably be to combine a continuation towards a reduction in the professions concerned by mandatory retirement with an increase of the age at which workers will

---

[41] However, the likelihood that an incipient economic recovery in Europe (particularly in the euro-zone) could also give a pretext for the continuation of widespread rules on mandatory retirement age should not be discounted.

[42] Commission 'Confronting demographic change: a new solidarity between the generations', Green Paper, COM (2005) 94 final.

[43] On the different impact of the ageing of the economy in well-educated and low skilled workers, see 'A billion shades of grey—An ageing economy will be a slower and more unequal one—unless policy starts changing now' The Economist (London 26 April 2014: http://www.economist.com/news/leaders/21601253-ageing-economy-will-be-slower-and-more-unequal-oneunless-policy-starts-changing-now) Accessed 21 October 2015.

[44] A general mandatory retirement age does not seem to exist in the USA, Canada, Australia or New Zealand.

[45] European Commission Annex III to the 'Joint Report on the application of the Racial Equality Directive (2000/43/EC) and the Employment Equality Directive (2000/78/EC)' SWD (2014) 5 final, 31–34.

be obliged to retire. Mandatory retirement age will possibly still exist in the future, but it will probably be set at an age higher than now, with a few exceptions for physically demanding jobs where the health and safety of other people are at stake.

3   Conclusion

In nine judgments on this matter, the Court has struck down national rules on mandatory retirement age in only two cases. Both cases regarded very specific situations, and one case concerned a collective agreement in one enterprise, not national legislation. Given the outcome of its case law, one could presume that the Court is quite flexible in its dealings with Member States and will normally be ready to accept national provisions on the mandatory retirement age.

This chapter argued that, on the contrary, the Court may be more demanding in the future when analysing national rules. On the one hand, the case law of the Court is more complex than may seem at first glance. Often the Court has made a very thorough examination of the national provisions and their justification and has shown it is ready to use its powers. On the other hand, future demographic evolution is likely to put pressure on the Court to be stricter in its scrutiny of national provisions.

The basic trend of the Court's case law in accepting national provisions may not change in the short term. However, as provisions on mandatory retirement age become gradually more the exception than the rule, the legitimacy of the Court to intervene will increase.[46]

---

[46] For an interesting insider's view of the legitimacy of the Court, see Koen Lenaerts (2013) 'The Court's Outer and Inner Selves: Exploring the External and Internal Legitimacy of the European Court of Justice', in Adams, Maurice and others (eds.), *The Legitimacy of the Case Law of the European Court of Justice* (Hart Publishing) 13.

Part II

The Issue of Retirement

3

Retirement and the Pension Crisis

Jo Grady

In many countries, the State Pension Age is rising.[1] Governments often present this as a reflection of increasing life expectancy and the need to extend working lives beyond the traditional retirement age, with individuals choosing, and also being required by law, to work longer. Indeed, in the UK, the government has also stressed that the increase in life expectancy presents them with no alternative other than to increase labour market participation of older workers.[2] As a result of this increase, the role of flexible working practices in providing a route for older workers with the ability to make choices regarding how long they choose to engage in work-related tasks[3] has become important and is being widely discussed. These working practices have often been held up as a way to improve employment choices for older workers,[4]

---

[1] OECD (2011) *Pensions at a Glance* (OECD Publishing).

[2] DWP (2006) *A New Deal for Welfare: Empowering People to Work* (Cm 6730, The Stationery Office).

[3] E J Hill, J G Grzywacz, S Allen, V L Blanchard, C Matz-Cpasta and S Shulkin (2008) 'Defining and Conceptualizing Workplace Flexibility', *Community, Work and Family* 11(2), 149–63.

[4] W Loretto, S Vickerstaff, and P White (2005) *Older Workers and the options for Flexible Work.* (Working Paper Series no. 31. Equal Opportunities Commission); W. Loretto, S. Vickerstaff, &

© The Editor(s) (if applicable) and The Author(s) 2016
S. Manfredi, L. Vickers (eds.), *Challenges of Active Ageing*,
DOI 10.1057/978-1-137-53251-0_3

or provide bridge jobs to ease older workers into retirement.[5] Indeed, the Department of Work and Pensions (DWP) have also identified this type of work as providing older workers with a choice where they may opt for a phased approach to retirement.[6] This has led to the suggestion that retirement is no longer seen as a life-defining event where workers leave the labour market for the final time but, instead, as a reversible state.[7] Moreover, research has demonstrated that 'financial security' is key in retirement planning,[8] suggesting that whilst it may be a choice to work past retirement, it may represent compulsion for those who have worked in low-pay occupations where pension coverage is poor.[9] This may well be the case—whilst we have seen increases in employment rates amongst the over-50s and over-60s, it is worth noting that this increase has been in full-time work, not part-time work.[10] This suggests that people are simply staying in the labour market longer, rather than bridging their way into retirement or 'un-retiring' via the use of flexible working practices. Thus, we have a growing life expectancy that has encouraged government to pursue a policy of increasing labour market participation of older workers alongside decreasing access to occupational pension provision.[11] Despite the importance placed on the role of flexibility by government and policy makers, research has revealed

---

P. White (2007) 'Flexible Work and Older Workers', in W. Loretto, S. Vickerstaff, & P. White, (eds.) *The Future for Older Workers: New Perspectives* (The Policy Press), 139–160.

[5] W Loretto et al, '*Older Workers*'; S Vickerstaff, (2010) 'Older Workers: the unavoidable obligation of extending our working lives?', *Sociology Compass* 4(10), 867–879.

[6] DWP (2006) *A New Deal for Welfare: Empowering People to Work* (Cm 6730 The Stationery Office)139; W Loretto, & S Vickerstaff (2015) 'Gender, age and flexible working in later life', *Work, Employment and Society* 29(2), 233–249.

[7] N Maestas (2010) 'Back to Work Expectations and Realizations of Work after Retirement', *Journal of Human Resources* 45(3), 718–748.

[8] C Price (2003) 'Professional Women's Retirement Adjustment: the experience of re-establishing order', *Journal of Aging Studies* 17, 341–355.

[9] V Beck & G Williams (2015) 'The (performance) management of retirement and the limits of individual choice', *Work, Employment and Society* 29(2), 250–267.

[10] ONS (2012) *Older Workers and the Labour Market* (ONS); ONS (2013) *Pension Trends 2013 Edition* (ONS); Loretto and Vickerstaff 'Gender, age and flexible working'.

[11] J Grady (2013) 'Trade Unions and the Pension Crisis: Defending Member Interests in a Neoliberal World', *Employee Relations* 35(3), 94–308.

that, when interviewed, older workers expressed the desire to reject flexible work,[12] much of which is characterised by low pay/skill and few prospects. Loretto and Vickerstaff have also demonstrated that amongst older and retired workers there is actually a feeling of 'release' that accompanies retirement, suggesting that individuals on the whole wish to be free from the labour market, and 'get off the treadmill' once they have 'done their bit'.[13] This research challenges the agenda of extending working lives, suggesting that many people are looking forward to ending paid employment where such a choice is possible.

What this chapter discusses is not the extent to which older workers wish to engage with the labour market beyond the State Pension Age—other contributions to this volume engage with that—but rather how the crisis, as a continued crisis in provision, coupled with low income in both working years and later life, will compel many to work beyond the traditional State Pension Age, as pensioner poverty increases and the value of pensions decreases. As such, it contributes to debates regarding choice or compulsion, as it is argued that unless we enact sustainable pension provision with adequate income in retirement, more individuals will be compelled to work in old age due to the increase in low-paid work, an increase use in zero hour contracts, closure of occupational schemes, and inadequate State Pension provision. With specific reference to the latter two, this chapter will examine how the pension crisis has been framed, and suggest that this dominant narrative is misleading. Moreover, it will then explore how the proposed solutions to the UK pension crisis will not provide adequate pensions for those it is intended; the New Auto-Enrolment pension will be directly discussed. In short, therefore, it places the debates surrounding active ageing in a very important context, namely that of the pension crisis that will compel many to engage with paid employment, whether or not they wish to. For many, therefore, active ageing may become more a typical requirement and less a choice.

---

[12] D Lain (2012) 'Working past 65 in the UK and the USA: segregation into 'Lopaq' occupations?' *Work, Employment and Society* 26(1), 78–94; W. Loretto & S. Vickerstaff, 'Gender, age and flexible working'.

[13] Loretto and Vickerstaff, 'Gender, age and flexible working', 239–240.

Obvious questions may seem to be how we will engage people in the labour market past traditional retirement ages, how we will ensure fair access to work with dignity, and how we will enable this. However, if what we are witnessing actually is people working beyond the retirement age because they are compelled to, then we need to understand the role of the pension crisis. Indeed, we need to ensure people have access to good pension provision rather than to work after retirement. With that argument in mind, this chapter turns its attention to the pension crisis, and demonstrates that the dominant understanding of the pension crisis is misleading. By demonstrating this, it argues that solutions other than those currently proposed are possible, whilst also arguing that the currently proposed policy will not have the promised impact of solving the pension crisis; rather, it will perpetuate a problem of state underfunding and short-termism regarding pension planning.

This chapter ties together themes from various literatures in order to advance a new understanding of the pension crisis. To engage with this synthesis, it is first necessary to analyse the constituent parts of the literatures that have given rise to it. A review of this literature that is orientated towards developing an understanding of the ideological aspects of the pension crisis swiftly reveals the utility of linking together various approaches to neoliberalism, pensions, and labour organisation in order to present an account of the pension crisis that runs contrary to the hegemonic one now dominant. This alternative account can be used as a lens through which to analyse the challenges that the dominance of neoliberal ideology has presented for pensions. Thus, it allows us to examine the growing dominance of neoliberal ideology and, in doing so, to ask why it has been so difficult to challenge neoliberal hegemony. Finally, we begin to understand better the push for people to work past retirement age as being linked to the adequacy of pensions.

To accomplish the above, the remainder of this chapter is structured thus: (i) a discussion of neoliberalism and the ways in which neoliberal ideology has been naturalised; (ii) a thorough analysis of the pension crisis (as represented both through conventional and alternative accounts); and (iii) a discussion of New Labour's neoliberal turn and how trade unions have responded to it.

1 The Role of Neoliberal Ideology and Discourse

The concept of ideology provides an alternative analysis of the pension crisis. In short, it argues that the pension crisis, as widely understood in the UK, is based on a number of misleading and/or narrow discourses. Building on the argument put forward elsewhere (Grady 2010, 2013), it is argued that the dominant (hegemonic) narrative of the pension crisis is based on a neoliberal construction of the crisis (rather than upon empirical fact), and that this construct is supported by a number of narrow, and often misleading, discourses. In addition, it is also argued that these discourses are constructed for, and work towards, ideological ends, principally the support of neoliberalism, which represents contemporary capitalism's ruling ideology.

According to Thompson,[14] dominant social groups or classes can use ideology to legitimate their dominance. Thus, for Thompson, to study ideology is to study the ways in which meaning (or signification) serves to sustain relations of domination, and it is this understanding of ideology in relation to neoliberal ideology that this chapter employs. Furthermore, Eagleton[15] outlines the process through which ideologies are legitimated and argues that a dominant power may legitimate itself through six different strategies. A dominant power may legitimate itself by (1) promoting values and beliefs congenial to it; (2) naturalising and (3) universalising such beliefs so as to render them self-evident and apparently inevitable; (4) denigrating ideas which might challenge it; (5) excluding rival forms of thought, perhaps by some unspoken but systematic logic [in terms of neoliberalism this is the often unspoken, but yet so often tacitly applied, logic of the market]; and (6) obscuring social reality in ways convenient to itself. This chapter uses the understanding put forward by Thompson, and the strategies outlined by Eagleton, to argue that neoliberalism performs as an ideology, and legitimates itself. Discourses and misleading narratives are deployed to achieve these strategies and, therefore, act as an

---

[14] J B Thompson (1990) *Ideology and Modern Culture: Critical Social Theory in the Era of Mass Communication*, (Polity Press).
[15] T Eagleton (1991) *Ideology: An Introduction*, (Verso) 5–6.

ideological vehicle to legitimate neoliberal values further, and serve those elites who best benefit from them.

Neoliberal ideology is, therefore, linked to power and to domination: power to control the terms of the discourse and, therefore, power to dominate the social world. In this sense, the pension crisis is transformed into more than merely a crisis regarding pension provision. It becomes a site where those seeking neoliberal reform of pension provision seek to construct and exploit a crisis in order to enact urgent reform. In other words, a crisis is constructed to which the obvious remedial steps are those consistent with the dominant neoliberal ideologies that run through contemporary capitalism.[16] This chapter maintains that neoliberal discourses represent the 'official' narrative regarding the pension crisis. In that context, neoliberal solutions—privatisation and individualisation—are offered and seem, at first glance, to be natural solutions to the crisis.

Further to the above, Jessop[17] argues that whilst all discourses are equal, some are more equal than others. Indeed, some discourses are able to reach the stage of naturalisation whilst others do not.[18] This helps us to understand why neoliberal discourses have formed the conventional narrative of the pension crisis; it is precisely because such discourses have become naturalised. Earlier work[19] identified the dominance of three main discourses (ageing, affordability, and responsibility) that are presented as explanations of the causes of the pension crisis. These discourses frame not only the terms of the debate but also the potential solutions. In that chapter, it was argued that whilst those discourses contain empirical truths, the way in which the evidence they contain is presented construes the pension crisis to be the consequence of a certain set of slim factors. In doing so, it ignores factors that either contradict or challenge this construct of the crisis, or which might suggest a solution other than

---

[16] P Pierson (1994) *Dismantling the Welfare State: Reagan, Thatcher and the Politics of Retrenchment* (Cambridge University Press).

[17] B Jessop (2010) *The Cultural Political Economy of Crisis*, paper presented at Leicester Business School, De Montfort University Department of Public Policy/Local Governance Research Unit Seminar Series, 2010.

[18] Eagleton (1991) *Ideology* 200.

[19] Jo Grady (2010) 'Trade Unions and the Pension Crisis'; J. Grady (June 2010) 'From Beveridge to Turner: Laissez-faire to Neoliberalism', *Capital and Class* 163–180.

a neoliberal one. Thus, an alternative account of the pension crisis was offered, one that argued that the conventional and hegemonic account, whilst not necessarily false, is certainly misleading. In short, the ideological discourses put forward to account for the pension crisis are true on one level, but they are not on another. Thus, they are true in their empirical content but deceptive in their force.[20] It is precisely for this reason that it is argued that those with a neoliberal agenda offer these discourses ideologically and aggressively in order to favour neoliberal pension reform. First, the nature of the crisis is manipulated through presentation, and this presentation is then exploited as a justification of urgent and radical reform along free market principles. Such reforms create yet further investment opportunities for the economic elite. Indeed, we have seen this before during the Thatcher governments.

It is, of course, worth nothing here that, herein, discourses are considered to be ways of not only representing the world but also of influencing it.[21] What is said or written can causally influence what we subsequently do. This makes discourse a potential cause of social action. Discourse influences action by selecting and emphasising certain linguistic and, hence, practical possibilities whilst deselecting, de-emphasising, or excluding others; thus, the former are far more likely to occur. Therefore, it is important to point out that just because discourse can 'construe' the world, it does not mean that discourse can re-construct the world. Remembering this allows us to retain the notion that what we say or write about practices related to pension provision can have causal efficacy without lapsing into an idealist trap whereby what we say or write creates or constructs these practices. Put simply, by selecting and emphasising certain linguistic possibilities (and hence action), and by de-selecting, de-emphasising or excluding others, some discourses relating to pension provision may become accepted as true—even if they are false.[22] Indeed, below, it will be argued that being forced to interact with these dominant discourses (even if they are recognised as fake) acts to legitimate their status.

---

[20] Eagleton (1991) *Ideology* 16–17.

[21] N Fairclough (2003) *Analysing Discourse: Textual Analysis for Social Research* (Routledge).

[22] S Fleetwood (2005) 'Ontology in Organization and Management Studies: A Critical Realist Perspective', *Organization* 12, 200.

1.1   A Brief Overview of Current Pension Provision in the UK

Within the field of employee relations there has been much written about pensions and the pension crisis. Many of these works have discussed employee perceptions of pension schemes;[23] pension scheme membership and its impact on employee retention rates;[24] power asymmetry in accessing the law in relation to pension schemes;[25] pensions and industrial conflict;[26] and, amongst other issues, international pension comparisons.[27] They all put forward important contributions in opening up the debate about pensions as part of the employment relationship, and provide the average person access to a subject that is often daunting (due to the technical nature of some terms).

This section will analyse in more detail the significant changes to pension provision that occurred from the late 1980s onwards, and will demonstrate that these changes reflect a neoliberalisation of pension provision, and further that it is this process of neoliberalisation that has in fact caused the current crisis, despite the conventional accounts claiming the contrary. It will be argued that the hegemonic construct of the crisis, as presented by the use of key discourses, is an artificial crisis. This is not to say that there is not a crisis of some form in relation to continued pension provision. Not only are two million pensioners due to retire into poverty[28] but, also, increased life expectancy means that issues such as the cost of schemes and age of retirement do need addressing. What needs to be considered, however, is the extent to which these legitimate questions are actually answered satisfactorily by conventional pension debates, and

---

[23] W Loretto, P White and C Duncan (2000) 'Something for nothing?: Employees' views of occupational pension schemes', *Employee Relations* 22(3), 260–271; O. Gough & R. Hick (2009) 'Employee evaluations of occupational pensions', *Employee Relations* 31(2), 158–167.

[24] S Taylor (2000) 'Occupational pensions and employee retention: Debate and evidence' *Employee Relations* 22(3), 246–259.

[25] R Nobles (2000) 'Access to the law of pensions: The lessons from National Grid v. Laws' *Employee Relations* 22(3), 282–285.

[26] C Nolda (2004) 'Industrial conflict in local government since' 1997 *Employee Relations* 26(4), 377–391.

[27] D Cooper (2000) 'A tale of two pension systems' *Employee Relations* 22(3), 286–292.

[28] H Osborne, '2 m pensioners live in poverty says ONS' *The Guardian* (27 January 2010).

the extent to which they are simply exploited to reform pension provision along neoliberal, free market lines.

The argument that pension provision has been subject to neoliberal attacks is not a new one, and has been put forward by a number of authors writing about a variety of countries and contexts.[29] However, prior to the onset of the pension crisis in the late 1990s and the early 2000s, pensions rarely made the news, and interest in them tended to be the preserve of statisticians and actuaries. This has obscured the central significance that pensions hold. Given the scope of this chapter, only a brief overview of the UK pension crisis, as widely understood, can be presented. Once this conventional account is established, it will explore what is referred to in this chapter as the 'real' pension crisis, and thus expose how the conventional crisis is in actual fact an artificial crisis.

It is accurate to state that historically, we have had a pension system in the UK that has relied upon providing individuals access to a pension scheme other than the British State Pension (BSP). Indeed, in 2007, the BSP represented just 15.9% of average wages. Hence, for many people in employment, workplace-based, collective pension schemes supplemented their incomes after retirement. Traditionally, this sort of scheme would be a 'final salary' defined benefit (DB) scheme contributed to by both employer and employee. A working life of contributing to such schemes usually provided adequate income in old age. The closure of these schemes—in favour of money purchase defined contribution (DC) schemes, or simply encouragement for employees to make their own pension arrangements—has left a significant number of workers without entitlement to a guaranteed and secure pension. This has caused a crisis of access to secure pension provision and, therefore, retirement income, and has resulted in state provision becoming the only form of income in retirement for more people. Without a commitment to improving alternative saving options, and ensuring these offer a guaranteed income

---

[29] M Townson (1994) *The Social contract for Seniors in Canada: Preparing for the 21st Century*, (National Advisory Council on Ageing); R Minns (2001) *The Cold War in Welfare: Stock Markets Verses Pensions* (Verso); R Blackburn (2002) *Banking on Death or Investing in Life: the history and future of pensions*, (Verso) J Williamson and M Williams (2005) 'Notional Defined Contribution Account Neoliberal Ideology and the Political Economy of Pension Reform' *American Journal of Economics and Sociology* 64(2), 485–506; J Morgan (2005) 'The UK pension system: the betrayal by New Labour in its neoliberal global context', *Research in Political Economy* 23.

in retirement (which neither the now abandoned NESTs—National Employment Savings Trusts—nor the new Auto-Enrolment pensions will), this is only set to continue.

The demise of DB schemes, and their replacement by less secure schemes funded by riskier investments, has revealed the inability of current pension arrangements to provide a decent and guaranteed retirement income. For those who have access to them, DB schemes provide a pension upon retirement based on years of service and salary at the time of retirement. Members of DB schemes usually accrue one-sixtieth or one-eightieth per year of service.

An additional factor related to DB schemes that has helped to create the perceived pension crisis is that of pension contribution holidays. It has been generally been the case that 70 % of the value of any DB scheme is invested in the stock market and the rest mainly in gilts, corporate bonds (company versions of gilts), and property. The returns on these investments serve as the basis of the liquidity and solvency of the scheme. As such, in principle, and if the returns are high, the employer can enjoy lower contributions so long as they maintain a solvent scheme that covers its liabilities. These lower contributions are also known as 'contribution holidays'. Contribution holidays, however, can only be taken by company DB schemes. For occupational DB schemes such as the University Superannuation Scheme or the local government pension scheme (LGPS), the employer has a contractual obligation to pay contributions; contribution holidays are illegal. The implications of pension holidays for the creation of the pension crisis are discussed below.

1.2   The Manufacturing of a Pensions Crisis

This section will provide a brief summary of how instabilities were introduced into the pension system. Thus, it will serve as the basis for the central argument of this chapter: the conventional construct of the pension crisis is misleading. Dissecting this construct is difficult; nevertheless, the work of Jamie Morgan is indispensable in helping us to see in broad perspective the ways in which the pension crisis has been constructed. The first potentially 'crisis causing' event for final salary schemes happened prior to the election of New Labour. It was the introduction of the 5% tax cap on DB pensions schemes by the Conservative Chancellor of the Exchequer, Nigel Lawson, in the 1986 Finance Act. The Act imposed a 5% cap on the value of assets over liabilities in DB pension schemes; any surplus is now subject to heavy taxation. This new tax cap was designed to deter organisations from avoiding tax by requiring them to make large contributions to the company pension scheme in years of high profit.

The problems that the 1986 Act caused were not immediately obvious.[30] Nevertheless, simply staying within the cap and avoiding paying tax became the motivation for organisations—not maintaining a healthy and slump-proof pension scheme. Morgan also points out that the new tax cap allowed organisations to decide how to distribute the 'benefits of the capital which would exceed that cap'.[31] It is unsurprising that CEOs chose to pay higher dividends rather than to improve pensions, as they had done heretofore. Larger dividends improve the attractiveness of equities; in turn, these enhance share prices and, as such, are immediately appealing. By contrast, attempting to carry on contributing to pension schemes by investing above the 5% cap would attract heavy taxation on those contributions; needless to say, companies were keen to avoid increasing their tax liabilities. The impact of contribution holidays is often left out of the hegemonic pension 'crisis' narrative; indeed, it is not even mentioned in either of Lord Turner's Reports on the state of pensions in Britain which were commissioned by New Labour and which form the basis of the state's response to the pension crisis.[32]

Neglecting the importance of employer contribution holidays hides the nature of the artificial crisis identified here, and in more detail by Morgan.[33] Employers who have closed schemes, or who are considering closing schemes, often cite the inherent instability and crippling unaffordability of final salary schemes, whilst quietly passing over the large deficits left by contribution holidays. For example, British Airways (BA), which enjoyed a sustained period of contribution holidays in the 1990s, accrued a £3.7 billion

---

[30] Morgan (2005) *The UK Pension System* 319.

[31] *The UK Pension System*.

[32] J A Turner (2005) *The Pension Commission: Challenges and Choices* (HMSO); J A Turner (2006) *The Pension Commission: A New Pensions Settlement for the Twenty-First Century*, HMSO).

[33] Morgan, *The UK pension system* 319.

pension scheme deficit. In 2003, the company closed their scheme to new members citing rising costs related to deficit reduction as the cause. British Airways claimed that the long-term viability of the scheme was in jeopardy if employees did not comply with the changes. But this account conceals the importance of key events (such as contribution holidays) that have led to the deficit. It does so by focusing on the discourse of affordability and responsibility, but principally of the employee to the company rather than the other way around. The BA case is not unique.

In addition to contribution holidays, in 1997, as part of his first budget as Chancellor of the Exchequer, Gordon Brown abolished the dividend tax credit (DTC) for pension schemes. Morgan[34] argues that this new tax regime ensured a quicker downturn in DB schemes; the thrust being that Brown's legislation exacerbated the problems that Lawson had introduced to workplace pension schemes and worsened the potential for a pension's crisis. Employers used the increased instability this created as an excuse for initiating pension scheme reforms profitable to them. Brown's legislative changes made matters worse in two ways. First, schemes were liable to tax on returns on equity investments established by Brown's law. Second, schemes were liable to taxation on total asset valuation if the 5 % cap was exceeded (Lawson's law). Overnight, the abolition of the DTC effectively increased the cost of maintaining a solvent pension scheme. In isolation, the abolition of the DTC[35] would have been a perfectly justifiable action for a Labour government, particularly if the revenue raised from the tax had gone to pensioners, and if it had been 'followed up with measures to make the funds accountable to social and economic priorities'.[36] However, this was not the case. Indeed, in the March 2000 budget, the BSP was increased by only 75 pence—a sum that would only cover the price of a packet of peanuts, as pensioners remarked at the time.

To make matters worse for potentially vulnerable pension schemes, the firms that were most affected by the abolition of the DTC were those that had become accustomed to taking contribution holidays. As we have seen, such behaviour was encouraged by Lawson's tax cap. In short, the

---

[34] *The UK pension system.*
[35] Blackburn (2002) *Banking on Death* 316.
[36] *Banking on Death.*

two laws, when combined, made a potential pension crisis more likely by encouraging irresponsible and short-termist behaviour by corporations and by fundamentally contradicting each other. It is also the case that neither tax channelled additional revenue to help pensioners. Instead, the BSP was allowed to decline.

Recognition of the instabilities that Lawson and Brown introduced to pension schemes is necessary if one is to understand fully the nature of the crisis facing DB schemes, and the neoliberal arguments presented in the face of this crisis. The dominant pension crisis narrative (endorsed by both Turner Reports) ignored the impact of Lawson and Brown's respective roles as Chancellor of the Exchequer and the important role that their respective taxation reforms to pension schemes have played in destabilising and then magnifying these instabilities. It also ignored how willing employers were to exploit the impact of these instabilities in order to accelerate the closure of schemes. As such, it will be argued that the pension crisis in DB schemes is manufactured (artificial) rather than a 'naturally' occurring one, as is so often the case presented by the hegemonic discourse.

In addition to the above, very substantial factors that contributed towards a downturn in DB schemes, other factors made matters worse. The new tax regimes depended, and were modelled upon, the existence of a sustained bull market (within which share prices are rising, which encourages buying). This in turn meant that the whole system of DB schemes also became susceptible to market volatility. Indeed, the very instabilities referred to above are these instabilities—the inherent instability of directly linking the solvency of a scheme to the maintenance of a bull market. This was an astoundingly short-term perspective[37] that ignored the historical development of capitalism, which has consistently demonstrated that by their very nature markets are volatile.

Unsurprisingly, these conditions presented employers with difficult choices. It is hardly surprising that employers began to question their financial commitment to a DB pension scheme; many investigated less costly pension alternatives. It must be stressed here that DB pension schemes are not necessarily inherently unstable, as is often presented. By

---

[37] Morgan, *The UK pension system*, 321.

examining in detail various tax regimes, and the irresponsible behaviour these encouraged, it can be demonstrated that this pension crisis is not a naturally occurring facet of DB schemes. The neoliberal discourse of unavoidable crisis is one that employers are happy enough to use, as it has meant that they can abandon their commitment to these types of schemes. These are the most expensive to maintain, because they do require long-term commitment to something other than maintaining share dividends. Moreover, some organisations were in serious deficit, and employers were able to exert a considerable amount of moral blackmail on employees who were called upon to help save the company rather than pursue their pension entitlements. In short, employees were expected to absorb the reckless behaviour of their employers by accepting a lower standard of pension and be thankful things were not worse.

In addition, vulnerabilities exploited by the end to tax dividend credit were further intensified by the introduction of FRS17 (financial report-ing standard 17) accounting procedures for DB pension schemes. Unlike previous accounting procedures that produced an overly optimistic view of asset valuation based on a long-term prediction of past stock mar-ket performance, FSR17 did not flatten out fluctuations into long-term growth. The new calculation of schemes assets and liabilities meant that further vulnerabilities were introduced into an already over-exposed sys-tem. Originally intended to be phased in over a three-year period, FRS17 (introduced by the non-government Accounting Standards Board) exposed the extent of underfunding of schemes and the subsequent shortfalls, and forced organisations to 'face up to' shortfalls and deficits. Combined with the above, the introduction of FRS17 was to have the effect of persuading firms to close their DB schemes in favour of less secure schemes such as DC.

The introduction of DC schemes (along with other inferior pen-sion saving arrangements such Stakeholder Pensions, the proposed and now defunct Personal Accounts, and the soon-to-be-introduced Auto-Enrolment) as a replacement for DB schemes has represented a decrease in the quality of pension provision for employees. Employers who have closed their DB schemes contribute little or nothing to the new DC and Stakeholder Pensions, and by the very definition of 'defined contribution' (DC), these pensions offer no guarantee of retirement income. Indeed, we know that the 'low cost' Stakeholder Pension has produced miserable returns for savers. Collinson[38] calculated this year that those who saved £100 a month from April 2001 (thus paying in total £13,300) have only accumulated £14,600 eleven years later (April 2012). Savers would have been better investing in a cash Individual Savings Account (ISA) rather than a government-backed Stakeholder pension.

Therefore, the wholesale closure of DB schemes, either entirely or else to new members, was a result of the combination of systematically irresponsible tax regimes from the Chancellors of both major political parties; the greediness of employers willing to enjoy the benefits of the stock market in good times by taking contribution holidays but not willing accept the consequences of their actions in economic downturns; and the introduction of a new accountancy procedure, the FRS17. Conventional explanations (that reflect neoliberal ideology and the neoliberal construct of the crisis) cite the inherent instabilities of DB schemes that were somehow responsible for their own 'downfall'. As we have seen, this understanding is not merely oversimplified but is in fact incorrect. The move away from DB schemes was also an implicit recognition by employers that the need to offer attractive benefits such a long-term DB pension provision was no longer necessary to attract and retain employees. Given that we know financial planning is key to retirement planning,[39] the pension crisis as outlined above has left many with inadequate pensions, so we can expect to see many compelled to remain in the labour market to augment this shortfall. This is a very different narrative to that of choice to engage with flexible working practices and extension of working lives as a bridge, as we have seen outlined elsewhere.

2   New Policy Changes

In response to the 'crisis' outlined above, a new pension policy has been enacted; Auto-Enrolment pensions. Space precludes discussion of the increases in retirement age, as this change is discussed in more detail by

---

[38] P Collinson, 'We Need to Order a Danish Pension', *The Guardian* (13 July 2012).
[39] Price (2003) 'Professional Women's Retirement Adjustment'.

others in this collection. This section will provide a brief outline of stated aims of Auto-Enrolment, as it is suggested that this policy represents an improvement on previous state-led arrangements,[40] whilst also providing solutions to the pension crisis. As was demonstrated in the previous section, it will be argued here that an alternative analysis of the pension crisis helps us question the extent to which new policies will actually solve the crisis

Traditionally the UK had a three tiered pension system: Tier 1, basic state provision provided via taxation; Tier 2, additional (opt-in) earnings-related state provision; and Tier 3, private provision (occupational or personal pension). Thus Tiers 1 and 2 were state funded, and Tier 3 privately funded. In May 2014, Parliament passed the Pensions Act (2014), which introduced a new flat rate State Pension for people reaching State Pension Age on or after 6 April 2016. In addition to this change, the Pension Act (2008) heralded the introduction and implementation of Auto-Enrolment pensions (a private and public partnership workplace pension) in October 2012. The Pensions Act (2014) also included provisions for an increase in the age at which people would be eligible for the State Pension, though there is insufficient space to discuss these proposals at any length here.

Since the introduction of Auto-Enrolment pensions, government has made it policy that those who reach State Pension Age on or after 6 April 2016 will no longer be eligible for additional State Pension, and thus it is being phased out. Instead, the Basic State Pension (Tier 1) will provide all state only provision. Thus, after 2016 the three Tier pension system that will be arranged accordingly: New Tier 1) state public pension provided via taxation; New Tier 2) public/private partnership of individualised savings; New Tier 3) Individualised private occupational provision. This represents a significant shift and restructuring of the provision of pensions in the UK, and a move towards a more market-ised and individualised savings regime.

---

[40] S Webb (2013) 'Pensions minister Steve Webb on welfare reforms—video *The Guardian*, available at: http://www.theguardian.com/politics/video/2013/apr/01/pensions-minister-steve-webb-welfare-reforms-video, [accessed: 1 August 2015].

Auto-Enrolment pensions are available to all workers aged between 22 and the State Pension Age so long as they earn the required salary threshold, currently £10,000. Employees are automatically enrolled into a pension scheme chosen by their employer but have the right to opt out. The required level of contribution is 8% (employees contribute 4%, employers contribute 3%, and the government contributes 1%). Like most workplace pensions some of it can be taken as a tax-free lump sum upon retirement. Of the pension, 25% will be tax-free, but income tax must be paid on the rest.

In a recent report from the DWP it has also been suggested that:

* Automatic enrolment is proving significantly more successful than previously predicted. With opt outs remaining low we now expect nine million people will be newly saving or saving more as a result of our reforms.

* Our reforms to pensions are working and have already proved a success. Now this is an extra million savers who will be helping to secure a better future for themselves and their families.[41] (DWP 2014a)

Due to low opt-out figures, Auto-Enrolment pensions have been heralded by the government as a success with 4 million workers enrolled since their establishment.[42] Membership of occupational pension schemes has traditionally been higher for men, so it is also expected that the introduction of Auto-Enrolment, open to all who earn over the threshold, will help address this imbalance, and bring women into workplace pension provision. As such, Auto-Enrolment pensions has been welcomed by the Trades Union Congress, but concerns have also been raised about the suitability of Auto-Enrolment for providing an adequate pension.[43]

[41] DWP (2014) *Press Release: Pension savings—9 million newly saving or saving more, says Pensions Minister*, available at: https://www.gov.uk/government/news/pensions-savings-9-million-newly-saving-or-saving-more-says-pensions-minister, [accessed: 1 August 2015] 2014a.

[42] J Ugwumadu (2014) 'Four million now auto-enrolled into workplace pensions', *The Actuary*, available at: http://www.theactuary.com/news/2014/08/four-million-now-auto-enrolled-into-workplace-pensions/2014 [accessed: 1 August 2015].

[43] H Osborne (2012) 'Warning over poor performing auto-enrolment pensions', *The Guardian* (11 Oct 2012); PWC (2012) available at: http://pwc.blogs.com/scotland/2012/09/millennials-pensions-will-fall-short-of-todays-pensioners-despite-auto-enrolment.html [accessed: 1 August 2015]; PPI (2013) 'What level of pension contribution is needed to obtain an adequate retirement income?'

An initial problem is that many of the poorest workers do not earn enough to qualify for enrolment. Given that women are more likely to be low paid,[44] we see a higher proportion of women being excluded. But we also know that income is key in retirement planning, so this pension provision is less likely to help the lowest earners strategically save for their retirement, because they simple do not earn enough to begin with. As such, they ideally need assistance, rather than access to a scheme. In addition, even for those enrolled there are concerns that the value of the pension will not to deliver sustainable retirement incomes.[45] The main cause of concern with Auto-Enrolment is that a contribution rate of 8% is just too low. Indeed, the DWP acknowledge that someone earning £28,900 would need to put away £3,250 a year (11.2% of salary), to even have a chance of a comfortable retirement.[46] As Auto-Enrolment only requires 8 % contributions, this leaves a 3.2 % gap for this salary group. Given that the Auto-Enrolment threshold is £10,000 we can see this will be a particular problem for low earners, as not only will their pension be significantly smaller due to their low income but also it is less likely that they will have any spare income to save additional amounts over the 8 % minimum contribution. If the value of the pension is allowed to fall, then this is most likely to impact on low earners who are unable to save as much privately, or may be denied access to Auto-Enrolment.[47]

Available at: http://www.pensionspolicyinstitute.org.uk/publications/reports/what-level-of-pension-contribution-is-needed-to-obtain-an-adequate-retirement-income [accessed: 1 August 2015]; A. Uren (2013) 'The 12 m workers who risk retiring on inadequate incomes with middle earners hit hardest by a pensions shock', available at: http://www.thisismoney.co.uk/money/pensions/article-2418601/12m-working-adults-face-retiring-inadequate-incomes.html, [accessed: 1 August 2015]; H. Roberts (2014a) available at: http://www.hrmagazine.co.uk/hro/news/1143906/staff-employers-concerned-retirement-savings, [accessed: 1 August 2015]; H. Roberts (2014b) http://www.hrmagazine.co.uk/hro/news/1146027/auto-enrolment-doesnt-provide-decent-income-low-paid-workers-tuc [accessed: 1 August 2015]; I UC (2014) 'Auto-enrolment pensions must do more for low-paid workers, says TUC, 2014', http://www.tuc.org.uk/economic-issues/pensions-and-retirement/auto-enrolment-pensions-must-do-more-low-paid-workers-says [accessed: 1 August 2015].

[44] M Saari (2013) 'Promoting Gender Equality without a Gender Perspective: Problem Representations of Equal Pay in Finland' *Gender Work and Organization* 20(1) 34–54; T Warren (2003) 'A Privileged Pole? iversity in Women's Pay, Pensions and Wealth in Britain', *Gender Work and Organization* 10(5), 605–628.

[45] PWC 2012; Uren, 'The 12 m workers'.

[46] K Morley (2014) 'Rethinking the Pension' *Investors Chronicle* (23 January 2014) 3.

[47] C Saunders (2013) 'Pot half full? How women lose out when it comes to pensions' *The Guardian* (1 May 2013) available at: http://www.theguardian.com/women-in-leadership/2013/may/01/

In addition, increased contributions from employees will not be matched with increased contributions from either employer or State, which leaves little incentive for very low earners to redirect salary to their pension pot. Thus, the Auto-Enrolment scheme is praised as a triumph because it offers access to workplace pension saving for many more people. However, as 8% contributions are unlikely to provide a sufficient retirement income for savers, Auto-Enrolment provides the illusion of adequate pension provision, rather than the delivery of it. The likely outcome of Auto-Enrolment, then, is increased working life as recipients will not be able to supplement fully their working income with their pension. This further demonstrates that for some non-retirement may well be representative of coercion rather than personal choice.

The account of Auto-Enrolment advanced by government also suggests that a level playing field has been created because the ability to save independently has been extended to women. This is only part of the narrative for women, however. At the same time, the increasing costs of childcare will prolong female breaks from the labour market as more new mothers decide to stay at home or work part-time.[48] This will additionally dilute the value paid into Auto-Enrolment pensions by women, further calling into question its suitability, which will obviously impact on the retirement choices of these workers when they are older, and indeed may compel them into longer working lives.

It should be noted that Auto-Enrolment is accompanied by the introduction of the New Flat Rate State Pension, which is intended to simplify the existing complex system. It is also expected that a simpler and fairer system will make it easier for individuals to plan their retirement savings. The features that differentiate it from the old State Pension are that it will be worth more than the current Basic State Pension and will be given to people with at least 35 years National Insurance (NI) contributions or credits. People will need at least 10 years of contributions to qualify for any new State Pension, and those with between 10 and 34 years of contributions

---

women-lose-out-on-pensions, [accessed 1 August 2015]; WRC 'Women's equality in the UK—A health check', CEDAW (2013) *Shadow report 2013* (Women's Resource Centre).

[48] G Cory & V Alakeson (2014) 'The Resolution Foundation, Careers and Carers', available at: http://www.resolutionfoundation.org/media/media/downloads/Careers_and_Carers_FINAL.pdf [accessed: 1 August 2015].

will receive a proportion of the pension. This clearly represents an advance on old arrangements, but given the limitations outlined of Auto-Enrolment and the scaling back of occupational schemes, alongside the increase in atypical employment, it is highly unlikely that this policy change will make much a difference for those that require help. Thus, as with Auto-Enrolment, the new flat rate pension system again represents the illusion of an adequate pension, not the delivery of it.

3   Compulsion, Non-Retirement, and Longer Working Lives

A re-examination of the pension crisis, and also proposed solutions to the crisis allow us to understand that, for many, longer working lives will not be the product of a choice but a result of economic compulsion due to their inability to amass enough savings to retire. This directly challenges the literature that extols the virtues of extending work, and in particular the notion that flexible working will be beneficial to older workers. Indeed, it is likely to extend low-pay work for those who have already endured a career of it.

This of course raises issues regarding how we deal with inequality. Recent research has demonstrated that increasingly older workers are 'performance managed' out of the workforce.[49] Moreover, workers with the greatest need or desire to continue working (for example those from low pay and poor pension coverage occupations) are not necessarily those that employers are choosing to keep.[50]

A key problem is that Auto-Enrolment does not address the pension crisis these workers will face, as it does not cover many low-paid workers, and even those that do qualify will not be able to save enough.[51] Another problem is the way in which the pension crisis is predominantly presented and discussed in mainstream debates; namely that individuals

---

[49] L Vickers and S Manfredi (2013) 'Age Equality and retirement: squaring the circle', *Industrial Law Journal* 42(1), 61–74; Beck and Williams 'The (performance) management of retirement'.
[50] Beck and Williams 'The (performance) management of retirement', 210.
[51] Morley, 'Rethinking the Pension', 3.

do not save enough privately and are living longer than ever before. As this chapter has demonstrated, the reality is much more complex than the dominant narrative, and moreover the proposed solutions will not actually do much to relieve poverty amongst pensioners, indeed, the new policies actually transfer risk on to them, and potentially guarantee the extension of working lives. Moreover it is not expected that this situation will improve any time soon because all mainstream parties broadly favour a neoliberal approach to managing the economy, and to inform the development of pension policy.[52]

The dominance of neoliberal thinking in economic policy is key in explaining the push towards privatisation of State Pension provision (as evident in the creation of Auto-Enrolment, a public/private partnership which replaces state only provision). Specifically, it helps us understand why a fundamental rethinking of the pension system in the UK is unlikely, as any such rethink would have to directly undermine the neoliberal preference for increased privatisation and transferral of risk to individuals.[53] Thus questions are asked instead about extending working lives and transforming what it means to retire. The fundamental reform required of pension provision is considered beyond the realms of what is possible within the current economic environment where neoliberal economic thinking is suspicious of state involvement.[54] Moreover, unless we implement policies that will ensure the protection of employment rights in older age, we are likely to see older workers 'performance managed' out of their jobs as Beck and Williams and Vickers and Manfredi have outlined. Thus we have a twofold problem; (1) compulsion to stay in the labour market rather than a choice, and (2) discrimination in that

---

[52] Blackburn, *Banking on Death*; R Blackburn (2004) 'How to Rescue a Failing Pension Regime: The British Case', *New Political Economy* 9(4),559–581; J Grady (June 2010) 'From Beveridge to Turner: Laissez-faire to Neoliberalism' *Capital and Class*, 163–180; J Grady 'Trade Unions and the Pension Crisis'; J Macnicol (1998) *The Politics of Retirement in Britain 1878-1948* (Cambridge University Press); Morgan 'The UK pension system'; J Myles (1984) *Old Age in the Welfare State: The Political Economy of Public Pensions.* (Scott Forseman and Company).

[53] J Grady (2010) 'From Beveridge to Turner'; J Hacker and P Peirson (2010) *Winner-Take-All Politics*, (Simon and Schuster); D Harvey (2005) *A Brief Introduction to Neoliberalism* (Oxford University Press); Morgan, 'The UK pension system'.

[54] Harvey, *Neoliberalism*; D Harvey (2010) *The Enigma of Capital: And the Crises of Capitalism* (Verso).

labour market impacting on the ability of certain workers to earn decent incomes (often those who require staying in labour market the most).[55] What we are likely to see is greater income inequality in old age and increased pensioner poverty.

4   Conclusion

The focus of this volume is important to those interested in how we construct sustainable working lives, and how we secure equality for workers who face discrimination. As life expectancy increases, and retirement ages rise we are likely to see a proliferation in research investigating the various topics discussed over the following chapters. What has been offered here is a reconceptualisation of the context that will frame these debates. Such a re-examination is important because work life sustainability will be an illusion for many if the choice to stay in the labour market after retirement is in fact a *Hobson's choice*.[56]

Thus if we would like to see genuine choice being exercised with regards to people's decision to stay in the labour market after the traditional retirement age, then this needs to be accompanied with access to pension schemes that will provide an adequate income in retirement for all workers. However, this seems unlikely given the current economic context as neoliberal economic doctrine which currently influences UK government prefers privatisation and individualisation of pensions. All of this, as has been demonstrated, will disproportionately affect low-paid workers, who are the most likely to need to work into retirement.

---

[55] Beck and Williams 'The (performance) management of retirement'.

[56] A *Hobson's choice* is a free choice, but in which only one option is offered.

4

The Challenges of Active Ageing in the UK: A Case Study of the Approach to Retirement in the UK

Simonetta Manfredi and Lucy Vickers

1   Introduction

In 2011, age discrimination legislation in the UK was repealed. As a result, it became unlawful for employers to have a contractual retirement age, unless this can be objectively justified in order to achieve a legitimate aim. This chapter will review the extent to which these legislative changes are helping to meet the challenges of active ageing. It will also consider the ways in which other aspects of the law are protecting older workers and supporting the extension of working lives. It begins by identifying five main challenges faced by policy makers in the UK when addressing the active ageing agenda, which aims to encourage and support the extension of working lives. It traces the evolution of age discrimination legislation in the UK, from a voluntary code, through the use of the right to request and the default retirement age, to the removal of retirement ages altogether in 2011. It then turns to assess when employers may be able to justify mandatory retirement under current UK legislation, in the light of the jurisprudence developed by the Court of Justice of the European Union (CJEU). It also considers the use of settlement agreements and

© The Editor(s) (if applicable) and The Author(s) 2016   **71**
S. Manfredi, L. Vickers (eds.), *Challenges of Active Ageing*,
DOI 10.1057/978-1-137-53251-0_4

performance management by employers to terminate older workers' contracts of employment. Finally, it discusses how we might meet the needs of older workers who wish to extend their working lives.

2   The Challenges of Active Ageing in the UK

As with many other countries, the UK faces a number of challenges which are connected with the active ageing agenda. Most of these challenges are discussed elsewhere in this volume, but will be briefly reprised here and considered within the specific national context.

The first challenge refers to demographic trends combined with early retirement and rates of work inactivity for people aged over 50, which amount to *de facto* early retirement. Projections from the UK Office for National Statistics[1] indicate that life expectancy at 65 is due to increase significantly over the coming years. For example since 1980, life expectancy has risen from just under 15 years to 21 years for men aged 65, and is forecast to rise to 27 years by 2060; for women, it has increased from 18 years to 24 years over the same period and is forecast to reach 29 years by 2060.[2] The proportion of people between the ages of 50–64 represent 41.5% of the total number of economically inactive people aged 18–64.[3] The fact that such a high proportion of older people are out of work and are not actively seeking employment can give 'the false impression that worklessness amongst older people is not a problem, as it masks a deeper problem with economic inactivity'.[4] This scenario is exemplified by what has been described as the 'the age/employment paradox',[5] which refers

---

[1] Department for Work and Pensions ('DWP') (June 2014) *Fuller working lives: Background evidence*, (DWP) 11 https://www.gov.uk/government/uploads/system/uploads/attachment_data/file/319948/fuller-working-lives-background-evidence.pdf [accessed 15 July 2015].

[2] *Fuller working lives* 11.

[3] Business in the Community (2015) *The Mission Million. Recommendations for Action.*,(Business in the Community: 12 http://www.bitc.org.uk/system/files/the_missing_million_-_rec_for_action_23-4-2015.pdf [accessed 20th July 2015].

[4] *Fuller working lives* 9.

[5] A Walker (29–30 November 2001) 'Towards active ageing in the European Union' Paper prepared for the *Millennium Project Workshop—Towards Active Ageing in the 21st Century* (Tokyo: The Japan Institute of Labour) 3.

to the fact that while life expectancy has increased, participation in the labour market has dropped due to early retirement trends. This in turn leads into a second challenge, which is the financial sustainability of pension benefits.

In response to an increase in life expectancy the UK government, similarly to other countries, has increased the State Pension Age (SPA): in 2011, the Pension Act was introduced, which provides for a gradual increase of the state pension age for both men and women to 66 by 2020 and to 67 between 2024 and 2026. This is to be complemented by an automatic review of the SPA to take place every five years, with the first review being planned to take place in 2017. It is estimated that the effect of these changes, together with demographic trends, will lead to a much larger working-age population driven by more people aged 50 and over. Currently, the proportion of people between the age of 50 and the SPA represents 27% of the working-age population but by 2020 the Office for National Statistics predicts that this is set to increase to 32% by 2020.[6] These figures demonstrate the importance of ensuring that older people remain active in the labour market.

In the past 10–15 years, there has been an increase in average retirement ages and, compared to other members of the OECD group of nations, the employment rates of older people aged 55–64 in the UK are in the middle of the range, at just below 60%.[7] Nonetheless, this is still below the 70% employment rate of older workers in countries like Norway, Sweden, Switzerland and New Zealand, and the employment rate of just under 80% achieved in Iceland.

A further challenge is that of intergenerational fairness. This is a complex issue that refers to two contrasting views: on the one hand, it refers to the idea that if older workers remain in their jobs past conventional retirement ages they may block the employment prospects of younger workers. Consequently, as a matter of intergenerational fairness, they should retire to allow younger workers to have a fair opportunity in the labour market. On the other hand, intergenerational fairness refers to

---

[6] *Fuller working lives* 12.
[7] *Fuller working lives*: 21.

concerns that older people are taking up too many public resources in the form of pension benefits at the expense of younger generations.

The first notion of intergenerational fairness, which advocates that older workers should hand their jobs on to younger workers in order to give them a fair chance in life has been criticised as based on a flawed economic model, although this remains contested.[8] For example, evidence from member states of the OECD[9] show that on average, those countries that do well at employing older people also maintain higher employment rates for younger workers. It is acknowledged, however, that at the micro level of individual organisations, unlike in the macro economy, resources are finite, and employers may not hire new employees until older ones retire and free up resources to take on new people. In the UK, labour market statistics show that while over the last 10–15 years employment rates of people over 50 have been increasing, at the same time employment rates for 25—49-year-olds have been broadly constant, with a 1–2 percentage point dip during the recession followed by recent improvement back to previous levels; instead, rates for people aged 18–24 years, who are not in full time education, have seen a decline. It was slightly steeper during the recession, but has been followed by a recent improvement.[10]

With regard to the second notion of intergenerational fairness, the debate is exemplified by the position taken by the Intergenerational Foundation, an independent UK think tank, which argues that, among other things, the costs of pensions and other benefits enjoyed by older people continue to rise,[11] and create a burden for younger generations. This view is echoed by the media,[12] which often portray older people as having had it all compared to the younger generations who instead are facing precarious employment, high university tuition fees and a shortage of affordable houses. Thus, organisations like the Intergenerational Foundation have called upon the UK government 'to embark on a

---

[8] S Fredman (2003) 'The Age of Equality' in S Fredman and S Spencer *Age as an Equality Issue: Legal and Policy Perspectives* (Oxford: Hart Publishing) 46.

[9] OECD (2012) *Live Longer, Work Longer* (OECD Publishing).

[10] *Fuller working lives* 26.

[11] See J Leech (2015) A. Hanton Intergenerational Foundation Index 2015 http://www.if.org.uk/wp-content/uploads/2015/07/2015-Intergenerational-Fairness-Index.pdf [accessed 24 July 2015].

[12] See for example 'Battle of the ages: Britain's new political divide' *The Guardian* 16 July 2015.

programme of intergenerational rebalancing'. The implications of this 'intergenerational rebalancing', among other things, are likely to involve the extension of working lives to reduce pension benefits.

These conflicting arguments create a tension between push and pull factors and, as argued elsewhere, older workers 'appear to be caught in a squeeze between governmental pressure away from retirement benefits and organisational pressure away from the workplace'.[13]

Another challenge is that of finding a way to meet the needs of older workers who will want to avoid discrimination and maintain dignity at the end of their careers. However, many may wish to extend their working lives because of inadequate pension income, for example, or adopt increased flexible working opportunities. Statistics show that older workers are more likely to work part-time or flexibly. There is however, a high demand from older workers for flexible working that research suggests has remained unmet.[14] Moreover, the proportion of people aged 50 and over who are unemployed and have been out of work for more than 12 months is significantly higher, 47.2%, than the 34.3% of all UK adults in the same situation.[15] This suggests that it may be more difficult for this group to find employment, and that they may be discriminated against because of their age.

A final challenge comes from employers. Research commissioned by the government prior to the abolition of mandatory retirement showed that, unsurprisingly, those organisations that did not have a contractual mandatory retirement age were favourable to the abolition of retirement whilst those organisations which had a contractual retirement age were against it. This study highlighted that these organisations found it useful to have a contractual retirement age as it provided 'a focal point to

---

[13] C Coupland, S Tempest and C Barnatt (2008) 'What are the implications of the new age discrimination legislation for research and practice?' *Human Resource Management Journal*, Vol 18(4), 423–431.

[14] Business in the Community (2015) *The Mission Million. Recommendations for Action* (Business in the Community) 20 http://www.bitc.org.uk/system/files/the_missing_million_-_rec_for_action_23-4-2015.pdf. Accessed 22 October 2015.

[15] Business in the Community (2015) *The Mission Million. Recommendations for Action* (Business in the Community) 12.

discuss an employee's future and plan resources'.[16] Furthermore, it was felt that if older employees' performance starts to decline, having a contractual retirement age would offer an opportunity to retire an employee compassionately without going through an arduous and potentially bitter performance management process.

The abolition of mandatory retirement was opposed by the Confederation of British Businesses (CBI). More recently, a review of employment law commissioned by the UK coalition government[17] suggested that 'there remains however, a concern that in the absence of a default retirement age (DRA), employers will be strongly deterred from hiring older workers, and that it will be difficult to remove older workers who are underperforming'. It recommended that practices relating to managing without a retirement age in the workplace should be monitored and, if it becomes clear that the concerns mentioned above turn out to be real issues for businesses, 'then it might be possible to show that a DRA, perhaps at a higher age than 65, could be objectively justified as a proportionate means of meeting the legitimate aims of encouraging businesses to hire older workers and improving the effectiveness of the workforce'.

In summary we have identified five key challenges which are linked to the active ageing agenda.

The first challenge requires the UK government to tackle the 'age/employment' paradox by increasing rates of labour market participation of older workers, aged 50 and above.

The second challenge relates to the need to ensure pension sustainability by changing retirement trends and creating the conditions for older workers to extend their working lives.

The third challenge about 'intergenerational fairness' is particularly complex, since it presents two conflicting aspects: on the one hand, it advocates that older workers should hand over their jobs to the younger generations; on the other hand, it portrays older people as a drain on public resources

---

[16] A Thomas, J Pascal (2010) *Default retirement age—employer qualitative research* Research Report 672. (DWP) 4.

[17] Beecroft, A. (2011) *Report on Employment Law* 6.https://www.gov.uk/government/publications/employment-law-review-report-beecroft [accessed 1 May 2015].

and argues that they should extend their working lives to reduce their dependency on pension benefits.

The fourth challenge relates to individual older workers and the need to ensure that their needs are met in order to enable them to extend their working lives.

The fifth challenge focuses more specifically on the workplace and the need for ensuring that employers 'buy into' the active ageing agenda and support the extension of working lives.

In the next section, the UK legal framework, together with its implementation in practice, will be briefly examined. This will be followed by an assessment of the extent to which the legal framework can be said to be successful in meeting the challenges identified above.

3   The UK Legal Framework

The first steps to tackle age discrimination in the UK came through soft law measures introduced prior to the creation of the EU Directive in 1999. These steps began with the introduction of a non-enforceable Code of Practice on Age Diversity in Employment, which aimed to raise awareness about age discrimination, highlight the benefits of employing an age diverse workforce and to reverse early retirement trends. However, this measure had little practical effect: awareness levels about the Code among employers remained very low, and few changes took place.[18] The next stage in the journey towards removing retirement ages came in 2006 when the UK government implemented the provisions of the EU Directive 2000/78 with regard to age discrimination. The Employment (Age) Regulations 2006 (the 'Age Regulations') made direct and indirect discrimination on the grounds of age unlawful and provided for a DRA of 65. This meant that employers could no longer retire employees before the age of 65, except in those instances where it could be objectively justified, for example for health and safety reasons.

---

[18] D Jones (June 2000) *Evaluation of the Code of Practice on Age Diversity in Employment, Research Brief* RBX 6/00 (Nottingham: Department for Education and Employment).

The 2006 Age Regulations introduced new rules for workers aged 65 and older, which aimed to address the complex issues surrounding retirement[19] by simultaneously encouraging employees to work beyond retirement while allowing employers to require them to leave. This was achieved by removing the bar on claiming unfair dismissal and redundancy for those over the age of 65, and introducing a right for all employees to request to continue to work past the age of 65 (or their contractual retirement age, if this was later than 65). However, employers only had to formally consider a request to continue to work past retirement; they were under no obligation to allow such requests or to provide a reason if they decided to refuse it. This 'right to request' procedure created a paradoxical situation. Employers had to formally notify employees approaching retirement age of their right to request to continue to work, a practice which gave the impression that they had a choice as to when to retire. Yet, if employees made such a request the employer could refuse with no explanation.

Perhaps unsurprisingly, given the rather mixed messages the procedure created, the right to request procedure was short-lived and, in 2011, it was abolished. This meant that in the UK, mandatory retirement would amount to direct discrimination, and would be lawful only if objectively justified as a proportionate means to achieve a legitimate aim of employment policy (this is known as an employer's justified retirement age (EJRA)). The changes in the law in the UK have not meant that retirement has been barred as a practice; instead, the changes relate to the default position regarding retirement. Prior to the implementation of the Directive, retirement was lawful. Since 2011, it is lawful only if it can be justified.

These changes were intended to meet some of the challenges highlighted earlier, and strike a balance between, on the one hand, socio-economic needs for extending working lives together with the needs of older workers not to be discriminated against by being made to retire once they have reached a particular age and, on the other, the needs of employers for effective workforce planning. This balancing exercise is carried out through the mechanism of the EJRA. The question of when retirement can be legally justified is considered next.

[19] S Fredman (2003) 'The Age of Equality' in S Fredman and S Spencer *Age as an equality Issue: Legal and Policy Perspectives* (Oxford: Hart):53.

3.1 Justifying Retirement

Justification of retirement under the Equality Act 2010 is a two-stage process: the identification of an aim which courts will accept as legitimate, as well as a factual finding that the use of the aim in the context was proportionate. In other areas of equality law, proportionality requires that the means chosen for achieving the aim or objective must correspond to a real need on the part of the undertaking, must be appropriate with a view to achieving the objective in question and must be necessary to that end.[20]

A number of cases have been heard by the CJEU which consider the justification of retirement, as discussed in chapters 1 and 2 in this volume. In the UK, the issue was discussed in some detail in *Seldon v. Clarkson Wright and Jakes*.[21] In this case, Mr. Seldon, the claimant, was a partner in a firm of solicitors which had adopted a mandatory retirement age for partners at 65. Once Mr. Seldon achieved the age of 65, according to the rules of the partnership agreement, he was made to retire. He claimed that this amounted to age discrimination. Although the case started under the Age Regulations (2006) when there was still a DRA, and applied to the context of a partnership agreement rather than the employment relationship, the legal question turned on whether the retirement could be objectively justified, and so it is still of relevance to the new legal context.

In the context of EU law, a number of objectives have been accepted by courts as legitimate, including enabling employers to manage workforce planning;[22] promoting better access to employment by means of better distribution of work among different generations;[23] and the aim of avoiding disputes relating to employees' ability to perform their duties beyond the age of 65.[24] These objectives were identified in *Seldon* as

---

[20] *Bilka-KaufhausvWeber von Hartz*[1986] ECR 1607-1631[1986] ECR 1607.

[21] Seldon v. Clarkson Wright and Jakes[2012] UKSC 16.

[22] Case 388/07 *The Incorporated Trustees of the National Council on Aging v. Secretary of State for Business* ('Age Concern').

[23] Case C-411/05 *Felix Palacios de la Villa v. CortefielServicios SA*;CJEU Case C341/08 *Petersen v. Berufungsausschuss fur Zahn fur den BezirkWestfalen-Lippe* Judgment 12 January 2010,; CJEU Case C-45/09 *Rosenblatt v. OellerkingGebaudereinigungsges.mbH* Judgment 12 October 2010 (*Rosenblatt*); CJEU Case C141/11, *Hörnfeldt v. MeddelandeCase* Judgment 5 July 2012 (*Hörnfeldt*).

[24] *Rosenblatt, Hörnfeldt*.

potentially justifying the mandatory retirement of Mr. Seldon. Among other things, the rule enabled associate solicitors to be given the opportunity of partnership after a reasonable period by ensuring a reasonable turnover of staff; facilitated workforce planning by having a realistic expectation as to when vacancies would arise; and limited the need to expel partners by way of performance management, thus contributing to a congenial and supportive culture in the respondent firm.[25] These aims were summarised by the Supreme Court as the 'dignity' argument and the 'intergenerational fairness' argument. While these aims were agreed to be legitimate, the Court did add a note of caution. First, the Supreme Court was clear that it was only the legitimacy of the aim that was being decided: the parties still had to show that, on the facts, the reliance on the legitimate aim was necessary and proportionate. Second, Lady Hale noted that the 'assumptions underlying these objectives look suspiciously like stereotyping'.[26] She therefore expressed sympathy with the position of Age UK, which intervened in the case, that such concerns should not be capable of justifying retirement. However, ultimately she allowed the claim to continue on the basis that the CJEU case law is clear that the aim of upholding dignity (that is, the avoidance of debates around older workers' capacity) is capable of being a legitimate aim for mandatory retirement. Nonetheless, Lady Hale was clear that although potentially legitimate, the aim of upholding the dignity of older workers by avoiding performance management should be applied very carefully in practice, and that it must be justified on the particular circumstances of the case.

4   Meeting the Challenges of Active Ageing?

The current legal framework in the UK thus seems to meet some of the challenges regarding active ageing identified above: the removal of default retirement encourages later working, and thereby addresses the first challenge, but the facility to justify retirement where there are legitimate

---

[25] See Seldon at para 9.

[26] *Seldon* at para 57.

reasons to do so allows for the other challenges to be met too. The need for employers to plan their workforce; the need to meet the competing needs of younger workers; and the need to safeguard the dignity of older workers are all accepted as legitimate aims for retirement in the UK.

However, as recognised in *Seldon*, these latter aims can be contested, in terms of both their legitimacy and of whether enforcing retirement is a proportionate means to achieve them. In terms of its inherent legitimacy, intergenerational fairness can be contested as it has not been proven that older workers block the career progression of younger workers.[27] Moreover, the idea of intergenerational fairness has also been criticised as its notion of fairness is predicated on the assumption that careers span around 40 years and culminate in pensioned retirement, despite the fact that such careers are not necessarily the norm, particularly for women and those in the secondary labour market of low-skill and low-paid jobs.[28]

The aim of preserving dignity via forced retirement is also contentious, as it is based on the assumption that performance deteriorates with age, and that older workers may need help in recognising this.[29] In the light of these concerns regarding legitimacy, we next consider in more detail the extent to which retirement can really be seen as an effective mechanism for meeting the challenges for active ageing set out above.

4.1   Challenging the Justification of Retirement

In addition to the inherent problems presented by a reliance on the needs of workforce planning, intergenerational fairness and dignity as legitimate aims for compulsory retirement a number of other concerns can be identified when the justifications for retirement are considered in more practical detail.

---

[27] S Fredman (2003) 'The Age of Equality' in S Fredman and S Spencer, *Age as an Equality Issue: Legal and Policy Perspectives* (Oxford: Hart Publishing) 46.

[28] M Reich, D M Gordon and R C Edwards (1982) 'Dual Labour Markets: A Theory of Labour Market Segmentation' *The Journal of Human Resources* 17/3: 359–365; See also S Manfredi (2011) 'Retirement, Collective Agreement, and Age Discrimination: Implications for the Higher Education Sector in the UK' *International Journal of Discrimination and the Law* Vol.11, No.1/2: 65–80.

[29] This was recognised by Lady Hale in the Supreme Court in *Seldon* [2012] UKSC 16 at para 58. See also E. Dewhurst (2015) 'Are Older Workers Past Their Sell-by Date? A View from UK Age Discrimination Law' 78 (2) *MLR* 189.

Dignity or Collegiality

The first concern relates to the use of dignity or collegiality as a justification for retirement. As referred to above, such arguments are implicitly suspect as they rely on an assumption that performance declines with age. Despite the fact that such an assumption relies on stereotypes of older workers, research suggests that such assumptions are made routinely by employers. It is arguable that rather than entrench such stereotypes into a potential defence to age discrimination claims, courts should instead be robust in challenging them.[30]

A second difficulty arises if the dignity approach is used in workplaces which have clear performance management processes. In *Seldon*, the use of retirement was accepted as legitimate on the basis that the partnership in which Mr. Seldon worked did not have clear performance management processes in place. However, in many workplaces, performance management or disciplinary procedures are in place, and so this aim is less appropriate. As Lady Hale pointed out in *Seldon*, if 'the business has sophisticated performance management measures in place, it may not be legitimate to avoid them for only one section of the workforce',[31] such as older workers. It may therefore be difficult to justify retirement on the basis of collegiality where workplaces have performance management processes in place. The fact that such processes are commonplace in many workplaces means that the dignity approach to justifying retirement may be much more limited in its practical application than at first appears.

General or Individual Justification?

Proportionality usually requires that an employer can justify not only the general rule but also its application to the individual. In other areas of discrimination law, justification has to be both general and individual: once a general justification has been identified, one must return to

---

[30] 'Are Older Workers Past Their Sell-by Date?' 189.
[31] 'Are Older Workers Past Their Sell-by-Date?' paragraph 61.

the facts of the particular case to see if there was any particular injustice involved in applying the rule to the individual.[32]

Yet this approach causes particular difficulties in the context of retirement, as retirement is the imposition of a general rule imposed for broad policy reasons which may not always fit with the needs of the particular person discriminated against. This gives rise to a tension in the use of proportionality in retirement cases where the employer wishes to justify a general retirement age for staff. Although the employer is likely to identify a legitimate aim, such as intergenerational fairness, in order to meet the requirements of proportionality it may be necessary to allow for exceptions where retirement is not fair on the individual. For example, in *Palacios*,[33] the use of mandatory retirement was justified as proportionate in part because the retirement provisions only applied where full pension had accrued. The fact that Mr. Palacios had accrued a full pension was therefore a relevant factor in determining the proportionality of the retirement provision.

This begs the question of whether retirement can be justified as proportionate in cases where the individual does not have much pension. Thus far, both the CJEU and the UK courts have accepted that general rules regarding retirement will be justified even where for the individual some hardship may result. In *Rosenbladt*,[34] the worker's pension provision was very low, but the Court upheld the general provision regarding mandatory retirement. Such an approach was taken by the CJEU also in *Hörnfeldt v. Meddelande*,[35] where the Court confirmed that a blanket rule on retirement could be justified, even if it resulted in some hardship to the individual.

This matter was discussed in *Seldon*. The question of whether the age discriminatory measure had to be justified in general as well as in its application to the particular individual was answered somewhat vaguely. Lady Hale suggests that if retirement rules are generally justified, then

---

[32] 'The very concept of proportionality is inimical to "one size fits all" solutions' Michael Rubenstein, EOR 01/02/11 p 25. See also *Cadman* v. *Health & Safety Executive* [2006] IRLR 969.

[33] *Case 411/05 Felix Palacios de la Villa v. Cortefiel Servicios* SA.

[34] *Rosenbladt.*

[35] *Hörnfeldt.*

their consequences are likely to be so too; otherwise, there is little sense in formulating the rules. Thus, the wider policy aims can justify retirement practices even if their implementation in the particular case causes hardship.

A further question arises regarding the need to justify as proportionate the particular age that is used for the retirement rule. The difficulty here is that whatever age is used will be difficult to justify *vis-à-vis* a different but similar age. Thus, although one might justify the need for a retirement age to allow for workforce planning, it is difficult to justify that the age should be 65, as opposed to 64, or 66. The courts have refused to be drawn into the difficulty; instead, they have been clear that as long as the need for an age-based rule can be shown, they will uphold the age—even though another age could do just as well. For example, when the case of *Seldon* returned to the tribunal for a hearing on the issue of proportionality following the decision of the Supreme Court, the tribunal had to decide whether the age of 65 for retirement was justified. The Employment Tribunal (ET) referred to the Employment Appeal Tribunal (EAT) the question of whether the fact that another age could be identified that would meet the legitimate aims meant that the use of the age 65 was not proportionate. The EAT held that the fact that the age could have been set at a different age such as 64 or 66 did not make it wrong in law to fix the age at 65. This approach can also be seen in the case of *Reynolds*,[36] where Lord Hoffman pointed out that 'a line must be drawn somewhere. All that is necessary is that it should reflect a difference between the substantial majority of the people on either side of the line.'[37]

This overview of the case law suggests that for organisations to adopt an EJRA may be seen as risky, since it can be complex to demonstrate that there is an objective justification for maintaining mandatory retirement if challenged on the grounds of age discrimination. Nonetheless, as we have seen before, many employers still see the abolition of retirement as problematic, and may look for ways to terminate the employment contracts of older workers.

---

[36] *R (Reynolds) v. Secretary of State for Work and Pensions* [2005] UKHL 37 ('*Reynolds*'). See also Hepple (2014) *Equality: the Legal Framework* (2nd Ed Oxford Hart Publishing) 80.

[37] *Reynolds* para 41.

4.2   Reinstating Retirement Through the Backdoor?

Even though mandatory retirement was abolished in 2011, there is some evidence that retirement has been continuing *de facto* through informal and formal processes adopted by employers.

In response to employers' opposition to the abolition of mandatory retirement—most notably from the CBI, as seen earlier—Business Secretary Vince Cable of the UK coalition government introduced a mechanism for employers to have what have been defined as 'protected conversations'. These would enable employers to discuss issues around performance or retirement with their employees in confidence and without fear of being sued at an employment tribunal. As a result, Section 14 of the Enterprise and Regulation Reform Act 2013 provides a statutory framework under which employers can initiate negotiations with an employee in order to reach agreement to terminate employment in a consensual way and in return for a payoff. What is discussed as part of these 'protected conversations' is inadmissible in most unfair dismissal claims, except where it can be demonstrated that the employer acted 'improperly'. This might be deemed to be the case if, for example, an employee is put under undue pressure to accept the terms on offer, or is not given reasonable time for considering the offer made by the employer. This provision was designed to address employers' concerns relating to the abolition of mandatory retirement, and to enable employers to achieve settlement agreements and pre-termination agreements to resolve issues around an employee's performance, or retirement, or both. Anecdotal evidence suggests that this type of agreement has been used especially in the manufacturing industry to make a deal with employees who it was felt should retire. It can be seen that not only is there a risk that, through this type of agreement, retirement practices may be reintroduced through the back door by employers, but also that these could lead to a weakening of employment rights. Employees selected for termination of employment may be pressured into an agreement even if they would like to continue to work. Only in extreme cases if an employee is able to prove that the employer acted 'improperly' during such negotiations would she be able to sue the employer for unfair dismissal. Moreover, taking employers to court has become much more difficult due to the introduction of fees to start an employment tribunal case.

Another way that could be used by employers to *de facto* retire an employee is through an increased use of performance management practices at the workplace, as identified by some empirical studies.[38] While clearly performance management processes are viewed as good practice within organisations, it is important to be mindful that performance management and capability procedures may be influenced by employers' negative stereotypical views about older workers. This is demonstrated by the case law. For example, in the case of *Dixon v. Croglin Estate Co Ltd*,[39] the employment tribunal found that age was a material factor in the employer's decision to dismiss on capability grounds a 58-year-old gamekeeper, although he was held in high esteem by his colleagues. When the estate earnings from grouse shooting started to fall, his employer saw Mr. Dixon, the head keeper, as being responsible for the loss. However, the employment tribunal found that the employer had formed the view that Mr. Dixon was 'set in his ways' and 'unlikely to change'. Stereotypical assumptions could be seen in other statements, such as 'you cannot see DD doing all the GPS computer work'. As no evidence was offered by the employer during the hearing to justify these remarks, the tribunal concluded in its judgement that the employer had formed the view that Mr. Dixon was 'old fashioned and either unable or unwilling to learn more modern methods' and they 'wanted a younger, fresher Head Keeper to replace the claimant'.[40] Similarly, in the case of *James v. Gina Shoes*,[41] a 58-year-old salesman was dismissed on grounds of capability; his employer made it clear that they felt that Mr. James's age had 'caused him not to meet their expectations'. During a meeting that the employer held to hear a grievance from Mr. James against his treatment, the employer resorted to stereotypical comments such as 'you can't teach an old dog new tricks'. Furthermore, in these cases, the threat of being sued for age discrimination may provide little by way of disincentive to employers to avoid discrimination against older workers since, as noted

---

[38] B Barrett and M Sargeant (2015) 'Working in the UK without a Default Retirement Age: Health, Safety, and the Oldest Workers' 44(1) *ILJ* 75; 'Pensioning off the mandatory retirement age: implications for the higher education sector', (2013) *Legal Studies* 289–311. See Bob Price at Chap. 13.

[39] (2011) ET No 2502955/2011 ('*Dixon*').

[40] *Dixon* para 9.10.

[41] *James v. Gina Shoes* [2011] UKEAT/0384/11/DM.

by Dewhurst,[42] the age of the claimant and their closeness to retirement can make compensation levels low.

Even if standard performance criteria exist, and are applied consistently across a company in what could be seen as a fair process to manage the workforce, care would need to be taken to ensure that the criteria used are age-neutral and not linked indirectly to age by being calibrated on the average performance of younger workers. Unless such care is taken, there is a risk of exposing older workers to indirect age discrimination. Such a situation could be reminiscent of the kind of disadvantage experienced by women with caring responsibilities when denied part-time work. The requirement of working full-time was calibrated on the experiences of working men and was treated as the norm, although it had the effect of disadvantaging women with caring responsibilities. In Canada, where mandatory retirement rules are also unlawful, there has been criticism of court decisions that have rejected claims for the need to accommodate age-related needs to performance management criteria.[43] This, however, highlights a potentially contradictory issue, which takes us into the next set of arguments that we can use to assess the extent to which the law is meeting the needs of individual older workers.

5 Alternative Means to Meet the Needs of Older Workers

As discussed earlier, assumptions that performance declines with age rely on stereotypes of older workers. Nonetheless, some argue that since the ageing process involves a gradual decline in some abilities, the duty of accommodation, which under current UK law applies only to disability, should be extended to older workers who suffer 'from an ailment, or a disadvantage linked to age'.[44] Although these conditions may not amount to a disability, it is argued that they still require protection because of

---

[42] E. Dewhurst 'Are Older Workers Past Their Sell-by Date?'.

[43] See for example P.Alon-Shenker (2012) 'The duty to accommodate senior workers: Its nature, scope and limitations', *Queen's Law Journal* Vol 38(1), 165–208.

[44] See on this point M. Sargeant (2008) 'Older Workers and the Need for Reasonable Accommodation' *International Journal of Discrimination and the Law* Vol 9(3), 176.

stereotyping. Counterarguments highlight[45] that if such protection is afforded by imposing a legal duty on employers to accommodate age-related needs, this might reinforce some employers' stereotypical views of older workers and make some organisations reluctant to employ them. However, this remains a grey area, as it could be further argued that an employer's failure to make a reasonable adjustment to meet age-related needs may amount to indirect discrimination, which is unlawful unless it can be objectively justified.

One way of trying to address the complexity of these issues is to make more flexible working opportunities available so that workers who have age-related needs can adjust their working practices to meet their needs. As we have seen earlier, there is a significant demand from older workers for flexible working. The UK coalition government tried to meet this need by extending the law to request flexible working[46] to all employees and not just those with caring responsibilities. It should be stressed that under this law, employees do not have the right to work flexibly but simply the right *to ask* to vary their contractual terms—for example, to reduce their working hours, in order to work more flexibly. Employers have a duty to consider such requests but they can refuse to accommodate them on business grounds such as, for example, the inability to reorganise work among existing staff or to meet customers' needs. Both research[47] and the government consultation[48] run prior to the extension to the right to request flexible working highlighted concerns expressed by employers about having to balance conflicting rights to flexible working once the right to change working patterns is extended to all employees. It ought to be noted that this right only applies to employees with 26 weeks of continuous employment. This means that it does not help those older workers who are seeking employment and need to work flexibly for all sort of reasons. Therefore, it remains to be seen to what extent this legislative change will help to meet older workers' demand for flexible working.

---

[45] 'Reasonable Accommodation: Time to Extend the Duty to Accommodate Beyond Disability?' (2011) 36:2 *NTM|NJCM*-Bulletin 186 at 191–92, online: SSRN: cited by P. Alon-Shenker 'The duty to accommodate', 94.

[46] Children and Family Act 2014.

[47] S Manfredi and L Vickers (2009) 'Retirement and age discrimination: Managing retirement in Higher Education', *Industrial Law Journal*, Vol. 38(4), 343–364.

[48] Modern Workplaces Consultation, 2012.

Finally, when considering the needs of older workers, it is also important to draw attention to the fact that extending working lives should be a choice and not a compulsion.[49] Linking pension ages to increased life expectancy, as the UK government is planning to do, overlooks the fact that although the quantity of life is generally increasing, the quality of life in later years is going to vary significantly depending on individuals' socio-economic circumstances. It has been argued that other indicators should be taken into account, such as healthy life expectancy and disability-free life expectancy, which are better predictors about the length of time individuals are likely to remain healthy and able to work later in life.[50] Research clearly shows that people in lower socio-economic groups are more likely to have lower life expectancies as well as lower healthy and disability-free life expectancy.[51] This has led the charity Age UK[52] to warn that average life expectancy should not be the only criterion on the basis of which an increase in pension ages should be determined, since there are 'huge disparities in life expectancy across the country'. For example, the Scottish First Minister, Nicola Sturgeon, noted that average life expectancy among the Scottish population is shorter and, therefore, higher pension ages stand to disadvantage people in Scotland.[53] Thus, there is a risk that pushing people with lower life expectancy or healthy life expectancy to extend their working lives could deepen inequality throughout their life course and deny them a dignified end to their working lives.

---

[49] See Chaps. 9 (Loretto) and 15 (Brett) for further discussion of the issue of choice and compulsion in the decision to retire.

[50] S Harper, K Howse, S Baxter (2011) *Living longer and prospering? Designing an adequate, sustainable and equitable UK state pension system* (Club Vita LLP and The Oxford Institute of Ageing, University of Oxford).

[51] D Sinclair, K Moore, B Franklin (2014) *Linking state pension age to longevity. Tackling the fairness challenge* (International Longevity Centre) http://www.ilcuk.org.uk/index.php/publications/publication_details/ageing_longevity_and_demographic_change_a_factpack_of_statistics_from_the_i [accessed 20 July 2014].

[52] H Osborne 'George Osborne confirms state pension age will rise to 67', *The Guardian* 29 November 2011.

[53] S McNab, 'Sturgeon vows to fight retirement age' rise http://www.scotsman.com/news/politics/sturgeon-vows to-fight-retirement-age-rise-1-3739364 (accessed May 2016).

6   Concluding Remarks

This review shows that extending working lives as a key aspect of the active ageing agenda presents a number of significant challenges, as social and economic policy aims need to be balanced against the interests of older workers for a dignified end of their working lives as well as against the interests of employers for an effective management of their workforce.

On the one hand, in some senses, abolition of mandatory retirement meets a number of the challenges identified at the start of this chapter. It has the potential to increase participation of older workers in the labour market and to ameliorate pension sustainability. It also has the potential to reduce the burden on younger workers to support an ageing population.

However, on the other hand, a number of concerns have been raised regarding the extent to which these challenges are really met. The fact remains that retirement can still be justified, and yet the idea of a single approach to justifying age discrimination is flawed at several levels. First, at a practical level, there is some inconsistency if we are trying to increase the number of older workers while also freeing jobs for younger workers. Conceptually, the different justifications for the age discriminatory practice of mandatory retirement are internally contradictory: we wish to achieve fairness, intergenerational or otherwise, by increasing work for younger workers while at the same time enabling older workers who wish or need to work to continue to do so. Legally, the need to justify a general rule such as a retirement policy—while also ensuring that the rule is proportionate for the individual—is so problematic in the context of age that the rule has generally not been applied. Perhaps as a result of these practical, legal and conceptual challenges the CJEU has not been particularly clear in terms of setting legal standards for employers. Instead, as is suggested in chapters 1 and 2, the CJEU has allowed a certain margin of discretion to member states in their approach to retirement; and the UK courts have followed suit by being reasonably generous in their approach to justifying age discrimination. For example in *Seldon*, Lady Hale notes the potentially discriminatory undertones of 'dignity' as an aim for retirement, but nonetheless allows that it can be legitimate.

In addition, the abolition of mandatory retirement as a strategy to support extended working lives may be undermined by the use of settlement agreements to terminate a contract of employment in return for a payoff or by performance management practices that could indirectly disadvantage older workers if calibrated on the average performance of younger workers. And, without strengthened remedies against age discrimination—in particular, increased levels of compensation regardless of an older worker's proximity to retirement—the scope for the Equality Act 2010 to protect older workers is much reduced.

Perhaps the greatest challenge for the law—as people expect and are expected to work longer—is that of meeting the needs of individual older workers in the workplace. The big question, therefore, is whether or not there should be a legal duty to accommodate age-related needs in the workplace. As seen earlier, views are divided between those who advocate in favour of the introduction of such a duty and those who believe that such a move would be counterproductive, since it would reinforce stereotypical views and make some employers reluctant to employ older workers, or make more employers more inclined to look for early termination of employment through settlement agreements. However, as seen earlier, if SPAs are linked to average life expectancy, and ignore the fact that older workers from low socio-economic backgrounds are likely to have lower healthy life expectancy, accommodating age-related needs in the workplace may become a necessity to enable this group to stay in employment until they reach the state pension age. There is a risk otherwise that this group may be exposed to an undignified end of their working lives.

One of the reasons for the difficulty in using retirement to meet the social policy aims related to active ageing, then, is that the older workforce is not a homogenous group, despite sharing a protected characteristic of age. Each attempt to address the needs of one group of older workers seems to cause difficulties for another group. Thus, some workers may not recognise a decline in ability, and compulsory retirement can meet their need to retain their dignity; the same policy may undermine the right for other older workers to avoid stereotypical assumptions about both their ability and their financial well-being. Given the wide range of situations of older workers, as well as the rather wide age range included in the category (Barret and Sargeant[54] point out that studies of older workers can cover workers from 50 upwards; other studies look only at workers over 65, or over 70), it becomes ever more clear that a single approach to justifying age discrimination is a key problem when it comes to the legal protection for older workers.

The use of retirement has been justified in the UK as well as the EU as a method to meet some of the challenges we face as our society ages. These challenges were identified above as the demographic changes towards an increasing number of older people capable of working longer, combined with trends of early retirement; the need to achieve intergenerational fairness; the challenge of ensuring that older workers maintain their dignity at the end of their careers; and the need for certainty in terms of workforce planning.

It seems, however, from the discussion above that retirement is an unreliable method for meeting the challenges of active ageing. Yet, employers will need nonetheless to meet the challenges of an older workforce while meeting the needs of younger workers. In the absence of clear legal standards being forthcoming from the courts, the way ahead for employers instead means being imaginative in their approach and developing greater 'pull factors' to encourage older workers to stay in the workplace. Some of these approaches are discussed in the contributions from Martin Hall, Bob Price and Sally Brett, in chapters 12, 13 and 15 respectively. If employers can develop working practices to allow for a sustainable extension of working lives, as well as to achieve equitable outcomes for workers in different occupations, it may be that choosing to remain in the workforce can become more of an active choice by workers. Moreover, we would suggest that greater involvement of the social partners may be beneficial in creating more age-friendly workplaces. This way, the legal remedies, which we have seen leading to an impasse when trying to address the double bind of the active ageing agenda, will become less significant as a method of managing an age diverse workforce.

---

[54] B Barrett and M Sargeant (2015) 'Working in the UK without a Default Retirement Age: Health, Safety, and the Oldest Workers' 44(1) *ILJ* 75.

Part III

The Challenges of Extending Working Lives

5

Intersectionality as a Tool for Analysing Age and Gender in Labour Law

Jenny Julén Votinius

1   Introduction

This chapter examines the value of applying an intersectional approach in analysing the position of older women in a labour law setting.[1] In the labour market context, and in this chapter, older persons are understood as those who are perceived as approaching their post-employment years.[2] Acceptance of the idea that the critical period with regards to old age and employment begins at the early end of a person's working life is reflected in EU policies on active ageing and in the age discrimination cases of the Court of Justice of the European Union (CJEU), which mainly concern employees from the age of just above 50 years of age and older.[3] It is also reflected in research on age discrimination, and on perceptions

---

[1] This chapter is part of an ongoing research project carried out within the Norma Elder Law Research Environment, Lund University, funded by Ragnar Söderberg's Foundation and the Marianne and Marcus Wallenberg Foundation.

[2] K Boudiny (2013) 'Active ageing': from empty rhetoric to effective policy tool' *Ageing & Society* 33, 1077 1082.

[3] The Active Ageing Index takes into account people from the age of 55, cf. *Active Ageing Index Concepts (2013) Methodology and Final Results (Vienna UNECE)*.

© The Editor(s) (if applicable) and The Author(s) 2016
S. Manfredi, L. Vickers (eds.), *Challenges of Active Ageing*,
DOI 10.1057/978-1-137-53251-0_5

and attitudes regarding employee age.[4] Today, both age and gender are established as important factors in EU labour law. Nevertheless, possible intersectional effects of these two factors are still disregarded in the legal rules, as are effects of other intersectionalities. The chapter acknowledges that the conditions under which men and women live may have legal implications for older persons in the labour market. It also explores how stereotypical perceptions of older employees, together with gendered expectations and perceptions on the labour market, work to influence the content and application of labour law. An important conclusion is that, both in the social context within which the law is shaped and in the law itself, age and gender intersect to the detriment of older persons in the labour market—and this is particularly true for women.

The chapter is composed as follows. Section 2 presents the conceptual and theoretical framework. Section 3 very briefly situates the topic of older women's position in labour law in relation to demographic development. Section 4 introduces the idea of EU employment policies with respect to active ageing. Section 5 deals with the prohibitions in EU law of discrimination in working life on the grounds of age and sex, from the perspective of multiple and intersectional discrimination. In Section 6, the legal analysis highlights and explores intersections of age and gender in labour law, through the lenses of gendered life courses and stereotyping, and with Sweden as a national example. Section 7 provides a concluding discussion.

2   An Intersectional Approach to Age and Gender in Labour Law

The origin and history of the intersectionality concept is well known. It was coined in 1989 by the legal scholar Kimberlé Crenshaw in an essay on the multiple oppressions that black women suffer by virtue of being both black

---

[4] H P Van Dalen, K Henkens & J Schippers (2009) 'Dealing with older workers in Europe: a comparative survey of employers' attitudes and actions' *Journal of European Social Policy* 19, 47; AM Ahmedab, L Andersson & M Hammarstedt (2012) 'Does age matter for employability? A field experiment on ageism in the Swedish labour market', *Applied Economics Letters* 19, 403; D Abrams, P S Russell, C M Vanclair & H Swift (2011) *Ageism in Europe: Findings from the European Social Survey* (Age UK).

and women.[5] By introducing the concept of intersectionality into discourses on gender discrimination and race discrimination, Crenshaw introduced a way to capture and acknowledge how two separate forms of oppression combine as one single experience: the specific oppression of black women, which is something greater than just the sum of racism and sexism.[6]

The important insight that the concept of intersectionality has provided is, thus, its recognition of the intersectional experience as a product of the intermeshing, or fusion, of two or more separate forms of oppression, rather than just simultaneous or parallel occurrences of these oppressions. Since the 1990s, feminist scholars from various disciplines have applied the intersectionality approach to analyse the interplay between different discursively and institutionally constructed categories—such as gender and ethnicity—in sociocultural hierarchies and power structures. Many scholars have emphasised that intersectionality includes a mutual process that affects social status, power, and level of inclusion.[7] This mutuality means that the understanding of one category and its social position will help to construct, transform, and enhance the understanding and positioning of the other category in the specific intersectional context in question.

Legal scholar Joanne Conaghan has criticised intersectionality for ignoring the historical and economic reasons for the rise of inequality, for its focus on identity politics and for its limited potential as a tool for the realisation of a feminist strategy.[8] There may be some merit in these observations, but I disagree that they must be considered as shortcomings in a feminist legal scientific context. The great benefit of the intersectionality perspective is that in a larger theory on discrimination, it can serve as an analytical instrument and can be used strategically to reveal previously ignored aspects of the law and its application.

---

[5] K Crenshaw (1989) *Demarginalizing the Intersection of Race and Sex: A Black Feminist Critique of Antidiscrimination Doctrine, Feminist Theory, and Antiracist Politics*, (University of Chicago Legal Forum) 139.

[6] Crenshaw's work linked up with a broader theoretical tendency within feminist theory, which until then had lacked a common frame of reference; A-M Hancock (2013) 'Empirical Intersectionality: A Tale of Two Approaches' *U.C. Irvine Law Review* 3, 259.

[7] P Hill Collins (2000) *Black Feminist Thought: Knowledge, Consciousness, and the Politics of Empowerment*, (2nd ed. Routledge).

[8] J Conaghan (2008) 'Intersectionality and the Feminist Project in Law', in: Davina Cooper (ed) *Law, Power and the Politics of Subjectivity: Intersectionality and Beyond* (Routledge Cavendish).

3   Demographic Developments and Older Women's Position in the Labour Market

Europe is experiencing a demographic development similar to that of the rest of the world—a development characterised by a growing population, longer lifespans, and decreased birth rates.[9] When declining mortality rates are not matched by a corresponding increase in nativity, the composition of the population in terms of age fundamentally changes. An ever-smaller share of the population must provide for more people and simultaneously take on the increasing care responsibilities accompanying an ageing community. In certain respects, the ageing of the population is a matter that concerns women in a particular way. Women live longer than men; above the age of 55, women outnumber men almost everywhere in the world. Women are the primary caregivers within the family; an increasing share of family care work is done for older persons. Meanwhile, in their capacity as taxpayers and providers of household income, women also play a key role in contributing to finance increasingly strained welfare systems and support family members.[10] In the labour market, women are more likely than men to be exposed to oppression caused by hierarchical structures and discrimination and, in this respect, older women seem to be hit especially hard. In a 2013 report, AGE Europe notes that age is quickly becoming the most commonly perceived disadvantage in the labour market, and that this particularly applies to older women 'who are among those most affected by the crisis and one of the groups most likely to lose their job and be unable to find new employment'.[11] Moreover, a recent comparative study on 12 EU Member States, carried out for the European Commission, shows that older women workers comprised one group of workers perceived as being at the highest risk for precarious

---

[9] On the demographic change see, for example, *The 2012 Ageing Report: Underlying Assumptions and Projection Methodologies: Joint Report* (Publications of the European Union, 2011) 94.

[10] I Ganguli, R Hausmann & M Viarengo (2014) 'Closing the gender gap in education: What is the state of gaps in labour force participation for women, wives and mothers?' *International Labour Review* 153(2); N Duvvury & C Finn (2014) 'Man-covery': recession, labour market, and gender relations in Ireland' *Gender, Sexuality & Feminism* 1(2), 59.

[11] AGE (2013) *Contribution to the European Commission's assessment of the transposition and application of Employment Equality Directive (2000/78/EC).*

work before groups such as interns, apprentices, women in general, older workers in general, and women who are pregnant or returning from maternity leave.[12]

The demographic development brings to the fore complex questions about the understanding and function of age in the societal context, but just as salient is how this development accentuates important questions about gender. In many ways, age aspects and gender aspects overlap and give rise to new questions about gendered understandings of age, gendered ageism and how age and gender interact in social and societal contexts. These questions all concern the *intersection* of age and gender, which is the approach that will be explored in this chapter from the perspective of labour law.

4 The Active Ageing Agenda in EU Employment Policies

While the importance of gender has long since been acknowledged in EU labour law, age was fairly invisible in this legal context until the introduction of the prohibition on age discrimination in 2000, through Directive 2000/78 (see further Sect. 4 in this chapter).[13] The recognition of age as grounds for discrimination coincided with a general shift within the EU towards policies that more actively addressed the looming demographic change in Europe.[14] In a short time, ageing and the situation of older persons became a central component of EU agendas regarding policies

---

[12] S McKay, S Jefferys, A Paraskevopoulou, J Keles (April 2012) *Study on Precarious work and social rights. Carried out for the European Commission (VT/2010/084)* (Working Lives Research Institute, London Metropolitan University).

[13] Council Directive 2000/78/EC establishing a general framework for equal treatment in employment and occupation. Earlier measures on older workers in the EU are few, and all have the form of non-legally binding acts. A very early example is the Council Recommendation 82/857/EEC on the principles of a community policy with regard to retirement age, p. 27. Compare Ellis E & P Watson (2002) *EU anti-discrimination law*, (2nd ed. Oxford University Press), M Bell (2002) *Anti-discrimination law and the European Union* (Oxford University Press); N ten Bokum & P Bartelings (eds.) (2009) *Age discrimination law in Europe* (Kluwer Law International).

[14] *Towards a Europe for All Ages* COM (1999) 221; *Europe's response to World Ageing* COM (2002) 143; *Confronting demographic change: a new solidarity between the generations* COM (2005) 94; *The demographic future of Europe—From challenge to opportunity*, COM (2006) 571; Council Resolution

for employment and economic growth, embodied in the key concept of *active ageing*.[15] Active ageing refers to a range of areas, but in effect it has been most developed in policies regarding active ageing in employment.[16] In 2001 and 2002, two general EU targets were adopted to increase labour market participation of older workers and promote sustainable pensions: the Stockholm target, to ensure that half of those aged 55–64 were in employment by 2010, and the Barcelona target, to increase actual retirement age by five years by 2010.

The active ageing policy of raising employment rates for older workers is part of the European Union's growth and job strategy Europe 2020, where it is addressed in the flagship initiative towards full employment— the 'Agenda for new skills and jobs'. In a recent, comprehensive survey of the development of the active ageing concept both within and beyond the EU policy sphere, along with an overview of the scholarly debate on the topic, EU policy discourses on active ageing are described as comprising two contrasting models.[17] The first, and predominant, model focuses more or less completely on extending working life; this model is based on considerations about productivity and economic growth.[18] The other model is less influential at the EU level, but is a leading one for the World Health Organization (WHO) and the United Nations (UN). It is much more comprehensive, in that it has equal focus on including

6226/07 *Opportunities and challenges of demographic change in Europe; Dealing with the impact of an ageing population in the EU (2009 Ageing Report)* COM (2009) 180.

[15] Council and Parliament Decision 940/2011/EU on the European Year for Active Ageing and Solidarity between Generations (2012). A Walker & T Maltby (2012) 'Active ageing: A strategic policy solution to demographic ageing in the European Union', *International Journal of Social Welfare* 21, 117; A Walker (2008) 'Commentary: The Emergence and Application of Active Aging in Europe' *Journal of Aging & Social Policy* 21, 75.

[16] Walker & Maltby (2012); c.f. European Commission (2012) *Commission Staff Working Document ex-ante evaluation accompanying document to the decision of the European parliament* and the *Council on the European Year for Active Ageing* SEC (2010) 1002 final.

[17] L Foster & A Walker (2015) 'Active and Successful Aging: A European Policy Perspective' *The Gerontologist* 55 (1), 83; E Carmel, K Hamblin & T Papadopoulos (2007) 'Governing the activation of older workers in the European Union' *International Journal of Sociology and Social Policy* 27 (9/10), 387.

[18] K Hamblin (2010) 'Changes to policies for work and retirement in EU15 nations (1995–2005): An exploration of policy packages for the 50-plus cohort', *International Journal of Ageing and Later Life* 5, 513.

quality of life, mental and physical well-being, and social participation.[19] In some EU policy actions and documents, there is a trend towards a certain convergence between these two models, such as in the launching of the European Year of Active Ageing and Solidarity between the Generations in 2012.[20] So far, this approximation towards a more comprehensive approach to active ageing on the EU side seems to have happened more on the rhetorical level.[21] In practice, the overall emphasis is still very much on promoting labour market opportunities and enhancing employment conditions and employability of older employees.

As an integrated part of the European Employment Strategy, the understanding of active ageing within the EU is closely connected to the discourse on employability and its emphasis on the responsibility of the individual employee to achieve and maintain his or her own power of attraction in the labour market.[22] The concept of employability also encompasses a requirement to adjust to an increasingly changing and insecure labour market, in relation to which policies for deregulation in order to allow for more flexibility for employers are seen as key.[23] In many EU countries, the level of insecurity on the labour market has increased during the years following the Great Recession.[24] From an immediate labour market participation perspective, the negative effects of economic crisis can be observed primarily in relation to young employees, among whom unemployment has risen sharply during the crisis years. However,

---

[19] L Foster & A Walker (2013) 'Gender and active ageing in Europe' *European Journal of Ageing* 10, 3.

[20] European Commission (2010) *Commission Staff Working Document* SEC 1002 final.

[21] K Hamblin (2013) *Active Ageing in the European Union Policy Convergence and Divergence,* (Palgrave Macmillan).

[22] A Fejes (2010) 'Discourses on Employability: Constituting the Responsible Citizen' *Studies in Continuing Education.*, 89; P Moore, *The International Political Economy of Work and Employability* 32, 27 (Palgrave Macmillan); B Casey (2012) 'The implications of the economic crisis for pensions and pension policy in Europe' *Global Social Policy* 12, 246.

[23] J Julén Votinius (2012) 'Having the Right Attitude: Cooperation Skills and Labour Law' *The International Journal of Comparative Labour Law and Industrial Relations* Vol. 28 (2), 223.

[24] S Laulom, E Mazuyer & C Escande Varniol (eds.) (2012) *Quel droit social dans une Europe en crise?* (Larcier); S Laulom, (2014) 'Dismissal Law Under Challenge: New Risks for Workers' *European Labour Law Journal* 5 (3–4), 231; C Degryse, M Jepsen & P Pochet (2013) *The Euro Crisis and its Impact on National and European Social Policies* ETUI working paper 201305; C Barnard (2012) 'The Financial Crisis and the Euro Plus Pact: A Labour Lawyer's Perspective' *Industrial Law Journal* 41, 98.

effects relating to the dismantling of employment security are a concern for every employee, especially for employees who belong to a group that typically is perceived as less attractive in the labour market—such as older women.[25] Within EU law, the longstanding tradition of legislation to safeguard the fundamental principles of equal treatment and non-discrimination in working life can provide a barrier against unfair management decisions. The following section introduces the relevant provisions of EU discrimination law, and addresses the question of the extent to which these provisions have the potential to handle intersectional discrimination.

5   EU Law on Work Life Discrimination

The area of non-discrimination has largely evolved in the context of gender equality in working life, which has had a place on the social policy agenda within the EU since the 1970s (although progress has been slow). A comprehensive body of secondary legislation and case law on sex discrimination began to develop in the 1970s, mainly on the basis of the provision in the Treaty of Rome regarding equal pay for men and women.[26] The promotion of gender equality also appears in various policy documents, such as the European Employment Strategy, the Community Action Programmes on equal opportunities for men and women, and several recommendations and resolutions from the Council.[27] Many times, these soft-law documents have expressed a more progressive approach than the binding law.[28]

---

[25] J Prassl (2014 'Contingent Crises, Permanent Reforms: Rationalising Labour Market Reforms in the European Union' *European Labour Law Journal* 5 (3–4), 211; Eurofound (2012) *Employment trends and policies for older workers in the recession.*

[26] Ellis & Watson (2013).

[27] Some recent examples are *Europe 2020, A Strategy for Smart, Sustainable and Inclusive Growth*, COM(2010)2020 final19; *Strategy for Equality between Women and Men 2010–2015*, COM(2010)0491 final; *Reconciliation of Work and Family Life in the Context of Demographic Change* 11841/11 SOC 584 (EPSCO).

[28] P Foubert (2002) *The Legal Protection of the Pregnant Worker in the European Community: Sex Equality, Thoughts of Social and Economic Policy and Comparative Leaps to the United States of America* (Kluwer Law International) 214; C McGlynn (2001) 'Reclaiming a Feminist Vision: the

In 2000, following the Treaty of Amsterdam, the existing directives on sex discrimination were accompanied by directives prohibiting discrimination on the grounds of racial or ethnic origin, religion or belief, disability, age, or sexual orientation. Through the ratification of the Lisbon Treaty, and its coming into force in 2009, promoting equal treatment and combating discrimination was acknowledged as a key aim of the European Union, and the fundamental right to equality became protected under the CFREU and the ECHR.[29] Today, the prohibitions against age and sex discrimination in working life are found in the Employment Equality Directive 2000/78 and the Equal Treatment Directive 2006/54, respectively.[30] Because the ban on discrimination has an almost identical design in the two directives, and the prohibition on age discrimination has been thoroughly described and analysed in Chap. 1 of this book, the following paragraph functions only to recall the pairing of direct and indirect discrimination in EU law, along with the comprehensive exceptions that apply to the ban on age discrimination.[31]

Both the Employment Equality Directive 2000/78 and the Equal Treatment Directive 2006/54 distinguish between *direct* discrimination and *indirect* discrimination. The former is at hand when a person is being subjected to less favourable treatment which is associated with a protected ground, such as age or sex.[32] The latter regards the case where the employer applies a condition or criterion that appears neutral, but in fact puts persons belonging to a protected group at a particular disadvantage, and where the criterion cannot be justified with reference to an objectively acceptable aim. A possibility for justification is built into the very

---

Reconciliation of Paid Work and Family Life in European Union Law and Policy' *Columbia Journal of European Law* 7, 242.

[29] Treaty of the European Union, Article 3, Charter of Fundamental Rights of the European Union, Chapter III, particularly Articles 21 (non-discrimination), 23 (equality between men and women) and 25 (the rights of the elderly), and European Convention on Human Rights, Art 14 and Protocol No 12.

[30] Council Directive 2000/78/EC establishing a general framework for equal treatment in employment and occupation; European Parliament and Council Directive 2006/54/EC on the implementation of the principle of equal opportunities and equal treatment of men and women in matters of employment and occupation (recast).

[31] Sexual harassment is conceptualized as a particular form of discrimination on the grounds of sex, and is thus covered only by the Equal Treatment Directive, Article 2.2, Directive 2006/54/EC.

[32] Article 2, Directive 2000/78/EC and Article 2.1, Directive 2006/54/EC.

construction of indirect discrimination, but normally direct discrimination is allowed in only the few cases that are specifically enumerated in the two directives. However, in relation to direct discrimination on the grounds of age, the possibilities for exemptions are particularly comprehensive; in fact, the possibilities for justification are similar to what otherwise applies in cases of indirect discrimination.[33] In relation to age, premise 25 of the Employment Equality Directive 2000/78 emphasises the importance of distinguishing between 'differences in treatment which are justified, in particular by legitimate employment policy, labour market and vocational training objectives, and discrimination which must be prohibited'. Accordingly, Article 6 justifies differential treatment on the grounds of age for various employment policy objectives.[34] To be permitted, differential treatment must be deemed appropriate and necessary but, in its case law, the CJEU imposes very undemanding requirements on Member States to prove that measures that disadvantage older workers actually provide the labour market benefits that are claimed as their justification.[35] It is clear that many times, collective and public interests that stem from the function of the labour market and societal considerations may be given priority over the interest of non-discrimination on the grounds of age.[36]

The exemptions that apply in relation to the prohibition against direct age discrimination are far more comprehensive than those that apply for other grounds; thus, in cases that involve more than one ground for discrimination, it could seem wiser for the individual to avoid age discrimination when formulating a claim. Therefore, it is not unlikely to believe that in some cases on discrimination against older women that are framed as sex discrimination; the plaintiff has in fact been equally exposed to age discrimination. Within EU law, discriminatory treatment

---

[33] See Chap. 1 of this book, written by Frank Hendrickx. Cf. A Numhauser-Henning (2013) 'The EU Ban on Age-Discrimination and Older Workers: Potentials and Pitfalls', *The International Journal of Comparative Labour Law and Industrial Relations* Vol 29 (4), 391.

[34] Article 6.1, Directive 2000/78/EC, interpreted by the CJEU in numerous cases.

[35] J Fudge & A Zbyszewska (2015) 'An Intersectional Approach to Age Discrimination in the European Union: Bridging Dignity and Distribution?' in A Numhauser Henning & M Rönnmar (eds) *Age Discrimination and Labour Law. Comparative and Conceptual Perspectives in the EU and Beyond* (Kluwer Law International).

[36] Compare Chap. 1 of this book.

that is associated with more than one ground of discrimination has been acknowledged as multiple discrimination. The CJEU has accepted claims of multiple discrimination, and several national legal systems within the EU have dealt with the issue in a similar way.[37]

However, the fact that multiple discrimination can be addressed in court does not mean that the same applies to intersectional discrimination. There is an essential difference between the cumulative effect which is recognised when the court acknowledges multiple discrimination and the effects stemming from the particular situation at hand for intersectional discrimination. In cases of multiple discrimination, the employer is made responsible for two different violations of the law at the same time. This situation can be compared with any other two concurrent legal infringements; for example, terminating an employee without cause and simultaneously failing to pay outstanding statutory holiday pay. Intersectional discrimination, on the other hand, is not about an additive or cumulative effect; it is about a *different* effect, stemming from what Crenshaw labels the synergistic character of intersectional discrimination. The synergies appear as two or more grounds for discrimination operating interactively to produce a separate ground for discrimination, thus forming a specific subject exposed to oppression and discrimination; with Crenshaw this is the black woman, and here it is the older woman.

The lack of an intersectional perspective in EU labour law has been highlighted and criticised by legal scholars as well as scholars in social and political science, mainly with regard to gender, ethnicity, and disabilities.[38] However, in the last few years, to a certain extent, an intersectional

---

[37] S Burri & D Schiek (2009) *Multiple Discrimination in EU Law. Opportunities for Legal Responses to Intersectional Gender Discrimination?* (European Commission); D Schiek & A Lawson (eds.) (2011) *European Union Non-Discrimination Law and Intersectionality. Investigating the Triangle of Racial, Gender and Disability Discrimination* (Ashgate).

[38] Among others, S Fredman (2009) 'Positive Rights and Duties: Addressing Intersectionality' in D Schiek, V Chege (eds), *European Union Non-Discrimination Law: Comparative Perspectives on Multidimensional Equality Law* (Routledge-Cavendish); E Lombardo & M Verloo (2009) 'Institutionalising intersectionality in the European Union? Policy developments and contestations' *International Feminist Journal of Politics* 11, 478; M Verloo (2006) 'Multiple Inequalities, Intersectionality and the European Union' *European Journal of Women's Studies 13*, 211; M Verloo & S Walby (2012) 'Introduction: The Implications for Theory and Practice of Comparing the Treatment of Intersectionality in the Equality Architecture of Europe', *Social Politics* 19, 433; J Kantola & K Nousiainen (2009) 'Institutionalising intersectionality in Europe: Introducing the

approach has been introduced in EU legislative development, in the emerging discussion about the need to recognise discrimination on multiple grounds.[39] Thus, the Commission's 2010–2015 action plan for gender equality briefly expressed an ambition to explore further the question of how other grounds for discrimination, such as age, may interact with gender.[40] In the proposed directive on equal treatment outside the labour market, which is currently under consideration by the Council, discrimination on multiple grounds is recognised for the first time in a legally binding act (albeit not in the enacting terms).[41] These documents and the discussions preceding them indicate a capacity, although still largely dormant, for a more nuanced approach to how different social hierarchical structures may interact in the area of law.[42]

In the wake of this development, and in asserting that EU non-discrimination law in fact allows for an intersectional approach, a number of legal scholars elaborate on strategies to capture this potential in EU law. Schiek and Mulder argue that EU law permits and calls for a change in focus, to avoid the current practice of redefining cases of intersectional discrimination as single-ground cases. These authors also

---

theme' *International Feminist Journal of Politics* 11, 459; M Schwalbe (2008) *Rigging the game: how inequality is reproduced in everyday life* (Oxford University Press).

[39] A Krizsan, H Skjeie & J Squires (eds.) (2012) *Institutionalizing Intersectionality: The Changing Nature of European Equality Regimes* (Palgrave Macmillan).

[40] European Commission (2011) *Strategy for equality between women and men 2010–2015* (Publishing Office of the EU) 32; *Green paper—Equality and non-discrimination in an enlarged European Union* COM (2004) 379 final; and Commission (2007) *Tackling multiple discrimination: practices, policies and laws* (Publishing Office of the EU).

[41] *Proposal for a Council Directive on implementing the principle of equal treatment between persons irrespective of religion or belief, disability, age or sexual orientation* COM (2008) 426 final; SEC (2008) 2180 and SEC (2008) 2181 recital 13, acknowledges that women are particularly at risk of being exposed to multiple discrimination. The Parliament has suggested that the proposed directive should be amended to explicitly prohibit multiple discrimination, *European Parliament legislative resolution of 2 April 2009 on the proposal for a Council directive on implementing the principle of equal treatment between persons irrespective of religion or belief, disability, age or sexual orientation* (COM(2008)426) P6 TA(2009)211.

[42] According to Bell, this process 'should have been fruitful terrain for law and policy to engage with inequalities linked to more than one ground', but 'remains a promise largely unfulfilled'. M Bell, 'The principle of equal treatment: widening and deepening', in P Craig & G de Búrca (2011) *The evolution of EU law* (Oxford University Press) 639.

emphasise the need for a fundamental reappraisal in which the harshness of the overall impact of central inequalities is acknowledged and where there is a recognition of the fact that multiple discrimination actually means greater harm.[43] Similarly, in a recent publication, Carneiro argues that there is a scope to frame intersectional discrimination within existing EU anti-discrimination law.[44] In respect of the intersection of race and gender, Ashiagbor states that if Member States were to fully implement the provisions of the non-discrimination directives, these would provide a framework that can serve as a starting point for the recognition of intersectionality.[45]

As for the question of how *age* as an intersecting ground for discrimination plays out in EU law, Fudge and Zbyszewska have provided a valuable contribution in their comprehensive analysis of CJEU case law in the area.[46] Their conclusion is that although it is very difficult to implement a truly intersectional approach to age-related discrimination in EU law, an intersectional analysis can nevertheless play an important role, not least by influencing the CJEU to accept age-specific policies intended to promote intergenerational solidarity, but only in cases where the Member State can demonstrate that it has considered whether the policy may have a particularly negative impact on specific groups in the labour market.

The following section changes the focus from policy level and EU law to intersections of age and gender in discriminatory working life practices in the national legal context where EU employment policies and non-discrimination provisions are implemented.

[43] D Schiek & J Mulder (2011) 'Intersectionality in EU Law: A Critical Re-appraisal', and 'Organizing EU Equality Law around the Nodes of 'Race', Gender and Disability' both in D Schiek & A Lawson (eds.), *European Union Non-Discrimination Law and Intersectionality. Investigating the Triangle of Racial, Gender and Disability Discrimination* (Ashgate).

[44] M Carneiro (2015) *Constructing Intersectionality in EU Anti-Discrimination Law* (Copenhagen University).

[45] D Ashiagbor (2009) 'Multiple Discrimination in a Multicultural Europe: Achieving Labour Market Equality through New Governance' *Current Legal Problems* 61.

[46] Fudge & Zbyszewska (2015), cf. S Bisom-Rapp & M Sargeant (2014) 'It's Complicated: Age, Gender, and Lifetime Discrimination Against Working Women—The United States and the U.K. as Examples', *Elder Law Journal* 22 (1).

6 Age and Gender in Working Life and Labour Law: Intersectional Observations

Gendered structures—in society, in working life, and in the home—expose women to obstacles in many areas and constantly subject them to the potential risk of sex discrimination. Although men's involvement in domestic work has increased in most countries since the 1960s, women still carry out the majority of unpaid housework, including child and elderly care. The implications of this persistent, gendered division of labour is visible across the life course, *inter alia* in terms of gender inequalities in working life and career.[47] Women's traditional life courses, in tandem with the male career pattern as the norm in working life, function to shape older women's positions in working life.[48] During their lives, women more often interrupt their careers than do men to tend to family care responsibilities. On this basis, it is assumed that female employees have a greater inherent tendency to give priority to family over work. This notion is part of the picture of women that influences the employer and to which the employer refers in dealings with female employees. To some extent, this perceived reluctance to give priority to work before family is a characteristic of every female employee until the opposite has been proved, and affects women's career chances and salaries because decisions about employment and promotion are part of employer expectations in terms of loyalty.[49]

---

[47] D Anxo, C Fagan, I Cebrian & G Moreno (2007) 'Patterns of labour market integration in Europe—a life course perspective on time policies', *Socio-Economic Review* 5, 233.

[48] D Grant (2011) 'Older Women in the Workplace' in M Sargeant (ed.), *Age Discrimination and Diversity Multiple Discrimination from an Age Perspective*, (Cambridge University Press). On the theory of gendered life courses within sociological research, see P Moen & S Sweet (2004) 'From "work–family" to "flexible careers"' *Community, Work & Family* 7 (2), 209. On the male norm in working life see, among many others, Fenwick & T K Hervey (1995) 'Sex Equality in the Single Market. New Directions for the European Court of Justice', *Common Market Law Review* 32, 443; JC Williams (2001) *Unbending Gender. Why Family and Work Conflict and What To Do About It* (Oxford University Press).

[49] J Julén (2001) 'A Blessing or a Ban. About the Discrimination of Pregnant Job Seekers' in Ann Numhauser-Henning (ed.) *Legal Perspectives on Equal Treatment and Non-Discrimination* (Kluwer Law International).

Studies on older persons' access to the labour market show that employers tend not to consider it worthwhile to invest in older jobseekers: older persons are perceived as more likely than young people to leave employment.[50] The very same perception—a perception that the employee will be absent or quit the job—has long since been identified as an important ingredient in working life structures that discriminate against women, mainly due to the social division of care responsibilities within the family.[51] Whereas the age-related perception that older employees are more likely to leave their employment contrasts sharply with what is generally expected of the male employee, for the female employee it adds to an already established expectation placed on women throughout their working lives. Similarly, sociological findings on employers' perceptions of older workers as unwilling to develop their competences and as limited in technical knowledge very much overlap with gendered notions of aptitude and performance, according to which women are perceived as less active and less naturally skilled in technical matters than men.[52]

The term 'double jeopardy' is sometimes used to describe how these kinds of parallel perceptions can mutually reinforce each other to the detriment of, for example, older women.[53] In scholarship outside the discipline of legal science, there is growing recognition of the insight that ageism in working life is not gender-neutral; on both perception-related and structural levels, age and gender synergise in ways that tend

---

[50] The Swedish National Audit Office (2009) *Arbetsgivares attityder till äldre yrkesverksamma*; C Krekula (2011) *Åldersdiskriminering i svenskt arbetsliv: om ålderskodningar och myter som skapar ojämlikhet* (Stockholm, The Equality Ombudsman).

[51] Williams (2001); J Julén Votinius (2006) 'On the Gendered Norm of Standard Employment in a Changing Labour Market', in J Fudge & Rosemary Owens (eds.) *Precarious Work, Women and the New Economy: the Challenge to Legal Norms* (Hart).

[52] Van Dalen, Henkens & Schippers (2009); HP Van Dalen, K Henkens & J Schippers (2012) 'Productivity of Older Workers: Perceptions of Employers and Employees' *Population and Development Review* 36, 309; C Krekula (2009) 'Age Coding—on Age-based Practices of Distinction' *International Journal of Ageing and Later Life* 4, 7; W Loretto & P White (2006) 'Employers' attitudes, practices and policies towards older workers', *Human Resource Management Journal* 16, 313.

[53] C Itzin & C Phillipson (1995) 'Gendered ageism: a double jeopardy for women in Organizations' in C Itzin and J Newman (eds), *Gender, Culture and Organizational Change: Putting Theory into Practice* (Routledge); C Krekula, (2007) 'The Intersection of Age and Gender—Reworking Gender Theory and Social Gerontology' *Current Sociology* 55, 155; FM Beale (1970) 'Double jeopardy: To be Black and female' in T Cade (ed.), *The black woman* (New American Library).

to discriminate against women.[54] The examples above show that certain negative perceptions in relation to age have a very similar content to that of negative perceptions in relation to gender. However, studies have also shown that managers and employers often perceive women to be older than their male colleagues of the same age.[55] Moreover, these studies indicate that women are perceived to reach the highest point in their careers about 10 years earlier than men (at 35 years of age instead of 45), and their perceived age-related decline in job performance is thought to begin earlier than for men.[56] The study of gendered ageism in the workplace provides an extensive and inviting basis for explorations of the intersection of age and gender in a wide range of labour law issues. Using examples from Sweden, an analysis of how gendered ageism may present itself in labour law, to the detriment of older working women, will be undertaken in the remainder of this section.

Swedish labour law is extensive, rich in detail, and uniform in scope. With the exception of wages, most areas of labour law are statutorily regulated. Collective agreements hold a significant position as a legal source in Swedish labour law; almost all employees are covered by collective agreements, and social partners are strong. Most of the comprehensive body of labour law legislation is 'semi-compelling', in the sense that otherwise mandatory rules may be deviated from in collective bargaining. The Discrimination Act of 2008, which is mandatory, has been designed closely on the EU Employment Equality Directive 2000/78 and the

---

[54] S Spedale, C Coupland & S Tempest (2014) 'Gendered Ageism and Organizational Routines at Work: The Case of Day-Parting in Television Broadcasting', Organization Studies 35 (11), 1585; W Loretto, C Duncan & P J White (2000) 'Ageism and employment. Controversies, ambiguities and younger people's perceptions' Ageing and Society 20, 279, 285 and 296; and J McMullin (1995) 'Theorizing Age and Gender Relations' in S Arber & J Ginn (eds.) Connecting gender and ageing. a sociological approach (Open University Press).

[55] C Itzin & C Phillipson (1993) Age Barriers at Work: Maximising the Potential of Mature and Older Workers (Metropolitan Authorities Recruitment Agency) and 'Gendered ageism: a double jeopardy for women in Organizations' in Itzin & Newman (1995); C Duncan & W Loretto (2004) 'Never the right age? Gender and age-based discrimination in employment' Gender, Work and Organization 11 (1), 95; R C Barnett (2005) 'Ageism and sexism in the workplace' Generations 29 (3), 25.

[56] J Drevenstedt (1976) 'Perceptions of onsets of young adulthood, middle age, and old age', Journal of Gerontology 31, 53; H Zepelin, R A Sills & M W Heath (1986), 'Is age becoming irrelevant? An exploratory study of perceived age norms' (1986) International Journal of Aging and Human Development 24, 241.

Equal Treatment Directive 2006/54.[57] In disputes about discrimination in working life, individuals who are not represented by their unions may be represented by the Equal Opportunities Ombudsman authority free of charge. Disputes are tried before the Swedish Labour Court, normally the first and only instance.[58] On the whole, the Labour Court rules on just under a hundred cases yearly, out of which only a few of these concern discrimination.

Since the coming into force of the prohibition against discrimination in January 2009, the Labour Court has tried four cases of discrimination on the ground of age. In two of these cases, action was brought on the multiple grounds of age and sex. The first case, from 2010, regarded a position as a job coach at the National Employment Agency. One of the applicants was a 62-year-old woman with a solid record of performance. At the time, she was registered as a jobseeker at the Agency.[59] The employer selected 10 persons for an interview, both men and women of various ages, but not one older woman. In the end, two women were hired, aged 27 and 36 years. The 62-year-old woman filed a report with the Equal Opportunities Ombudsman, on the basis that she had been neither selected for a job interview nor hired. In its defence, the National Employment Agency claimed that during the recruitment process, the Agency had received information that the 62-year-old woman was arrogant and lacked humility, and that she was thus not suitable for employment as a job coach. The information had been provided in an informal way from two of the Agency's own administrators who had been in contact with the woman earlier in her capacity as a jobseeker. The administrators doubted that the woman was empathic enough for the job in question. The Swedish Labour Court rejected this explanation, and stated that the National Employment Agency had discriminated against the 62-year-old woman on the parallel grounds of age and sex, by refusing to invite her to the job interview, and on the ground of age by not hiring her. However, the Court also stated that the finding of two grounds of discrimination

_____

[57] Discrimination Act (2008:567).

[58] When the employee chooses to not be represented by the union or the Equal Opportunities Ombudsman, action must be brought to the District Court in first instance; Ch. 2 Sec. 1 of the Labour Disputes Act (1974:371).

[59] Swedish Labour Court judgment AD 2010 No 91.

in this case should *not* increase the level of the damages. Instead, the Court explained that damages should be determined on the basis of the *immediate result* of the discrimination, i.e., that the woman was never considered for employment. From an intersectional perspective, this is a problematic standpoint. A basic idea of damages in discrimination cases is that the damage shall provide redress for suffering and emotional distress caused by degrading treatment that results from the discriminating act. As has been argued by legal scholars, multiple discrimination has a stronger effect of exclusion than discrimination on only one ground; consequently, it should attract higher damages.[60]

The second case, which came in 2013, regarded wage discrimination in relation to a 64-year-old female social assistant working in a short-term residential facility for young children.[61] During her 30-year career in the profession (out of which 20 years were with the employer in question), she continuously pursued studies to increase her competences in different therapeutic methods and, in periods, was granted leave of absence to hold temporary employments in management positions in both the facility and in the public sector. The subject of the dispute was that a newly recruited 33-year-old male social assistant, with five years of experience in the field, was given an initial salary at a level well above that of the 64-year-old woman. When the dispute was triggered, the woman was one of the highest-paid social assistants in the facility. The Equal Opportunities Ombudsman brought action on behalf of the woman, claiming discrimination on the parallel grounds of sex and age. In the proceedings, the employer claimed to have only reluctantly accepted the man's high salary requirements at the time of his recruitment, and only because he had mastered a particular evaluation method that the company was about to implement in its business at that time. The Swedish Labour Court accepted that explanation, and concluded that the wage difference in this case was based on the outcome of market forces, not on discrimination. The fact that the wage gap between the 62-year-old woman and the 33-year-old man persisted for two years following the man's recruitment was not seen as problematic in this context.

---

[60] Burri & Schiek (2009).
[61] Swedish Labour Court judgment AD 2013 No 64.

Ageist attitudes and presumptions are rarely displayed openly in discrimination disputes. This is to be expected, because such expressions would indicate age discrimination, which is prohibited by law. Ageist stereotyping with a gendered bias is more clearly visible in sex discrimination cases from the Swedish Labour Court stemming from the era before the ban on age discrimination was introduced. For instance, in 2006, when recruiting for a position as sergeant, the Swedish Police ranked a male applicant with 11 years of service higher than a female applicant who, with 30 years of service, was formally more qualified.[62] The decision was based on claimed deficits in the woman's decision-making ability and natural leadership skills. The woman's leadership style was described in terms of an 'old-fashioned school teacher' or a 'mother'. Likewise, in 2005 when a church bypassed a highly qualified 55-year-old woman to the benefit of a 35-year-old man in appointing a vicar, references were made to the woman's lack in personal suitability.[63] Here, the negative terms used to portray the woman were 'self-confident' and 'condescending'. In 2004, when recruiting for a position as director of investigations for the Swedish Police, a qualified female applicant with 30 years of service, uncontested extensive experience in conducting investigations, and a fine record was turned down in favour of a man who had graduated from the Police Academy only five years earlier. The Swedish Police claimed that doubts had been expressed regarding the female applicant's courage and strength to act as well as her ability to earn respect from subordinates.[64] In all of these cases, the Labour Court dismissed the discrimination claim.[65]

The understanding of intersectionality as mutual process, where one category and its social position help to construct the understanding and positioning of the other category, with implications for social status,

---

[62] Swedish Labour Court judgment AD 2006 No 126.

[63] Swedish Labour Court judgment AD 2005 No 69.

[64] Swedish Labour Court judgment AD 2004 No 44.

[65] In the first case, the Labour Court stated that despite her formally better merits, the woman had less personal suitability for the position. In the second case, the Labour Court acknowledged that the woman was at least of equal merit as the man in respect of education, professional experience and personal suitability, but that the church had preferred the male applicant's leadership style. In the third case, a divided Labour Court found that the woman's superiority in respect of education and experience was outweighed by the male applicant's presumed much greater personal suitability for the position, and thus rejected her claim.

power, and level of inclusion, is well illustrated in these cases. Within the police force and within the church, female gender implies a lower status, while age is a more neutral factor. In this setting, the understanding of female gender makes becoming older problematic in relation to women; they are described in deteriorating and diminishing terms, or as being mean and patronising. In a labour market where flexibility, responsibility, teamwork, social skills and responsiveness are key, the words used to describe the women in the cases above represent the opposite of these values. The gendered ageism that these words reveal is quite obvious in 'old-fashioned school teacher' and 'mother', but also appears in the description of the woman's 'self-confidence' as something negative, which makes her 'condescending'. This description fits closely with the stereotype of the older woman as a 'shrew', described in psychological scholarship to capture attitudes towards older women which encompass characteristics such as bitter, inflexible, stubborn, demanding, nosy and selfish, in contrast to the stereotype of the 'perfect grandmother' as women who are kind, serene, trustworthy, nurturing, and helpful.[66]

7   Conclusions

In EU and Swedish labour law, age, and gender are not identified as intersecting, nor are other discursively and institutionally constructed categories. In certain cases, gender and age issues may be treated as part of the same legal matter—for example, in cases regarding different retirement ages for men and women, or in cases of multiple discrimination. However, labour law does not address in a more general and comprehensive way the intersection of age and gender as a question of legal significance in its own right. It is thus only in parallel to each other that the 'age factor' and the 'gender factor' have been recognised as important in the labour law context. From a labour law perspective, it is also important

---

[66] M L Hummert, T A Garstka, J L Shaner & S Stram, (1994) 'Stereotypes of the Elderly Held by Young, Middle-Aged, and Elderly Adults', *Journal of Gerontology* 49 (5), 240. Cf. D F Schmidt & SM Boland (1986) 'Structure of perceptions of older adults: Evidence for multiple stereotypes', *Psychology and Aging* 1 (3), 255; M E Kite & B T Johnson (1988) 'Attitudes toward older and younger adults: a meta-analysis' *Psychology and Ageing* 3 (3), 233.

to acknowledge intersectional outcomes of the interplay between these categories. These outcomes are of interest in relation to the interpretation of legal rules whereby all kinds of managerial decisions are made—such as assessments of the employee's qualifications and suitability for a position or a task, wage setting, and also in relation to investments in the employee's professional development and lifelong learning.

In light of the ongoing demographic change in Europe, where the proportion of older people in the labour market is rapidly growing, the need to examine this intersection between the 'age factor' and the 'gender factor' in labour law is taking on new urgency. In the end, regulatory activity that overlooks the complexity of age and gender may prove unable to provide the legal protection that was originally intended. From a labour law perspective, this means that older women are at risk of experiencing obstacles to and deteriorations in their capacities as jobseekers or employees, despite existing legislation intended to prevent such a course of events. Such impairments may be due to discrimination, but they may also have other, less obvious explanations related to unchallenged perceptions about age and gender—perceptions that permeate the organisation of both work and labour law.

6

Active Ageing in Italy: Labour Market Perspectives and Access to Welfare

Luciana Guaglianone and Fabio Ravelli

Luciana Guaglianone is associate professor of Labour Law at the University of Brescia. Fabio Ravelli is Lecturer of Labour Law at the University of Brescia. Although this article is the result of the authors' shared observations on active ageing, Sects. 2, 3, 4 and 9 are the work of Fabio Ravelli, while Sects. 1, 5, 6, 7, 8 were written by Luciana Guaglianone.

1   Introduction

The quantitative data describing the participation of older workers in the Italian labour market shows, without any doubt, that Italy's performance is unsatisfactory when compared not only with the most virtuous countries but also with the EU average. According to *Eurostat* (2013), the employment rate for older Italian workers (aged 55–64) is 42.7%, while the EU average is 50.1%.[1] More recent data, published by Confindustria (the biggest employers' association), show that the employment rate for older workers has further

---

[1] See http://ec.europa.eu/eurostat/statistics-explained/index.php/Employment_statistics [Accessed 30 May 2014].

© The Editor(s) (if applicable) and The Author(s) 2016   **117**
S. Manfredi, L. Vickers (eds.), *Challenges of Active Ageing*,
DOI 10.1057/978-1-137-53251-0_6

increased (46.9%), which puts Italy in fourth place for the 2007–2013 period in the EU ranking as regards this indicator. However, Italy's performance, while encouraging, is still unsatisfactory in absolute terms.[2]

The above data clearly show the importance, for Italy, of developing an effective and consistent active ageing strategy in order to comply with the European Employment Strategy guidelines. Despite this, Italian active ageing policies are characterised by an overall lack of strategy. There are multiple reasons for this lack of strategy, and they can be analysed by taking into account two different aspects that are particularly significant within the Italian context. The first involves the development of appropriate retirement policies, with implications in terms of age discrimination. This is discussed in the first part of this chapter. The second relates to the adoption of inclusion measures aimed at extending working life based on legal rules, collective agreements and good practices. This is discussed in the second part of this chapter.

2   Retirement Age

2.1   Active Ageing and Retirement Policies

In order to properly address the issue of retirement policies, it seems appropriate to recall the three goals set in the EU Commission's White Paper on Pensions[3] that have a considerable impact on active ageing policies and were supposed to have guided the action of the Italian government in this field: first, to link retirement age with increases in life expectancy; second, to equalise retirement age between men and women (by increasing women's retirement age); and third, to restrict access to early retirement schemes and other early exit pathways.

As will be explained in more detail in the following sections, the measures adopted by the Italian legislature over the past five years have been consistent with both the first and second goals while, as to the third, the picture is mixed. In particular, the following sections will focus on three

---

[2] Confindustria 'In Italia più occupati anziani e meno giovani', *Commentary Centro Studi Confindustria*, no. 1/2015 (see www.confindustria.it). [Accessed 30 May 2015].

[3] See EU Commission, White Paper *An Agenda for Adequate, Safe and Sustainable Pensions*, 16.2.2012 COM (2012) 55 final.

topics: retirement age; age and termination of employment; and early retirement schemes and other early exit pathways.

Between 2009 and 2011, the retirement age was progressively increased. The last increase was established in 2011 by the 'Monti Reform' (contained in the so-called 'Save Italy Decree',[4] according to which workers are entitled to retire at 66 in the case of men and women in the public sector; and at 66 in the case of men and (now) at 63 and 9 months in the case of women in the private sector. However, women's pensionable age will increase to 66 by 2018). Moreover, the 'Monti Reform' has introduced a mechanism for the periodic adjustment of the retirement age in line with increases in average life expectancy.[5] These reforms clearly have a significant impact on active ageing policies. Indeed, raising the retirement age can be considered the most effective instrument used by the Italian government to comply with the goal of retaining the elderly in the labour market. While active ageing policies may have been a concern in the pension reform, to find its prime mover it would be better to look elsewhere.

The increase in retirement age was mainly the result of financial concerns. The financial sustainability of the pension system has been the main focus of Italian social security policies for well over 20 years—since 1992. With specific regard to the equalisation of the retirement age between men and women, the task was initiated by the Berlusconi government and finally accomplished by the Monti government (2011–2013).[6] In order to explain what happened in Italy, two powerful driving forces must be taken into account: on the one hand, the state budget,[7] and on the other hand, the Court of Justice of the European Union (CJEU). In *Commission v. Italy*,[8] the Court of Justice ruled that different pension ages for male and female civil servants violated the principle of equal pay.

---

[4] See Article 24 of Law Decree no. 201/2011.

[5] For example, by 2021 the retirement age will be 67 years and 2 months.

[6] The activity of the Monti government covered the period 16 Nov. 2011–28 Apr. 2013. More specifically, the reform of pensions was effected in December 2011 under Law Decree nos. 201/2011 and 211/2011 respectively.

[7] A crucial role was played by the letter calling for reforms that Mario Draghi, the President of the European Central Bank, sent to the Italian Government in the summer of 2011. Although far from being legally binding, this letter had a more powerful effect on Italy than any EU directive.

[8] C-46/07 *Commission v. Italy*. Judgment of 13 November 2008.

That decision had a snowball effect: measures aimed at equalising the pensionable age between men and women were introduced not only in the public sector, as the Court had requested, but also in the private sector. The equalisation of the retirement age between men and women cannot, therefore, be attributed to a conscious active ageing strategy; instead, it was determined by external factors. In other words, equalisation was imposed by circumstances rather than actively pursued.[9]

Concluding on the issue of retirement age, it can be observed that the pension reforms have not only enabled the government to save money but also increase the number of old persons in work. So far, raising the retirement age can be seen as the most effective instrument used by the Italian government to comply with the goal of retaining older workers in the labour market, as proposed by the EU Employment Guidelines. However, since it is an instrument based on coercion rather than on incentives, it is one of the weakest points of the Italian active ageing policy.

3   Age and Termination of the Employment Contract

Under Italian law, age can be relevant to the termination of an employment contract in various respects. Age may be taken into consideration

- for the purpose of mandatory retirement;
- for the purpose of 'at-will' dismissal of pensionable workers;
- as a justification, provided for by collective agreements, to terminate the employment contract; or
- as a criterion for the identification of the workers to be laid off as a result of a collective dismissal procedure.

---

[9] It is worth pointing out that at the time the equalisation of the retirement age between men and women was not on the political agenda. Since it was considered a thorny issue, no government really wanted to deal with it. Moreover, the idea that a lower retirement age should be a compensation for the disadvantages experienced by women in the labour market was still a powerful one. The 'compensation argument' was even used by the Italian Constitutional Court (see Decision nos. 137/1986, 335/2000 and 256/2002).

3.1   Mandatory Retirement

Mandatory retirement is a controversial issue in various European social security systems, and Italy is no exception.[10] On the one hand, mandatory retirement, especially when the compulsory exit of the elderly from the labour market seeks to promote the inclusion of the young, puts social cohesion to the test and raises a number of questions in terms of inter-generational fairness.[11] On the other, it can be conceived as a limitation on the individual's right to work beyond pensionable age, in particular under Article 4.1 of the Italian Constitution, as well as discrimination on the grounds of age insofar as it is not adequately justified by the objective reasons provided for by Article 6 of Directive 2000/78.[12]

With specific regard to the Italian situation, it is worth distinguishing between the private and public sector, since different rules apply.

Private Sector

In the private sector, mandatory retirement is excluded: there is no legal obligation on workers to retire and, similarly, no legal obligation on employers to dismiss pensionable workers. Therefore, in principle, employees can decide when to retire without being subject to external constraints either from the legislature or the employer.

However, under Article 4 of Law no. 108/1990 employers can, if they wish, dismiss pensionable workers without providing any justification, notwithstanding the general principle establishing that dismissals must be justified. The rationale of this rule lies in the idea that the employer

---

[10] D Izzi (2014) 'Invecchiamento attivo e pensionamenti forzati' *Rivista italiana di diritto del lavoro* 1584;ff and F. Ravelli (2015) 'Alcune questioni in tema di pensioni e turn-over generazionale' *Rivista giuridica del lavoro* 2, 347 ff.

[11] H Sheppard (1978) 'The Issue of Mandatory Retirement', *Annals of the American Academy of Political and Social Science*, 438, and also 'Planning for the Elderly' *Annals of the American Academy of Political and Social Science,* 40.; M. Gunderson and J. Pesando (1988) 'The Case for Allowing Mandatory Retirement', *Canadian Public Policy* XIV 32 ff.

[12] F Hendrickx (2013) 'Age and European Employment Discrimination Law' in F Hendrickx (ed.), *Active Ageing and Labour Law* (Intersentia) 3; M. Schlachter (2011) 'Mandatory Retirement and Age Discrimination under EU Law', *The International Journal of Comparative Labour Law and Industrial Relations* 3, 287 ff.

should be entitled to plan and implement workforce renewal through the dismissal of (older) workers who are considered to be less productive.[13]

A number of scholars[14] have raised doubts about the compatibility of this provision with the Framework Directive, given that the alleged lower productivity of older workers is more a stereotype than a fact[15] (see also Frank Hendrickx at Chap. 1).

In spite of this, judges have so far shown little sensitivity to this argument. However, a decision recently issued by the Tribunal of Genoa[16] is worth mentioning in this context. The judge stated that the rule allowing the employer to dismiss 'at-will' pensionable workers is contrary to Article 6 of the Directive, and held that Article 4 of Law no. 108 did not pass the legitimacy test insofar as it protects a 'purely individual interest particular to the employer's situation' instead of a public interest.[17] This decision has raised some criticism. In particular, it is questionable whether the provision at issue is only functional to the individual employer's interest or not. The judge did not seem to take into consideration a number of other possible legitimate aims identified by the CJEU.[18]

The rule allowing the employer to dismiss pensionable workers at will, while formally still in force, has been considerably toned down by Law no. 211/2011 under which employees can postpone their retirement until the age of 70, enjoying statutory protection against at-will dismissal (at-will dismissal is still applicable to 70-year-old workers).[19] This seems

---

[13] The 'productivity argument' is described (and criticized) by W Eichhorst et al. (2014) 'How to combine the entry of young people in the labour market with the retention of older workers?' IZA Journal of European Labour Studies 3 (19), 6.

[14] O Bonardi (2007) 'Le discriminazioni basate sull'età' in M. Barbera (ed.), *Il nuovo diritto antidiscriminatorio. Il quadro comunitario e nazionale*, (Giuffrè)125 ff.

[15] C O' Cinneide (2013) 'The Growing Importance of Age Equality', *The Equal Rights Review* 11,99, according to whom 'age [is] used as a 'proxy' for other personal characteristics such as maturity, health or vulnerability'.

[16] Tribunal of Genoa 3 December 2012, no. 1605. For a comment see L Guaglianone, F Ravelli (2015) 'Young and Old: Age Discrimination in Italian Case Law', *European Labour Law Journal* 2 (forthcoming).

[17] The judge referred explicitly to C-388/07 *The Queen, on the application of The Incorporated Trustees of the National Council for Ageing (Age Concern England) v Secretary of State for Business, Enterprise and Regulatory Reform* [2009] ECR I 1569 ('Age Concern England').

[18] See the leading case C-411/05 *Palacios de la Villa v Cortefiel Servicios SA* [2007] ECR I 8531 ('*Palacios de la Villa*') para 53, and the subsequent case law.

[19] Article 24.4 of law no. 211/2014.

to confirm the attitude of disfavour that the Italian social security system has towards mandatory retirement and other equivalent forms, at least in the private sector.

Public Sector

The rationale employed in the public sector is different. Mandatory retirement applies.[20] Retirement age is normally envisaged as a 'maximum age' and its attainment determines the automatic termination of the employment. Retirement age in the public sector is 66 for civil servants in general, 70 for some special categories such as judges, public prosecutors, state lawyers and university professors, and 75 for notaries. Until 2014, civil servants could ask to have their employment relationship prolonged by up to two years. The final decision was up to the administration, which had broad discretion in this respect. However, a certain degree of flexibility was attached to this mechanism. This flexibility has been progressively reduced in recent years. In 2012, the government significantly limited the discretionary power of the public administration to keep pensionable workers on duty[21] and then, following Law no. 144/2014, the extension of working life beyond statutory retirement age has become a residual possibility.

One could ask whether the Italian way to mandatory retirement is compatible with the Framework Directive. According to the CJEU's jurisprudence, the answer is in the affirmative.

The termination of the employment of pensionable civil servants is clearly designed to pursue two aims: (1) reduce spending, in order to ensure financial sustainability in times of severe economic crisis; and (2) foster intergenerational turnover between young and old, in order to have a more balanced workforce in terms of age and increase the employment rate of young workers, in a context characterised by dramatic levels of youth unemployment.

---

[20] Article 72 of decree no. 112/2008. This rule was confirmed by article 24 of law no. 214/2011 and then by law no. 144/2014.

[21] Decree no. 95/2012.

In terms of legitimacy, both aims seem to be consistent with the decisional standards adopted by the CJEU and, as to the compliance with the proportionality principle, the measures adopted by the Italian government seem to pass the test of necessity and appropriateness as applied by the Court.[22] In this respect scholars have pointed out that 'the standard of judicial review is rather lenient, allowing for all measures short of those that are clearly arbitrary'.[23] In the light of the CJEU's stance, it can therefore be concluded that the legitimacy of mandatory retirement in the public sector should not be questioned.

3.2   Clauses on Automatic Termination of Employment

Until recently, the social partners used to insert into collective agreements age-related clauses regarding automatic termination of employment contracts. Indeed, such clauses were very common. Over the last few years, the Supreme Court of Cassation has constantly stated that the insertion of such clauses is to be considered illegitimate.[24] However, it is worth noting that, contrary to what one might expect, the Supreme Court does not decide such cases by applying the principle of non-discrimination. Italian judges tend not to use the tools provided by anti-discrimination law, preferring to stick to the traditional line of reasoning based on the so-called principle of 'typicality' of the reasons for fair dismissal. The reasons for fair dismissal are, basically, of two types: either a serious infringement of the obligations deriving from the contract, or an economic reason. No other type of reason is permitted. Therefore, 'atypical' reasons, such as the attainment of a certain age (e.g. retirement age) are unlawful.

Interestingly, the Italian judges' tendency to set aside the anti-discrimination approach also has implications for the outcome of the

---

[22] See for example, C-341/08 *Domnica Petersen v Berufungsausschuss für Zahnärzte für den Bezirk Westfalen-Lippe* [2010] ECR I-47 ('Petersen'), and C-250/09 & C-268/09 *Vasil Ivanov Georgiev v Tehnicheski universitet - Sofia, filial Plovdiv* [2010] ECR I-11869; C-159/10 & 160/10 ('Georgiev').

[23] M Schlachter (2011) 'Mandatory Retirement and Age Discrimination under EU Law', *International Journal of Comparative Labour Law and Industrial Relations* 27 (3) 287–299, 292.

[24] See, for example, Court of Cassation 18.10.2011, no. 21554.

decision-making process: were they to follow the anti-discrimination approach, then clauses on automatic termination might be seen as being legitimate (see *Palacios* and *Rosenbladt*).[25] On the contrary, relying on the principle of 'typicality' leads to the opposite outcome, and thus provides more protection to an individual's right to work.

3.3   Age as Selection Criterion for Dismissal of Redundant Employees

In order to identify workers to be made redundant, terms and conditions of collective dismissals negotiated at company level and set out in collective agreements always establish a number of selection criteria. 'Proximity-to-retirement' is often one of those.

The rationale behind this criterion is that workers who have nearly reached retirement age can be protected more easily than younger ones, either by specific social security cushions, such as the so-called '*mobilità lunga*' (a social allowance aimed at bridging the gap between redundancy and retirement) or by early exit schemes (particularly popular in recent decades).

Some local courts have called into question the validity of the 'proximity-to-retirement' criterion for violating the principle of non-discrimination on grounds of age.[26] In particular, it has been pointed out that a selection criterion based solely on proximity-to-retirement (therefore on age), irrespective of further 'employment policy, labour market and vocational training objectives' (cf. Article 6 of the Directive), is inherently illegitimate. On the contrary, for several years the Court of Cassation has held that 'proximity-to-retirement' is to be considered a legitimate criterion insofar as it complies with the principle of reasonableness and/or the principle of good faith (in other words, insofar as it is not applied arbitrarily).[27] This solution relies on a common-sense argument that the

---

[25] *Gisela Rosenbladt v. Oellerking Gebäudereinigungsges* judgment of 12 October 2010 (*Rosenbladt*).
[26] See, for example, Court of Appeal of Florence 27.3.2006, with commentary by L. Calafà (2006) 'Licenziamenti collettivi alle Poste e discriminazioni in base all'età: la prima applicazione nazionale della sentenza Mangold', in *D&L – Rivista Critica di Diritto del Lavoro* 915 ff.
[27] See Court of Cassation 21.9.2006, no. 20455; 24.4.2007, no. 9866; 26.4.2011, no. 9348.

dismissal of older workers who are about to retire is to be considered the lesser evil. However, it is questionable whether this legal approach is consistent with the Directive.

3.4   Judges' Reluctance to Rely on Anti-discrimination Law Tools

In the previous sections, it has been observed that Italian judges seem to be reluctant to make use of anti-discrimination law, as can be noted by the small number of decisions issued by the courts. It is worth investigating the reasons for this reluctance.

One possible, superficial explanation is the traditional slowness of the Italian judicial apparatus. The majority of cases handled by higher courts originated from lawsuits filed before the entry into force of the Directive. As a consequence, only a few decisions address the legal issues at stake from the perspective of anti-discrimination law.

However, this cannot be true when it comes to cases handled by the courts of first instance. Therefore, there must be another, and stronger, reason.

An analysis of the courts' legal reasoning shows that the reason is ultimately 'cultural'. First, judges tend to use their old toolbox instead of new tools (although it is questionable whether in 2015 age discrimination can be seen as something 'new'); in this respect, Italian jurisprudence appears a bit conservative. Second, the plaintiffs themselves, knowing the judges' attitude well, are inclined to make use of legal arguments that proved to be effective in the past.

If this is the general framework, it must nonetheless be stressed that tribunals and courts of appeal, or at least some of them, have been changing their methodological approach, showing an increasing sensitivity to the issue of age-related discrimination.

However, again, a distinction has to be drawn:

(a) judges are more inclined to use anti-discrimination law when it comes to factors such as nationality, race, religion or personal beliefs. In relation to these factors a significant body of case law has developed;

(b) on the contrary, there is relatively little case law in relation to age-related discrimination.

Observing the Italian situation, we can note that, with regard to its judicial implementation, anti-discrimination law is still characterised by a two-speed development.

4 Early Retirement Schemes and Other Early Exit Pathways

As to the goal of restricting access to early retirement schemes and other early exit pathways, we have a mixed picture. No doubt the Monti Pension Reform of 2011 has considerably limited the access to early retirement schemes. The old 'seniority retirement', allowing workers with at least 35 years of pension contributions to retire early, has been repealed, except in the case of those workers who perform strenuous work, and replaced by a new early retirement scheme characterised by more restrictive access requirements.[28] These measures are clearly consistent with the EU goals, in particular with the goal of retaining employees in work for a longer period in order to increase the employment rate of older workers.

At the same time, in Italy a counter-trend can also be observed. Notwithstanding the EU Employment Guidelines calling for the extension of elderly working life, Law no. 92/2012 (the so-called 'Fornero Reform') tried to re-launch, though not very successfully, early exit collective agreements designed to encourage older workers to exit the labour market. This has always been a typical way to manage redundancies in Italy. In the past, exit agreements played a crucial role, but their importance had been declining in recent years. The main reason was a lack of money rather than a reconceptualisation of the strategies for active ageing. This can be seen as a classic exemplification of the paradox pointed

---

[28] In particular, the minimum contributory period has been significantly extended: the minimum required contribution is 42 years and 6 months for men and 41 years and 6 months for women; besides, those who retire before the age of 62 are penalized through a reduction of the amount of the pension.

out by Alan Neal[29]: public policies often envisage two divergent strate-gies—the former aimed at retaining workers in the labour market, and the latter at subsidising their early withdrawal.

5   Inclusion Measures Aimed at Extending Working Life

5.1   The Legal Perspective: Is Labour Law Too Inflexible to Promote Active Ageing?

The Italian legislature has never introduced active ageing policies targeted solely at older workers. The main reason for this is the desire to avoid com-petition between young and older workers, even though several sources[30] give the lie to this risk. The two groups occupy different and very distinct segments of the job market in terms of skills and experience.[31] However, the Italian legislature appears to share the view of those that claim that 'fathers are stealing jobs from their children'.[32]

An example of active ageing policies for both categories is Article 33 of Legislative Decree no. 276/03 (as amended by Article 1, Section 22 of Law no. 92/2012) 'individuals aged over 55 and under 24' may be hired using job-on-call contracts.[33] The legal technique used in this provision,

[29] A Neal (2012) 'Active Ageing and the Limits of Labour Law' in F. Hendrickx (ed.), *Active Ageing and Labour Law*, (Intersentia) 31 ff.
[30] The ISTAT (Italy's National Institute of Statistics) Report for 2014, which documents the changes affecting the country's economy and Italian society. indicates that the work profiles of the two generations do not overlap (www.istat.it). [Accessed 30 May 2014].
[31] See S Fredman (2011) *Discrimination Law* (Oxford University Press. Blaming elderly workers for the low level of young people in work is, therefore, the result of a simplistic interpretation of the labour market, which sees the two groups competing against each other.
[32] See L. Mariucci (2013) 'The real sins of the fathers: wrong reforms and missed reforms', *Economia e società regionale* XXXI (3), 84.
[33] The job-on-call contract, introduced under Article 34 of Decree no. 276/2003, is an employment contract without pre-established working hours. The employee puts himself at the employer's dis-posal and awaits his call. The worker may choose to answer some or all of the employer's calls. If the employee undertakes to answer all of the employer's calls, he is entitled to receive an availability indemnity. The law allows an employer to unilaterally decide the conditions of the employment contract provided that the worker in question is younger than 25. The fact that this requisite per-mitted a job-on-call contract with a ground of discrimination raised doubts among legal scholars about its legality. Some had found it to be discriminatory from the very beginning, but Italian lawmakers failed to take notice.

which was proposed again in the decree bill of Law no. 81/2015, is a combination of legislative and contractual provisions. The rules regulating the legal relationship are laid down by Italian law,[34] while collective agreements determine the cases in which job-on-call may be used.

The technique used to draft the legal rule has implications that go beyond the value of the provision itself, which until now has been little used by social partners. What is more, a recent judgment by the Appeal Court of Milan[35] found the provision to be in violation of the prohibition of age discrimination. More specifically, it raises the question of whether legislation is the most appropriate means of proposing active ageing policies or if labour law regulations are too inflexible to fully protect older workers.[36]

Until February 2015, the Italian legislature seemed to share this uncertainty. It had delegated to the social partners the duty to indicate or modify all the types of contract which, in theory, were capable of constituting the legal bases for policies in favour of older workers, as these could tailor work to their needs, or make it more flexible.[37] These included not only job-on-call, but also part-time[38] and job-sharing contracts.[39] The social partners have never shown any interest in using flexible working hours to promote active ageing policies. Job-on-call has only been regulated in

[34] In Italy, collective bargaining is a private form of agreement, but Italian law also grants social partners the right to derogate from legal provisions or supplement them. The essential rules regarding collective bargaining are to be found in agreements (inter-confederal agreements of 2009 and 2012 and the memorandum of understanding of 2013) signed by the main Italian trade unions (CGIL-CISL-UIL). Collective bargaining takes place at two levels, industry and local (either district or company). National collective bargaining establishes the rules regulating the employment relationship, while local collective bargaining adapts the general regulations to the specific contexts.

[35] In its decision of 14 April 2014, the Court of Appeal of Milan found the dismissal of a worker hired using job-on-call on the sole ground of the worker's age (under 25) to be discriminatory insofar as it was in breach of Article 3 of Legislative Decree no. 216/2003.

[36] See A Neal (2012) '"Active Ageing" and the Limits of Labour Law' in F Hendrickx (ed.) *Active Ageing and Labour Law*, (Intersentia).

[37] The findings of a recent study on the subject of work preferences after 50 clearly show a close correlation between an increase in age and a decrease in the desire for a full-time job. Moreover, one of the recommendations proposed at the European level to Member States to promote work among over 50-year-olds is the use of part-time work tailored to older workers. See Eurofound (2014) *Work preferences after 50* (Publications Office of the European Union).

[38] See Legislative Decree no. 61/2000 in www.camera.it/parlam/leggi/deleghe/00061dl.htm [Accessed 22 October 2015].

[39] See Article 41 of Legislative Decree no. 276/300 in www.camera.it/parlam/leggi/deleghe/00061dl.htm [Accessed 22 October 2015].

tourism and commerce, while job-sharing and part-time work have never been used to promote active ageing. The reasons for this are complex. Italian trade unions have for years favoured the indefinite duration contract model believing it offered workers greater protection. This has led to a failure to collectively regulate forms of work considered to be excessively flexible such as job-sharing and job-on-call. Other reasons, and this applies to part-time work, are exclusively related to trade unions' lack of interest in engaging with active ageing policies.

Since February 2015, the relationship between legal and contractual rules has changed. The draft bill approved by the Council of Ministers on 20 February 2015 (Jobs Act) will repeal job-sharing contracts and reduce the role of collective bargaining in the case of part-time work. The proposed new rules bear the mark of an obsession to restrict the regulatory freedom enjoyed by collective bargaining to a minimum. This will make it impossible for the social partners to include active ageing policies by making the various types of contracts more flexible. As a result, Italy will distance itself even more from those countries that have been most successful in Europe in promoting the inclusion of older workers, namely France, in the form of the *contrat de generation,* and Germany.[40]

6   The Contractual Perspective: Trade Unions' Lack of Interest at National and Company Level

6.1   The National Contract

While the social partners have never engaged in active ageing initiatives, they have been actively involved in the regulation of 'defensive' policies to protect older workers. Most company crises over the last 20 years have, to some extent, been solved through exit procedures targeting workers close

---

[40] On *contrat de generation*, see B Barbareschi (2014) 'Gestire le differenze d'età nel mercato del lavoro e in impresa: il caso francese', *Sociologia del lavoro*,134. Some Nordic countries (Denmark, Finland, Sweden) use a combination of collective bargaining rules and corporate social responsibility guidelines. See H Piekkola (2008), 'Nordic policies on active ageing in the labour market and some European comparisons', in *Country and Regional development,* (UNESCO).

to retirement, and managed by the social partners at company level. This mechanism worked until 2011, the year in which changes in pension rules pushed the retirement age up significantly, making it much more complex and costly to use early retirement procedures (see below). A different form of interaction became necessary on the issue of older workers.

Starting in 2012, some national collective bargaining agreements[41] included a joint declaration calling on the government to enact measures to promote intergenerational balance. The tool proposed was part-time work as a technique to promote voluntary flexible working conditions, aimed at workers nearing retirement, and as a way of hiring younger workers. The choice went in the right direction. Labour market researchers[42] have pointed out that part-time work is one way of tackling problems associated with ageing. But again, the social partners showed little real interest in promoting active ageing. The initiatives proposed did not include any to train or re-train older workers for new work opportunities. Further, there have been no measures for older and younger workers to interact through, for example, tutoring or mentoring schemes. The trade union organisations, therefore, propose using older workers as facilitators of youth employment, but do not recognise that they too may have an interest in work. Mental prejudice, such as the idea that young and old compete in the same labour market, and stereotypical attitudes about the ability of older employees to work, continue to dominate the types of contracts that are available. Also, the increased attention paid to ageing has not changed the attitudes of the social partners. Since March 2015 the so-called *contract of credit* has allocated resources to initiatives aimed at re-employing workers who have been laid off on the basis that such initiatives focus on intergenerational solidarity. In the same month, the contract for the service sector, which employs mainly young people, went further and focused explicitly on policies aimed at this group. Students and young people under 25 can be employed at weekends on part-time contracts lasting a maximum of eight hours. Even if the legal

---

[41] For an analysis of contracts see M. Corti (2013) 'Active ageing e autonomia collettiva. "Non è un Paese per vecchi", ma dovrà diventarlo presto' *Lavoro e Diritto 3*, 383.

[42] P Ilmakunnas and S Ilmakunnas (Spring 2011) 'Diversity at the workplace. Whom does it benefit?', *De Economist* (Berlin). They suggest that incentives are necessary to encourage this form of flexibility to be accepted.

provision is not in itself particularly important, what heralds a change in the attention social partners pay to young people's needs is the greater desire to negotiate these issues. The wording of the agreement originally also included the unemployed and persons aged over 55, but was subsequently amended to focus on young people.

Notwithstanding internal difficulties, the possibility of including contractual clauses to promote youth employment is consistent with European Community policy. When the CJEU has been asked to rule on alleged age discrimination suffered by the elderly in favour of young people, it has (almost) always ruled in favour of the latter. *Petersen* was a case in point.[43] Here, the CJEU held that the difference in treatment between older and younger workers was a tool to rebalance the market.

Given these conditions, the search for forms of contract to promote active ageing must follow new routes and operate on several levels—in particular, awareness campaigns to tackle prejudice against older workers and fulfilment of the duty to train and update the skills of older workers. Whatever the individual initiatives, the national social partners must change their attitudes not only towards ageing, but age in general. It should no longer be seen as an event to be combated/managed, at best through improvised measures. It should, instead, be seen as a phenomenon requiring constant attention, given that it is closely linked to the life cycle of employees.

6.2   Company-Level Contracts

Company-level contracts have not shown any greater interest in active ageing policies either.[44] The approval of the pension reform law has led to the substantial reduction of voluntary retirement agreements: employers no longer have an incentive to make up for the time period between the termination of employment and the start of retirement age. Moreover, older workers are no longer of interest as a category in bargaining agreements.

This lack of interest on the part of national trade unions, which is already incomprehensible at the national level, cannot be accounted for at

---

[43] *Petersen* See fn 22.

[44] As also shown by an analysis of company-level bargaining in the province of Brescia, based on data collected by the University of Brescia Labour Law research group (OSMER).

the local level. Many active ageing initiatives satisfy needs also frequently expressed by employers, which should make their negotiation simpler.

One of the many points of common interest could be the reorganisation of production activities. For example, the recent debate about lean production shows the benefits of this mode of working.[45] The management techniques involved implies the end of traditional workplace hierarchy and a greater focus on teamwork. The role of teamwork as a key component in decision-making acknowledges the skills possessed by older workers—that is, their greater knowledge of related activities as well as greater authority and ability to manage a group. Moreover, the need to achieve the best results requires a reorganisation of the working environment and the use of machinery requiring less physical effort on the part of employees.[46] Taken together, these two elements also imply greater attention to workplace ergonomics, with clear benefits for older workers. Organising on the basis of lean production criteria would lead not only to increased productivity, but also make maintaining an ageing workforce easier.[47] This would, therefore, strike a balance between protective ageing policies and productivity. More generally, work organisation as a whole could be an area of interest for company-level bargaining. This could include the introduction of team working and the balancing of skills.

7   Are Trade Unions Losing Ground in Corporate Governance?

The repercussions of this lack of interest in ageing initiatives are potentially very serious for trade unions. They run the risk of being left behind by the growing number of age management programmes in medium and large companies that are offering interesting, non-exit solutions.

---

[45] As shown by P Zanoni (2010) 'Diversity in the lean automobile factory: Doing class through gender, disability and age', Organization org.sagepub.com [Accessed 22 October 2015]; G Berta (2014) *Produzione intelligente* (Einaudi).

[46] See J Rifkin (2013) *La fine del lavoro* (Mondadori).

[47] G. Gosetti (2012) 'Dalla qualità del lavoro alla qualità della vita lavorativa: persistenze e innovazione nel profilo teorico e nelle modalità di analisi' *Sociologia del lavoro* 17.

A study conducted in 2014[48] analysed the best practices in some Italian companies, mostly located in Northern Italy and mainly in the manufacturing industry. The practices fall into three main categories: harnessing the experience of workers aged over 50 (skills balance, specific training courses, mentoring and coaching activities); making the most of generational differences (reverse mentoring and generational relay); and age management in difficult working conditions (e.g., creating a production line dedicated to older workers; reduction in working hours). In these cases, the decision to introduce measures to promote ageing is not the result of agreements with trade unions, even though all employers have expressed an interest in discussing these issues with them. Frequently, instead, the companies that promote ageing do so as part of their commitment to corporate social responsibility (CSR).

The study also showed that even when companies do not have active ageing policies, they do run individual initiatives that promote active ageing. Most frequently, these include recruiting personnel without regard to age, or even hiring older workers, and providing specific training and protecting their health.

Summing up, only trade unions appear to be indifferent to the issue of active ageing. This lack of attention motivated, in part, by a simplistic reading of the labour market as a battleground between young and old means that trade unions are losing ground in corporate governance.

8   Is the Local Dimension the Right Perspective for the Future?

But is the arena of collective bargaining still the right one to promote ageing policies?

The issue of age requires a balancing between individual and collective interests. The trade unions are probably no longer the most appropriate actors to protect an interest that does not revolve around a collective

---

[48] A study conducted by M. Aversa, P. Checcucci, L. D'Agostino, R. Fefè, S. Marchetti, M. Parente and G. Scarpetti for ISFOL in 2014, *Il fattore età nelle imprese italiane*, Paper for the Espanet Conference "*Sfide alla cittadinanza e trasformazione dei corsi di vita: precarietà, invecchiamento e migrazioni*" University of Turin, Turin, 18–20 September 2014.

identity, but around individual characteristics. There is a need for a less confrontational arena of negotiation in which to experiment with less traditional and more creative initiatives,[49] one where the value of diversity (age, skills, experience) is acknowledged to achieve a win-win outcome.[50] Adapting this idea to industrial relations and to ageing in particular, it could be argued that there is a shared inclusive interest among the social partners, an interest which ought to be promoted through age-independent work. However, to achieve this goal, it is necessary to widen its territorial geography and involve new collective actors that can identify solutions to smoothen out market difficulties.[51] Indeed, tackling active ageing means tackling labour market issues not only at the national level but, above all, at the local or regional level. Neither labour law nor collective bargaining, be it at national or company level, can achieve this satisfactorily. There needs to be a change of focus, and territorial bargaining could be one solution. This level of bargaining is able to propose across-the-board and cross-industry solutions, as Regalia[52] points out, and above all also addresses the needs of small businesses (that make up the backbone of Italy's production system), some of which have no trade union representation.

One of the most interesting initiatives in the field of active ageing has been a territorial development programme called 'Senior @ Work', which was promoted by the Provincial Authority of Livorno in 2008–10.[53] The programme involved various local stakeholders, including social partners, a local university, not-for-profit associations, equality bodies, training agencies, as well as some foreign partners (from Denmark, Ireland and Belgium). Although the programme is not very recent, it may be considered one of the most successful in promoting active ageing. The choice of

---

[49] F Hendrickx, 'Age and Employment Discrimination Law' in F. Hendrickx (ed.), believes that it is necessary to adopt an approach that promotes social justice and solidarity as values. On this basis, he suggests that it would be interesting to try out, also in the case of age, policies that are similar to those devised for disability.

[50] These terms are based on the negotiating method developed in 1985 by F. Fischer and W. Ury (1985) L'arte del negoziato (Mondadori).

[51] Both B Hepple and A Neal 'Active Ageing and Labour Law in the United Kingdom' in F Hendrickx (ed.), 275 ff., question the future role of the trade unions in relation to ageing.

[52] See I. Regalia (2014) 'Azione del sindacato nel territorio' Economia e società regionale, 39.

[53] http://www.mutual-learning.eu/documenti/en/pub_w_23.pdf [Accessed 30 May 2014].

initiatives to undertake was made after analysing local needs and profiling the labour market characteristics of the older workers. The purpose of the initiatives was to encourage older workers to stay in work by improving working conditions and providing ongoing training. To achieve this final objective the programme sought to promote the re-training of workers, eliminate the age limits related to measures promoting hiring and increase entrepreneurship.

The local/regional level may, therefore, offer a solution. Confirmation of this comes from the recent (February 2015) 'Memorandum of understanding for joint action' signed by the Provincial Authority of Bergamo, trade unions and employers, which aims to encourage people aged over 45 to return to work. The participants intend to understand the professional and employment needs of the territory, quantify the number of workers aged over 45 laid off by companies and verify the active ageing policies available within the province.

The proposals put forward in the European Parliament Resolution[54] on information and consultation of workers, and the anticipation and management of restructuring make very interesting reading in relation to widening the territorial level of confrontation and negotiation and, therefore, of adopting different approaches. The Resolution hopes that a change of approach on the subject of restructuring will lead to more stakeholders being involved in preliminary consultation procedures. In addition to workers' representatives, public authorities too could be party to the negotiations 'as well as other relevant stakeholders' (Recommendation 5, Point 1). This mechanism of involvement engages traditional local stakeholders (public authorities) but also opens the door to various organisations, depending on the interests at stake. In the case of ageing, these could be non-governmental organisations (NGO) or associations representing 'older workers'. The approach marks a profound change of direction by encouraging companies to design human resource development strategies tailored to their own individual circumstances, as well as mechanisms that anticipate and plan for future employment and skills needs.[55]

---

[54] European Parliament Resolution of 15 January 2013 concerning Information, consultation of workers, anticipation and management of restructuring. (P7 TA (2013) 0005).

[55] As stated in recommendation no. 5 point 1 of the Resolution.

9   Conclusions

The brief survey of the Italian active ageing policies provided in the previous sections shows quite clearly a lack of strategy at every level. So far, the Italian legislature has adopted very few initiatives in the field of active ageing. Moreover, the approach has been based more on coercion than on incentives and promotional measures, which make it ineffective in many respects. Without doubt, the most incisive measure has been the increase in the statutory retirement age, which has achieved a substantial improvement in terms of the employment rate of older workers. However, what has been achieved so far still does not seem to be enough to tackle the challenge of active ageing.

For a long time, the national legislature delegated the task of developing policies in the field of ageing to social partners, whose response has not been very enthusiastic. Although there have been interesting experiences at a local level, such initiatives have mostly been sporadic and lacking a coherent design. Moreover, recently there has been a significant change in the regulatory framework, which is set to further reduce the social partners' scope for action in the field of ageing policies. Since February 2015, modifications in the relationship between labour law and contract, and new rules on the types of contracts available have greatly diminished the self-regulatory autonomy enjoyed by collective bargaining. At the same time, it does not seem that collective bargaining, either at national or company level, is interested in changing its attitude either towards active ageing or age in general. Consequently, the trade unions run the risk of being left behind by the growing number of age management programmes in medium and large companies that are offering interesting, non-exit solutions.

The truth is that the issue of age requires a balancing between individual and collective interests. There is a need for a less confrontational arena of negotiation in which to experiment with less traditional and more creative initiatives, one where the value of diversity (age, skills, and experience) is acknowledged to achieve a win-win outcome. The trade unions are probably no longer the most appropriate actors to protect an interest that does not revolve around a collective identity, but around individual characteristics, which require new negotiation strategies.

As a final remark, it is worth saying something about the judiciary's approach. As shown above, when it comes to handling age-related cases, judges are a bit reluctant to apply the categories and principles of anti-discrimination law which, in other EU legal contexts, have been opening up new perspectives. The above mentioned attitude has clearly had a significant impact on the way the legal system as a whole deals with ageing, because the lack of strategy at the decision-making level is not sufficiently counterbalanced by more action at the judicial level through anti-discrimination law. This could be seen as another sign of the extreme caution shown by the Italian system as a whole towards active ageing strategies.

7

Older Workers in the Nursing and Midwifery Profession: Will They Stay or Will They Go?

Nicola Johnson and Simonetta Manfredi

1   Introduction

One of the challenges posed by increased life expectancy is to ensure the financial sustainability of pension provisions. In response to these demographic changes, the UK government has taken three major policy steps. The first has been to remove mandatory retirement in 2011, unless the need to maintain a contractual retirement age can be objectively justified by an employer (see Manfredi and Vickers at Chap. 4 and Ashtiany at Chap. 14). The second relates to pension arrangements with the introduction of a system where employees will be automatically enrolled in a pension scheme unless they decide to opt out of it, and the third to carry out reforms of public sector pensions. With regard to the latter, an Independent Public Service Pensions Commission was set up. In 2011, it published a report[1] that recommended a change to public sector pensions that addresses the balance between, on the one hand, the need to reward

---

[1] HM Treasury (2011) *Independent Public Service Pensions Commission: Final Report March 2011* (HM Treasury London public.enquiries@hm-treasury.gsi.gov.uk). Available at: http://webarchive. nationalarchives.gov.uk/20130129110402/http://cdn.hm-treasury.gov.uk/hutton_final_100311. pdf (Accessed: 9 March 2013).

© The Editor(s) (if applicable) and The Author(s) 2016   **139**
S. Manfredi, L. Vickers (eds.), *Challenges of Active Ageing*,
DOI 10.1057/978-1-137-53251-0_7

workers' loyalty and, on the other hand, to secure 'value for money' for taxpayers. One of the main implications of these changes for the UK National Health Service (NHS) is that, from 2015, nurses will no longer have the option of retiring at the age of 55. Members of the NHS Pension Scheme will be entitled to draw their pension without reduction only once they have reached the state pension age (SPA), which will be linked to their birth date. For example, the SPA for people born between 1954 and 1960 will be the age of 66, while for those born between 1961 and 1977 will be 67[2]; and these changes are intended to be reviewed and kept in line with increased life expectancy.

As well as recommending changes to public sector pensions in order to make them more financially sustainable, the report also recommended that public sector employers should take steps to assist public sector workers to work longer until they reach their pensionable age. In response to this, NHS Employers launched a call for evidence in June 2013 to contribute to the *NHS Working Longer Review*.[3] The purpose of this was 'to identify issues that may make working to a higher retirement age more difficult and to capture examples of good practice that enable staff to continue working'. The review sought feedback from NHS employers, trade unions and individuals to provide an insight on current working practices, flexible working arrangements and support mechanisms to assess what changes need to be made to enable NHS employees to work longer. The outcome of this work demonstrated the need for a real change in thinking that will have to take place for both NHS employees and employers. Traditionally, both parties have had a clear line of sight on when a working life moves into a retirement phase. As a result of changes to the NHS Pension Scheme, the 'retirement phase' will be based on the individuals' ages and will differ from that of colleagues they work alongside. Any adjustments to working patterns to accommodate longer working lives will have to be balanced against the demands of the service which needs to meet stringent quality indicators adopted by the NHS to ensure the very best patient care.

---

[2] HM Government Pensions Act 2011, revised version 30/11/14. Available at http://www.legislation.gov.uk/ukpga/2011/19/introduction (Accessed 2 October 2015).

[3] NHS Employers (2013b) *Working Longer Review*. Available at: http://www.nhsemployers.org/PayAndContracts/NHSPensionSchemeReview/ImpactofWorkingLongerReview/Pages/NHSWorkingLongerReview.aspx (Accessed: 15 June 2013).

It is against this background that this chapter discusses the finding from a study that sought to investigate the views of nurses and midwives in the 45–55 age group and of those over the age of 56 about retirement and extended working lives, as well as the views of clinical managers about staff in these age groups.

This chapter is articulated as follows. It starts with an overview of key themes emerging from academic literature about older workers and extending working lives. In order to set the context for the study, this overview of themes is followed by an overview of changes to the NHS Pension Scheme, and of the NHS response to these changes in setting up a tripartite Working Longer Group (WLG) between nationally recognised NHS trade unions, NHS employers and health department representatives. The group's remit was to review the implications for NHS employees of working longer as a result of increases to pension ages in line with SPA. Then, the findings of the research are discussed: first, we examine the result of a survey with a sample of nurses and midwives, which highlight that greater work flexibility is seen as being of key importance to this group of staff to work for longer. Second, we consider the findings from the interviews with clinical managers. These suggest that although older workers are overall viewed as an asset, there also seem to be some views held by some clinical managers that perceive older workers as finding it difficult to use new technology and being resistant to change. The chapter concludes by highlighting some of the challenges faced by the NHS sector in the UK to support the extension of working lives.

2   Debates About Older Workers and Extending Working Lives

There is a vast body of academic literature focusing on older workers and on the implications of extending working lives. Several strands of this literature have already been reviewed in some of the chapters included in this collection. Therefore, here we will focus only on some key aspects of the debate around older workers and extending working lives in order to put the findings from the study discussed in this chapter into context.

First of all, it is important to highlight that older workers are not a homogeneous category. For example, McNair[4] has categorised older workers into three main groups. The first one is defined as the 'choosers', who are considered to be a privileged group of older workers with positive working experiences and more inclination to work for longer. Conversely, the second group, defined as the 'survivors', are those who may have been forced into job changes by circumstances out of their control and their motivation for working longer is driven mainly by financial circumstances. The final group, the 'jugglers', tend to make decisions about extending their working lives in conjunction with domestic and caring responsibilities and are likely to be predominantly women. Moreover, views about at what age a person may be considered an older worker can vary depending on retirement norms existing in different sectors of the economy. Another variable that can be added when looking at older workers and their likelihood of wanting to extend their working lives is gender. Winkelmann-Gleed[5] found that as workers age, the desire to match work with non-work commitments intensifies and that this seems to be particularly the case for women who wish to use 'any healthy lifespan left to meet non-work related commitments'.[6] Loretto and Vickerstaff[7] suggested that not all women want to 'have it all', as their research indicated that some women see retirement as an opportunity to be released from the 'gender contract, that of combining paid work and domestic commitments'[8] and, therefore, these women were unlikely to intend to continue to engage with paid work. They also found that job satisfaction played an important part for women, and retirement decisions are brought forward if they feel dissatisfied with their work. Furthermore, their work highlighted that men, too, may look forward to retirement, as they see this as their 'reward', and as an opportunity to spend more time with their families.

---

[4] S McNair (2006) 'How Different is the Older Labour Market? Attitudes to Work and Retirement among Older People in Britain', *Social Policy and Society* 5 (04), 485–494.

[5] A Winkelmann-Gleed (2011) 'Retirement or committed to work?: Conceptualising prolonged labour market participation through organisational commitment', *Employee Relations* 34 (1), 80–90.

[6] 'Retirement or committed to work?', 84.

[7] W Loretto and S Vickerstaff (2013) 'The domestic and gendered context for retirement', *Human Relations* 66 (1), 65–86.

[8] 'The domestic and gendered context' 77.

Another important factor that can influence older workers' decisions about extending their working lives is the possibility of working flexibly and changing working patterns. Flynn[9] pointed to a survey undertaken by the Centre for Research into the Older Workforce which focused on the impact of job changes (including changing of employer, hours, role and skills) on workers aged 50 and older. This survey found that 80% of those employees who responded to it would like to stay in work past retirement age, and only 9% of them wanted to continue to work full-time. Similar findings emerged from research undertaken in higher education, which indicated that there was a lot of interest about flexible working options among older workers.[10] It follows that adjustments to work, such as reducing hours or workloads in the lead-up to retirement, could encourage many more people to continue to work for longer (Flynn 2011).

However, to what extent employers are able and willing to meet older workers' demands for flexible working also depends on existing working norms, business needs and service requirements, which will vary in different sectors. For example, Winkelmann-Gleed (2011) found that in the NHS, employers were unable to offer the flexibility of shifts that older nurses would need. As a result, older nurses would take retirement as soon as possible, but continue to work for the same NHS organisation through an agency. This gave the older nurses desirable working hours and less responsibility, as well as an income in addition to that from their pensions. This however, means that in order to retain valuable skills, expertise and adequate levels of staff the NHS needs to incur higher costs by employing agency staff.

This suggests that flexibility in redesigning jobs and working patterns is crucial in order to retain older workers. Research undertaken in a Danish hospital[11] showed how this organisation had made special provisions for older workers by allowing them to opt out of shift work and on-call duties, and work part-time, while protecting full-time pension

---

[9] M Flynn (2011) 'Ageing populations: time to get ready' *Training Journal*. 56–59.

[10] S Manfredi and L Vickers (2009) 'Retirement and Age Discrimination: Managing Retirement in Higher Education', *Industrial Law Journal* 38 (4), 343–364.

[11] F Frerichs, R Lindley, P Aleksandrowicz, B Baldauf. and S Galloway (2012) 'Active ageing in organisations: a case study approach', *International Journal of Manpower* 33 (6), 666–684.

contributions for them. It also adjusted its age-related policy to a life-stage policy that takes into account the differing domestic commitments (for example, from childcare during early career stages to eldercare in later career) giving fair access to all employees should they require the support. This approach resonates with the work that Ilmarien[12] developed for the Finnish Institute of Occupational Health in the late 1990s around the concept of 'work ability'. This concept is underpinned by the idea that an individual's capabilities have to be matched with work demands: balancing the two will increase older workers' participation in the workplace. Furthermore, it has been highlighted that as employees' wishes and plans will vary, a standardised response will waste resources and not lengthen the working lives of employees.[13] Likewise, it can be argued that standardised responses would not suit employers either. The case of the NHS demonstrates the importance of developing strategies to retain older workers which fit with the operational requirements within the sector and, above all, the need to deliver high-quality health care. The next section considers the NHS response to the challenges of active ageing and extending working lives.

3   Extending Working Lives in the NHS

The NHS Pension Scheme arrangements from April 2015 set the normal pension age (NPA) under the scheme directly in line with its members' SPA. The proposed Final Agreement of the NHS Pension Scheme[14] recognises that this increase in pension age may impact certain categories of staff, in particular those in the 'frontline' and physically demanding roles (nurses and midwives would be included in this category). In order to address this, the NHS WLG has been formed as 'a tripartite partnership

[12] J E Ilmarinen (2001) 'Ageing workers. Occupational and Environmental Medicine', 58, 546–552.

[13] L D Sargent, M D Lee, B Martin and J Zikic (2013) 'Reinventing retirement: New pathways, new arrangements, new meanings', *Human Relations* 66 (1), 3–21.

[14] Department of Health (2012) *Reforming the NHS Pension Scheme for England and Wales: Proposed Final Agreement* https://www.gov.uk/government/uploads/system/uploads/attachment_data/file/216219/dh_133003.pdf [Accessed 23 September 2015].

group between national recognised NHS trade unions, NHS employers and health department representatives, established to review the implications of the NHS workforce working to a later, raised retirement age'.[15]

The WLG was formally commissioned in October 2014 after a NHS Working Longer Review ran a 'Call for Evidence' campaign in 2013 from June to September. Following this, a summary report of findings was compiled by researchers at Newcastle University[16]; it listed three areas for further investigation. Firstly, the need to undertake a review of working patterns, in particular the impact of working long shifts and taking part in 'on-call' arrangements at an older age. Secondly, the report addressed physical capability and recommended that retirement before SPA did not carry a stigma or financial penalty for a NHS Pension Scheme member. Finally, it recommended reviewing the management of flexible working, as it identified misunderstandings about the possibilities for working flexibly, its financial implications and a lack of knowledge about the actual demand from employees for it. The WLG was instructed to take forward this report's findings. They began by compiling a report that presented preliminary findings and recommendations in March 2014.[17] This report identified four areas of focus.

1. Data challenge: They found a rich source of data can be collected from the NHS organisations, but it had all been collected in different ways for differing reasons. The WLG want to formulate a consistent data set so that the implications of working later in life can be analysed.
2. Pension options and retirement decision-making: Helping members understand the NHS Pension Scheme and flexibilities available to them is essential to enable them to work longer.

---

[15] NHS Employers (2015) *Working Longer Group* http://www.nhsemployers.org/your-workforce/need-to-know/working-longer-group [Accessed 23 September 2015].

[16] M Flynn and S McNair (2013) 'Annex 7' *Working Longer in the NHS, Call for evidence interim findings report* http://www.nhsemployers.org/-/media/Employers/Documents/Pay%20and%20reward/WLR%20Prelim%20Report%20-%20Annex%207 %20-%20Call%20for%20evidence%20interim %20findings%20report.pdf [Accessed 23 September 2015].

[17] NHS Employers (2015a) *Working Longer Group: Preliminary findings and recommendations report* http://www.nhsemployers.org/your-workforce/need-to-know/working-longer-group/preliminary-findings-and-recommendations-report-for-the-health-departments [Accessed 23 September 2015].

3. Appropriate working arrangements and work environment: There is a need to break down barriers that prevent NHS employees from moving between organisations and geographical areas.
4. Occupational health, safety and wellbeing: It is important to continue to develop good practice of staff wellbeing in the context of an older workforce.

By January 2015, project plans for workstreams had been agreed by the WLG Steering group[18] to deliver specific objectives. These include addressing pension options and retirement planning. A toolkit is being compiled for human resources (HR) departments in NHS organisations to enable them to gain more knowledge and awareness of the NHS Pension Scheme and to support managers in workforce planning as well as employees' retirement choices. This is complemented by another workstream to develop a manager's toolkit for 'development conversations' to encourage regular career and retirement planning discussions with employees. Then, on a strategic level, a toolkit is being developed for employers to work with their staff representatives to embed strategic responses to an ageing workforce. The objectives of these work streams are important to ensure that employees fully understand the implications of their pension schemes, and also to encourage employers in NHS organisations to develop strategic responses to an ageing workforce as well as introducing regular 'development conversations' between line managers and employees about these issues.

A further work stream relates to 'Early Retirement Reduction Buy out Assessment Framework' (ERRBO). Once implemented, this will provide guidance for employers to use a mechanism to discharge older employees who may no longer be able to comply with the requirements of the job. This mechanism will offer employers the option to pay additional contributions to an employee's pension to eliminate or reduce the actuarial reduction that would be applied should they need to retire prior to their NPA. Guidance will be developed to support NHS employers to apply such measures fairly to older employees when there is no option of keeping them in employment.

---

[18] NHS Employers (2015b) *Working Longer Group: Steering Group meetings—key messages* http:// www.nhsemployers.org/your-workforce/need-to-know/working-longer-group/steering-group-meetingsDOUBLEHYPHEN-key-messages [Accessed 23 September 2015].

There is also a work stream on the issue of redeployment. The WLG acknowledges the 'stigma attached' to employees being moved from one department to another within an NHS organisation with the label of 'redeployee'. This workstream sets out to 'change the beliefs and opinions of the NHS workforce'.[19] This suggests that a significant change in culture may be needed to achieve these objectives, and that it will require much more than the provision of a toolkit to achieve this. This work stream could also help address the objective of facilitating the movement of NHS employees not only between departments within their own NHS organisation, but also to other NHS organisations in other geographical locations.

Finally, in order to maintain credibility with NHS employees and managers and secure their engagement, the WLG is committed to communicate its progress and achievements with the workstreams and make them visible via the NHS Employers website. The WLG was introduced in tandem with the implementation of the NPA for the NHS Pension Scheme being linked to the SPA. Its work will be of key importance to both support NHS Pension Scheme members (the employees) as well as to ensure that the NHS, as an employer, assesses the impact of having to work for longer on its workforce and retains the skills and expertise to provide its vital service.

4   Will They Stay or Will They Go?

The research discussed in this chapter took place in an acute teaching NHS Trust hospital in the UK where 34% of the employees are nurses and midwives. The overall annual turnover rate of staff in this category is 12.4%. This study took place after the UK government had removed mandatory retirement and at a time when changes to the NHS Pension Scheme were about to be implemented. Its main objectives were to investigate the views of nurses and midwives in the age group of 45–55 and of

---

[19] NHS Employers (2015c) *Working Longer Group: Changing Attitudes Towards Redeployment, Task and Finish Group Terms of Reference* http://www.nhsemployers.org/-/media/Employers/Documents/Pay%20and%20reward/WLR%20Prelim%20Report%20-%20Annex%207%20-%20Call%20for%20evidence%20interim%20findings%20report.pdf [Accessed 23 September 2015].

those over the age of 56 on working for longer, especially in view of the changes being made to their pension scheme; and to explore the views of a sample of clinical managers about managing older nurses and midwives in the 45–55 age group as well as those above the age of 56. The research involved an online survey that was sent to 1065 nurses and midwives identified in these age groups; 286 responses, representing 26% of the total sample, were received. This survey was complemented by 15 one-to-one in-depth semi-structured interviews with clinical managers (also referred to as matrons). The following sections present the key results from a descriptive analysis of the survey's responses and from the interviews with the clinical managers, which were analysed by using a thematic approach.

5   Responses from Nurses and Midwives

Most of the nurses and midwives who responded to the survey, 42%, were in the 51–55 age group, which is not surprising, given their proximity to pensionable retirement age. The next largest proportion of respondents was 37.7%, in the 45–50 age group. In terms of gender, 95% of respondents were women, which reflects the fact that this is a highly feminised profession, with 85% of them describing their occupation as 'nurse' and 15% as 'midwife'. Almost all of them, 97%, belonged to the NHS Pension Scheme, and just over half of them, 52%, indicated that they would be able to claim their NHS pension at the age of 55—15% at the age 60, 14% at 65, 5% over the age of 65—but 14% stated that they 'did not know' when they would be able to claim their pension. When asked whether they were aware of the changes taking place with the NHS Pension Scheme, 79% indicated that they were, but a significant proportion, 17%, said that they were 'not sure' and 3.5% responded that they 'did not know'. More mixed results were obtained when respondents were asked whether they knew how much pension they were likely to be entitled to: only 18% responded affirmatively to this question, with the largest proportion, almost 49%, indicating that they knew 'approximately', with the remaining respondents indicating that either they were 'not sure' or that they 'did not know'. Uncertainty also prevailed in the responses to the question as to whether they thought that the amount of pension that they would receive would be sufficient for their retirement plans: the largest proportion 48.5% stated that they were 'not sure'; 33% thought that it would 'not be sufficient' and only 18.6% responded affirmatively. When asked what would be their main activity once they retired, a significant proportion, 28% of them, indicated that they would continue to work for the NHS but on a different contract, 16% that they would continue to do paid work but outside the NHS, while the largest proportion 43% responded that they 'did not know'. A significant proportion, 25%, indicated leisure as their main post-retirement activity and only 2.5% childcare, the latter suggesting that they may be planning to help with looking after grandchildren as their main post-retirement activity. Finally, respondents were given the option to specify in an open question what would help them to work for longer, and the great majority of them indicated flexible working. The most popular options were reduced hours, shorter days and shorter shifts; a few said that they would be prepared to work on lower grades in return for more flexibility. One respondent put forward the suggestion that older workers themselves should be involved in finding solutions to make working practices more manageable, such as '… the opportunity to job share with another colleague who is due to retire at the same time so that we can share 12 hours shift to fit in with service needs'. Others indicated that less stress, allowing older workers not to do night shifts, a lower staff/patient ratio with more staff on the wards would help them to work for longer in the NHS. A further important factor that was mentioned in responses to this question by several respondents was the need to continue to work for financial reasons.

Finally, the importance of looking holistically at working patterns and pension arrangements as well as acknowledging that people are likely to age in different ways is well captured by the following response:

> As the workforce ages, not all individuals can work clinically till 65 or even 60. There needs to be greater flexibility with pension and perhaps the ability to leave the NHS and return but not have to start at the bottom again (if you are out for a year then you come back in on the lowest increment.)

Although this is a relatively small sample, it provides, nonetheless, a useful snapshot about some of the challenges of extending working lives in the nursing and midwifery profession. Most of the respondents belonged to the NHS Pension Scheme, and were aware about the changes taking place. There was, however, a significant level of uncertainty about the level of pension people would be entitled to once they retire, which suggests the need for better financial education to ensure that people can make well-informed decisions about their retirement plans. A significant proportion of nurses and midwives in this sample indicated that they are planning to continue to work for the NHS past retirement, although many others were unsure whether they would continue to engage with paid work. The most significant finding is the overwhelming demand for greater flexible working, which was seen by many respondents as important to enable them to extend their working lives. This highlights the importance for the sector to develop more flexible working solutions to enable older employees to continue to work under the terms of their new pension scheme until they reach their pensionable age. Other suggestions included a lower staff to patient ratio with more staff on wards, which would have significant cost implications. This highlights a potential tension between, on the one hand, the need to create the conditions for staff to work for much longer and, on the other hand, a push towards greater work intensification driven by insufficient financial resources[20] to support the NHS. As discussed elsewhere in this book (see Brett), greater workloads and working additional hours can run counter to the aim of extending working lives and instead make working longer unsustainable.

6   Senior Clinical Managers' Perceptions of Older Workers

Senior clinical managers were asked for their views about the attitudes and work motivation of nurses and midwives who are in the 45–55 and in 56+ age groups and what they thought the advantages and disadvantages were of employing older workers over the age of 56.

---

[20] The King's Fund, an independent charity working to improve health care, has pointed to the growing financial pressure in the NHS http://www.kingsfund.org.uk/projects/funding-and-finances Accessed 25 September 2015. It has also been reported that the NHS is facing its worst financial crises in a generation, 'NHS facing £2bn deficit and 'worst financial crises in a generation', *The Guardian* 9th October 2015.

When discussing the 45–55 age group, two main themes emerged. The first one could be described, in the words of one of the interviewees, as 'resurgence'. It was felt that often nurses and midwives in this age group had seen a change in their home life, after the children had grown up, and therefore were likely to have 'more time'. Therefore, managers saw these nurses and midwives to have won a 'second lease of life' and to be interested in 'taking on new roles and challenges that they wouldn't have done previously' due to constraints of family responsibilities. It was noted, for example, that some would think more about their personal development and satisfaction. Examples were given of staff in this group studying for Master's degrees or even undertaking PhDs. It was also commented by several interviewees that if workers in this age group are still working in the NHS, either full-time or part-time, '[they] are genuinely doing it because they want to be here'. The second theme, however, highlighted that there were also some nurses and midwives in this group who were seen as 'biding time' and waiting for their pensionable age to arrive. People in this group were described as being 'increasingly tired' and 'looking forward to retirement', and were perceived as being less motivated. For example, some clinical managers felt that this was reflected in some of these workers' attitudes to training. Some managers said that although this group of older workers would be still willing to complete the statutory and mandatory training required, they did not show much enthusiasm to carry out what was deemed as 'academic education' and to explore new ways of working or put themselves forward for training seen as important for 'career development'.

With regard to nurses and midwives aged 56 and over, many interviewees held very positive views about nurses in this age group who were seen as committed to continue to provide patient care. Some had formally retired but came back to work because they really like their job; it was pointed out that 'there is a small number that just love the job'. Conversely, some clinical managers observed that those who continued to work in this age group were doing so mainly for financial reasons, as it was noted that 'it is a financial thing that has brought them back and they need to earn … that income'.

When asked about advantages and disadvantages of employing older workers, the majority of comments were very positive and overall this group of workers was seen as a 'huge asset'. Several managers highlighted that for this group 'patients are first priority', they have a 'greater work ethos' and, as seen above, often their love for the job and a commitment to providing patient care is their main drive for continuing to work. As one manager described it, 'they come and do their job and do it really well'. Some interviewees also talked about the positive influence that this attitude to work can have on other team members by highlighting that ' … the NHS is coming back to compassionate care, the basics of nursing … and I think, generally, that group of nurses can bring those qualities to perhaps younger people starting out with all the challenges and demands that nursing puts on them'.

Other qualities that were commonly associated with older nurses were having many years' experience, and being loyal and reliable, which instils confidence in patients about the care they are receiving. Experience was one aspect that was especially valued by managers. Reference was made to the basic training that had been carried out by this age group in the twentieth century as one that focused more on caring for patients compassionately rather than the more academic side of nursing. It was acknowledged that experience encompassed a mixture of job and life experience, as exemplified by this quote: 'There is a clinical knowledge and a situational knowledge and there is very little that will faze an older nurse.'

It was also commented that this age group 'are very good teachers, they pass that onto younger staff' and that 'you have got wise heads to mentor the junior nurses to support them through their little emotional crises … '.

But challenges emerged in formalising this teaching relationship with more junior colleagues as illustrated by this matron's example:

> … it is an NMC[21] requirement that we mentor and preceptor and I have older members of staff, because they don't see themselves moving on with their careers … they see it as being academic and they really don't want to do it.

Another advantage associated with older workers was that they have lower rates of absence from the workplace, especially compared to their younger colleagues. This point was partly corroborated by an analysis

---

[21] Nursing and Midwifery Council.

of the hospital staff absence records at the time when this research was undertaken. This confirmed that nurses and midwives in the 46–55 age group had a lower number of short sickness absences, but they also showed that if they took time off work due to sickness, this was likely to be for a higher number of calendar days compared to those in the younger age groups.

There was also a perception about this age group that they have a 'greater work ethos' and are highly motivated towards their work; on the other hand, some of their younger counterparts are perceived as still trying the profession and undecided as to whether this is the right career choice for them. It was also noted that this age group tends to have a more settled personal life, having reduced or no childcare commitments to juggle, and it was felt that this in general can contribute to a higher level of commitment and stability in the workplace.

One manager talked about the importance of having a balance of younger and older workers, as she thought that the younger nurses bring energy and the ability to change rapidly, while the older nurses keep her more grounded and challenge her. Others described older nurses as bringing 'wisdom' and 'calmness' within their team, and that they were good role models.

Although older workers were seen overall mainly as an asset, some disadvantages relating to staff in these age groups were also identified. One is about the physical as well as physiological demands of nursing work especially in acute patient areas like intensive care. For example, one matron commented 'I know that physically, the older nurses over 50, definitely over 55—you are starting to struggle with the internal rotation to nights', while another said that 'There is an element at 63, 64 are you physically able to run around the ward, juggle all those jobs, have an early (shift) followed by a late?'

Moreover, it was noted that night shifts could also become too challenging. It was reported that 'relatively frequently' older nurses would say 'I just cannot cope with the number of nights'. From the perspective of a manager, 'that's a really challenging conversation because they are contractually obliged to fill that number of nights', as in some levels they are expected to do half of their contracted working time in night shifts. Other disadvantages identified with older workers were difficulties in mastering new technology, reluctance to change and the fast pace of change which appeared to be interlinked.

Some managers felt that the older age group generally struggles more with grasping new technology in the workplace. For example, it was commented that 'Yes, they can get their heads around it but it takes them much longer to learn.' One matron believed that the way in which technology has been introduced to the workplace has had a detrimental effect on older workers retention as she said that '…I just think a lot of nurses would have stayed on the ward…but technology has pushed a group of nurses out of nursing, we could have perhaps done more to retain them.' Some of those interviewed held the view that older workers can become 'ingrained in practice' and 'cynical' about change and resist it by not engaging fully with it. The 'fast pace of change' in the NHS was also seen as problematic for the older age group, who were viewed as being unable to 'keep up with it'. One matron attributed this to nurse training before it became a graduate profession, when 'it was very much hands-on':

> …you did your placements on the ward and learn on the job, so there will be a group that think 'Why should I?—I am a perfectly good nurse as I am.

7   Retaining Older Workers and Flexible Working

At the time this research was undertaken, new legislation was about to come into force which would extend the right to request flexible working to all employees.[22] All matrons who were interviewed were already

---

[22] From 30 June 2014, every employee has the statutory right to request flexible working after 26 weeks employment service. (Before 30 June 2014, the right only applied to parents of children under the age of 17 (or 18, if the child is disabled) and certain carers.) Once a request has been received, the employee should arrange a meeting to discuss the request. This should be done as soon as possible. This is not a statutory requirement, but is good practice. The law requires the process to be completed within three months of the request being received, which includes any appeals. If the employer is willing to grant a request, then meeting may not be necessary, but it still may be useful to discuss a request to ensure that the proposal made by the employee is the best solution for both employer and employee. http://www.acas.org.uk/index.aspx?articleid=1616 (Accessed 2 October 2015).

open to, and used to, considering requests from all employees. This suggested that a widespread culture of flexible working already existed in the hospital ahead of legislative changes. It was clear, however, that the parameters within which flexibility could be agreed were strict, and limited to predetermined start and finish times of shifts. Doubts were expressed about part-time employees being able to carry out specialist and senior manager roles successfully. Requests to opt out of on-calls, shift work and other physically demanding working patterns were being managed through the occupational health department. Examples were given where, upon advice from this department, matrons were able to move some of their team members to less demanding areas of work, and agree to more flexible working patterns. This was also made possible by the fact that these matrons were responsible for different types of service; therefore, it was easier to move staff around.

Nonetheless, it appeared that still not enough consideration is being given to the need to address the physical implications of carrying out the role of a nurse or midwife and make adjustments to enable older workers to continue to work in these roles past the age of 55. This was probably because, by and large, nurses and midwives, at the time when this research was carried out, were still expected to retire at the age of 55—although, as a result of changes to pension provisions, as discussed earlier, after 2015 these workers will no longer be able to retire at 55 without paying a financial penalty.

8   Concluding Remarks

The findings from this study have highlighted some of the challenges that the NHS is likely to face in supporting nursing and midwifery staff to work longer. The results from the survey clearly indicate that nurses and midwives see increased work flexibility as a key factor to enable them to work longer. The findings from the interviews with clinical managers have also highlighted that flexibility is not the only issue, as some older workers find it increasingly difficult to cope with the number of night shifts they are contractually obliged to do. This suggests that the sector will need to rethink how to organise working patterns, and shift work in particular, in a way that matches individual capabilities—for example, by using the work ability model proposed by Ilmarien. Such adjustments, however, will also raise issues around equitable treatment of staff of all ages. Working a certain number of nights may be too physically demanding for older nurses and midwives, but it might be argued that it could be equally demanding for younger nurses with small children or with other caring responsibilities—for example, for a disabled adult or older parents. Moreover, the current limitations on offering nurses and midwives greater flexibility may be explained by the necessity to interact with other staff groups (for example, doctors and associated professions such as physiotherapy). Therefore, the possibility of generating solutions to achieve greater flexibility of working patterns cannot be examined for one staff group alone.

An important finding that emerged from the survey suggested that although the great majority of respondents were aware of changes being made to their pension scheme, a significant proportion did not have sufficient knowledge about these changes. A high proportion of respondents also indicated that they had only an approximate knowledge of their pension entitlements. These results highlight the importance of educating the staff on the provisions of their pension scheme and their likely pension income. As seen earlier, the NHS WLG is taking steps to address these issues. They are creating tools to develop awareness among NHS HR teams, and are introducing the concept of 'development conversations'. Managers in the NHS are expected to have these conversations with employees regularly. These can help managers to establish an ongoing dialogue with staff in order to respond to their needs and enable them to work longer.

Overall, senior clinical managers displayed positive attitudes about employing older workers, especially those whose description matched that of McNair's 'choosers'—workers who were motivated to work and delivered excellent patient care and achieved individual self-fulfilment. Reference was also made to staff in the 45–55 age group described as the 'resurgence' types who—having experienced major changes in their home life after their children had grown up—were keen to take on new roles, responsibilities or undertake further studies that previously they would not have been able to do due to constraints of family responsibilities. This highlights the importance for the sector to harness this renewed energy and motivation for staff in mid-career and to enable them to fulfil their aspirations. Regular 'development conversations' could help to achieve this. As highlighted by the work of Loretto and Vickerstaff, discussed earlier, job satisfaction plays a very important role in motivating people to work for longer.

Concerns, however, were expressed about dealing with those described by McNair as 'survivors', who were motivated to remain in work mainly by financial necessity. It is clear that maintaining work motivation for this group will be more challenging. Some clinical managers also expressed concerns as to whether older nurses and midwives will remain physically able to meet some of the most onerous aspects of their jobs. As discussed elsewhere in this book (see Manfredi and Vickers at Chap. 4), it should be added to this that although people may be living longer, their quality of life will vary, as some may develop age-related impairments or illnesses which will undermine their capacity to remain engaged in paid work. In this respect, the 'Early Retirement Reduction Buyout Assessment Framework' and opportunities for redeployment across different units being developed, as discussed earlier, by the WLG can potentially be important tools to meet these challenges, but they will need some careful consideration. In particular, the WLG needs to be vigilant about potentially ageist views which may result in unfair assessments about the capacities of older workers to the detriment of both the organisation and of the individuals themselves. Overall, clinical managers displayed positive attitudes towards older workers; nonetheless, some negative stereotypes also emerged, such as the view that older workers are likely to find it hard to keep up with technological changes, being set in their ways and unwilling to engage with new training and change.

It is clear from this study that changes to the retirement age for NHS employees brings with it a wholesale change in working practices. The tripartite partnership approach taken by the WLG acknowledges the importance of involving trade unions, NHS Employers and health department representatives in developing solutions that strike a balance between the needs of the service, patient care and the needs of individual workers, especially that of developing good practice to maintain staff wellbeing at all ages. In this respect, research undertaken in healthcare organisations outside of the UK could provide insight on useful practices that have been adopted in order to achieve such balance.

Finally, the findings discussed in this chapter clearly demonstrate that the implications of working longer will differ significantly depending on the organisational context and culture. They highlight the importance for employers and trade unions of working together to develop practices that will enable people to work longer but also have a dignified end of career and a decent retirement.

8

Emerging Options for Extending Working Lives: Results of a Delphi Study

Alysia Blackham

There are a range of legal and policy reforms that may help to extend working lives. However, it remains unclear whether these reforms are important and practicable in the UK context. To develop these proposals for change further, this chapter presents the results of expert discussions conducted via the Delphi method. The Delphi method offers an effective means of achieving reliable consensus between different expert views and developing and analysing future policy scenarios. Using this method, a group of UK experts were asked to consider a range of scenarios that may help to extend working lives. These scenarios included:

- industries developing work ability strategies to be implemented by individual workplaces;
- workplaces adopting an age management approach;
- employees being given the right to request flexible working arrangements;
- easily accessible information and guidance about managing and working in an ageing workforce being made available to employers and employees;
- effective leadership;
- a national dialogue regarding what rights, obligations and privileges should be granted to individuals at different ages;

© The Editor(s) (if applicable) and The Author(s) 2016
S. Manfredi, L. Vickers (eds.), *Challenges of Active Ageing*,
DOI 10.1057/978-1-137-53251-0_8

- employers having a positive duty to achieve employment equality, including for older workers; and
- employers having a responsibility to consult with employees and/or their representatives in relation to equality matters.

The experts were asked to evaluate whether these reforms would be desirable, important and practicable in the UK context. While most scenarios were regarded as impracticable under a deregulatory governmental agenda, the respondents regarded some changes as being important, desirable and practicable. Given this consensus, I argue that these reforms should be seriously considered and vigorously pursued.

1   The Delphi Method

The RAND Corporation first used the Delphi method during the Cold War to estimate Soviet nuclear capabilities for the US Air Force.[1] The Delphi method has since been used a handful of times in legal and socio-legal research, including for examining the impact of legal rules and how laws operate in practice,[2] offering solutions to law-related problems,[3] developing taxonomies and definitions of legal phenomena[4] and criteria to evaluate policy initiatives,[5] and exploring the future of interactions between law and society.[6]

---

[1] Norman Dalkey and Olaf Helmer (1963) 'An Experimental Application of the Delphi Method to the Use of Experts', *Management Science* 9, 458.

[2] John P van Gigch and Rudolf Hommes (1973) 'A Study of How Correctional Counsellors and Psychologists Agree upon Pre-Sentence Recommendations', *Canadian J Criminology & Corrections* 15, 93; Bogdan Dziurzyński (1996) 'FDA Regulatory Review and Approval Processes: A Delphi Inquiry', *Food & Drug LJ* 51, 143.

[3] H Graham McDonald and Clifford P Kirsch (1978) 'Use of the Delphi Method as a Means of Assessing Judicial Manpower Needs', *Just Sys J* 3, 314; Sarah J Young and others (2004) 'Best Case Scenario: The Development of a Teaching Tool for Sport Law', *J Legal Aspects Sport* 14, 1.

[4] Margaret F Hudson (1991) 'Elder Mistreatment: A Taxonomy with Definitions by Delphi' *Journal of Elder Abuse & Neglect* 3, 1.

[5] Evgeny Guglyuvatyy (2010) 'Identifying Criteria for Climate Change Policy Evaluation in Australia', *Macquarie J Bus L* 7, 98.

[6] Kevin N Wright (1982) 'A Delphi Assessment of the Effects of a Declining Economy on Crime and the Criminal Justice System', *Fed Probation* 46, 36; Lawrence F Travis and others (1985) 'The Future of Sentencing and Parole: A Delphi Reassessment of Sentencing and Parole Reforms', *Crim Just Rev*

The Delphi method is a structured group communication process that allows individuals to deal with complex problems as a group.[7] Where knowledge is uncertain or imperfect, the Delphi method can achieve reliable group consensus[8] and identify divergence of opinion on hypothetical future scenarios.[9] The Delphi method is effective for exploring solutions in policy areas with high levels of uncertainty,[10] and can eliminate distractions and distortions in group discussion.[11] The method is therefore more effective at generating new ideas and exploring future scenarios in areas of uncertainty than traditional face-to-face communication.[12] At a practical level, the Delphi method allows participants to think through responses, which promotes careful and thoughtful contributions, while the anonymity of responses ensures open and honest discussion.

While a range of Delphi structures can be used, the 'policy Delphi', the structure adopted for this study, is designed to identify, examine and estimate the impact, consequences and acceptability of particular policy options.[13] Further, it allows respondents to react to and assess different viewpoints on policy issues.[14] Therefore, it is particularly well suited to coordinating and structuring respondents' thinking around

---

10, 45; Sarah J Young and Lynn M Jamieson (1999) 'Perceived Liability and Risk Management Trends Impacting Recreational Sports into the 21st Century', *J Legal Aspects Sport* 9, 151.

[7] Harold A Linstone and Murray Turoff (1977) 'Introduction' in Harold A Linstone and Murray Turoff (eds), *The Delphi method: techniques and applications* (Addison-Wesley) 3.

[8] Georg Aichholzer (2009) 'The Delphi Method: Eliciting Experts' Knowledge in Technology Foresight' in Alexander Bogner and others (eds), *Interviewing experts* (Research methods, Palgrave Macmillan) 252–53.

[9] Mary Kay Rayens and Ellen J Hahn (2000) 'Building Consensus Using the Policy Delphi Method' *Policy, politics, & nursing practice* 1, 308, 308.

[10] See Armando Rotondi and David Gustafson (1996) 'Theoretical, Methodological and Practical Issues Arising out of the Delphi Method' in Michael Adler and Erio Ziglio (eds), *Gazing into the oracle: the Delphi method and its application to social policy and public health* (Jessica Kingsley) 42.

[11] Aichholzer (n 8) 252–53.

[12] Erio Ziglio (1996) 'The Delphi Method and Its Contribution to Decision-Making' in Michael Adler and Erio Ziglio (eds), *Gazing into the oracle: the Delphi method and its application to social policy and public health* (Jessica Kingsley) 22.

[13] Murray Turoff (1977) 'The Policy Delphi' in Harold A Linstone and Murray Turoff (eds), *The Delphi method: techniques and applications* (Addison-Wesley) 83.

[14] Turoff (n 13).

how complex legal issues might develop and evolve in the future[15] and provides a constructive forum for discussion, the building of consensus[16] and the clarification of different ideas and viewpoints.[17] Thus, the Delphi method offers distinct advantages over reliance on face-to-face interviews alone.

2   Research Procedures

The policy Delphi method adopted in this study was a multistage process with two asynchronous rounds of online surveys. The process involved:

- initial measurement of opinions (Round 1);
- data analysis;
- design of a subsequent questionnaire based on initial responses; and
- second measurement of opinions (Round 2).[18]

Between rounds, participants were provided with statistical group feedback about the beliefs of other participants as a means of promoting consensus[19] before the second survey was completed.[20] This process is depicted in Fig. 8.1.

The respondents in the Delphi survey were a group of 17 UK experts representing government, academia, the judiciary, unions, business groups and lobby groups. For the purposes of this research, 'experts' were defined as those who were active participants in ageing issues and likely to have special knowledge regarding older workers.[21] Experts

---

[15] Aichholzer (n 8) 259.

[16] Rayens and Hahn (n 9) 309.

[17] Wolf Rauch (1979) 'The Decision Delphi' *Technological Forecasting and Social Change* 15, 159, 163.

[18] Rayens and Hahn (n 9) 309.

[19] Rayens and Hahn (n 9) 309.

[20] Murray Turoff and Starr Roxanne Hiltz (1996) 'Computer-Based Delphi Processes' in Michael Adler and Erio Ziglio (eds), *Gazing into the oracle: the Delphi method and its application to social policy and public health*, (Jessica Kingsley) 58; Aichholzer (n 8) 252.

[21] Michael Meuser and Ulrike Nagel (2009) 'The Expert Interview and Changes in Knowledge Production' in Alexander Bogner and others (eds), *Interviewing experts* (Research methods, Palgrave Macmillan) 24.

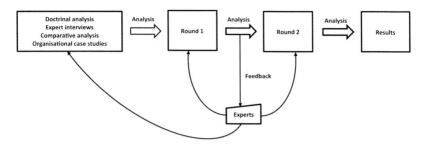

Fig. 8.1 The Delphi process

were initially purposively sampled to identify respondents who were most likely to contribute meaningfully to the research.[22] As the study progressed, theoretical sampling was used to identify further respondents who were likely to extend or further develop emerging concepts and theory[23] in conjunction with snowball sampling (where experts identify other potential respondents).[24] Qualitative semi-structured expert interviews were conducted with the experts between September and November 2012 as part of an earlier study.[25] At the conclusion of the interviews, the same experts were invited to participate in an online Delphi survey.

The survey instrument used in Round 1 of this Delphi study drew on doctrinal analysis, expert interviews and comparative analysis to create and test meaningful scenarios which might represent the future of employment security for older workers.[26] These scenarios acted as 'straw models' and presented different perspectives on how the employment of older

---

[22] Robert Stake (2008) 'Qualitative Case Studies' in Yvonna Lincoln and Norman Denzin (eds), *Strategies of qualitative inquiry* (3rd edn, SAGE) 130.

[23] Kathleen M Eisenhardt (2002) 'Building Theories from Case Study Research' in A Michael Huberman and Matthew Miles (eds), *The qualitative researcher's companion* (Sage Publications) 13; Juliet M Corbin and Anselm L Strauss (2008) *Basics of Qualitative Research: Techniques and Procedures for Developing Grounded Theory* (3rd edn, Sage Publications) 117.

[24] Tim May (1993) *Social Research: Issues, Methods and Process* (Open University Press) 100; Lisa Webley (2010) 'Qualitative Approaches to Empirical Legal Research' in Peter Cane and Herbert M Kritzer (eds), *The Oxford handbook of empirical legal research* (Oxford University Press) 934.

[25] See Alysia Blackham (2014) 'Extending Working Life for Older Workers: An Empirical Legal Analysis of Age Discrimination Laws in the UK' (University of Cambridge) ch 4.

[26] Aichholzer (n 8) 262. These methods are reported elsewhere: see Blackham (n 25).

workers might evolve to promote deep discussion among participants.[27] Participants were also given the opportunity to suggest additional or different policy options during the first survey round.[28]

In the survey, experts were asked to identify scenarios that were likely to be important, desirable and feasible.[29] Definitions of these terms were provided to ensure respondents had a similar understanding of what the terms meant.[30] Questions were assessed on a four-stage assessment scale (1 = very low or negative, 4 = very high or positive).[31] Participants were also asked to rate their confidence in their assessment of each scenario (1 = no confidence, 4 = high confidence). Self-rating is a meaningful way of identifying expertise and can improve the accuracy of responses.[32] Participants were invited to make comments regarding their selection and/or suggest other scenarios[33] and/or suggest changes to the wording of existing scenarios.[34]

Round 2 included four key elements[35]:

1. Reworded scenarios from the first survey to clarify or further develop scenarios in response to participant comments. Changing the wording of a policy option is often necessary in a policy Delphi, and can impact positively upon the level of consensus achieved.[36]
2. Repetition of scenarios that led to disagreement in the first round, with the aim of allowing participants to revisit or reconsider their original opinions in light of the feedback provided.
3. New scenarios posed by respondents in the first survey round.
4. New implementation scenarios, posing possible means of implementing scenarios that achieved a strong level of consensus in the first round.

---

[27] Rotondi and Gustafson (n 10) 43; Ziglio (n 12) 20.
[28] Rayens and Hahn (n 9) 310.
[29] Ziglio (n 12) 19; Aichholzer (n 8) 263.
[30] Murray Turoff (1970) 'The Design of a Policy Delphi' *Technological Forecasting and Social Change* 2, 149, 157; Turoff (n 13) 85.
[31] Aichholzer (n 8) 263.
[32] Harold A Linstone and Murray Turoff (1977) 'Evaluation—Introduction' in Harold A Linstone and Murray Turoff (eds), *The Delphi method: techniques and applications* (Addison-Wesley) 234.
[33] Aichholzer (n 8) 264.
[34] Turoff (n 13) 93.
[35] A fifth element, related to 'goal' items, will be reported elsewhere.
[36] Turoff (n 30) 161.

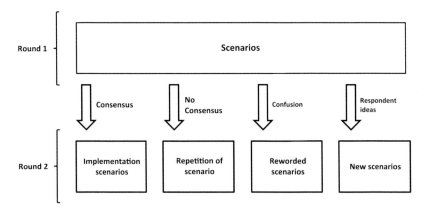

Fig. 8.2   Relationship between Round 1 and Round 2 Delphi survey instruments

Table 8.1   Response rate for Delphi method by survey round

Round	Number of participants	Response rate	Period of survey
1	13	77%	May–July 2013
2	8	62%	October 2013–January 2014

The process of developing the Round 2 survey is depicted in Fig. 8.2.
In other reported Delphi studies, three survey rounds have been sufficient to attain stable responses from participants; more rounds only antagonised participants, because they found the repetition excessive.[37] In this study, consensus appeared to have been achieved on many issues following the second survey round. This is consistent with previous studies, which have found that changes to participant responses tend to be limited to the early rounds of a Delphi.[38] Further, as found in other studies, the motivation and commitment of participants declined during the second round of the Delphi,[39] making a third round impracticable. The response rate for each round of the Delphi is included in Table 8.1.

---

[37] Linstone and Turoff (n 37) 229.
[38] Aichholzer (n 8) 267.
[39] Aichholzer (n 8) 267.

3   Means of Analysis

Rayens and Hahn recommend two criteria to measure the degree of consensus in a Delphi survey.[40] First, it is necessary to consider the inter-quartile range (IQR) of an item.[41] On a four point Likert-type scale, an IQR of more than 1.00 indicates a degree of disagreement.[42] However, the IQR is not sufficiently sensitive to distinguish between degrees of agreement when IQR = 1.00.[43] Therefore, the percentage of respondents who are generally positive about a scenario may be used as a secondary criterion of consensus.[44] Following Rayens and Hahn,[45] this study regarded both:

- scenarios having an IQR of more than 1.00; and
- scenarios having an IQR of 1.00 and receiving positive responses from between 40% and 60% of respondents

as having a degree of disagreement worthy of further exploration in Round 2. Scenarios that did not satisfy this definition were regarded as achieving consensus.

Prior to analysis, responses were adjusted to exclude respondents who self-identified as having 'no confidence' in their response to ensure a minimum level of knowledge about each area.[46] Following this adjustment, the answers of two respondents were excluded for two scenarios in Round 1 (four answers in total); and the answers of one respondent were excluded for five scenarios in Round 2 (five answers in total).

---

[40] Rayens and Hahn (n 9) 312.

[41] The IQR is the difference between the upper and lower quartiles (that is, the range within which the middle 50% of responses fall). Rayens and Hahn (n 9) 312 describe this as the 'inter-quartile deviation' (IQD), which is calculated by halving the IQR. However, in the authors' calculations, it is clear that they are using the IQR, *not* the IQD.

[42] Rayens and Hahn (n 9).

[43] Rayens and Hahn (n 9) 312.

[44] Rayens and Hahn (n 9) 312.

[45] Rayens and Hahn (n 9) 312–13.

[46] Aichholzer (n 8) 267.

4   Scenarios and Results

4.1   Round 1 Scenarios

The Round 1 survey instrument included eight scenarios. A brief description and justification for each scenario is provided below.[47]

Each Industry Develops a Work Ability Strategy to Be Implemented by Individual Workplaces

Work ability is concerned with the physical, mental and social capacities of an individual to manage their role in the workplace,[48] balancing personal factors with the demands of the job itself.[49] Work ability encompasses individual characteristics such as education, knowledge, skill, experience and motivation,[50] and targets four key areas: work demands and the environment; work organisation and the work community; workers' health and functional capacity; and workers' professional competence.[51] Policies to enhance work ability can embrace areas such as training and professional development, occupational health and safety, workplace (re)design, employee engagement and autonomy and physical and mental wellbeing.

Activities to promote work ability are common in Finnish workplaces.[52] Promoting work ability is thought to lower absence rates and disability costs, increase productivity, improve management, secure competent manpower and improve individual quality of life and wellbeing, both

---

[47] For further justification, see Blackham (n 25).

[48] J Ilmarinen and K Tuomi (1992) 'Work Ability of Aging Workers' *Scandinavian Journal of Work, Environment & Health* 18, 8, 8.

[49] J Ilmarinen (2001) 'Aging Workers', *Occup Environ Med* 58, 546, 548.

[50] Ilmarinen and Tuomi (n 48) 8; see also J Ilmarinen and others (2005) 'New Dimensions of Work Ability', *International Congress Series* 1280, 3.

[51] K Tuomi and others (2001) 'Promotion of Work Ability, the Quality of Work and Retirement' *Occupational Medicine* 51, 318, 318.

[52] Ibid.

during work and during retirement.[53] Improved work ability is associated with enjoyment in staying in work, fewer thoughts of retirement[54] and lower levels of later disability.[55] Therefore, work ability promotion is seen as a positive measure to reduce premature retirement and extend working lives.[56]

Each Workplace Adopts an Age Management Approach to Its Workforce

Age management is a key means of improving the psychosocial work environment within a 'work ability' approach. Age management involves the consideration of age-related factors in the daily management, design and organisation of individual work tasks and the work environment.[57] Good age management tends to include: a positive attitude towards ageing; support for teamwork and group work; finding individual solutions which fit with changing strengths and weaknesses during ageing; and open-minded communication within organisations.[58]

Age management is a key feature of the Finnish approach to older workers. Further, the adoption of age management strategies in Member States is one of the Guiding Principles for Active Ageing and Solidarity between Generations, as jointly agreed by the EU's Social Protection Committee and the Employment Committee.[59] Work on age management has been undertaken in the UK, resulting in various sources of information and

---

[53] J Ilmarinen and J Rantanen (1999) 'Promotion of Work Ability during Ageing' *American Journal of Industrial Medicine* 36, 21, 23.

[54] Tuomi and others (n 5) 322.

[55] Ilmarinen and Tuomi (n 48) 9; K Tuomi and others (1977) 'Summary of the Finnish Research Project (1981–1992) to Promote the Health and Work Ability of Aging Workers', *Scand J Work Environ Health* 23, 66, 68; Ilmarinen and Rantanen (n 53) 21.

[56] Tuomi and others (n 5) 318.

[57] J Ilmarinen (2005) *Towards a Longer Worklife!: Ageing and the Quality of Worklife in the European Union* (Finnish Institute of Occupational Health) 120.

[58] Ilmarinen and Rantanen (n 53) 22.

[59] See Council of the European Union (2012) *Council Declaration on the European Year for Active Ageing and Solidarity between Generations (2012): The Way Forward...*

guidance for employers.[60] Much of this work on age management has originated from non-governmental organisations, such as The Age and Employment Network (TAEN) and the Chartered Institute of Personnel and Development (CIPD), and the concept continues to '[strike] British ears rather awkwardly'.[61] Therefore, this scenario tested the possibility of adopting age management ideas in the UK context. By focusing on *workplaces*, it reflects an emphasis on employers as agents of change and the broader role of employers in supporting older workers. This scenario was given to respondents with a short definition of 'age management' to ensure respondents had a similar understanding of what the term meant.

Each Employee Is Given the Right to Request Flexible Working Arrangements

Flexible working arrangements and changes to working time are seen as having significant potential to extend working lives. Previous studies have found that many older workers prefer flexible work arrangements, and that the presence of flexible working would encourage older workers to stay at work.[62] Similarly, a real or perceived lack of working time flexibility may encourage older workers to retire involuntarily.[63] Reduced working time may also help older workers to manage health issues[64] and caring responsibilities.[65]

---

[60] See, for example, Chris Ball (2007) 'Defining Age Management: Information and Discussion Paper'; Chris Ball (March 2013) 'Age Management at Work: Adopting a Strategic Approach' (Employment Relations Comment); Emma Parry and Lynette Harris (December 2011), 'The Employment Relations Challenges of an Ageing Workforce' (Acas Future of Workplace Relations discussion paper series); CIPD (May 2011) 'Managing Age: New Edition 2011'.

[61] Ball 'Defining Age Management: Information and Discussion Paper' (n 60) 1.

[62] Diane-Gabrielle Tremblay and Émilie Genin (2010) 'Aging, Economic Insecurity, and Employment: Which Measures Would Encourage Older Workers to Stay Longer in the Labour Market?' *Studies in Social Justice* 3, 173 & 181.

[63] Andreas Cebulla and others (2007) 'Working beyond the State Pension Age in the United Kingdom: The Role of Working Time Flexibility and the Effects on the Home', *Ageing & Society* 27, 849 & 852.

[64] Nathalie Burnay (2011) 'Ageing at Work: Between Changing Social Policy Patterns and Reorganization of Working Times', *Population Review* 50, 150 & 161.

[65] Tony Maltby (2009) 'The Employability of Older Workers: What Works?' in Wendy Loretto and others (eds) *The future for older workers: new perspectives* (Policy Press) 170–71.

In the expert interviews, 13 respondents independently identified flexible working as a key area of focus for employers and government in the UK, demonstrating the relative importance of flexible work for extending working lives. Further, there was a general consensus that flexible workplaces were more likely to retain older workers. The experts strongly endorsed flexible working for older workers, and the extension of the right to request flexible working to older workers.

After the conclusion of the expert interviews and the Delphi survey, this scenario actually came to fruition: from 30 June 2014, all employees (and not just those with caring responsibilities) with 26 weeks' service have had the right to request flexible working from their employer.[66] Employers may only refuse a request due to a 'sound business reason'. Thus, each employee has actually been given the right to request flexible working arrangements. Scenario 3 tested this possibility prior to the legislative reforms.

Easily Accessible Information and Guidance About Managing and Working in an Ageing Workforce Is Available to Employers and Employees

During the expert interviews, respondents suggested that additional guidance be created to assist employers in managing their obligations towards the ageing workforce. The experts emphasised that this guidance needed to be accessible, available and understandable by employers. Respondents also suggested the creation of an (online) 'one-stop-shop' to signpost relevant information, and the provision of opportunities for employers to collaboratively work through issues, including through facilitated opportunities to network, discuss issues around ageing and share best practice. Alternatively, organisations could be given access to tailored advice from advisors about how to adapt legal provisions to their workforce. In this context, Scenario 4 tested the relative desirability and importance of enhancing information provision in this area. Again, following the conclusion of the

---

[66] *Employment Rights Act 1996* (UK) c 18 s 80F; *Children and Families Act 2014* (UK) c 6 s 131.

Delphi survey, this scenario was implemented to some extent with the creation of the Age Action Alliance Employer Toolkit for managers of older workers.[67]

Effective Leadership Ensures the Ageing Workforce Is an Issue of High Priority

The expert interviews also identified a need to build employer capacity and leadership skills generally. Governmental leadership was also identified by one expert as being important for changing employer attitudes towards older workers and encouraging organisations to adopt best practice. Therefore, leadership at a governmental and organisational level may be a key driver of better age-aware practices. Scenario 5 therefore tested the relative desirability and importance of leadership in the context of an ageing workforce. The question was framed broadly on purpose, to allow respondents to interpret 'leadership' as that at a governmental, organisational and/or sectoral level.

A National Dialogue Regarding What Rights, Obligations and Privileges Should Be Granted to Individuals at Different Ages Is Undertaken

The expert interviews and broader literature identified the need for a social dialogue regarding what is acceptable age discrimination, what rights and obligations should be provided at different ages and what exceptions should be allowed to age equality provisions. A dialogue of this nature may promote better social policy.[68] Therefore, Scenario 6 tested this suggestion.

---

[67] See Age Action Alliance 'Employer Toolkit: Guidance for Managers of Older Workers' (no date) http://ageactionalliance.org/employer-toolkit/ accessed 1 July 2015.
[68] See further Alan Walker (2002) 'Ageing in Europe: Policies in Harmony or Discord?' *Int J Epidemiol* 31, 758 & 760; Hedva Sarfati (2006) 'Social Dialogue: A Potential "Highroad" to Policies Addressing Ageing in the EU Member States', *International Social Security Review* 59, 49 & 53.

Employers Have a Positive Duty to Achieve Employment Equality, Including for Older Workers

The imposition of positive duties on employers to achieve employment equality or fair participation would be a key means of encouraging a more proactive and less compliance-focused organisational response to the equality framework.[69] Further, it would shift the responsibility to organisations to identify and address unlawful discrimination, irrespective of whether an individual complaint has been received,[70] and encourage a renewed focus on changing organisations to accommodate individual needs, rather than just adapting individuals to fit existing structures.[71] By not imposing such duties on the private sector, the Equality Act 2010 (UK) c 15 does not go far enough to achieve equality[72]: positive duties would change 'the whole landscape of discrimination law'[73] through a 'radical strategy for tackling deep-seated discrimination'.[74]

Imposing a positive duty on the private sector would be likely to generate significant consternation among employers and substantial political resistance, as it would be seen as increasing the 'regulatory burden' on employers.[75] The *Equality Act 2010* (UK) c 15 currently limits positive duties to public bodies, on the assumption it would be 'unfairly onerous' to apply them to the private sector.[76] However, the private

---

[69] Bob Hepple and others (2000) *Equality: A New Framework—Report of the Independent Review of the Enforcement of UK Anti-Discrimination Legislation* (Hart) 59–65, 69–72; Linda Dickens (2006) 'Equality and Work-Life Balance: What's Happening at the Workplace' *Ind Law J* 35, 445, 447; Linda Dickens (2007) 'The Road is Long: Thirty Years of Equality Legislation in Britain' *British Journal of Industrial Relations* 45, 463 & 474; Sandra Fredman and Sarah Spencer (June 2006) 'Delivering Equality: Towards an Outcome-Focused Positive Duty—Submission to the Cabinet Office Equality Review and to the Discrimination Law Review', 6–7.

[70] Fredman and Spencer (n 69) 6–7; Sandra Fredman (2012) 'Breaking the Mold: Equality as a Proactive Duty', 60 *Am J Comp L* 265, 266.

[71] Dickens, 'The Road is Long' (n 69) 472.

[72] Bob Hepple (2011) 'Enforcing Equality Law: Two Steps Forward and Two Steps Backwards for Reflexive Regulation', *Ind Law J* 40, 315, 319.

[73] Fredman (n 70) 271.

[74] Anne CL Davies (2009) *Perspectives on Labour Law* (Law in context, 2nd edn, Cambridge University Press) 135.

[75] Bob Hepple (2003) 'Age Discrimination in Employment: Implementing the Framework Directive 2000/78/EC' in Sandra Fredman and Sarah Spencer (eds), *Age as an equality issue: legal and policy perspectives* (Hart) 85.

[76] Sandra Fredman (2002) *Discrimination Law* (Clarendon law series, Oxford University Press) 178.

sector has 'potential strategic importance' in addressing inequality, given it employs the vast majority of the UK workforce.[77] Private and public sector equality duties 'harness the energy' of those in the best position to promote equality and achieve structural change.[78] Therefore, the imposition of positive duties to achieve employment equality on private sector employers should be seriously considered. Scenario 7 considered whether this duty could or should be introduced in the UK.

Employers Have a Responsibility to Consult with Employees and/or Their Representatives in Relation to Equality Matters

Hepple, Coussey and Choudhury also propose a duty on employers to engage with other groups in decision-making on equality matters.[79] This proposal was tested in Scenario 8.

4.2 Round 1 Results

The results for the Round 1 scenarios are presented in Table 8.2. Positive consensus is indicated with a tick (✓), negative consensus with a cross (X), and a lack of consensus with (≈).

Table 8.2 Results for Round 1 of the Delphi survey

Scenario	Desirable	Feasible	Important
Age management	✓	✓	✓
Information and guidance	✓	✓	✓
Leadership	✓	✓	✓
Work ability	✓	X≈	✓
Right to request flexible working	✓	X≈	✓
Responsibility to consult	✓	✓≈	✓
National dialogue	X	X	X
Positive duty	✓	✓	✓≈

---

[77] Fredman and Spencer (n 69) 8; see also Dickens, 'The Road is Long' (n 69) 474.

[78] Fredman (n 76) 176; Fredman (n 70) 271.

[79] Hepple and others (n 69) 71.

At the end of Round 1, positive consensus had been achieved regarding three scenarios: age management, information and guidance and leadership. Four scenarios failed to achieve consensus, and were re-tested in Round 2. The respondents' comments on two scenarios (national dialogue and positive duty) indicated a degree of confusion. Thus, these scenarios were reworded for Round 2. This process is explained in more detail below.

4.3   Round 2

Reworded Scenarios

Two scenarios were reworded for Round 2 to clarify or further develop the scenarios in response to participant comments.

Positive Duty

The respondents generally regarded this scenario positively in Round 1, and saw it as being both desirable and feasible. However, there was no consensus regarding whether it was important. This response was surprising, as imposing positive duties on the private sector was predicted to generate significant consternation among employer groups. It was therefore anticipated that the scenario would generate far less consensus.

The respondents' comments suggested that confusion or multiple interpretations may have led to an artificially positive response. Indeed, one respondent noted that the positive duty was already in place under legislation, perhaps confusing it with public sector equality duty. Other respondents felt the question was unclear, and asked for clarification regarding how the duty might be implemented, enforced and defined.

The scenario was therefore rewritten for Round 2 to clarify its meaning and reflect the respondents' comments. The reframed scenario explicitly noted that the duty would be imposed by statute, and would apply to public and private sector employers. Examples were also given of how the duty might be implemented and enforced, drawing on the framework developed by Hepple, Coussey and Choudhury.[80]

---

[80] Hepple and others (n 69) 71.

Table 8.3 Results for reworded scenarios, Round 2 of the Delphi survey

Amended Scenario	Desirable	Feasible	Important
There is broad-ranging discussion and awareness-raising regarding the needs of older workers	✓	✓≈	✓
A statutory duty is imposed on all employers (public and private) to achieve employment equality	✓	X≈	✓≈

Following its rewording and clarification, the scenario received a markedly less positive reception (see Table 8.3). While respondents still saw the scenario as desirable, there was no consensus regarding whether it was feasible or important, and most respondents felt it would not be feasible. Therefore, a positive duty may not be a priority for governmental reform or, alternatively, other reforms should take precedence. These responses also reflect the perceived impact of a deregulatory governmental agenda on the viability of legal reform.

National Dialogue

The vast majority of respondents regarded the suggestion of a national dialogue negatively, and there was consensus that the suggestion was not desirable, feasible or important. This was unexpected, given that the scenario was derived from interviews with the same expert respondents. However, the comments revealed significant concern that a dialogue could perpetuate discrimination, or be ineffective at achieving concrete change. Further, respondents felt the question was unclear, which was reflected in the low percentage of confident responses.

The scenario was rewritten for Round 2 to clarify its meaning and integrate the respondents' comments. The scenario was reframed to focus on discussion and awareness-raising, rather than dialogue more broadly. The reworded scenario was received far more positively in Round 2, indicating that the issues in Round 1 were at least partly attributable to a lack of clarity. However, there was still a lack of consensus on whether the scenario was feasible, and respondents again expressed concern that the discussion may fail to achieve meaningful outcomes. Therefore, expert views indicate that broad discussion and awareness-raising is not a scenario that should be prioritised.

The results for the reworded scenarios in Round 2 are presented in Table 8.3.

Repetition of Scenarios

Scenarios that led to disagreement in Round 1 were repeated in Round 2 with the aim of allowing participants to revisit or reconsider their original opinions in the light of the feedback provided. The lack of consensus in Round 1 related largely to feasibility—given, particularly, the government's deregulatory agenda. The results for the repeated scenarios are presented in Table 8.4.

As Table 8.4 demonstrates, consensus was achieved when respondents reconsidered the feasibility of the scenarios: respondents saw a responsibility to consult and the right to request flexible working as desirable, feasible and important. However, there was consensus that the work ability scenario was not feasible.

New Scenarios

In Round 1 of the survey, respondents were asked to suggest new or different scenarios for testing in Round 2. The scenarios suggested were:

1. introduction of a statutory right to take paid time off to fulfil caring responsibilities; and
2. do nothing and maintain the status quo.

Table 8.4 Results for repeated scenarios, Round 2 of the Delphi survey

Scenario	Feasible
Responsibility to consult	✓
Work ability	X
Right to request flexible working	✓

Table 8.5 Results for new scenarios, Round 2 of the Delphi survey

New Scenarios	Desirable	Feasible	Important
Introduction of a statutory right to take paid time off to fulfil caring responsibilities	✓	X≈	✓
Do nothing and maintain the status quo	X	✓≈	X

The results for these scenarios are presented in Table 8.5. Consensus was not achieved for either scenario. However, while the right to take time off was seen as desirable and important, respondents did not endorse doing nothing to respond to the ageing workforce. No respondent saw doing nothing as desirable (with the original proponent of the scenario failing to participate in Round 2), and the majority of respondents did not regard the scenario as important. Further, there was no consensus regarding whether the scenario was feasible. Therefore, while it may be difficult to achieve change in this area, it is clear that respondents regarded doing nothing as neither desirable nor feasible.

Implementation Scenarios

Finally, the scenarios that achieved significant consensus across the experts in Round 1 (age management, and information and guidance) were explored further in Round 2 via a series of 'implementation scenarios'.

Age Management

For this scenario, a range of measures were presented, from persuasion and education to incentives and statutory regulation,[81] to examine how age management approaches could be achieved at the workplace level. Respondents were also asked who should be responsible for each implementation scenario. The results for these questions are presented in Table 8.6.

---

[81] See DC Walsh and NP Gordon (1986) 'Legal Approaches to Smoking Deterrence', *Annual Review of Public Health* 7, 127.

Table 8.6 Results for age management implementation scenarios, Round 2 of the Delphi survey

Scenario	Desirable	Feasible	Important
Further promotion of the business case for adopting an age management approach to workplaces	✓	✓	✓≈
Further information and guidance regarding how to adopt an age management approach is made available to employers	✓	✓	✓
Additional training and development opportunities are provided to ensure employers have the skills to implement age management approaches	✓	✓≈	✓
Effective leadership ensures age management is an organisational priority	✓	✓	✓
Incentives are introduced to reward workplaces that adopt an age management approach	✓≈	X	X≈
Regulations promoting practices consistent with an age management approach are introduced	✓≈	X≈	X

Using confidence-adjusted results, there was consensus among respondents that providing additional information and guidance, and effective leadership were desirable, feasible and important implementation measures for securing organisational age management. While training and development opportunities were seen as desirable and important, respondents disagreed regarding their feasibility, perhaps due to the potential cost of such programmes. When asked who should be responsible for implementing such initiatives, respondents placed emphasis on the role of employer bodies, industry bodies and professional organisations in leading change. While some respondents identified government as playing a role in this area, more reliance was placed on non-governmental bodies.

In contrast to the broad support and consensus regarding information and persuasion measures, respondents were far less supportive of regulation and the use of financial incentives in this area: neither financial incentives nor regulations to promote age management were seen as being feasible or important. Respondents questioned where funds would come from to finance incentives, and doubted whether there would be sufficient

Table 8.7 Results for information and guidance implementation scenarios, Round 2 of the Delphi survey

Scenario	Desirable	Feasible	Important
An online 'one-stop shop' provides links and references to relevant information and guidance	✓	✓≈	✓≈
An advisory service provides tailored information and guidance to workplaces upon request	✓	✓≈	✓
Further information and guidance about managing and working in an ageing workforce is developed	✓	✓≈	✓
Existing information and guidance is rewritten to ensure its accessibility and relevance	✓≈	✓≈	X
Employers are given facilitated opportunities to network, discuss issues around ageing and share best practice	✓	✓	✓

political will to introduce regulations. Therefore, respondents appeared far more supportive of 'persuasion' measures and non-governmental activity to promote age management approaches at the workplace level. This is consistent with the traditional 'hands-off' approach to governance in the UK and the prevailing reliance on 'soft law' and exhortation in the area of equality.[82] However, while soft law is a useful adjunct to legal regulation, it is 'a poor substitute' for legal intervention.[83]

Information and Guidance

The implementation scenarios for this topic reflected the respondents' suggestions and ideas for how information and guidance on ageing could be made more accessible. The results for these questions are presented in Table 8.7.

The majority of implementation scenarios generated limited consensus: an online 'one-stop shop' was seen as desirable, but there was no consensus regarding whether it was important or feasible; an advisory

---

[82] Linda Dickens and Mark Hall (2006) 'Fairness—up to a Point. Assessing the Impact of New Labour's Employment Legislation', *Human Resource Management Journal* 16, 338, 348.
[83] Dickens and Hall (n 82).

service, while desirable and important, was seen as unfeasible, perhaps due to the difficulties of securing funding in an austerity climate; the development of further guidance failed to generate consensus regarding its feasibility; and the redrafting of existing guidance was not seen as desirable or important and did not achieve consensus regarding its feasibility.

The striking exception was the provision of facilitated opportunities for employers to network, discuss issues around ageing and share best practice. All respondents felt this implementation scenario was important, feasible and desirable. However, most experts felt responsibility for this reform should lie with employer or industry bodies and professional bodies, again indicating that government should play a limited role in this area.

5   Analysis and Conclusions

Over the two rounds of the Delphi, respondents endorsed five scenarios as being desirable, feasible and important:

* adoption of age management approaches by workplaces;
* making information and guidance available and easily accessible to employers and employees;
* effective leadership;
* employers having a responsibility to consult with employees and/or their representatives on equality matters; and
* extension of the right to request flexible working.

While consensus was achieved on these scenarios, it is less clear how they should be implemented in practice. In relation to age management, respondents only supported implementation via persuasion measures rather than through incentives or regulation. It is unclear whether persuasion alone will be effective for achieving positive change for older workers. Respondents also placed emphasis on non-governmental activity in implementing these initiatives, and regarded government as having a more limited role.

Further, for information and guidance, most implementation scenarios were not seen as being important, desirable or necessary. Consensus was only achieved on the provision of facilitated opportunities for employers to network. Again, responsibility for providing these opportunities was seen as lying with professional organisations and employer or industry bodies, rather than government. Similarly, while respondents supported the leadership scenario, 'leadership' was interpreted as organisational leadership, rather than leadership at a governmental level. At the same time, respondents expressed concern that individual managers lacked the capacity and skills to lead change.

The results of the Delphi survey indicate that experts feel government should play a limited role in this area, and that regulation and statutory intervention is not the preferred course of action. Therefore, based on the results of the Delphi study, legal reform appears unlikely to garner support. Instead, employer and industry bodies and professional organisations may need to play a larger role in promoting positive change.

The results of the surveys also hint at the impact of government austerity measures and a deregulatory agenda on the perceived viability of legal reform. The former coalition government 'set a clear aim' to reduce 'the overall burden of regulation'[84] and eliminate 'unnecessary burdens on business'[85] to pursue the government's 'vision' of a labour market 'with minimal intervention by the Government'.[86] In this context, the respondents' concern about reform feasibility is wholly reasonable: it is unlikely that new regulations would be imposed on business in this climate. This will severely limit the UK's capacity to respond to demographic change. It is unlikely that these concerns will be any less significant with the election of a Conservative government, which has vowed to 'extend the fight against red tape' even further.[87]

---

[84] Cabinet Office, 'About Red Tape Challenge' (*Red Tape Challenge*, no date) http://www.red-tapechallenge.cabinetoffice.gov.uk/about/ accessed 7 March 2014.

[85] BIS (October 2011) 'Flexible, Effective, Fair: Promoting Economic Growth through a Strong and Efficient Labour Market' 7.

[86] BIS (October 2011) (n 85) 4.

[87] Larry Elliott (19 May 2015) 'Tories Vow to Slash "Burdensome" Red Tape for Business by £10bn', *The Guardian* (London) http://www.theguardian.com/business/2015/may/18/conservative-party-cut-red-tape-business-sajid-javid accessed 1 July 2015.

In sum, then, the Delphi study highlights a range of scenarios that might be pursued in the UK to address the implications of ageing for labour law, and demonstrates that experts support the adoption of these scenarios. Indeed, respondents firmly rejected doing nothing as a viable course of action. Therefore, this study strongly supports the case for targeted change to address demographic ageing. More particularly, actions that should be pursued include

- Providing further information and guidance to employers regarding how to adopt an age management approach;
- Effective leadership to ensure age management is an organisational priority;
- Giving employers facilitated opportunities to network, discuss issues around ageing and share best practice;
- Introducing a right to request flexible working arrangements for each employee; and
- Ensuring employers have a responsibility to consult with employees and/or their representatives in relation to equality matters.

Some of these actions are already in place, or are being actively pursued. For example, the Age Action Alliance and the Department for Work and Pensions (DWP) have produced an employer toolkit, which touches on some issues relevant to an age management approach.[88] Further, opportunities for employers to network and discuss matters related to ageing are already being facilitated to some extent by the Age Action Alliance, TAEN, the Employers Network for Equality & Inclusion (enei), and the CIPD. Finally, as noted above, legislation has been introduced to provide a right to request flexible working for all employees: from 30 June 2014, all employees (and not just those with caring responsibilities) with 26 weeks' service have had the right to request flexible working from their employer.[89] Thus, good progress is already being made in some of these areas. However, there is still significant work to be done on promoting effective leadership on ageing, and facilitating consultation and/

---

[88] Age Action Alliance (n 67).
[89] *Employment Rights Act 1996* (UK) c 18 s. 80F; *Children and Families Act 2014* (UK) c 6 s. 131.

or employee input on equality matters. These are areas that should be seriously considered in government policy going forward.

These results also indicate that the Delphi process is a successful method for achieving consensus. Across the survey, three of the eight scenarios achieved consensus in Round 1, and a further three scenarios achieved consensus in Round 2. This study, then, demonstrates the significant benefits of using the Delphi method to identify and evaluate policy responses to the ageing workforce. The method is an excellent tool for exploring solutions in policy areas with high levels of uncertainty and divided opinion, including those related to ageing. It is particularly well suited for developing long-term solutions and hypothetical scenarios for the advancement of ageing policy, and provides new opportunities to constructively consider and generate consensus around policy options. Thus, it could be of significant assistance to policy makers and researchers considering ageing issues.

However, at the same time, it is worth acknowledging the practical challenges involved in using the Delphi method: the process can be time-consuming and demanding; maintaining response rates and participant enthusiasm is a constant challenge; scenarios may be misinterpreted or lead to confusion; and administering an online survey requires a level of technical expertise.

While the method offers significant benefits, it also raises practical methodological challenges. Even with these difficulties, the Delphi method still has significant potential for developing consultative and collaborative solutions to long-term challenges, like demographic ageing. As a result, the Delphi process is a worthy adjunct to traditional legal doctrinal methods in developing policy and law reform in this area.

Part IV

The Perspectives of Workers

9

Extended Working Lives: What Do Older Employees Want?

Wendy Loretto

Across most western nations, the assumption that individuals will be working for longer and delaying retirement has come to dominate discussion of policies and practices around later working life. The OECD's (2006) publication, *Live Longer, Work Longer*,[1] captured the relationship between increased longevity and extended working lives, and paid work has become a key component of the active ageing agenda. Legal restrictions around compulsory retirement ages have been lifted in many countries, facilitating greater choice over working for longer (see for example Manfredi and Vickers in Chap. 4). In addition, concerns relating to the inadequacy of pension provision have led to an expectation that people will need to work for longer because they cannot afford to retire as early as previous generations. Data from the OECD on trends in 24 countries illustrates an effective rise in retirement age, with the average retirement age for men in 2012 reaching 65 years or over in 11 countries, and for women in nine countries.[2] This compares to only four countries in

---

[1] Organisation for Economic Co-Operation and Development (OECD) (2006) *Live Longer, Work Longer*, (OECD Publishing).

[2] http://www.oecd.org/els/public-pensions/ageingandemploymentpolicies-statisticsonaverageeffectiveageofretirement.htm (Accessed 15 October 2015).

© The Editor(s) (if applicable) and The Author(s) 2016   **187**
S. Manfredi, L. Vickers (eds.), *Challenges of Active Ageing*,
DOI 10.1057/978-1-137-53251-0_9

2007.[3] Within the UK, the country focused on in this chapter, national statistics show rising employment rates for people aged 60+. However, these increases are typically modest, and the majority still retire at, or before, the age of eligibility for state old age pension (currently 65 years for men, and rising from 60 to 65 years for women).

Despite legal changes, policy initiatives, and so on, this chapter argues that we do not fully understand the relationships between individuals' behaviour and opportunities and the constraints around working for longer. In part, this is because the voices of those at the very centre of the debates, the 'older' workers themselves, have been relatively neglected. Through a secondary analysis of existing national datasets, as well as of primary quantitative and qualitative research, this chapter will examine the attitudes and expectations of people aged 50+ (the age group most often deemed to be 'older' workers in policy debates) in the UK. It will seek to understand what people want from their later working lives, and when and how they might wish to work for longer or to retire. The implications of the findings for employers and policymakers will be discussed, along with the experience of the UK, as a nation located within a wider, international context.

1   Employment Patterns Among the Over-50s in the UK

Against a background of population ageing and concerns over funding for state pensions and eldercare costs, successive UK governments have clearly voiced a need for individuals to work longer. The discourse has changed over time, from reversing early retirement, to extending working lives, to most recently encouraging fuller working lives.[4,5] However, the intention remains firmly focused on delaying permanent withdrawal from paid work. A series of initiatives in the last 15 years has seen the

---

[3] P Clayton (2010) 'Working on: choice or necessity?' in *Working and Ageing: Emerging Theories and Empirical Perspectives*, (European Centre for the Development of Vocational Training) 227–252.

[4] Department for Work and Pensions (DWP) (2014) *Fuller Working Lives—A Framework for Action* (DWP).

[5] R Altmann (2015) *A New Vision for Older Workers: Retain, Retrain and Recruit*, (London: DWP).

introduction of legislation prohibiting discrimination in grounds of age in 2006 and the subsequent abolition of a default retirement age in 2011 (see Chap. 4). There has been a steady raising of age of eligibility for state old age pension and a reduction in benefit and pension regimes which encouraged early retirement or following ill-health or disability pathways out of work. These changes have been accompanied by active, supply-side, labour market policies which encourage or subsidise long-term economically inactive people back into work, such as making work pay through tax incentives or increasing training to improve employability. Following the OECD's (2006)[6] tripartite model of barriers to employment of older workers (which classifies barriers according to their causes: employers ignoring, undervaluing or discriminating against older workers; financial disincentives to working longer; and weak employability skills of the older workforce), much of the emphasis is couched in terms of offering or extending individuals the *choice* to work longer by removing barriers. This is set against a general shift away from 'mass fixed age retirement'[7] to a more diverse set of individual experiences and pathways. Certainly, before the abolition of the default retirement age of 65 years, surveys[8] routinely showed a demand for the choice to work longer. In particular, flexible working has been proffered as a way of extending working lives[9] and offering a range of opportunities and widening pathways into retirement by down-shifting; providing bridge jobs; enabling gradual returns to employment for those who had been out of work for some time; and 'unretirement'.[10]

UK official labour market statistics show that employment rates for men, and especially women, have increased in the 2000s, with particular rises seen in the over-60 age group. However, although much lauded in

---

[6] OECD (2006) *Live Longer, Work Longer.*

[7] I Rees Jones, M Leontowitsch and P Higgs (2010) 'The Experience of Retirement in Second Modernity: Generational Habitus among Retired Senior Managers' *Sociology* 44 0 (1), 103–120.

[8] See, for example, D. Smeaton and S Vegeris (2009) *Older People Inside and Outside the Labour Market: A Review*, Research Report 22, (Equality and Human Rights Commission) www.equality-humanrights.com/en/policyresearch/pages/default.aspx (Accessed 15 October 2015).

[9] Chartered Institute of Personnel and Development/International Longevity Centre (CIPD/ILC) (2015) *Avoiding the Demographic Crunch: Labour Supply and the Ageing Workforce*, (CIPD/ILC).

[10] N Maestas (2010) 'Back to Work Expectations and realizations of Work after retirement' *The Journal of Human Resources*, 45 (3), 718–748.

media coverage of labour market trends, such rises are modest and steady, and as Table 9.1 demonstrates, the vast majority of men and women aged 60+ are not in paid work.

Moreover, there is little evidence of a wide-scale uptake of more flexible forms of work. As an illustration, the proportion of those engaging in part-time employment has remained steady or even fallen slightly over the past 10 years. Taking the 65–69 year old age group as an illustration: in 2004, 64% of men working in that age group did so on a part-time basis; by 2013, the percentage had fallen to 54%. For women aged 65–69, the percentage of women who worked part-time, from among all working women in that age group, fell from 85% to 74% over the same time period. A more detailed analysis of people working beyond 65 years (the state pension age)[11] shows that most of these people occupy jobs they have held for ten or more years in permanent posts. These findings from the British case are echoed in a comparative review, which found that across a range of European and North American countries, there were only limited 'signs of flexibilisation of work patterns' for older workers, especially in comparison to changes in the youth labour markets.[12]

All in all, it appears that the policy thrust and legal changes have not, as yet, had a transformational effect on extending working lives. While there are likely to be multiple reasons for this (for example, see Loretto[13] for a review of the role of workplace policy and practices), this chapter explores the position of those at the heart of the debates, the older workers themselves, by providing insight into their plans and ambitions. Two particular studies are considered here—one focuses on reinvention in retirement; the other interrogates why, to paraphrase Warhust et al.,[14] flexible work may be more topical than typical.

---

[11] D Lain and W Loretto (2015) *Workers over 65 in the UK: The new 'precariat'?* Presentation given at British Society of Gerontology conference, Newcastle 1–3 July 2015.

[12] D Hofacker (2015) *Older Workers in a Globalizing World. An International Comparison of retirement and Late-Career Patterns in Western Industrialized Countries,* (Edward Elgar).

[13] W Loretto (2010) 'Work and retirement in an ageing world: the case of older workers in the UK' *21st Century Society: Journal of the Academy of Social Sciences,* 5 (3) Special edition: The Ageing World.

[14] C Warhurst, D R Eikhof and A Haunschild (2008) 'Out of balance or just out of bounds? Analyzing the relationship between work and life' in C Warhurst, D R Eikhof and A Haunschild (eds) *Work Less, Live More? Critical analysis of the work-life boundary* (Palgrave Macmillan) 1–21.

Table 9.1 Percentage of men and women in employment, by age, 2004–2013

		25–29	30–34	35–39	40–44	45–49	50–54	55–59	60–64	65–69	70plus
Men	2004	85.9	89.1	89.8	88.8	87.9	84.0	75.0	54.0	18.0	4.0
	2013	84.0	88.0	88.7	88.7	86.5	82.8	75.4	55.6	24.4	6.2
Women	2004	72.4	71.9	73.3	76.6	77.7	75.0	61.0	30.0	10.0	2.0
	2013	69.2	72.0	73.3	75.9	77.8	77.0	66.3	35.8	15.0	2.8

Source: UK Labour Force Survey (GB figures) 2004 and 2013 (author's analysis)

2   Reinvention in Retirement

As part of a publicity campaign for a national financial services provider, an independent survey of 1500 individuals was carried out in November 2013.[15] The sample included 1200 people aged above 50 years, of whom 39% were still working and 45% were retired. All the retired respondents were asked if they considered that they had 'reinvented' themselves in their retirement. The term 'reinvention' was included in the survey, but its interpretation was left open to individual respondents. Of the participants, 187 people (15.6%) felt their retirement had involved some form of reinvention, and the analysis which follows focuses mainly on these people. Although an equal number of men and women said that they had reinvented themselves, striking gender differences emerged in behaviours and attitudes. In line with national patterns, the modal age group for women retiring was 56–60 years (40% retired in this age range), as compared to 61–65 for men (50%). Marked gender differences appeared in respondents' expectations around their retirement age. As illustrated by Table 9.2, men were significantly more likely to state they had retired close to their expected retirement age, with women more likely to say they had expected to retire earlier.

In other related questions, around a quarter of men and women said they would have retired earlier if they could have afforded to, with men being nearly three times more likely than women to say they had retired at the age at which they wanted to stop working.

Table 9.2 Retirement expectations of men and women (numbers and percentages)

	Women		Men	
		%		%
I expected to retire earlier	49	44.95	29	37.18
I expected to retire later	24	22.02	15	19.23
I retired close to my expectations	36	33.03	34	43.59

---

[15] Further details of survey available from author on request.

2.1   Reinvention Activities

So, what forms did reinvention take for these people? Respondents were invited to nominate activities in a free-text response; these were subsequently coded into 21 categories by the author. Although paid work activities were included as options, these were not very popular: 26.7% of respondents' reinvention involved starting a new hobby or leisure activity, and 22.5% had opted for reinventing themselves through voluntary work. Figures 9.1 and 9.2 present the 'top 5' activities for women and men separately.

While there were several common categories, only men included an activity associated with paid work (career change) as one of their popular choices. It is also clear that caring activities (especially caring for grandchildren) featured more for women than for men. As an aside, when those in the sample who were still working (all ages) were asked what their dream retirement would be, caring for grandchildren was the fifth most popular activity for women, while volunteering was number three for men and number four for women. Currently, noncustodial grandparenting and its effects on later-life working is very under-researched. We know that a third of workers with children under the age of 15 receive

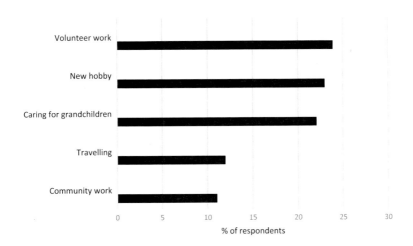

Fig. 9.1 Most popular reinvention activities among women

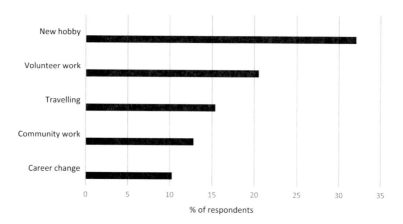

Fig. 9.2 Most popular reinvention activities among men

regular help with childcare from their parents.[16] The pressure to provide this care will remain significant, given the high costs of UK childcare and the increasing employment of working mothers.[17]

2.2   Reasons for Reinvention

Respondents were also asked about the reasons for their reinvention. Again, this was a free response question, with the answers falling into 12 categories. The most popular reasons given were 'keeping active' (36.9%) and 'following a passion' (24%), with women markedly more likely than men to give reasons around keeping active. Figures 9.3 and 9.4 contain the top five most popular reasons by gender—giving back to one's community was popular among both men and women. Each list contained a reason connected with paid work, but these were rather different for

[16] K Glaser, E R Montserrat, U Waginger, D Price, R Stuchburg and A Tinker (2011) *Grandparenting in Europe* (Grandparents Plus). Available from: http://www.grandparentsplus.org.uk/wp-content/uploads/2011/03/Grandparenting-in-Europe-Report.pdf (Accessed 15 October 2015).

[17] A Koslowski (2009) 'Grandparents and the Care of their Grandchildren' in J Stillwell, E Coast and D Keele, (eds) *Fertility, Living Arrangements and Care: Understanding Population Trends and Processes* (Springer) 171–190.

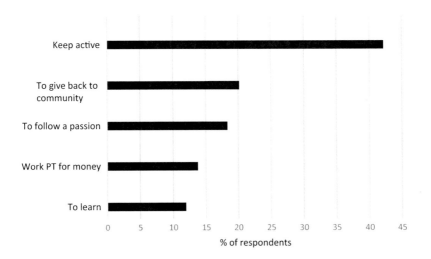

Fig. 9.3   Most popular reasons for reinvention among women

Fig. 9.4   Most popular reasons for reinvention among men

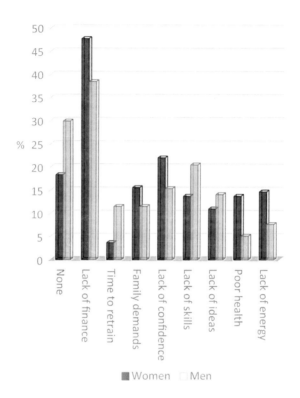

Fig. 9.5 Barriers to reinvention

women (who needed to work part-time for financial reasons) and men (who did not want to give up paid work completely).

2.3   Barriers to Reinvention

Those respondents who were retired but considered that they had not reinvented themselves in retirement were asked about possible barriers to reinvention. This was a fixed response question, and the distribution of answers is displayed in Fig. 9.5. Once again, gender differences are pronounced, with men more likely than women to say they had experienced no barriers. On the other hand, women were more likely to cite a range of practical barriers, including a lack of money, family demands, poor health and a lack of energy. Motivationally, although women were more likely to count a lack of confidence as a barrier, they were less likely to reckon that a lack of skills or ideas was holding them back.

In summary, the messages from these findings are two-fold. First, the survey showcased the wide range of activities undertaken by retirees, most of which were outside the realm of paid work. Future retirees too were also likely to express a desire to undertake activities other than paid employment in the future. As such, their 'working lives' were more likely to be extended in ways other than continuing to remain in the labour force. Second, the findings highlight some key gender differences, in terms of the nature of activities undertaken in later (working) life, in the reasons for these, and in the barriers to choice relating to 'reinventing' oneself in retirement. These key themes of heterogeneity in expectations and gender differentiation are now explored in more detail in the second part of this chapter that focuses on the extent to which men and women engage with flexible working as a way of extending working lives.

3   Flexible Work and Extending Working Lives

As mentioned in the introduction, there appears to be substantial gaps between the rhetoric and reality of flexible working among older workers in the UK. Possible reasons for these gaps will now be explored by drawing on data from a wider qualitative project commissioned by the UK government's Department for Work and Pensions (DWP) to investigate the factors encouraging labour market activity among people aged 50–64 years.[18] In total, 96 people in three contrasting British locations were interviewed. The study focus was on people and households with low-medium income levels, with the spread of household income in each of the three locations reflecting the socio-economic characteristics of that region. Within each location, the sample was purposively selected to

---

[18] S Vickerstaff, W Loretto, J Billings, P Brown, L Mitton, T Parkin P and White (2008) *Encouraging Labour Market Activity among 60–64 year olds* DWP Research Report No. 531. (DWP). Available from: http://www.dwp.gov.uk/asd/asd5/rrs-index.asp (Accessed 15 October 2015).

capture a range of personal (age, gender, marital status), health, financial, caring and employment statuses. Of the total number of respondents, 42 individuals were still in employment, 16 were unemployed or economically inactive and 38 were retired (all self-definitions).

3.1   Overview of Prevalence of Flexible Working

Although the sample exhibited heterogeneity of behaviours and attitudes towards flexible working in later life, overall, among the men, there was a relatively low incidence of flexible working, while amongst the women, part-time working was more common. Typically, women stopped work when their first child was born and then had returned to work, often different work, part time as the children got older. Many then further modified their hours in later life to undertake further caring for elderly parents, an ailing partner or grandchildren. Flexible working as a transition to retirement, as a way of working longer or a possible source of unretirement, was most often articulated as a 'wee part-time job'—usually in a different occupation from one's current employment. However, although often viewed as an attractive abstract concept, there was little evidence of uptake in practice or in terms of practical plans to make it happen in the future. Reasons were grouped together in five categories. Although separated for analytical purposes, it should be noted that these reasons do overlap in practice.

3.2   Reason 1: No Appetite to Work Longer in Any Capacity

This was a dominant viewpoint among the interviewees, whether retired or still working. Partly reflecting their own experience of retirement, most respondents in the retired group said they would not consider returning to work, even on a flexible basis. Some gave health reasons; others (mainly men who were in receipt of a defined benefit pension) said they had no financial need to return to work. However, these more straightforward reasons were often underpinned by issues associated with respondents' constructions of retirement. The key issues in this respect were 'freedom' and 'control'. These often superseded more rational financial drivers and constraints.

The importance of time sovereignty[19] was one of the strongest recurring themes across the interviews—many respondents were strongly attracted to the freedom that release from work had given, or was expected to give them. For several women who were retired, this freedom manifested itself as escape from a low quality and unsatisfying job.

There was a strong feeling among many, especially the men, that they had 'done their bit'. The majority had left school at 15 or 16 years and had been working continuously since then, so by their mid-50s, they had completed 40 years of working life. Some men also strongly felt that they wanted to focus on their families as they had missed out on this earlier in their lives. It was also clear that concerns about the real possibility or risk of deterioration in status, and the sense that 'I could drop dead tomorrow', coloured the way respondents were thinking about work and retirement, and in many instances, reinforced the traditional notion of 'cliff-edge' retirement[20]:

> We want to retire together because neither of our parents had any retirement together so I mean my mum died at 48 and my father died at 65 and his mum died at 60 … while we've got good health, touch wood, we want to enjoy it. (female_working)

Several people still working (mainly women) referred explicitly to 'bed blocking', that is, they felt they should retire in order to make room for younger employees. This resonates with recent decisions made by the European Union Court of Justice to accept that there is a need to enable younger workers to have access to work and employment opportunities; and that this is a valid reason for setting a compulsory retirement age, as discussed elsewhere in this volume.

---

[19] C Atkinson and L Hall (2009) 'The role of gender in varying forms of flexible working', *Gender, Work and Organization* 16 (6), 650–666.
[20] See P Brown and S Vickerstaff, (2011) 'Health Subjectivities and Labour Market Participation: Pessimism and older workers' attitudes and narratives around retirement in the United Kingdom', *Research on Aging* 33 (5), 529–550 for a further discussion of this health pessimism.

3.3   Reason 2: Quality of Flexible Work Options

The second key barrier to the uptake of, or planning for, flexible work related to the concerns expressed by many respondents about the quality of jobs that might be available to them on a flexible basis. There was a widely-held view that flexible working options for older workers equated to low-skilled, low-paid jobs with few prospects, for example, pushing trolleys in a supermarket. Such views were frequently based on media coverage of well-known retail chains who had received national publicity for their positive stance towards the older workforce, but respondents, especially women, were sceptical (or suspicious)[21] that such jobs would offer them much. These reservations are underpinned by empirical evidence.[22, 23]

In many cases, respondents' previous negative experiences of flexible working also made them wary of working flexibly in the future, or sometimes, even contributed to them stopping work altogether. For example, a former security guard described his previous employer's approach to flexibility: 'they shoved me wherever they thought they could shove me'; while a college lecturer in Nottingham recounted how an organisational restructuring led to him working via 'hot-desking', a 'flexible' work practice he found exceedingly stressful. Recent research has suggested that older workers' perceptions of job quality in general (not just related to flexible working opportunities) has declined over a long-run period, since the 1990s.[24] Analysis of national data sets has showed a persistent decline in satisfaction with both, the extrinsic and intrinsic, aspects of work, with the decline being more pronounced among older as compared to younger workers.

---

[21] M Simpson, M Richardson and T Zorn (2012) 'A job, a dream or a trap? Multiple meanings for encore careers', *Work, Employment and Society* 26 (3), 429–446.

[22] D Lain (2012) 'Working past 65 in the UK and the USA: segregation into 'Lopaq' occupations?' *Work, Employment & Society* 26 (1), 78–94.

[23] P McGovern, D Smeaton, and S Hill (2004) 'Bad Jobs in Britain: Nonstandard Employment and Job Quality' *Work and Occupations* 31 (2), 225–249.

[24] D Smeaton and M White (2015) 'The growing discontents of older British employees: Extended working life at risk from quality of working life', *Social Policy and Society*, online 1st, July 2015.

It is also important to note that for some older workers, in the main women, there was still a desire to continue building their careers, to upgrade rather than downgrade. For some women who had put their careers on the back-burner to raise their families, later working life was viewed as the time to renew or even start a new career.

3.4 Reason 3: No, or Limited, Opportunities to Work Flexibly

A key limitation to the potential for flexible working was the lack of available opportunities or at least a very limited awareness of opportunities. Respondents recounted very few examples of good practice, whereby employers had encouraged people towards gradual retirement—these were either in the public sector or in small (family) businesses. Previous research[25] has also shown that these types of employers are those most likely to be positive towards older workers and accommodate flexible working.

In the main, however, people were not aware if their employer offered the option to retire gradually or assumed that no options would be available. Thus, it may be that opportunities to work flexibly exist, but the awareness or willingness to ask is low. This interpretation is consistent with findings from other studies which have indicated that awareness of the right to request flexible working as carers is low.[26, 27] Moreover, there were several people in the study—mainly women—who felt that they could not ask for more flexibility in their work as their employer was already being kind to them in 'allowing' them to work part-time in the first place. They did not want to upset their employer by making any further requests. Another common refrain from respondents was that the decision was not theirs to take—it was up to their employer. Such perceptions could help explain why, in a study of employer responses to an ageing workforce,

---

[25] E Alden (2012) *Flexible Employment: How employment and the use of flexibility policies through the life course can affect later life occupation and financial outcomes* (Age UK).

[26] A Maitland (2010) *Working Better. The Over-50s, the New Work Generation* (EHRC).

[27] S Vickerstaff, W Loretto, A Milne, E Alden, J Billings, and P White (2009) *The Employment Support Needs of Carers*, DWP Research Report No. 597 (DWP). Available from: http://research.dwp.gov.uk/asd/asd5/rports2009-2010/rrep597.pdf (Accessed 15 October 2015).

Barnes et al (2009: 106)[28] found that employers reported little demand for flexible working options from older workers.

There were only a few respondents who had been able to work flexibly to accommodate health problems and these were all men. Most were men, working in white-collar jobs, who had taken ill-health retirement from their principal job, for example the police force, and were now working in quite different jobs. Flexible working for these people was characterised by a high degree of control and autonomy, achieved by being self-employed, for example as a taxi driver. There were only four cases (all men) where people had been able to work flexibly in their current jobs to allow them to deal with their health.

3.5   Reason 4: Mismatch Between Employers and Employees

The study also revealed that many of the older workers put severe limitations on the flexibility that they were willing or able to offer. These limitations centred around health restrictions, caring responsibilities and the strong desire for time sovereignty. The reality for several respondents was that their own, and often, partner's health constrained the type and amount of work that they could do. For example, one man aged 60 years described himself as semi-retired, or 'retired with PT dabbling'. He had a long history of arthritis which had meant he was no longer attractive to employers. At the time of the interview, he was volunteering for an arthritis charity and undertook some examination invigilation 'now and again'. As well as the limitations imposed by his own health, his decision not to work more had been influenced by his wife being diagnosed with cancer. Respondents with poor health often fully recognised that their limitations made them difficult to employ·

> They're running a business, they're not running a charity. (female_economically inactive)

Following on from health-related issues, many of our respondents, most often women, were caring for partners or parents who were ill.

[28] H Barnes, D Smeaton, and R Taylor (2009) *The Ageing Workforce: The Employers' Perspective* Report 468 (Institute for Employment Studies).

While in theory flexible working should offer a way to combine employment and caring needs, the reality showed a mismatch between employee and employer needs. The overarching issue here was that the existing flexible working options did little to accommodate the often unpredictable nature of caring needs, a finding supported by other studies of carers.[29]

Among other respondents, the salience of time sovereignty discussed earlier contributed to a mismatch between their needs and those of employers. The 'wee part-time job' that many thought they might be willing to do turned out to be a fantasy job in terms of pay, location, flexibility in hours and job satisfaction that they aimed for.

> So I won't be doing regular work but I won't necessarily be stopping altogether. It's just so that it enables us if we want to go on holidays for six weeks to Spain in term time we can go because we've got a caravan so we take it abroad … (female_working).

Similarly, when articulating the kind of flexible work that they might consider after retirement, a number of retired respondents suggested jobs or work patterns that were unlikely to be obtainable:

> … but the thing is about any job that I would want, is the sort of job where I can say … I'm maybe just on the internet and looking at flights and things and "God, look at … I could fly to so and so next week for that" and I'll go and on the meantime you're on the shift that they need you at B&Q [British retailer well-known for employing older workers] or whatever … I would need to be able to say "oh I'm not coming in next week" and very few employers would give you that flexibility. (male_retired)

3.6   Reason 5: Narrowness of Notions of 'Flexible Work'

A final set of possible explanations as to why the reality of flexible working appears not to live up to the rhetoric is related to the narrow ways in which flexible work has been conceptualised and is measured. Two

---

[29] S Vickerstaff et al (2009) *The Employment Support Needs.*

aspects of this narrowness emerged through the accounts presented by the poorest respondents, and through those presented by many of the women in the sample.

Firstly, looking at the poorest respondents, many of whom were economically inactive, few in this group had any hopes of being officially employed again for reasons mainly connected with their often extensive health problems. While some said they might like to work on a part-time or other flexible basis, none felt this was practically feasible. Some had investigated part-time work, a couple even went as far as accepting jobs, such as this man who had taken up part-time low-paid and low-skilled work as a cleaner after an industrial accident ended his career as a welder:

> I just wanted to get back to work…now we're screwed again…should have stayed on the sick. (male_working)

He could not increase his hours because his GP had put a limit on the hours he can work, and he had ended up being worse off financially than when he was on benefits. His experience was echoed by others and resulted in people staying on benefits and not taking up opportunities for flexible work.

Several of these respondents were also disadvantaged by a lack of basic literacy skills and confidence, and in the case of a couple of respondents, criminal records. Many of these reasons echoed those found in other studies of the long-term older unemployed.[30] As a consequence of all these constraints, flexible working for people in this group most often meant working in the informal economy, such as 'private' work in the building trade, or earning money via car boot sales, or cash-in-hand cleaning jobs.

Further considerations of flexible working in the informal economy were seen among several women in our sample, many of whom, as well as caring for dependants, cared for neighbours and friends, all on an unpaid basis. One woman, who described herself as retired, was looking after a couple of elderly neighbours, doing their shopping, cleaning and personal care: 'it's unpaid as we've been friends for a long time' (female_retired).

---

[30] L Porcellato, F Carmichael, C Hulme, B Ingham, and A Prashar,(2010) 'Giving older workers a voice: constraints on the employment of older people in the North West of England', *Work, Employment and Society* 24 (1), 85–103.

Others did not even conceive of their work as such, preferring instead to refer to 'helping out'. As discussed elsewhere,[31] for many older workers, especially women, flexibility has meaning far beyond standard labour market definitions.

This qualitative investigation of flexible working as a way of extending working lives offers insights into why official labour market statistics are not showing higher prevalence of flexible working and challenges the dominant policy thinking that flexible working is widely available to, and/or desired, by the older workforce. In addition, the analysis has also explored gender differences in more detail, highlighting fundamental differences in the ways in which men and women may experience opportunities and constraints around later-life working. The wider implications of these findings are considered in the final section of this chapter.

4   Discussion and Policy Implications

Overall, people are working longer and retiring later than in recent decades, and the nature of later working life is undoubtedly changing, but the key argument presented in this chapter is that policy assumptions—or even exhortations—that extending working life is inevitable or universally desirable may be overstated. This final section brings together findings from the various studies covered in this chapter to draw out implications for future policy approaches in this area.

Firstly, as the analysis of the British Labour Force Survey confirms, traditional 'cliff-edge' retirement, that is, moving from full-time work to full-time retirement at, or before, the age of eligibility for the state old age pension or normal pension scheme retirement dates, is still common, especially for men. Women are more likely to retire from part-time jobs, but these are jobs they have held for some time, not taken up as part of a gradual transition to retirement. Only a minority of both sexes are in paid employment beyond the age of 65. On this basis, one could question the extent to which people actually wish to extend their working

---

[31] W Loretto and S Vickerstaff, (2015) 'Gender, age and flexible working in later life', *Work Employment and Society* 29 (2), 233–249.

lives. The abolition of the default retirement age is still in its infancy, and there is likely to be a lag in behaviours, not least due to a lack of awareness of the change. Those fortunate enough to have defined benefit pensions may still be working towards their pension scheme retirement date. However, the ongoing decline of such schemes is likely to loosen retirement ages. Moreover, other research currently being conducted by the author suggests that the ability of people to draw their pension while remaining in work—a legislation which was introduced in 2006—is now starting to have an effect on decisions to remain in work for longer, so the number of people in employment in their 60s and beyond is likely to retain its upward trajectory. Nevertheless, from the material presented in this chapter, it is important to note that pensions and the financial afford-ability of retirement, while important, are often not the primary drivers of older workers' decisions and behaviours. This seems to be overlooked by policymakers. Choice is hugely important to people, but as the quali-tative work reported here illustrates, choice is very unevenly distributed and is constrained by a myriad of interrelated factors including health, caring responsibilities, gender and social class. Aggregated labour market figures mask the significant heterogeneity of experiences, situations and preferences.

The second discussion point to emerge is that the almost exclusive focus on paid work in policy debates serves to undermine older workers' situations and their wider contributions to societies and economies. As the reinvention in retirement survey suggested, people may wish to leave paid work in order to contribute more to local communities or to volun-teer. In addition, many women, and increasingly men, make a significant contribution to the economy through caring, either eldercare, or as was suggested here, via grandparenting. In this way, the boundaries between paid and unpaid work may blur more in later life, especially for women.[32]

A third, and related, point is that the notion of active ageing has become similarly constrained (or hijacked) by the focus on paid work. Respondents in the reinvention survey confirmed the importance of remaining active as a reason for reinventing themselves in retirement, but it was clear that most of these reinventions were not related to paid work.

---

[32] W Loretto and S Vickerstaff (2015) 'Gender, age and flexible working'.

As well as reflecting the heterogeneity of circumstances, preferences and needs, these 'choices' also highlight another flaw in assumptions which appear to underpin policy thinking—that people make these choices as individuals.[33] As argued elsewhere,[34] and demonstrated in the qualitative investigation of flexible work in later working life, decisions around later-life working and retirement are made in conjunction with partners and families, and reflect a combination of long-held domestic roles and assumptions which are often highly gendered.

In the UK and elsewhere, there is increasing attention paid to the concept of i-deals, or individually negotiated deals between an employer and employee, in connection with decisions around later working life and transitions to retirement.[35, 36] Such moves are welcome in that they recognise individual choice and heterogeneity of circumstances. Extending the concept beyond paid work would represent a real revolution in the ways in which we conceive of longer working lives. A holistic i-deal would recognise options beyond paid employment, to include contributions to economies and societies through caring and voluntary work. It would bring together policymakers, employers and older workers. Recent work across a range of European countries[37] has emphasised the importance of this type of multi-level approach in moving forward agenda around employment in later lives. In conclusion, this chapter wholly endorses that perspective, and maintains that it is crucial to avoid perpetuating myths and bias around older workers' attitudes and behaviours. A further key aspect of a holistic i-deal would be a life course analysis,[38] necessary to recognise the interconnectedness of different patterns of paid and

---

[33] J Lewis (2007) 'Gender, Ageing and the 'New Social Settlement': The Importance of Delivering a Holistic Approach to Care Policies' *Current Sociology* 55,271–286.

[34] W Loretto and S Vickerstaff (2013) 'The Domestic and Gendered Context for Retirement' *Human Relations* 66 (1), 65–86.

[35] P M Bal, S B De Jong, P G W Jansen and A B Bakker (2012 'Motivating employees to work beyond retirement: A multi-level study of the role of i-deals and unit climate', *Journal of Management Studies* 49 (2), 306–331.

[36] C Atkinson and P Sandiford (2015) 'An exploration of older worker flexible working arrangements in smaller firms', *Human Resource Management Journal*. Accessed via Early On-Line.

[37] H M Hasselhorn and W Apt (eds) (2015) *Understanding Employment Participation of Older Workers: Creating a knowledge base for future labour market challenges* (Federal Ministry of Labour and Social Affairs and Federal Institute for Occupational Safety and Health).

[38] Hasselhorn and Apt (2015) *Understanding Employment Participation.*

unpaid work throughout life and how these affect decisions around later-life work and retirement. Failure to embrace this perspective merely risks reinforcing existing inherent structural inequalities between (older) men and women, and makes a mockery of the very notion of older worker choice.

The aim of this chapter was to offer some insight into what older workers in the UK want from their later working lives. It has questioned the dominant policy thrust that this is necessarily more paid employment, whatever the format. It has drawn attention to the diversity of experiences and expectations of older workers, focusing in particular on the differences between men and women. The conclusions support a small, but growing, body of work which calls for more nuanced analysis of the realities of the contemporary labour market in making predictions about the nature of the future work landscape. Longevity is indeed increasing and bringing with it both problems and opportunities. To address these, we now need to decouple living longer from working longer.

10

Work and Careers: Narratives from Knowledge Workers Aged 48–58

Karen Handley and Birgit den Outer

1   Introduction

A weakness of the burgeoning policy-related literature on older workers is a tendency to treat 'older workers' as a single, homogenous group,[1] overlooking the influence of intersectional factors such as income, education, social background, occupation, age and the type-of-work on individual experience. Only 'gender' has attracted sustained research attention, yet other socio-demographic characteristics are likely to have effects which are just as important. To take one example, professionally qualified accountants have very different opportunities in later life compared with car assembly workers whose activities are tied to 'the track' and therefore lack portability. Age itself is a key variable in older worker research. The experiences, motivations and aspirations of a 50-year-old are likely to be barely comparable with those of an 85-year-old; the 35-year gap is almost a generational difference. This heterogeneity of older worker experiences, contexts and situations

---

[1] S Vickerstaff, W Loretto and P White (2007) 'The future for older workers: opportunities and constraints' in W Loretto, S Vickerstaff and P White (eds) *The Future for older workers: new perspectives* (Polity Press) 203–226.

suggests that research should be more attentive to variations. This can be partly achieved by investigating sub-groups within the broader 'older worker' category. The potential advantage of doing so is a greater understanding of older workers, which may lead to more targeted policymaking. This study seeks to contribute to this broader agenda by focusing on one particular group of workers: those aged between 48 and 58 years employed in, or studying at, a higher education institution. People in this group are getting older, but are certainly not elderly, and they potentially have many years of work ahead of them. In the literature and the media, they are often referred to as the 'sandwiched' generation with caring responsibilities for their offspring as well as for longer living parents.

In the next section, the chapter proposes a narrative approach to older worker research, and then introduces the research context, including the 15 participants in our study. The chapter then presents the similarities in participants' narratives, as well as four variants in the types of narratives they tell (renewal; seeking progression; winding down; and reorienting the 'self' away from work). Key implications are then discussed—in particular, the possibility that older workers are diverting their productive capabilities away from work as they search for a meaningful narrative for their future lives.

2   Bringing the 'Narrative Turn' to Older Worker Research

The narrative turn in the social sciences[2] has expanded and enriched the repertoire of approaches by which we can explore older worker experiences, identities and decision-making. It is not that new narratives have been 'discovered', but rather, the value of narrative approaches is becoming appreciated and acknowledged. Alongside conventional survey methods and statistical data, narratives offer complementary insights. By hearing others' narratives of their pasts as well as their imagined futures, we can broaden our understanding of how they perceive the work-related

---

[2] B Czarniawska (2003) *Narratives in Social Science Research* (Sage Publications).

choices they believe are feasible or appropriate for themselves. Narratives thus provide a framework for the temporal dimension of our lives, within which we 'craft'[3] our identities. Narratives give insights about how we think, and not just what we think; they reveal the options we consider, and not just the actions we finally take.

Narratives also offer insights into socialisation processes. This is because the way individuals talk about their imagined futures reveals something of the range of cultural stories or 'scripts' they believe to be available to them. Taken together, collected narratives produce what Czarniawska calls the 'history of narratives'. As she explains, 'to understand a society or some part of society, it is important to discover its repertoire of legitimate stories and find out how it evolved'.[4] Narratives provide insights into the identity positions that people feel are available to take on (such as 'grey-haired sage'), or which they feel constrained by (such as the 'old dear'). They shine a light on how individuals construct their work 'potential', as well as how that potential might be interpreted by others. Thus, narrative methods open up the space for critical enquiries into the politics of cultural discourses about what is 'normal' behaviour as an older worker, and whether idealised identities are accessible to everyone.

3   Insights from Existing Narrative Research

Although contemporary narrative research has tended to focus on young people's decision-making,[5] another strand of research has investigated individuals' experiences in periods of transition. These include experiences of redundancy among senior managers over 50 years of age,[6] narratives of unemployment,[7] and research on the narrative identity

---

[3] D Kondo (1990) *Crafting selves: Power, Gender, And Discourses Of Identity In A Japanese Workplace,* (University of Chicago Press).

[4] Czarniawska (2003) 5.

[5] For example, J Brannen and A Nilsen (2002) 'Young people's time perspectives: from youth to adulthood', *Sociology* 36/3, 513–536; M Anderson, F Bechhofer, D McCrone, L Jamieson, Y Li and R Stewart (2005) 'Timespans and plans among young adults', *Sociology* 39/1, 139–155.

[6] Y Gabriel, D Gray and H Goregaokar (2010) 'Temporary derailment or the end of the line? Managers coping with unemployment at 50' *Organization Studies,* 31/12, 1687–1712.

[7] D Ezzy (2001) *Narrating unemployment* (Ashgate).

of knowledge workers in times of organisational change.[8] A dominant theme in this work is the performative value of individuals' narrative strategies to maintain, revise and mediate their personal and social identities. For example, Mallett and Wapshott's study of a fast-expanding and increasingly commercial design studio showed how workers adjusted their personal narratives in order to retain a sense of the value of their knowledge work, for example, by re-positioning their career as 'developing' even in the midst of troubled organisational change.

Narrative analysis is less prevalent in research with older workers. Instead, perhaps due to the influence of gerontology and labour market studies, there has been a tendency towards creating typologies of decision-making.[9] McNair,[10] for example, identified three clusters of older workers' retirement behaviour and work orientations: choosers, survivors and jugglers. In a study of UK managers aged over 50 years, Bown-Wilson and Parry[11] identified a typology of four career orientations: stick, switch, slow down, and strive. Interestingly, their sampling strategy was still framed by retirement, since they selected managers who were in the process of planning for that event.

This chapter seeks to contribute to the debates on older workers by addressing some of the limitations of previous studies. Firstly, to counter-balance the tendency to homogenise 'older workers', this study looked at a particular group of workers: those aged between 48 and 58 years involved in knowledge work. Secondly, to counter the emphasis (especially in policy research) on surveys and statistical approaches, this study took a narrative approach and explored individuals' stories of their past working lives and their imagined futures. Thirdly, although involved in the knowledge economy, our participants represented a wide diversity of older workers in terms of career

---

[8] O Mallett and R Wapshott (2012) 'Mediating ambiguity: narrative identity and knowledge workers' *Scandinavian Journal of Management* 28, 16–26.

[9] This tendency is to some extent replicated in our study, which has created a typology of participants' narratives.

[10] S McNair (2006) 'How different is the older labour market? Attitudes to work and retirement among older people in Britain' *Social Policy & Society* 5/4, 485–494.

[11] D Bown-Wilson and E Parry (2013) 'Career progression in older managers' *Employee Relations* 35/3, 309–321.

stage, work history, educational background, and in factors such as having co-dependents, carer responsibilities, and so on.

4   The Field Research

The methodology was based on narrative and situational approaches, drawing on scholars such as Gabriel, Clarke, Czarniawska and Ezzy.[12] Participants were invited as part of an open call to staff and (mature) students at a post-1992 British university. The call invited individuals aged 48–58 years who were working, or between jobs, in the knowledge sector to take part in the interview-based research to discuss their working lives and how they saw the future of work for themselves.

During interviews, we asked participants to reflect on their decisions, aspirations, hopes and fears, in order to explore not only what they did, but also what had shaped their decisions. This is because we wanted to know what discursive and cultural resources they drew on as they constructed their identities, work trajectories and imagined futures. Interviews lasted from one to two-and-a-half hours, and all conversations were recorded and subsequently transcribed.

A key aspect of analysis was its iterative and dialogic nature. As collaborative researchers, we spent considerable time reading transcripts and then discussing and comparing our interpretations and impressions. Long summaries (each of about four pages) were then written up for each participant, combining condensed notes, interpretative memos and illustrative quotations. The proprietary software MAXQDA was used for data management and indexing purposes. Table 10.1 provides the socio-demographic profiles of our participants.[13] Of the 15 participants, 12 were employed at the university, and three were mature students with backgrounds in the knowledge economy, taking computing or psychology degrees. Most of our participants were women.

---

[12] Gabriel, 2010; Czarniawska, 2003; Ezzy, 2001; A Clarke (2005) *Situational analysis: grounded theory after the postmodern turn*. (Thousand Oaks: Sage).

[13] Pseudonyms and age-ranges have been used, to protect confidentiality.

Table 10.1 Demographic profile of participants

Category of 'career'	Reference		Age group	Current occupation
Frequent job moves	Julia	F	48–51	Senior administration, HE
	John	M	52–55	Senior administration, HE
	Jenny	F	52–55	Senior administration, HE
	Rebecca	F	48–51	Academic
	Maddy	F	52–55	F/t mature student, after career in software engineering and project management
	Richard	M	48–51	P/t mature student and A/V technical engineer
	Nicola	F	48–51	Academic
	Cathy	F	56–58	Senior administration, HE
	Simon	M	52–55	P/t mature student and electrical engineer
Worked in few organisations	Debbie	F	56–58	Senior administration, HE
	Maria	F	48–51	Senior administration, HE
	Susan	F	56–58	Senior management, HE
	Emma	F	52–55	Academic
	Bronte	F	48–51	Senior administration, HE
	Sylvia	F	52–55	Academic

5   Some Core Similarities in Participants' Narratives

A central feature of the narratives was the complexity of the career trajectories. These were narratives of accidental career turns and serendipitous opportunities, especially in participants' early careers but also to a lesser extent in their later career paths. Nine of the 15 participants reported frequent job moves, identifying two or more career shifts among those jobs. Of the other six participants, those who had worked in only a few organisations, not one person had begun their working life in the occupation they now inhabited. A feature of the narratives was the often casual nature of early career [post-education] decisions. Most participants talked of their first jobs as accidents: 'just a place to start'; 'almost a non-decision'; 'I simply went for jobs I thought I could pull off'.

Some participants were firm in labelling their narratives as 'not a career' but [merely] a series of jobs. This raises questions about how the meaning of 'career' is personally understood and socially constructed, and relates to reflexive issues around self-worth. In our interviews, the word 'jobs' was used more than 'career', the latter being associated with progressive ladders, or scripts one could follow, or a broader sense of work which carried status because of its impact on society. There seemed a reluctance to presume that one had a 'career', but also some ambivalence. Sylvia, for example, talked of moving into lecturing from accountancy, but said she did not see it as a career because she had no plans to seek promotion. She explained:

> I didn't think, 'Oh, I want to be Dean one day.' No. I saw it as a really interesting job that I could combine with family life.

A core theme in these work narratives was a sense of crafting a journey. The journey involved responding to serendipitous events and circumstances, or more proactively deciding to initiate an exciting change of direction. What was rare was a sense of planning far ahead. Rather, there seemed a preference for crafting a journey that made sense in the here-and-now, referred to by Nowotny[14] as the 'extended present'. Planning was resisted because it closed down the imagined space of future opportunities—the possibility and hopefulness that 'things might turn up that are interesting' [Sylvia]. Improvisation, rather than planning, allowed for the crafting of one's own destiny. We can see this perhaps as a strategy of resistance to what Gullette[15] calls the 'master narrative of decline'. By avoiding a long-term plan, one avoids having to demarcate the end-point or the dead-end.

There were, of course, influences and life events which shaped how participants crafted their career journeys. Women who became mothers made the greatest adaptations, such as changing to part-time work (or withdrawing from work for limited periods), or changing jobs to increase family income. Now in their late 40s or 50s, the women who had continued to work flexibly were able to increase their hours and commitment as their children became independent, thus avoiding some

---

[14] H Nowotny (1994) *Time: the modern and postmodern experience* (Polity Press).
[15] M Gullette (2004) *Aged by Culture* (University of Chicago Press).

Table 10.2 Dominant narratives in our sample, shown alongside profile of participants

Category of 'career'	Ref		Age group	Current occupation	Dominant narrative	Current outlook/story
Frequent job moves	Cathy	F	56–58	Senior administration, HE	[Waiting for] Renewal	Despondent, feeling 'stuck' in current role and capable of much more. Remains in current role because it suits family constraints. Once these are lifted, she feels her life (and work) can 'start again'
Frequent job moves	Rebecca	F	48–51	Academic	Renewal	Has a portfolio career and enjoys the freedom and space it brings. Sense of renewal (e.g., move into education) is accompanied by awareness of consolidating her sense-of-purpose around 'transforming care'. Public service motivation
Frequent job moves	Maddy	F	52–55	F/t mature student, after career in software engineering and project management	Renewal	Sees the UG degree as a 'lifebelt' opportunity which she grabbed without knowing where the experience would take her. Enjoying the journey
Frequent job moves	Richard	M	48–51	P/t mature student and A/V technical engineer	Renewal	Has almost completed p/t MSc in computer science. Is coming to understand why he became disillusioned with work [in media/advertising] and with low-calibre managers. Looking forward to improved freelance job prospects in IT-related roles

	Name		Age	Sector	Transition	Description
Worked in few organisations	Emma	F	52–55	Academic	Renewal	Recently completed her doctorate and is full of excitement about the research and development opportunities ahead. Feels she has 'only just started'
Worked in few organisations	Sylvia	F	52–55	Academic	Renewal	Consolidating her move into academic research, by doing doctorate. Excited by prospects of this transition and the impact that her research might have
Frequent job moves	Nicola	F	48–51	Academic	Renewal	Positive about the future. Has almost completed her doctorate. Looking forward to developing her teaching and research, and describes her work/role as a 'new career'
Frequent job moves	Julia	F	48–51	Senior administration, HE	Reorientation from work to other projects	Questioning her tendency towards continual striving and development - 'for what purpose?' Epiphanous moment when passed over [for a job for which she was 'exceptionally qualified'] for younger person. Coming to terms with 'not going anywhere', and reorienting her energies towards other projects such as writing
Worked in few organisations	Maria	F	48–51	Senior administration, HE	Reorientation from work to other projects	Work is tedious. Professionalism and 'my own dignity' mean she maintains high standards in her work. Enjoyment is 'outside work'; and pleasure-at-work is from the environment and social relationships

(continued)

Table 10.2 (Continued)

Category of 'career'	Ref	Age group	Current occupation	Dominant narrative	Current outlook/story
Worked in few organisations	Bronte	F 48–51	Senior administration, HE	Reorientation from work to other projects	Enjoys her work but is not passionate about it. Enjoys the social relationships and the atmosphere of trust and respect. Has important interests outside of work
Frequent job moves	John	M 52–55	Senior administration, HE	Seeking progression	5 years since last job move, and feels it's time to step back and let others through. Facing dilemma of staying put (where he feels he's 'doing good') vs. trying to progress (which his 'conscious' tells him to do)
Frequent job moves	Jenny	F 52–55	Senior administration, HE	Seeking progression	6 years since last job move. Feeling left behind as younger managers pass her on the career ladder. Wants to progress, but not optimistic
Worked in few organisations	Susan	F 56–58	Senior management, HE	Seeking progression	Enjoys current role and has opportunities to progress. Feels she has potential for one more significant role, and wants to make a contribution 'on a broader scale'
Frequent job moves	Simon	M 52–55	P/t mature student and electrical engineer	Seeking progression	Has almost completed p/t MSc in computer science. Hopes his MSc credentials will enhance his employability in his current sector, but is open to some renewal, e.g., IT consultancy work
Worked in few organisations	Debbie	F 56–58	Senior administration, HE	Winding down	Clearly sees her retirement horizon and wants to gradually reduce hours from 60, and retire at 65. Looks forward to the possibilities of interesting activities and projects in retirement. Apologises that the 'pottering' sounds 'really boring'

of the confidence problems associated with long-term absence from the workplace. More generally, for many of our research participants, the meaning and salience of work had changed since their early entry into the workplace. Some questioned their work's value and contribution to society; some were tired of the merry-go-round of IT consultancy 'solutions' they had seen repeatedly fail; some could now see (and wanted to begin) the next steps of a career trajectory which had hitherto been 'shrouded in mystique' [Emma]. This reorientation was significant for many of our participants, and provided a critically important platform for their future as 'older workers', opening doorways or prompting a reassessment of one's work-life balance. From our analysis, we categorised the ways in which participants responded to this reorientation using the typology provided in Table 10.2. The typology relates to the participants in our sample and so cannot be generalised beyond that, but nevertheless, it offers a conceptual contribution to research in the area of older workers. Before elaborating on this typology in a later section, some illustrations will be given to show how participants conceptualised work.

5.1   Changing Meaning of Work

Narratives are crafted in the context of cultural discourses and shared (or contested) understandings about the meaning of work. Our participants were reflecting on their working lives in the context of these discourses, and these influences can to some extent be seen in participants' assessment of where they were in their trajectories.

One theme from our interviews was the reassessment of the value of different types of work. Sylvia was one of several participants who had moved from teaching or the professions into higher education. Initially a part-time lecturer, Sylvia had extended her involvement as her children grew up, taking on programme roles as well as several innovative teaching projects. She explained that her turn towards research about four years ago was initiated because she felt she 'ought to; because of increased pressure to do research, but not because I was terribly interested'. She described how, over time, working in a university city, she had imbibed the discourse of academia and now felt she wanted to be able to say she was an academic, not just a lecturer, and she realised that that meant doing serious research and starting a doctorate. For Emma too, the route to respectability in academia was to do a doctorate, which she also saw as opening a pathway to professorship. For both participants, this reassessment of social worth initiated a renewed momentum in their career paths, and brought with it immense enjoyment and excitement.

Others asked questions about the wider impact of their work. Talk of one's contribution to society was prompted by various reasons, including prolonged exposure to one sector. Maddy, with 25 years' experience in software engineering, and later, in outsource consulting, talked of her decision to start a full-time undergraduate degree in the social sciences:

> There was an element of the futility of all this. [I thought] 'Why am I wasting my time, my human effort, everybody else's human effort on something that actually contributes nothing? OK, so there's a new ISA[16] on the market, big deal!' It just seems an unproductive use of human endeavour [Laughs].

Alongside this cynicism was boredom at work. In the past, Maddy used to be excited by the possibilities of new initiatives and new technologies, but had now seen the recycling of these initiatives too many times to have any faith in them as productive endeavours. She sorely needed a change to find renewed meaning in her working life. Richard told a similar story of becoming disillusioned with the media and advertising sector where he worked as an audio, visual, and graphics engineer. He had come to see the vacuousness of a consumer industry designed to seduce, sell and deceive, and could not bear any more of it. His response was to take up a part-time master's course in computer engineering, a welcome return to 'hard' science.

Another theme linked to meaning and contribution concerned shifting views about how to create positive change. There was a sense of seeing a bigger picture, and taking a more systemic perspective on social change. However, the consequences of this changed viewpoint differed. Rebecca, for example, had worked on multiple projects in health and

---

[16] An ISA is a tax-exempt savings vehicle in the UK.

social care, and was increasingly frustrated by the sector's bureaucracy, and the ineffectual chaos created by perennial reorganisations. She was now taking freelance roles to achieve her desire of transforming social care. This was 'scary' financially, but gave her freedoms beyond a 'job title':

> I was fed up with being in a subordinate role and not being able to make enough decisions about things, and being in a structure which actually needs reorganising and you can't do anything about it. I would have more freedom as a freelance and could also use different skills with different organisations and not be just channelled in one direction.

Richard made a similar shift, though this was more symbolic than real. His working life had always been about short-medium term contracts, but he explained that his career orientation had now changed, largely owing to his project management education in his master's. He discarded what he realised was an 'employee mentality', and felt he was now moving towards a consultancy mindset that was more professional and independent.

Whilst Richard and Rebecca epitomise the shift towards independence and working outside the organisation, John and Susan relished their work and influence within the organisation context. For John, work had changed its meaning because of a reappraisal of the value of people and relationships. In his youth, as an apprenticed carpenter and painter, he liked the satisfaction of seeing the concrete product of his labours. Now, after many years as a senior manager in estates management, he talked of networks, relationships and responsibility for others' development. One might even say he had become 'institutionalised' in the way he spoke about his management role.

6 Core Differences Between Participants' Narratives

Although participants shared similar tales of crafting a future trajectory of hope and possibilities, there were stark differences in their stories. Four categories were identified from our sample of 15 participants: narratives of renewal, of seeking progress, of winding down, and of reorienting the 'self' away from work. Table 10.2 summarises participants' individual narratives.

6.1   Narratives of Renewal

The spark that initiated a trajectory of renewal was often traceable to a reassessment of the meaning of one's work and life. As indicated earlier, reassessments of work tended to follow prolonged exposure to particular ways of working in an organisation or sector, provoking feelings of frustration, disillusionment, boredom or stagnation. For the disillusioned, 'progression' along the same path would have been anathema; they wanted to get away from the sector and start afresh in a new one, or at least (in the case of Rebecca) take a different position within the sector. For the three participants doing their doctorates, renewal was about making a serious commitment to a sector they had earlier joined as lecturers, from a professional career outside of academia, which would give them the status, identity and enjoyment of doing serious research 'as academics'.

A positive sense of renewal was palpable in participants' responses. Richard spoke of divesting himself of the employee mentality and regaining control as an independent consultant (albeit still with a client or contracting employer). Maddy called herself 'a teenager' starting afresh on her career journey. For Cathy, what sustained her tedious work was a vision that once her frail relative passed away and she no longer had caring responsibilities, she could retrain:

> It will be the end of an era, and I will literally cross into my next stage of life. I will be in control. I won't have anybody who—if the lawn doesn't get mowed, nobody will tell me when I get in the door, I can just leave it and hope the neighbours don't notice. And then I'll be able to focus on what's important to me.

Participants in this category were excited and emboldened by new challenges and new ventures. Novelty was important, as Nicola implied when commenting on her transition into higher education:

Whether I would be happy now if I'd done [the career move] earlier, I don't think so, because I think one of the reasons I'm quite happy and content in the roles that I've got at the moment is **because it's effectively a new career that's only five years old. I haven't had time to get disillusioned with the place.** [emphasis added]

She, and some others, reflected that the more one saw of an organisation, and the more one saw its 'rough edges', the less one idealised the job. It was as though this tarnished viewpoint had not yet infected those on a renewal pathway. Thus, the optimism of 'renewal' challenges conventional notions of midlife being a time of decline. These interviewees saw the future very differently and more positively. Several commented that they had 10–15 years ahead of them, which meant that the career they were embarking on might be the longest period of time they had ever spent in the same job. This was no mere 'bridge' job before retirement.

6.2   Narratives of Seeking Progression

Progression was the intended career trajectory of four participants. The narrative here was about staying in the same sector or organisation, and moving up a fairly clearly defined ladder. This is not to say that an upwards move was inevitable. Jenny, for example, talked of wanting to progress but seeing younger managers pass her by. She sensed that the organisation wanted 'fresh blood'; a theme we return to later regarding the notion of 'potential'. Susan, in her late 50s, felt she had the capacity for 'another big job', and was already networking and engaging in extracurricular posts in order to demonstrate (when a job opportunity arose) that she still had the energy and motivation to do an important job well. She feared that after 60, she might be seen as 'past it'.

6.3   Narratives of Winding Down

An orientation towards 'winding down' was dominant in only one of our participants. Debbie, in her mid-50s, had worked in higher education for about 15 years, and talked of a gradual reduction in her contractual hours, moving to part-time work at 60, and retiring at 65. Her fears, which were also articulated by another long-serving employee, were about the implications of 'going part-time'. Her fears were primarily about loss: of involvement, social interaction, and having one's fingers on the pulse. Alongside loss might come intensification of work, driven by the fear that the same job would have to be done in reduced hours. Neither participant who talked of these worries raised any concerns about loss of status. One [Bronte] ascribed this to the normalised prevalence of part-time working in the public sector. However, their responses may reflect a gendered effect, and warrants further investigation.

6.4   Narratives of Reorienting 'Self' Away from Work

The fourth orientation category concerns a reorientation of the sense of self, away from work and towards other sources of enjoyment and self-worth. It seems reasonable to ask why these participants (there were three) did not seek renewal. The main distinction is that 'renewal', as defined in our proposed typology, concerns a renewal of career. The participants in the 'reorienting' category were directing their attentions away from work and towards other sources of interest, including self-development. Perhaps the main driver behind this reorientation was that these participants shared a lack of intrinsic enjoyment from their current job. All three were in senior administrative roles, and perhaps did not see the sort of alternative career path which the lecturers in our sample envisioned through doing doctoral research. Their work was important, but felt tedious at times; pleasure came from the workplace environment and from relationships with people.

Participants in this category made a point of assuring the interviewer that they performed their jobs well and were conscientious. Their sense of dignity and professionalism were maintained by ensuring that their work and the work of their teams were of a high standard. But, as one person explained: 'that doesn't mean I find it interesting to do; I do it because that's what you do'. There was perhaps some identity positioning in the way participants distanced themselves from work which they did not value. One person asserted that she was not defined by her job, and thought it was rather sad when others did so. She also talked of not wanting a 'higher-up job' because that would mean more stress 'and reporting', as though not necessarily more valuable than what she contributed currently. Another participant talked of an epiphanous moment in her recent past where she tried for a job for which she was 'exceptionally qualified', only to see it given to a young person without dependents because (as her job interviewer rather rashly admitted) she was likely to give less discretionary effort to the work than the younger candidate without children. Her reaction was to start reorienting herself towards other pursuits that were enjoyable, such as extending her involvement in local music and artistic groups. Others, too, reoriented their attentions and sense of self homewards, investing in activities that were not 'new', but that might have been dormant, such as writing, crafts, music and dance.

7   Potential

Many participants in our study reflexively considered their own potential, and talked of how they might appear to others. When asked what they felt they contributed 'as an older worker', there were common themes: they felt they had a broader perspective, were able to question strategies and not just implement them, were more sanguine and less hot-headed, had more skilful communications skills, and were more empathetic and therefore able to understand what others wanted and needed. There was also disappointment that experience and expertise built up over many years in an occupation or sector did not seem to be appreciated by others, such as those with the power to influence career progression and those with less experience. The ability to learn similar processes and technologies quickly—by building on pre-existing knowledge—seemed unappreciated. Cathy reflected on why this situation might persist:

> I've learnt in life that people can only see as far as their experience allows them to see; they can only understand the value of something if they know

what the value is, anything else will just not be noticed because we all evaluate the outside world according to our standards and the highest we can go in those standards. So if somebody has a great insight into something, those witnessing it will only perceive if it they can understand it.

Cathy talked of how she learnt to bite her tongue rather than intervene to suggest alternative ways of doing things to her colleagues: she'd been 'pushed down too many times'. Others were more sanguine, recognising that experience can't be 'taught', but acknowledging that avoidable mistakes might be made by others. This apparent passivity—watching predictable mistakes unfold—might seem irresponsible, but interviewees seemed unsure of what to do instead. There was recognition that organisations wanted 'fresh ideas; fresh blood'—graduates who were 'malleable' and could be socialised easily. Older workers, almost by definition, could not offer that. Some talked of their growing irritation about being asked to mentor and develop others who would soon overtake them. This situation seemed more prevalent in senior administrative roles. Cathy illustrates the frustrations of this double-speak:

> I'm so tired of him [manager] coming to me and saying, 'Oh, so and so wants the younger ones, I'd like you to work with her [the younger recruit], because it's an opportunity for her growth,' and I said to him, 'What about my growth?' … It seems like there are two languages, the young get this and people are put into positions as an opportunity for growth, but with the older ones, suddenly they say, 'Well you didn't have this or that.' And so you don't go to [selection] interviews.

On the other hand, John, a senior manager already, talked of wanting to let others come in with new ideas, but perhaps because he was more positive about the likelihood that he could seek out and get a promotion. 'Potential' was seen as an attribute of the young, and if you were stuck in the same job for too long, your potential (based on prior experience and knowledge) would become invisible. There was a vicious circle of invisibility as one got older, and also a visibility of getting older. This was especially problematic for women. Rebecca pondered whether she needed to have a certain level of seniority before she could stop dyeing her hair and become grey. Maddy felt that older women are respected and valued in the workplace, but only if they have a senior role, and in any case, the respect would be 'for clichéd reasons' and not necessarily desirable. Cathy talked of a potential new role in the future if she could make herself invisible and only 'virtually present' so that she could hide her age whilst producing work of the quality of an 18-year-old. A rather different strategy was adopted by Susan, who endeavoured to signal her continued energy and commitment by taking on more discretionary responsibilities, including non-executive leadership roles.

The narratives show that 'potential' can be rekindled, but perhaps only in certain circumstances. It is interesting to note that the three participants embarking on or finishing their doctorates had a strongly positive sense of their own potential. This seemed linked to the possibility, in higher education, to [re]start a career with a doctorate. One could be an older 'early career researcher', and as such, the benefits of presumed potential were more attainable.

8   Retirement

'Retirement' seemed remote for most participants. It was part of the temporal horizon, but not necessarily attractive because of its connotations of finality. Retirement was in some ways more of a mental challenge than a practical one; and many participants were ambivalent about it.

Less than half mentioned any concerns about finances. Among those who did, none seemed to have translated this concern into a work-to-retirement plan for financial security. Even those who described themselves as largely motivated by money were unsure of their pension provision. One person worried about the further dismantling of the welfare state, implying that focused planning was fairly futile given this uncertainty. More generally, finances were 'in the background': none of the participants had yet made specific retirement plans based on financial calculations of future income and expenses. For some, their future was populated by 'pensionable age' dates. Debbie, for example, spoke of going part-time at 60, and retiring at 65. Age as a 'stepping-off point' featured in the conversations of long-serving employees, albeit with some uncertainly as to the State Pension Age that applied to their cohort. But more generally, interview questions about retirement prompted some ambivalence. Retirement was about freedom, flexibility and time.

> [Retirement means] being in a position financially, emotionally, to be able to say …'yes' or'no' to what you wanted to do…. And it's certainly **nothing** about **not** doing things, it's all about doing what you want to do. [Nicola]

Retirement gave one options and opportunities, but also a restfulness that was almost mentioned in hushed tones as though inappropriate. Debbie apologised for admitting that she might actually spend time 'pottering' in the garden—'it sounds really boring'. Earlier in the conversation, she had reeled off a number of possible activities such as helping children read, doing things in the village, talking to people in a hospital, and looking after dogs. Her later admission implies that some 'identity work' was going on.[17] What seemed important was to convey (to oneself, or the interviewer) a positive sense of opportunities and options, creating a positive image of one's future 'possible self',[18] and presenting a range of possibilities rather than a cliff-edge of decline and misery after work. Others said they would be 'bored at home'; the solution was 'voluntary work in the community; anything really' [Jenny], and 'charity work or whatever' [Richard], implying a sense of bits-and-pieces which was rather vague as though something had to be there to fill a possible, but unacceptable, void. A few, such as Rebecca, talked of wanting to work for as long as they could:

> I think I'll just keep working at whatever I can work at for as long as I can.
>   I: Where do you picture yourself at 75/80?
>   Well I hope by 80 I would be retired! < Laughs > But I would like to still be involved. I would probably volunteer for charities, I would probably be a trustee for something. I'd probably be running little, local things in my community, I wouldn't want to just be sitting at home. [I'll be] taking up

---

[17] M Alvesson H Willmott (2002) 'Identity regulation as organizational control: producing the appropriate individual' *Journal of Management Studies* 39/5, 619–644.

[18] H Markus and P Nurius (1986) 'Possible Selves' *American Psychologist* 41, 954–969.

new hobbies and doing things which I haven't had a chance to do before. So I could see my retirement being very busy' < laughs >.

9 Conclusion

This exploratory study, grounded in the specific setting of university employment and education, has generated a number of themes with implications for the active ageing agenda, and for understanding the experiences of 'younger' older workers. Themes include: the prevalence of narratives of hope, renewal and reorientation; resistance to the 'master narrative of decline'; leakage of energies away from the workplace; and the problematic discourse of 'potential'.

In their conversations about work, life and the future, participants in our study were crafting narratives which constructed for themselves something positive, something to look forward to. Even the gloomiest story of being 'stuck' was interspersed with slivers of hope: Cathy was staunchly optimistic that her life would re-start once her caring responsibilities were completed. The narratives were hopeful and varied. Those who saw a pathway of career renewal, for example becoming a research academic through the transitional step of doing a doctorate, or who had taken opportunities to re-educate themselves, told very different stories from those who felt stuck in a department with limited scope for job movement. The latter participants could not see a development path at work, and instead talked of taking up new pursuits outside of work, of diverting their creative energies elsewhere whilst retaining a professional commitment to performing their work well. The dominant theme across all participants was a drive to create a (future) narrative which offered opportunities to flourish, to deflect identity threats signalled by the 'master narrative of decline',[19] and to push back the boredom of retirement. Restfulness seemed to be non-permissible and almost frightening in its cavernous emptiness, pushed back by the possibilities for 'bits-and-pieces' of other activities.

---

[19] Gullette, 2004; H Vough, C Bataille, S Noh and M Lee (2015) 'Going off script: how managers make sense of the ending of their careers' *Journal of Management Studies* 52/3, 414–440.

This human need to hope, dream and create an imagined future is a theme which resonates in the arts and literatures of all cultures. It is exemplified in literature such as Viktor Frankl's *Man's Search for Meaning*,[20] an account of extreme suffering and hope in Nazi concentration camps. What our study shows is that in searching for meaning, some participants were withdrawing their energies and discretionary efforts from paid work to seek a more positive sense of self elsewhere, for example in voluntary work, creative endeavours or social activities. An implication of this is the risk that the productive capability of older workers may be seeping out of the paid-work sector of the economy. Our findings point to a tension between older workers' desire for interesting developments and to create a strong sense of their working self, and the positions that are culturally available or assigned to them by their organisations. This is perhaps ironic given that a legacy of the human relations movement, following Maslow and others, has been 'a continuous effort [from employers] to co-opt the individual's mental and spiritual energies in the service of profit'.[21] These co-opting processes seem to be focused on younger workers, neglecting the energetic potential of older workers. What our participants did not want was merely to be asked to 'look after' others who were being promoted in their place—to be unpaid (and undervalued) workplace carers. A key message from our participants was that as older workers, they have much to offer. They feel capable of doing more, and are far from 'past it'.

---

[20] V Frankl (2004/1946) *Man's search for meaning: The classic tribute to hope from the Holocaust* (Rider).

[21] A Lait (2012) *Telling tales: work, narrative and identity in a market age* (Manchester University Press) 120.

11

Function, Flexibility, and Responsibility: Differences Between the Former Professional Job and Post-retirement Activities

Leena Pundt, Jürgen Deller, Kenneth S. Shultz, and Ulrike Fasbender

1   Introduction

This chapter highlights the differences between retirees' former professional jobs and their present post-retirement activities. To date, there are no empirical findings with regard to retirees' comparative perceptions of experienced differences. Understanding retirees' views would allow organizations to develop adequate transition plans as well as design post-retirement activities that are both attractive and beneficial to retirees. This is particularly important as the value of working retirees—and the necessity of integrating working retirees into organizations—is likely to increase in the future. Therefore, we pose the following overall research question:

> What are the experienced differences between retirees' former professional jobs and present post-retirement activities?

In order to acquire an unbiased perspective on the perceived differences between former professional jobs and activities in retirement, we present a qualitative-quantitative approach using two samples of German active

© The Editor(s) (if applicable) and The Author(s) 2016
S. Manfredi, L. Vickers (eds.), *Challenges of Active Ageing*,
DOI 10.1057/978-1-137-53251-0_11

retirees. In this chapter, we aim at revealing relevant job dimensions in addition to those identified in the research literature. Furthermore, we share additional insights gained about the target group of active retirees in Germany.

With regard to the context in which post-retirement activities take place, it is important to note that the nature of retirement has become more dynamic and diverse.[1] New concepts, such as successful aging at work, are being developed as a consequence of economic and political pressure to retain older people at work for as long as possible.[2] At the same time, aging populations and increasing life expectancy present policymakers with challenges, in particular, regarding social security schemes.[3,4] Many highly developed countries' pension systems are becoming increasingly difficult to sustain financially as a result of changing population compositions. As such, the percentage of older people in relation to the total population will significantly grow in the coming years.[5] For instance, Germany, one of the biggest economies in the world, is facing a strong upward trend from 16% (12.7 million) of people aged 65 years and older in 1995 to 21% (17.3 million) in 2015 to 30% (23.2 million) in 2035, as indicated by the Federal Statistical Office of Germany.[6] Several other countries will encounter a similar increase, assuming continued birth rates, migration trends, and the estimated life expectancy of newborn children. Also, the lifetime remaining after formal retirement is further rising in many

[1] K S Shultz & M Wang (2011) 'Psychological perspectives on the changing nature of retirement' *American Psychologist*, 66,170–177 doi: 10.1037/a0022411.

[2] H Zacher (2015) 'Successful Aging at Work' *Work, Aging and Retirement* 1(1), 4 25. doi:10.1093/workar/wau006.

[3] Organization for Economic Cooperation and Development [OECD] (2006) *Live longer, work longer*, (OECD Publishing) Retrieved from: http://www.oecd.org/document/42/0,3343 ,en_649_34747_36104426_1_1_1_1,00.html [Accessed 21 October 2015].

[4] OECD (2013) *Pensions at a glance 2013: Retirement-income systems in OECD and G20 countries*: (OECD Publishing).

[5] Eurostat (2015) 'Population structure and ageing' Retrieved from http://ec.europa.eu/eurostat/statistics-explained/index.php/Population_structure_and_ageing Accessed 21 October 2015.

[6] Federal Statistical Office of Germany (2015) '13th coordinated population projection for Germany'. Retrieved from https://www.destatis.de/bevoelkerungspyramide/ Accessed 21 October 2015.

developed countries.[7] Some economists note that this aging trend will prove to be an enormous burden on people of working age (often people aged 20 to 65 years), who would have to contribute to social expenditure related to a range of health, care and leisure services required by the people of retirement age (often people aged 65 and older). As a result, this has led to a series of politically difficult and controversial reforms, such as the increase of the retirement eligibility age (e.g. from 65 to 67 in Germany).[8]

In addition, the existing shortage of skilled workers in some industries will continue to grow in the coming years. For instance, Germany is expected to encounter an increased demand for intermediate and high-skilled labor as well as to develop an increasingly service-oriented economy in the long-term future. Up until 2030, the country is expected to face labor shortages in the electrical, mechanical and plant engineering sectors (e.g., engineers, mechanics and technicians), and also in the health and care sectors (e.g., doctors, nurses and midwives), while other areas of the economy, such as the manufacturing sector, are likely to decline.[9] It is to be expected that skills shortages will become particularly visible as the largest number of baby-boomers (i.e., people born approximately 1946–1964) enter retirement.

At the same time, however, many people remain able to contribute beyond the traditional retirement age,[10] and are also willing to continue to deploy their productivity. In Germany, a recent representative study[11] investigating transitions and old age potential indicated that 36% of

---

[7] OECD *Live longer, work longer* (OECD Publishing 2006). Retrieved from: http://www.oecd.org/document/42/0,3343,en_649_34747_36104426_1_1_1_1,00.html Accessed 21 October 2015.

[8] OECD (2015) *Silver economy and ageing society: An opportunity for growth and job creation in the G20 countries* (OECD Publishing).

[9] European Commission (April 2015) EU Skills Panorama 2015. Analytical Highlight Prospects for Germany. Retrieved from http://euskillspanorama.cedefop.europa.eu/AnalyticalHighlights/ Accessed 21 October 2015.

[10] U Lehr and A Kruse (2006) 'Extending working life—a realistic perspective?' *Zeitschrift für Arbeits- und Organisationspsychologie*, 50, 240–247. doi:10.1026/0932.4089.50.4.240.

[11] Fasbender, U., Deller, J., Zohr, M., Büsch, V., Schermuly, C., & Mergenthaler, A. (2015). Absicht zur Erwerbstätigkeit im (zukünftigen) Ruhestand [Intentions to work in (future) retirement]. In N. F. Schneider, A. Mergenthaler, I., U. M. Staudinger, & I. Sackreuther (Eds.), *Mittendrin? Lebenspläne und Potenziale älterer Menschen beim Übergang in den Ruhestand [Midcourse? Life plans and potentials of older people in transition to retirement]*, pp. 121–138. Opladen: Budrich.

older workers (aged 55 to 70) were willing to continue working in retirement, while only 4% of their non-working counterparts had the same intention. This, however, depended largely on socio-demographic, individual, and job-related factors. In Germany also, the actual number of people working beyond retirement age has increased. As recent data shows, the labor force participation rate has roughly doubled across various age groups over the last ten years.[12] Also, the number of older people engaging in volunteering activities has substantially grown over the last few decades.[13] As a result, it can be argued that people's engagement in post-retirement activities contributes a great deal to society.

In addition to the economic relevance of post-retirement activities, several studies have demonstrated the individual benefits of staying active in retirement—older people engaging in paid or unpaid work activities report higher life satisfaction, health, and well-being.[14] For example, Morrow-Howell et al.[15] have investigated five different activity levels across various domains (e.g., personal leisure, civic and religious activities, exterior household chores, working) among people aged 55 and older. As a result, the authors found that older people who indicated a high level of activity, whether working or physically active, reported higher rates of health and lower rates of depression compared to older people with a low or moderate level of activity. Another study[16] found that working retirees had an even higher rate of work satisfaction compared to older workers (pre-retirement).

[12] For example, labor force participation rate changed from 2004 to 2014 for people aged 55–59: 71.5% to 81.0%; 60–64: 28.1% to 55.8%; 65–69: 5.2% to 14.0%; 70–74: 2.5% to 5.9%; 75+: 0.9% to 1.7%. OECD. StatExtracts. Dataset: Labour force statistics—Sex and age indicators. (2015) Retrieved from http://stats.oecd.org/Index.aspx?DatasetCode=LFS_SEXAGE_I_R# Accessed 21 October 2015.

[13] N Morrow-Howell (2010) 'Volunteering in later life: Research frontiers', *Journals of Gerontology—Series B Psychological Sciences and Social Sciences*, 65 B(4), 461–469. http://doi.org/10.1093/geronb/gbq024.

[14] P Warr, V Butcher, I Robertson, & M Callinan, (2004) 'Older people's well-being as a function of employment, retirement, environmental characteristics and role preference', *British Journal of Psychology* 95, 297–324.

[15] N Morrow-Howell, M Putnam, Y S Lee, J C Greenfield, M Inoue, & H Chen (2014) 'An investigation of activity profiles of older adults', *Journal of Gerontology: Social Sciences* 69B, 809–821. http://doi.org/10.1093/geronb/gbu002.

[16] T K McNamara, M Brown, K Aumann, M Pitt-Catsouphes, E Galinsky & J Bond (2013) 'Working in Retirement: A Brief Report', *Journal of Applied Gerontology* 32(1)1, 20–132. doi:10.1177/0733464811408085.

This might reflect the importance of role preference (i.e., the choice to work or not to work, assuming working post-retirement to be rather voluntary compared to working pre-retirement for various reasons (e.g., financial necessity or social expectations). Similarly, longitudinal research[17] demonstrated improved physical and mental health outcomes for working retirees. Post-retirement activities may also be beneficial in providing a supplementary income, daily or weekly routine, and support during the transition and adjustment process in retirement.[18] Against this backdrop, post-retirement activities are described as having great potential benefits for individuals, organizations, and society.

In this chapter, we aim to identify the underlying factors that differentiate retired workers' individual experiences of their former professional jobs and the characteristics of activities chosen in retirement. Specifically, we focus on the experienced differences in an individual's comparative perception that go beyond solely a description of post-retirement activity characteristics. According to Beehr and Nielson,[19] retirees' retrospective reports of their former jobs strongly agree with their prior reports of the same jobs. The target group of our investigation consists of skilled individuals who were formally retired from their former career job and started to engage in post-retirement activities. Based on two samples of German active retirees, we investigated the differences between retirees' former professional jobs and post-retirement activities using a qualitative-quantitative approach. Study 1 ($N = 133$) was conducted using a qualitative research design with the purpose of creating an in-depth picture of the individual perceptions of experienced differences. Study 2 ($N = 618$) was conducted using a quantitative research design to tie in with, and extend, the exploratory findings of the qualitative study. As a result, we present a framework of differences between retirees' former professional jobs and post-retirement activities that can help

---

[17] Y Zhan, M Wang, S Liu & K S Shultz (2009) 'Bridge employment and retirees' health: A longitudinal investigation', *Journal of Occupational Health Psychology* 14, 374–389.

[18] M Wang (2007) 'Profiling retirees in the retirement transition and adjustment process: Examining the longitudinal change patterns of retirees' psychological well-being' *Journal of Applied Psychology* 92, 455–474. http://dx.doi.org/10.1037/0021-9010.92.2.455.

[19] T A Beehr & N L Nielson (1995) 'Descriptions of job characteristics and retirement activities during the transition to retirement', *Journal of Organizational Behavior* 16, 681–690.

guide older people's retirement transition and adjustment process, and in designing jobs for skilled and motivated retirees.

2   Post-retirement Activities

2.1   Conceptualization of Post-retirement Activities

In a traditional sense, work and retirement have been opposing concepts.[20] However, recent approaches have re-conceptualized retirement as a late career development stage in which work-related activities play a prominent role.[21] In particular, this applies to retirees who still can, and want to, devote time and energy to post-retirement activities. As aging is no longer exclusively associated with general decline,[22] many retirees are in good mental and physical health when leaving their professional jobs.[23] Also, they benefit from skills they acquired in their previous working lives.[24] In line with the current research literature, we define post-retirement activities as productive engagement in work-related activities after a mandatory or median retirement age. Research literature suggests comparable concepts of post-retirement activities that are either synonyms or related, such as post-retirement work, post-retirement employment, bridge employment, and silver work.

Post-retirement activities, as part of the changing nature of retirement (e.g., the US phenomenon of bridge employment), have been a well

---

[20] N Kim & D T Hall (2013) 'Protean career model and retirement' in M. Wang (Ed.) *The Oxford Handbook of Retirement* (OUP) 102–11.

[21] M Wang & J Shi (2014) 'Psychological research on retirement', *Annual Review of Psychology* 65,209–233. http://doi.org/10.1146/annurev-psych-010213-115131.

[22] C Hertzog, A F Kramer, R S Wilson, & U Lindenberger (2008)'Enrichment effects on adult cognitive development. Can the functional capacity of older adults be preserved and enhanced?' *Psychological Science in the Public Interest* 9, 1–65.

[23] J Ilmarinen (2006) *Towards a longer worklife! Ageing and the quality of worklife in the European Union* (Finnish Institute of Occupational Health).

[24] L Maxin & J Deller (2010) 'Activities in retirement: Individual experience of Silver Work' Comparative Population Studies 35, 801–832. doi:10.4232/10.CPoS-2010-18en.

established area of research in North America for more than two decades.[25] In Germany, empirical research on so-called silver work has produced the first insights over the last few years.[26] Silver work embraces all kinds of post-retirement activities, both paid and unpaid work-related activities, including possible temporal intermissions.[27] Bridge employment refers to work after full retirement from career jobs.[28] Paid post-retirement activities can be carried out on an employed basis or in the context of self-employment.[29] In international research going beyond the North American scope, the originally exclusively paid post-retirement activities were broadened in definition, as tasks in the context of bridge employment also encompass unpaid or rather voluntary work-related activities.[30] Given this emerging definition, bridge employment and silver work clearly overlap. The two samples in this study, however, consist of older workers in unpaid work-related activities in retirement. Either way, both paid and unpaid or voluntary post-retirement activities are strongly related to people's evaluation of their former professional job.[31] When approaching retirement age, people who strongly identify with their professional job tend to maintain their work role identification and well-being (i.e., life satisfaction, and satisfaction with retirement)

[25] M Wang, Y J Zhan, S Q Liu, & K S Shultz (2008) 'Antecedents of bridge employment: A longitudinal investigation' *Journal of Applied Psychology* 93, 818–830.

[26] J Deller, P M Liedtke & L Maxin (2009) 'Old-age security and Silver Workers: An empirical investigation identifies challenges for companies, insurers, and society' Geneva Papers on Risk and Insurance 34, 137–157.

[27] J Deller & L Pundt (2014) 'Flexible transitions from work to retirement in Germany' in C M Alcover, G Topa, E Parry, F Fraccaroli, & M Depolo (eds.), *Bridge employment: A research handbook* (Routledge) 167–192.

[28] D C Feldman (1994) 'The decision to retire early: A review and conceptualization' *Academy of Management Review* 19, 285–311.

[29] P B Doeringer (1990) 'Economic security, labor market flexibility, and bridges to retirement' in P B Doeringer (Ed.) *Bridges to Retirement* (Ithaca Press) 3–32.

[30] B Griffin & B Hesketh (2008) 'Post-retirement work. The individual determinants of paid and volunteer work' *Journal of Occupational and Organizational Psychology* 81, 101–121.

[31] B Griffin & B Hesketh (2008) 'Post-retirement work. The individual determinants of paid and volunteer work', *Journal of Occupational and Organizational Psychology* 81, 101–121.

by engaging in work-related activities.[32] Further, for organizations, knowing the differences in work design between former professional jobs and post-retirement activities can help with designing jobs for skilled and motivated retirees who still want to contribute. As a result, the engagement in post-retirement activities can constitute a valuable source of managers and professionals needed in many industries as well as in charitable organizations, in particular, in times of good economic conditions with high labor demand.

2.2   From the Former Career Job to Post-retirement Activities

The process of retirement, which includes the decision to retire as well as the decision to engage in any kind of post-retirement activity, is complex and influenced by various factors at multiple levels, including individual, job-related or organizational, and societal level factors.[33] Beehr[34] initially distinguished between the personal factors (e.g., skill obsolescence, health, economic well-being) and environmental forces (e.g., attainment of occupational goals, job characteristics, marital family life, leisure pursuits) leading to the preference to retire, and finally, to the act of retirement. Since then, many researchers have investigated the relationship between personal characteristics and the decision to retire. However, one alternative to full retirement is engaging in any kind of post-retirement activity.[35] Feldman and Kim[36] emphasize that work-related activities in

---

[32] S Kim & D C Feldman (2000) 'Working in retirement: The antecedents of bridge employment and its consequences for quality of life in retirement', *Academy of Management Journal* 43, 1195–1210.

[33] M Wang & K S Shultz (2010) 'Employee retirement: A review and recommendations for future investigation' *Journal of Management* 36, 72–206.

[34] T A Beehr (1986) 'The process of retirement: A review and recommendations for future investigation' *Personnel Psychology* 39, 31–55.

[35] J Deller, P M Liedtke, & L Maxin (2009) 'Old-age security and Silver Workers: An empirical investigation identifies challenges for companies, insurers, and society', *Geneva Papers on Risk and Insurance 34*, 137–157.

[36] D C Feldman & S Kim (2000) 'Bridge employment during retirement: A field study of individual and organizational experiences with post-retirement employment', Human Resource Planning 23(1) 14–25.

retirement facilitate a smoother adjustment to retirement and increase overall life satisfaction as well as satisfaction with retirement. The possible activities available to older workers after formally entering retirement are manifold. One can distinguish between career-oriented activities and activities carried out in a different field, also referred to as non-career-oriented activities.[37] Either way, post-retirement activities do not necessarily constitute less demanding or challenging tasks as senior volunteers and workers exhibit a wide range of skills, interests, and experience. These need to be addressed by organizations in formulating post-retirement activities.[38] The various manifestations of individual transitions show either a quantitative or a qualitative deviation from the former professional job, which is expressed in changes in the invested hours, a new organization, or another type of activity.[39] Further, the majority of post-retirement activities develop from previous work and contacts from a former professional job, from external enquiry, and from an individual's own initiative and active search.[40]

2.3   Determinants of Post-retirement Activities

Several decisive components are identified as being associated with post-retirement activities, such as individual and organizational level factors. On the individual level, the intention to engage in post-retirement activities is driven by different motivational elements (e.g., social, financial or generative reasons)[41] and individual work values (e.g., self-transcendence,

[37] M E Von Bonsdorff, K S Shultz, E Leskinen & J Tansky (2009) 'The choice between retirement and bridge employment: A continuity theory and life course perspective', *International Journal of Aging and Human Development* 69, 79–100.

[38] J Warburton, J Paynter & A Petriwskyj (2007) 'Volunteering as a productive aging activity: Incentives and barriers to volunteering by Australian seniors', *Journal of Applied Gerontology* 26, 333–354.

[39] R L Pleau (2010) 'Gender differences in postretirement employment', *Research on Aging* 32, 267–303.

[40] L Maxin & J Deller (2010) 'Activities in retirement: Individual experience of Silver Work' *Comparative Population Studies* 35, 801–832. doi:10.4232/10.CPoS-2010-18en.

[41] A M Wöhrmann, J Deller, & M Wang (2013) 'Outcome expectations and work design characteristics in post-retirement work planning', *Journal of Vocational Behavior* 83, 219–228. doi:10.1016/j.jvb.2013.05.003.

such as altruism and relationship values).[42] Madvig and Shultz,[43] for example, found that retirees' perceptions of the organization, perceptions of retirement, and factors related to the meaning of work predicted post-retirement behaviors directed toward the organization individuals retired from. Although often highlighted in research, the financial meaning of work seems to be less relevant for people's decision to engage in post-retirement activities than other factors. Recent research indicated that the financial meaning of work seems to be only relevant for people with a low subjective socioeconomic status, while the social (e.g., having contact with others) and personal (e.g., finding personal satisfaction) meanings of work were relevant for people of different financial backgrounds.[44] There are other relevant individual attributes that impact the retirement process—including the decision to engage in post-retirement activities—which incorporate knowledge, skills and abilities, attitudes toward work and retirement (e.g., job involvement, work centrality), as well as health and work ability measures.[45]

There are also organizational level factors, such as scheduling flexibility and targeted equal opportunity statements, that affect older people's decisions to engage in post-retirement activities.[46] Also, the decision of retirees to return to work depends on the human resource practices of organizations, which ideally should be tailored to the needs and desires of older workers.[47] The positive aspects of the work

[42] Wöhrmann, A. M., Fasbender, U., & Deller, J. (2016). Using work values to predict post-retirement work intentions. *Career Development Quarterly* 64, 98–113.

[43] T L Madvig & K S Shultz, 'Modeling individuals' post-retirement behaviors toward their former organization' (2008) 23 Journal of Workplace Behavioral Health 17–49.

[44] Fasbender, U., Wang, M., Voltmer, J.-B., & Deller, J. (2016). The meaning of work for post-retirement employment. *Work, Aging and Retirement* 2, 12–23. doi: 10.1093/workar/wav015..

[45] M Wang & K S Shultz (2010) 'Employee retirement: A review and recommendations for future investigation', *Journal of Management* 36, 72–206.

[46] B L Rau & G A Adams (2005) 'Attracting retirees to apply: Desired organizational characteristics of bridge employment', *Journal of Organizational Behavior* 26, 649–660.

[47] M Armstrong-Stassen (2008) 'Organisational practices and the postretirement employment experience of older workers', *Human Resource Management Journal* 18, 36–53; M Armstrong-Stassen & F Schlosser (2011) 'Perceived organizational membership and the retention of older workers' *Journal of Organizational Behavior* 32, 319–344.

environment could serve as a retention tool for organizations address-ing older workers considering bridge employment.[48] In addition, inflexible pre-retirement work schedules are a predictor of an indi-vidual retiring completely.[49] Certain job characteristics, such as autonomy at work, prevent older workers from retiring or encourage them to engage in post-retirement activities.[50] Important organiza-tional frameworks for post-retirement activities are flexible working hours, working conditions tailored to age, and a consideration of needs.[51] Recognition and appreciation, using experience and know-how, exchange between young and old, involvement in further and advanced training, and active involvement in the employer's business are also important organizational framework aspects of post-retire-ment activities.[52]

Based on the identified research literature, we hypothesize that differences between retirees' former professional jobs and present post-retirement activities can be found in the following areas:

(a) *Individual attributes:* Use of knowledge, skills, and abilities, as well as positive attitudes toward work.
(b) *Organizational policies:* More flexibility, framework tailored to the needs and desires of older workers, more decision-making opportu-nities, as well as more recognition and appreciation.

---

[48] J R Weckerle & K S Shultz (1999) 'Influences on the bridge employment decision among older USA workers', *Journal of Occupational and Organizational Psychology* 72, 317–329.

[49] C Pengcharoen & K S Shultz (2010) 'The influences on bridge employment decisions', *International Journal of Manpower* 31, 322–336.

[50] S Zaniboni, G Sarchielli, & F Fraccaroli (2010) 'How are psychosocial factors related to retire-ment intentions?', *International Journal of Manpower* 31, 271–285.

[51] J Deller, P M Liedtke & L Maxin (2009) 'Old-age security and Silver Workers: An empirical investigation identifies challenges for companies, insurers, and society', *Geneva Papers on Risk and Insurance* 34, 137–157.

[52] L Maxin & J Deller (2010) 'Activities in retirement: Individual experience of Silver Work', *Comparative Population Studies* 35, 801–832. doi:10.4232/10.CPoS-2010-18en.

3   Study 1: Qualitative Approach

3.1   Method for Study 1

The purpose of Study 1 was to develop an in-depth picture of the individual perceptions of experienced differences of retired professional workers with regards to their former professional job and their present post-retirement activities. To this end, an open-ended question for a past-present comparison about the differences between retirees' present activities and their former job was used. We chose this qualitative approach because we were not interested in yet another description of post-retirement activity characteristics, but rather in experienced differences in individual comparative perception. Data was collected as part of a larger explorative investigation on active retirees in Germany.[53] A total of 133 retirees in unpaid work, aged 60 to 85 years ($M = 67$, $SD = 4.2$), were surveyed in telephone interviews lasting an average of 60 minutes. The sample consisted of 31% women and 69% men. Almost 60% of the interviewees held a university degree. Content analysis was used to evaluate the qualitative categories in Study 1. Semantic validity and construct validity were guaranteed through multi-person codebook development by a team of between two and six developers, and in some cases through triangulation.

3.2   Results for Study 1

Content clustering of the qualitative answers from Study 1 resulted in five main categories of differences between respondents' former professional jobs and their post-retirement activities as presented in Table 11.1. The largest category (32.2% of total mentions) was 'extent of freedom', with the majority of answers (30.5% of total mentions sorted in this category) reflecting more freedom today than in the former professional job. Another important category was 'allocation of time'. It accounts for 23% of the total occurrences. The majority (16.7% of total mentions

---

[53] L Maxin & J Deller (2010) 'Activities in retirement: Individual experience of Silver Work', Comparative Population Studies 35, 801–832. doi:10.4232/10.CPoS-2010-18en.

Table 11.1 Differences in activity before and after retirement

Answer Category	Mentions (%)
Extent of freedom	**32.2**
Today more freedom	30.5
Today less freedom	1.7
Allocation of time	**23.0**
More time today and free timing	16.7
Today lower working hours	4.6
Today longer working hours	1.7
Comparability	**19.5**
No differences	7.5
Great differences	6.9
Not comparable	5.2
Content of task and demands	**16.1**
Different task definitions and occupational field	9.8
Less stress today	4.0
Different competencies required	2.3
Perceived responsibility	**9.2**
Today less responsibility	6.9
Responsibility in general/less significant tasks	2.3

Note. Open-ended question: "If there are differences between your current and your former activity: What are they?" Multiple answers were allowed. Mentions = 174

sorted in this category) suggest that older workers have more time and freedom in post-retirement activities. One-fifth (19.5%) of total occurrences refer to the general 'comparability' of their former professional job and their activities in retirement. Almost one-third of total mentions sorted in this category (7.5%) assert that there are no differences between the activities, almost one-third (6.9% of total mentions sorted in this category) see great differences, while almost one-third (5.2% of total mentions sorted in this category) observe that the activities are not comparable.

Also, 'content of task and demands' appears to be an important element in differentiating between post-retirement activities and former professional jobs, with 16.1% of total mentions. One out of ten statements (9.8% of mentions in this category) reflects different task definitions and different competencies used in post-retirement activities, whereas only 4% of statements identify less stress today. Another field for differentiation between respondents' former working lives and their current post-retirement activities was the area of 'perceived responsibility', where 9.2% of total entries emerged, with 6.9% reporting less responsibility in their current activities compared to that in their career job responsibilities.

4   Study 2: Quantitative Approach

4.1   Method for Study 2

From the results presented in Study 1, we derived ten items which we used within the framework of the quantitative survey methodology in Study 2. Items used to measure the comparison between the former professional job and post-retirement activities were: 'Compared to my previous professional job:

(a) I have considerably more freedom in my current post-retirement job.
(b) I have more control over the way time is organized in my current post-retirement job.
(c) I have considerably lower working hours in my current post-retirement job.
(d) There are no differences to my current post-retirement job.
(e) I have completely different task definitions in my current post-retirement job.
(f) I am working in a completely different occupational field in my current post-retirement job.
(g) I have considerably less stress in my current post-retirement job.
(h) Completely other competencies are required in my current post-retirement job.
(i) I have considerably less responsibility in my current post-retirement job.
(j) I have considerably less significant tasks in my current post-retirement job.'

Table 11.2 Item statistics comparison, former and today

Today compared to the past...	M	Mdn	SD	Skew	Kurtosis
More freedom	3.49	4	0.93	−0.50	−0.19
Free timing	3.37	4	1.02	−0.47	−0.41
Lower working hours	2.98	3	1.19	0.11	−0.96
No differences	2.82	3	0.98	0.14	−0.76
Different task	2.24	2	1.01	0.87	0.29
Different occupational field	2.38	2	1.09	0.70	−0.31
Less stress	3.44	4	1.00	−0.41	−0.36
Different competencies	2.72	3	1.02	0.15	−0.86
Less responsibility	2.92	3	1.01	0.02	−0.97
Less significant tasks	2.75	3	1.08	0.38	−0.64

Note. All the described items were answered on five-point Likert scales ranging from 1 (completely disagree) to 5 (completely agree)

Further, we asked for differences in tasks (e) as well as in occupational field (f) in the 'content of tasks and demands' category. We asked also for differences in both responsibility (i) and significance (j) in the 'perceived responsibility' category. Item statistics are presented in Table 11.2.

Further, we used a series of five, one-item measures to measure attitude toward work (i.e., work ability, willingness to continue working, estimated work capacity today and expected in two years) as presented in Table 11.3. Our aim was to identify the relationship of these person-related variables to the identified factors which differentiate between former professional life and post-retirement activities.

Data was collected from 618 professionals, who had fully retired from their career job. The response rate was 36%. Participants engaged on a voluntary and unpaid basis in a non-profit organization named Senior Experts Service,[54] which offers retirees the opportunity to work on projects, both abroad and within Germany in their former professional career field. The weekly working hours during a project were on average 37.3 h (SD = 18.2), with 82.2% working abroad. Participants' average age was 69 years (SD = 4.1). The sample comprised 49.3% respondents with a university degree, 84.5% married and 91.8% men.

Factor analysis was used to determine the underlying structure of both the comparison variables and the person-related variables. We

---

[54] SES, www.ses-bonn.de/en Accessed 20 October 2015

Table 11.3 Item wording and distributions for person-related variables

Variable	Item	M	Mdn	SD
Work ability[a]	Current work ability compared to highest work ability ever: assume that your work ability at its best has a value of ten points. How many points would you give your current work ability? (Zero means that you currently cannot work at all)	7.35	7	1.29
Work involvement[b]	Most things in my life are more important than my post-retirement job. (r)	2.93	3	0.87
Willingness to continue working[c]	I want to stay active as long as I can	4.04	4	0.85
Work capacity[d]				
Estimated today	How do you assess your current work capacity?	3.87	4	0.68
Expected in two years	How do you assess your work capacity in two years?	3.55	4	0.68

Note. All the described items were answered on five-point Likert scales ranging from 1 (completely disagree/very low) to 5 (completely agree/very high) except for the work ability item
[a]Work ability index (Hasselhorn and Freude 2007; Ilmarinen 2007). Item selected due to highest correlation with scale
[b]Item selected due to highest correlation with scale, selected due to highest correlation with scale
[c]J Deller, P M Liedtke & L Maxin (2009) 'Old-age security and Silver Workers: An empirical investigation identifies challenges for companies, insurers, and society' Geneva Papers on Risk and Insurance 34,137–157.
[d]Developed on the basis of the work ability index and in cooperation with HR responsible of the Senior Experts Service (SES)

applied the principal axis factoring extraction method, because we wanted to explain the common variance of the variables through factoring and used varimax rotation with Kaiser normalization. The Kaiser-Meyer-Olkin measure of sampling adequacy showed that the partial correlations among variables ($r=.74$) were large enough to apply factor analysis. Further, Bartlett's test of sphericity was highly significant ($p < 0.001$), confirming the appropriateness of applying factor analysis.

4.2   Results for Study 2

Table 11.4 presents the correlation of results for the ten before and after retirement activities, as well as the five person-related variables. The results of the correlation analyses suggest that person-related variables could constitute an additional factor in relationship to the items measuring differences between the former professional job and post-retirement activities. Table 11.5 shows the results of the exploratory factor analysis with all ten items measuring differences between an individual's former professional job and today's post-retirement activity, as well as with the five person-related variables. This analysis resulted in a four-factor model (explaining 49.5% of the common variance) with the person-related variables, except work involvement, constituting the first factor. The strongest item loading on the first factor was 'Current work ability compared to highest work ability ever?' We labeled this factor 'person-related variables' (α =.76).

The second factor constituted differences in the job field itself. These concerned the task, individual skills or job function. The strongest item loading on this factor was 'Compared to my previous professional job I have completely different task definitions in my current post-retirement job' (λ =.92). We labeled this second factor 'different function' (α =.81). Differences were also found regarding the perceived responsibility and significance in the job activity. The item 'Compared to my previous professional job I have considerably less responsibility in my current post-retirement job' showed the highest factor loading (λ =.76). This third factor was named 'less responsibility' (α =.76).

Finally, the experienced degrees of freedom in time allocation and flexibility in job practice was another aspect that differentiated post-retirement jobs and former professional activity. The marker item here was 'Compared to my previous professional job I have more control over time in my current post-retirement job' with a factor loading of λ =.80. We labeled this fourth factor 'more flexibility' (α =.75).

Table 11.6 shows the correlations between the three factor scores and person-related factors. Only the 'less responsibility' factor correlated significantly (r = −.19, p < 0.01) with the person-related factor, whereas

Table 11.4 Correlations among study variables

	1.	2.	3.	4.	5.	6.	7.	8.	9.	10.	11.	12.	13.	14.	15.
1. Work ability	—														
2. Work capacity today	.60***	—													
3. Work capacity expected in two years	.60***	.73***	—												
4. Willingness to continue working	.33***	.34***	.42***	—											
5. Work involvement	.14**	.15***	.13**	.12**	—										
6. Different task	.00	.01	.00	−.06	.01	—									
7. Different occupational field	.04	−.03	.01	−.08	.03	.75***	—								
8. Different competencies	−.02	−.05	−.07	−.07	.02	.55***	.49***	—							
9. Less responsibility	−.13***	−.09	−.14***	−.13***	−.16***	.10*	.07	.14***	—						
10. Less significant tasks	−.14***	−.10*	−.09*	−.14***	−.13**	.26***	.24***	.24***	.53***	—					
11. Lower working hours	−.14**	−.07	−.08	−.13**	−.14***	.25***	.25***	.16***	.41***	.39***	—				
12. Less stress	−.08*	−.02	−.07	−.06	−.11**	.05	.06	.01	.40***	.38***	.51***	—			
13. Free timing	.03	.07	.02	.05	−.05	.15***	.13**	.13**	.09**	.02	.28***	.28***	—		
14. More freedom	−.05	−.02	−.09*	−.03	−.01	.13***	.13***	.21***	.15***	.10*	.30***	.31***	.61***	—	
15. No differences	.02	−.02	.01	.08	.05	−.31***	−.23***	−.15***	−.15***	−.20***	−.16***	−.08	−.10*	−.14***	—

$*p < 0.05$; $**p < 0.01$; $***p < 0.001$

Table 11.5 Factor analysis of differences between activity before and after retirement and with person-related variables

Item	Factor			
	1	2	3	4
Work ability	.91	.03	-.15	-.02
Work capacity today	.56	-.01	-.01	.02
Work capacity expected in two years	.58	.00	-.03	-.03
Willingness to continue working	.38	-.07	-.01	.04
Work involvement	.14	.03	-.17	-.02
Different task	.00	.90	-.05	.06
Different occupational field	.02	.86	.05	.07
Different competencies	-.05	.64	.07	.08
Less responsibility	-.11	.10	.75	.02
Less significant tasks	-.10	.29	.72	-.09
Lower working hours	-.11	.25	.68	.34
Less stress	-.02	-.01	.63	.31
Free timing	.07	.11	.09	.82
More freedom	-.04	.12	.15	.68
No differences	.01	-.35	-.14	-.06

Note. Numbers in boldface are primary factor loadings and indicate the factor assignment for the item. Explained variance: 49.5%. Proposed factor labels: (1) Person-related variables ($\alpha=.76$); (2) Different function ($\alpha=.81$); (3) Less responsibility ($\alpha=.76$); and (4) More flexibility ($\alpha=.75$)

Table 11.6 Correlations of person-related variables with job-related factor scores

Factors		α	1.	2.	3.	4.
1.	Person-related variables	.76	–			
2.	Different function	.81	-.01	–		
3.	Less responsibility	.76	-.19***	.04	–	
4.	More flexibility	.76	.03	.03	.07	–

***$p<0.001$

the 'different function' and 'more flexibility' factors were uncorrelated with the person-related factor. Thus, persons who experience lesser responsibility in their current post-retirement activity compared to their former professional job have lower work ability, lower work capacity, and a lower willingness to continue working.

5   General Discussion

The purpose of this research project was to identify experienced differences between retirees' former professional jobs and their present post-retirement activities. Based on the identified research literature, we hypothesized that differences can be found in individual attributes (e.g., use of knowledge, skills and abilities, as well as positive attitudes toward work) and in organizational policies (e.g., more flexibility, framework tailored to the needs and desires of older workers, more decision-making opportunities, as well as more recognition and appreciation). The results of this qualitative-quantitative approach showed experienced differences in three areas: first, in the job field itself with regard to the task, individual skills, or job function (i.e. 'different function'); second, the experienced degrees of freedom in time allocation and flexibility in the job practice (i.e., 'more flexibility'); and third, differences with regard to the perceived responsibility and significance of the job activity have been found (i.e. 'less responsibility'). The identified 'person-related variables' constituted an additional factor, inversely related to the less responsibility factor. Thus, our assumptions were mostly confirmed with three factors referring to organizational policies (i.e., different function, less responsibility, and more flexibility) and one factor referring to individual attributes (i.e., person-related variables). The focus is clearly on organizational, job-related attributes as all areas of interest gained from the qualitative in-depth Study 1 account for this aspect.

The five categories resulting from the content analysis in Study 1 for the most part correspond to factors that were associated with post-retirement activities in previous research.[55] Only the social support factor did not emerge in the open-ended question, whereas it was found in other empirical studies.[56] It may be the case that working retirees have already established their personal network, and so do not experience a difference between their former professional working life and their activities in retirement with regard to their personal contacts. Further, the

---

[55] For example, D C Feldman (1994) 'The decision to retire early: A review and conceptualization', *Academy of Management Review* 19, 285–311

[56] For example, T L Madvig & K S Shultz (2008) 'Modeling individuals' post-retirement behaviors toward their former organization', *Journal of Workplace Behavioral Health* 23, 17–49

factor analytical structure of experienced differences in former professional jobs and post-retirement activities in Study 2 largely confirmed the conclusions of the content-analytical evaluation of the qualitative Study 1: only the extent of experienced stress and working hours were allocated to different areas. Lower working hours and less stress co-constitute the 'perceived responsibility' factor and only load slightly on the other factors. These results are consistent with a large-scale investigation based on data from 15 European countries which showed that self-reported stress among older workers was dependent on schedule flexibility.[57]

The present research contributes to further determining the job characteristics of post-retirement activities. The qualitative-quantitative approach to studying the differences between pre- and post-retirement work-related activities helped understand these differences to the benefit of both individuals and organizations. In particular, the findings highlight that organizations need to provide opportunities for older people with a range of skills, interests and needs. One way of doing so could be to design post-retirement activities which relate to older workers' former jobs, whilst in line with their current needs and taking their present situation fully into account.

In addition to the valuable insights that the present research project revealed, future research should investigate relevant contextual factors that extend organizational or job-related attributes. For example, family and social network factors might be relevant in terms of providing material and immaterial support, offering anchoring points, role modeling opportunities, and providing a socially desirable setting. These together may guide an individual's decision to engage in post-retirement activities which connect to the former professional job. Also, cultural norms can influence behavioral arrangement after formally entering into retirement. One example, with regard to post-retirement activities, is the concept of 'active aging', which was introduced in the 1990s by the World Health Organization and subsequently promoted by political institutions, such as the European

[57] K S Shultz, M Wang, E M Crimmins, & G G Fisher (2010) 'Age differences in the demand-control model of work stress: An examination of data from 15 European countries', *Journal of Applied Gerontology* 29, 21–47

Union.[58] The concept of active aging describes a broad approach of later life engagement, including paid and unpaid, or voluntary, activities in society. Certain images of older people are created to promote inclusion, health and well-being outcomes, and at the same time, older people are implicitly expected to behave in a socially desirable manner. This in turn encourages post-retirement activities among older people. Future research should address these contextual features to further extend our understanding of factors underlying post-retirement activities.

6   Conclusion

Knowing the differences in the work design of regular professional jobs and post-retirement activities can help craft jobs for skilled and capable retirees who intend to continue to contribute to organizations and society. The call in research and practice for a shift from managing threats to creating opportunities requires a new, positive way of looking at the capacities of older workers. Increasing healthy life expectancy in aging populations prolongs individuals' remaining lifetime after retirement. As activities in retirement are beneficial to individual life satisfaction and well-being, provided that a person is in good health, it seems crucial to meet an individual's needs when creating employment opportunities for older workers. Thus, due to labor shortages and the lack of specialists in many areas, as well as a dependency on older people's community presence and involvement, society has an interest in how post-retirement activities can be crafted to attract people after entering formal retirement. In addition, organizations, including charitable and for-profit businesses, should provide tasks different from the individual's former professional job. Individuals want to experience reduced responsibility, lower working hours, less significant tasks, and more flexibility in the allocation of time and decision-making. Doing so is most likely to lead to positive psychosocial and physical outcomes.

---

[58] P H Jensen & A Principi (2014) 'Introduction: Enhancing volunteering in later life in Europe' in A. Principi, P. H. Jensen, & G. Lamura (Eds.) *Active ageing: Voluntary work by older people in Europe* (Bristol Policy Press) 3–20.

The value of working retirees and the necessity of integrating working retirees into organizations may increase, not only due to labor shortages. Macro-social changes (e.g., demographic changes and the pressure to innovate) create challenges for organizations for recruiting experienced workers, such as retirees who have worked for most of their lives.[59] Previous research has highlighted 'the importance of understanding retirement as a new career stage rather than simply as complete labour-force withdrawal' (p. 128).[60] Experienced individuals can help to fill new work roles in order to help organizations stay competitive, but also in accordance with individual role preferences. For instance, retirees could serve as mentors for younger colleagues. Also, serving as specialists on particular projects, following the models of Senior Expert Service or Bosch Management Support GmbH,[61] can be a valuable new work role. Placing emphasis on social or cultural competencies, skilled and motivated retirees can, for example, serve as guest advisors available as required by a certain institution where senior expertise is a valued competence. These exemplarily described work roles can be filled with a combination of more flexibility and less responsibility, and can occupy a new function. Thus, people engaging in post-retirement activities can be a valuable resource for organizations and society wanting to benefit from this experienced group of individuals. Finally, the positive psychosocial and physical outcomes of engaging in post-retirement activities are likely to support transition and adjustment to retirement.

[59] M A Taylor, K S Shultz & D D Doverspike (2015) 'Academic perspectives on recruiting and retaining older workers' in P T Beatty & R M S Visser (Eds.) *Thriving on an aging workforce: Strategies for organizational and systemic change* (Krieger Publishing Company) 43–50.

[60] T K McNamara, M Brown, K Aumann, M Pitt-Catsouphes, E Galinsky, & J Bond (2013) 'Working in Retirement: A Brief Report', *Journal of Applied Gerontology* 32(1), 120–132 doi:10.1177/0733464811408085.

[61] J Deller & L Pundt (2014) 'Flexible transitions from work to retirement in Germany' in C M Alcover, G Topa, E Parry, F Fraccaroli, & M Depolo (eds.) *Bridge employment: A research handbook* (Routledge) 167–192.

Part V

The Perspective from Practice

12

BMW Group Case Study: Help a Workforce to Age

Martin Hall and Andrea Rathbone

1 Introduction

In 2007, in response to demographic changes challenging the performance of their workforce, the premium car manufacturer, BMW Group, launched the 'Today for Tomorrow' programme designed to manage and support the ageing workforce. This case study is based on the BMW Group in the UK. This consists of four manufacturing plants: MINI Plant Swindon, BMW Plant Hams Hall, MINI Plant Oxford and the Rolls Royce Plant in Goodwood. The BMW Group in the UK employs 18,000 people and there are over 160 apprentices currently employed across its manufacturing sites. The company makes a significant contribution to the UK economy, and £1.6 billion has been invested in the UK manufacturing operations at Oxford, Hams Hall, Swindon and Goodwood between 2000 and 2015. More than three million MINIs have been produced by the Oxford plant, and two million have been exported to over 110 markets contributing £1.2 billion per annum to the UK gross domestic product.

This case study outlines BMW's implementation of the 'Today for Tomorrow' programme in the UK via its Value Added Production System

© The Editor(s) (if applicable) and The Author(s) 2016   **257**
S. Manfredi, L. Vickers (eds.), *Challenges of Active Ageing*,
DOI 10.1057/978-1-137-53251-0_12

(VPS). This programme is aimed at managing demographic change effectively in order to support the workforce and to give the company a competitive edge by retaining experienced and skilled workers and by ensuring that older workers remain as productive as their younger counterparts. At the core of this programme is the aim of helping the workforce age well and remain active, rather than retrospectively managing an ageing workforce. In order to achieve this aim, the programme is based on a series of measures which include:

- Creating an ergonomically friendly work environment
- Managing health and offering preventative healthcare
- Changing working patterns and responding to the needs of associates[1]
- Training to keep up the skills of the workforce

The key features of these measures are explained in the following sections.

2   Creating an Ergonomically Friendly Work Environment

The company has invested in technology to design an ergonomically friendly working environment in order to minimise physical stress and strain for its workers. The organisation employs external occupational therapists to assess the physiological demands of working at particular work stations on the factory floor. Each station is fully anthropomorphically tested in order to ascertain how much strain it would exert on any particular joint in the worker's body. The amount of strain is quantified numerically and built into a web-tool that can be used to quickly compare the activity level which any particular work station requires. This tool, which was adopted two years ago as part of a 'fit for work' strategy and to reduce absenteeism, is particularly useful for associates who have muscular skeletal issues as they can be placed on work stations which

---

[1] Employees at the BMW Group are defined as associates.

exerts less physical strain on the worker's affected area. Additionally, a Reintegration Forum was also established to support associates with medical constraints so that they can be redeployed to different parts of the factory to help support their medical condition. This strategy has proven to be a very effective way of managing older workers who may be affected by age-related muscle degradation or back conditions, as it can avoid excessive strain which could cause these conditions to deteriorate. This measure ensures that as the workforce ages, they can be redeployed into less physically demanding roles, than having to stop working on the basis of medical capability.

Assistors are used to move and fit heavy components and vehicles are moved into position using rotary slings so that it is comfortable for associates to work on them, thus avoiding a situation where the worker would have to bend and twist in order to fit parts. Work stations in the assembly building have a special type of flooring which is used because of its properties which minimise fatigue on leg joints. Job rotation among associates is also used to ensure that no set of muscles or joints are overworked.

3   Managing Health and Offer Preventative Health Care

The company has introduced the concept of 'biological age' as opposed to chronological age, since the former can be a better predictor of an individual's work ability. This is central to the organisation's health management strategy, which recognises that individuals can influence their ageing process through their lifestyle choices. A booklet has been produced and distributed among the workforce to raise awareness about health issues, which also contains a questionnaire to assess an individual's 'biological age' and provides advice for keeping healthy. Moreover, monthly initiatives are undertaken to involve and engage workers in preventative healthcare, which aligns with national health promotion issues such as a 'dryathon' to encourage individuals to abstain from alcohol for a month; 'healthy hearts'; no smoking in March; bowel cancer and allergy awareness; walking and mental health awareness in May; diabetes awareness and sun and fatigue awareness. Other initiatives include health checks, an on-site occupational health department which also provides counselling and physiotherapy, healthy eating options at work, a 'cycle to work' scheme, and gym membership subsidies.

A key tool for managing workforce health is the 'Fit for Work Index' (FWI). This measure was originally introduced to reduce absenteeism, which has decreased significantly from over 5% in 2009, to less than 3% in 2015. The FWI helps to quantify how physically capable an associate is to work on certain production lines. This is complemented by a Reintegration Forum to accommodate those workers who, for example, have come back from extended medical leave after an operation. This measure combines absence, medical constraints and rehabilitation to provide a total assessment of how many working hours had been lost over the month, and it is used to determine an associate's capability to work in the plant. Associates are allocated to a more or less demanding assembly line that can accommodate their needs without affecting their utility and output. Thus, this system ensures that the labour of the workforce is distributed effectively, appropriately, and efficiently.

Furthermore, the metric produced by the FWI can be used to adjust working conditions according to associates' needs and ensure that the company complies with legislation around age and disability discrimination as well as flexible working. Finally, in the event of consistent under-performance, the results from the FWI and the Reintegration Forum can be used to undertake capability proceedings in a fair way and to justify dismissal on medical or performance related grounds if needed.

4   Changing Working Patterns and Responding to the Needs of Associates

Shift work, which is a key feature of the car manufacturing industry, can be very demanding on associates, and the BMW Group recognises that individuals will all respond differently to shift work across their life-course. From this perspective, the challenge for the company is to maintain a high level of production volume for the plant whilst cutting down the hours of working shifts for individual plant workers. The shift model at the Oxford plant was realigned to a shorter 7.5 hours over a five day period to ensure that the plant's output is kept at the same level as the one under the previous system of longer working shifts which requires associate to work shorter shifts, but more of them during the working week. Furthermore, to complement these changes to the shift system, a 'buddy arrangements' programme is in place where associates can pair up and agree on which shifts to work and to cover each for other's shifts if one of them has other commitments. This works very well for the company since it allows for a smooth transition from one working shift to the next, ensuring that production is only minimally disturbed at shift change. It also works well for the associates and especially for the older ones who are more comfortable working in the morning or afternoon shifts, as it enables them to pair up with a younger associate who is comfortable with working the night shifts.

Flexible working practices are also available and include part-time working and job share options to help associates manage their work-life balance.

5 Training to Keep Up the Skills of the Workforce

The company recognises the importance of training all associates to operate any new equipment in the plant regardless of their age. As associates are likely to have longer working lives, it is essential that older associates keep up their skills on par with younger associates in order to allow for the plant to run efficiently as the average age of the workforce increases. Furthermore, the technology related to the production of vehicles evolves very fast, and the company is well aware of the potential skill gaps that could arise as a result of current demographic trends, and this provides an even more compelling case for keeping up the skills of older workers.

The process of keeping up the skills of the workforce can also be facilitated by the engineers who design the manufacturing equipment and the cars themselves. The company recognises that an essential aspect of their strategy to manage an ageing workforce is the need for the engineers to focus their attention on the human factors and physiological aspects of the assembly process itself, rather than just the individual tasks associated with the assembly of the cars.

6   Supporting Associates with Plans for Retirement

The company offers a generous pension scheme to its associates and supports associates who plan to retire by offering pre-retirement seminars. These seminars provide guidance on pensions, financial management, and health. Ill health early retirement options are also available for those associates who are confirmed as not being medically fit to perform their duties.

7   Conclusions

The introduction of the 'Today for Tomorrow' programme is a timely and forward thinking initiative to meet the challenges of an ageing work force. The BMW Group's philosophy is that workplace design starts with the engineers. This means that they need to plan and design the assembly process with workers in mind to ensure that the job is fit for people of all ages. Supporting the workforce as they age is of key importance for the organisation in terms of maintaining its competiveness in spite of current demographic trends. Moreover, from a broader perspective, this approach helps meet one of the challenges of active ageing identified elsewhere in this book (see Manfredi and Vickers in Chap. 4). This relates to the fact that although average life expectancy is increasing, the quality of people's later years in life is likely to vary significantly. As several governments, including the one in the UK, are gradually raising pensionable ages to link them to increased average life expectancy, this creates a need for employers to think 'today' about meeting the needs of an older workforce 'tomorrow' and to help workers to remain in employment until their reach their pensionable ages. The sustainability of working lives is important to businesses and to society as a whole, and the BMW Group sees its 'Today for Tomorrow' programme both as part of its business strategy as well as its corporate social responsibility.

13

Managing Older Workers in a Local Authority: The Case of Oxford City Council

Councillor Bob Price

1   Introduction

Oxford City Council is one of the larger district councils in England, with a workforce of some 1300 office and manual staff.[1] The Council has adopted, as one of its core objectives, the aim of becoming an employer of choice with excellent HR policies and good terms and conditions of employment. In pursuing that objective, the Council has become a Living Wage Employer, adopting an Oxford Living Wage that is linked directly to the London Living Wage, in recognition of the high cost of housing in Oxford.[2] The Council has also achieved the Investors in People Gold and Champion accreditations, and was recently awarded the distinction of International Investors in People Champion.[3]

---

[1] District councils provide most local services in English counties, other than education, social care, libraries and transport, which are the responsibility of county councils.

[2] Living Wage is a concept based on an assessment of the minimum wage level required to support independent living in a particular area. It is significantly higher than the statutory minimum wage and is based on local transport costs, housing costs and access to basic facilities.

[3] The Investors in People accreditation scheme is a national scheme which allows employers to benchmark their employment practices against a set of criteria that cover, inter alia, management effectiveness, communication, training, equality and employee involvement. The scheme has several levels, starting at 'Bronze' and rising to 'Champion' at the highest level.

© The Editor(s) (if applicable) and The Author(s) 2016   **263**
S. Manfredi, L. Vickers (eds.), *Challenges of Active Ageing*,
DOI 10.1057/978-1-137-53251-0_13

The Council has retained its housing stock, and its housing maintenance is undertaken by an in-house workforce; waste and refuse collection, street-cleaning services, and the parks and countryside services are also managed in-house, following successful bidding in competition with external tenderers.[4] The Council's Direct Services workforce is therefore relatively large for a district council, with between 400 and 500 employees at any one time. Those services are now also bidding for, and winning, external contracts with other employers and businesses.

The Council's relationship with the two recognised unions, UNISON and Unite, is very good, and an innovative collective agreement was signed with them in 2012. This took Oxford out of the national pay bargaining group for five years and created a local pay structure which guarantees minimum annual increases plus a John Lewis style annual bonus linked to the Council's success in meeting the expenditure reduction targets that have been built into its annual budgets to meet the cuts in grant income imposed by central government.[5]

2   Managing the Workplace Without Mandatory Retirement

The abolition of the DRA has had a limited impact on the Council's office-based workforce. The Local Government Pension Scheme is still a high quality defined benefit scheme, with many employees able to count on pensions from significant periods of service which, for pension calculation purposes, are assessed on a final salary rather than on an annual average basis. This group's experience has been that those who wish to continue employment past the old retirement age of 65 years can usually be accommodated on either a full-time or, more often, a part-time basis, which allows them to spend more of the working week on activities

---

[4] Since the Thatcher government in the 1980s, public bodies have been encouraged, and at certain times required, to put service provision out to a competitive tendering process. In many local authorities, as a consequence, services such as refuse collection, street-cleaning, parks and leisure management, pest control, benefits and IT are provided by private companies rather than by directly employed local authority staff.

[5] The austerity programme of the coalition government (2010–15) hit local governments particularly hard, with reductions in annual grants of up to 40% over the five-year period. These reductions are expected to continue.

of their own choice. The reason the office-based workforce has (thus far) had such an unproblematic experience with the pension scheme is that the Council implements rigorous performance management policies and has undertaken a series of restructurings over the past decade to reduce the net budget to cope with cuts in government grants. This has raised the quality of the Council's service provision and has created high performing teams—reflected in the International Investors in People Award commendation.

The Council's Direct Services workforce is markedly different from the office-based workforce, and this creates significant challenges in relation particularly (but not exclusively) to older workers.

2.1 Turnover

The Direct Services workforce consists of a wide range of skilled, semi-skilled and unskilled workers, including electricians, gas fitters, carpenters and joiners, plumbers, mechanical fitters, drivers, painters and decorators, civil engineering technicians, refuse collection workers, street cleaners and gardeners. These are all functions that are in demand from a wide range of employers, and are also extensively offered on a self employed basis to private householders and to businesses. As a consequence, there is a greater flow of staff in and out of the Council's employment than among the office-based workforce, and this is particularly true in areas where formal skill qualifications are not required, such as street-cleaning and refuse collection. The effect of the higher turnover levels is to substantially reduce the average length of local authority service for these categories of employees, and hence, to reduce the size of their pension entitlements.

2.2 Opting Out from the Local Government Pension Scheme (LGPS)

Despite the attractiveness of the Local Government Pension Scheme and the advent of Automatic Enrolment, the level of opting out from a pension scheme is much higher among this group. Migrant workers feature strongly in this context.

2.3   Second Jobs

The ability to use craft and craft-based skills outside the framework of formal employment means that many of these employees are able to offer their services elsewhere.

2.4   Pay Directly Linked to Productivity

For a significant number of employees in this group, pay is linked to the number of jobs completed within the working week; housing maintenance workers, for example, can go beyond the expected standard work allocation and, in doing so earn additional income in what amounts effectively to voluntary 'overtime'. This rate of work and the use of overtime may become more onerous and less attractive as the years go by.

3   Alternative Work Trajectories for Employees as They Get Older

Against this background, the Council has adopted a portfolio of policies that can offer alternative trajectories for employees as they get older.

3.1   Part-Time Employment

Probably the most popular and straightforward option for the older worker is to reduce the number of working hours either in the working week or the working month, depending on the nature of the service area. In combination with a pension payment, where it is available, this provides a continuing level of income that can support a quality of life and standard of living that is often not substantially lower than when in full-time work. While this option can also be attractive to the employer, it also creates complications for the management of shift patterns, the creation of stable work teams and consistent staff availability, particularly in periods of excessive demand or emergencies. There is a point at which the balance in the workforce swings away from full to part-time hours contracts, and this becomes a challenge to managers in the delivery of the quality and consistency of service that is expected, particularly when they are delivering against a contract.

3.2   An Alternative Job or Role Within the Council

Where the physical demands of a job are significant, and older workers find these demands less easy to cope with, it is often possible to identify other roles where the demands are less onerous but which require similar skill and knowledge levels. A housing maintenance worker, for example, can move from the pressurised world of day-to-day housing repairs to small contract work or support roles in the depot. Street-cleaning and bulky items collections offer very different work routines compared to the daily round of household waste collections and mixed and green waste recycling. Redeployment to caretaking and similar roles can also be considered. The Council provides a wide range of training and retraining opportunities; this commitment lies at the heart of the Investors in People successes that were mentioned earlier. These opportunities are available to re-skill staff at any age if there is a wish to move to a different type of work; in relation to older workers, a wish to continue in employment in an office-based role can also be accommodated where there is an appropriate level of the required aptitudes.

As a Council which wishes to be considered as a good employer, Oxford City has made two core policy commitments in relation to the management of its employees: an insistence on effective performance management, supported by extensive line management training to embed the principles of good leadership and management; and a high degree of flexibility in the management of teams and in the provisions of job descriptions and contracts of employment. Both of these have been of value in dealing with the issues which arise in relation to the wishes and capacities of older workers. As indicated above, the effects of the changes in the statutory framework around age have been relatively limited in scale and significance so far, but the Council has sought to plan ahead and to develop policy responses which can be deployed on a limited scale in the current conditions, but which will provide experience to cope satisfactorily with the longer term changes in the workforce that are likely to occur as the years go on.

Two such changes are the gender and role composition of those employees seeking to extend their occupational life with the Council. As the age of entitlement to state pensions and related benefits rises, it is likely that female employees, who are disproportionately represented in the office-based workforce, will want to work longer. A similar portfolio of options to those outlined above can be provided to facilitate this wish, but it will have to be adapted to meet specific contexts. In housing management teams, for example, handling complex tenant enquiries and complaints can be seriously compromised if the responsible officers are working part-time and a robust case handling system is not in place. Additionally, if the demand for extended working lives comes increasingly from professional staff in, for example, planning, environmental development, asset management or treasury management functions, there will be a vital requirement to increase the availability of continuous professional development.

4   Conclusion

To summarise, Oxford City Council is dealing effectively with the current limited impact of the change in the law on age discrimination, and takes the view that its commitment to good employment practices, a strong commitment to training and professional development, and good collective bargaining relationships with the recognised unions will enable it to adapt further in future years.

14

What Scope for an Employer Justified Retirement Age? A View from Practice

Saphieh Ashtiany

Visiting Professorial Fellow (QMUL) and Principal (Ashtiany Associates).

This paper is based on anecdotal evidence from practice and from a range of employers. It does not purport to be a systematic examination of data relating to retirement practice.

This contribution offers a view from the perspective of a lawyer with many years' experience of the challenges that the removal of the Default Retirement Age (DRA) could raise. It questions the UK Government's decision to abolish the DRA on the basis that a fixed end-date for employment is by no means a social ill: it has many benefits for orderly planning of the employment market and work opportunities. It obviates intergenerational difficulties and removes the source of some workplace conflicts. Fixed retirement can also promote diversity.

Employers are currently feeling their way towards possible solutions to the issues emerging from the removal of the DRA, and some interesting formulations of a valid Employer Justified Retirement Age (EJRA) are emerging. However, the general picture remains mixed and there is little by way of systematic response. Moreover, the issues remain largely under the radar as far as case law is concerned.

As discussed elsewhere in this collection, the DRA was finally abolished in 2011, after the introduction of what turned out to be a short-lived process whereby retirement was justified, provided the employer strictly followed the notification regime set out in the Employment Equality (Age) Regulations 2006.

The primary governmental impetus for the abolition was almost certainly not the pursuit of an equality agenda, but rather, the specific wish to encourage later retirement for fiscal reasons: to enhance GDP and to reduce pressure on public services. The DRA was abolished in the face of opposition from employer organisations such as the Confederation of British Industry (CBI), which criticised the rapid legislation of the proposed changes, saying it would leave firms "with many unresolved problems" and little time to prepare.[1] Indeed, the general employer response was that it would add to overall costs and complicate the job of managing a workforce. Anecdotally, it remains the case that UK employers are largely bemused by and opposed to the measure.

Ironically, the developing jurisprudence under the 2006 AGE Regulations was already demonstrating a capacity to protect older workers and to limit the rights of employers to act without due regard to their interests. Thus, in *Ayodele v. Compass Group*,[2] the EAT had upheld a tribunal's finding at first instance that an employer had to consider requests for continued working beyond the DRA properly and in good faith: it was not just a tick-box exercise. In *Bailey v. R&R (Peterborough) Plant Ltd*,[3] the Court of Appeal made it clear that the employer must follow procedures with care, ensuring that the employee was aware it was initiating a statutory procedure under which the employee had certain rights. These cases clearly indicate the willingness of the Courts to apply robust criteria for the protection of individual employees wishing to challenge their retirement. At the same time, use of a DRA remains widely accepted within the European Union and there is nothing in the jurisprudence of the Court of Justice of the European Union (CJEU) to suggest that a specified retirement date is either in letter or spirit against the Directive. This is discussed in detail, in Chap. 2.

---

[1] http://www.cbi.org.uk/media-centre/press-releases/2011/09/.

[2] UKEAT/2011//0484/10. An important decision by the then president of the EAT, Underhill J, who is now in the Court of Appeal.

[3] [2012] EWCA Civ 410.

Thus, there was nothing preventing the government from allowing the statutory regime to continue in place in the UK. Instead of swiftly abolishing the DRA, it could have commissioned robust research on the impact of its removal across a range of criteria and in comparison to modelled alternatives. This would have enabled a proper examination of the issues. However, the developing picture in the UK was effectively stopped in its tracks with the repeal.

The new measures came fully into force in October 2011. So far, we have little data on its impact, and this is almost certainly because there are still very few people in the relevant age-group, i.e. people seeking to work beyond the age of 65. The age at which people stop working in the UK is still usually short of 65. As of December 2014, the average age of retirement was 64.7 for men (static 2012–2014) and 63.1 for women (up slightly from 62.7 in 2012). However, in the coming years, pressures (or incentives) to work longer will mount with a steady increase in the State Pension Age,[4] a decline both in eligibility for and quantum of pensions generally, and an increase in the 65+ years population in England.

The abolition of a legally mandated general fixed retirement age has implications for issues not directly related to retirement *per se*, such as workforce planning, salary and benefits systems, performance management, etc. In the absence of an EJRA, and therefore a fixed-end point to employment related to age, there is potentially little lawful scope even for discussions about altering the role of, say, a senior professor or head of department or reducing responsibilities or workloads: *any* mooted change is potentially an age-related detriment. If there is a lawful and valid end-date, then it is possible for the employer lawfully to initiate discussion about a range of options including part-time working or role changes without running the risk of claims of unlawful discrimination. Without such a provision, any workplace policy that considers an end point of employment is potentially at risk of being deemed to be unlawful age discrimination as are decisions based, whether directly or indirectly, on service, experience or longevity. Although the Equality Act permits

[4] Those now in their twenties can expect not to be eligible for a state pension (assuming these still exist) until after their 70th birthday. In its most recent business plan, the Department for Work and Pensions said that it would like the average age at which people retire to rise by as much as six months every year to offset the costs of an aging population.

distinctions in the provision of 'a benefit, facility or service' based on the length of employment over five years, provided the employer reasonably believes this fulfils a business need,[5] the scope of this exception has not been tested and is not clear. The provision is aimed at permitting service-related benefits that an employee has built up during employment, rather than planning decisions based on the premise of an end-point in the employment. In the absence of a specified end-point, any decision or policy which impacts work opportunities, training, or access to work experience, and which takes into account a view about reasonable periods of payback, is challengeable and risks being unlawful. Should employees start to exercise a right to remain in their jobs into their late 60s and 70s in any significant numbers, and given that any directly or indirectly age-related measure risks being unlawful unless objectively justified, there will be plenty of scope for disputes.

The removal of the DRA left employers with the choice of dealing with such issues as they arose. These choices include introducing more draconian performance management across the board, considering whether they could themselves establish an EJRA for some or all of their staff, or considering whether there were other alternatives such as the wider use of fixed-term contracts. The picture is currently confused and in a state of flux. Some employers have chosen to maintain or establish an EJRA. This is the case generally for police forces, emergency services, the armed forces and the judiciary. Many in the professional services sector have also taken the view that some fixed end-date is required, at least for partners. These are not the only sectors where the employer operates a fixed end-date, but it may be relevant that they are all characterised byhigh status roles, lack of turn-over at senior levels with almost no scope for expansion, entrenched rights, and a practice of working right up to retirement age. Some employers have also considered side-stepping the issue by using fixed-term contracts. Thus, in some higher education institutions, senior academic staff are employed on fixed-term contracts which set the expectations of both parties as to longevity. However, there is by no means a uniformity of approach, and many employers have simply been advised to remove any reference to a retirement date and manage situations as best they can when they arise.

---

[5] Equality Act 2010 Schedule 9 Clause 10.

An analysis of court judgments also shows little interest in retirement as an issue *per se*. There is only one Supreme Court decision,[6] discussed in Chap. 4. That case reviewed carefully the CJEU jurisprudence which has established a number of potential legitimate aims, and held that a fixed retirement age was a proportionate means of achieving the legitimate aims of dignity and collegiality, retention and intergenerational fairness and succession planning. The Supreme Court left open the question of whether the specific age of 65 was proportionate: this was upheld in further litigation in *Seldon (2)*.[7] Since *Seldon (1)*, there have been very few cases. The sole appeal level case directly concerned with retirement policy, *Chief Constable of West Midlands Police v. Harrods* (UKEAT/0189/14), upheld the decision of a number of police forces to terminate the jobs of police officers on the grounds that they were eligible for adequate pensions.[8] Three other cases have been heard at tribunal (first instance) level. In two of them, EJRAs were upheld. The England and Wales Cricket Boards' policy of retiring umpires at the age of 65 was upheld in a careful decision by the London ET, as was the Ministry of Justice's policy of retiring judges at 70. Conversely, in the third case, the tribunal which felt unable to uphold a retirement age of 70 for parking adjudicators because of insufficient evidence from the employer, made a plea for more guidance from the appellate courts about how to approach the issue of justification of an EJRA.[9]

There is little soft law guidance either. The Advisory Conciliation and Arbitration Service (ACAS), a quasi-governmental public body which provides guidance on a range of employment issues, produced a booklet, *Age and the Workplace*,[10] in 2011. It includes a couple of pages of general information which understandably leaves it entirely to an employer to decide how and why it might consider an EJRA and warns of the

---

[6] *Seldon v Clarkson Wright and Jakes [2012] UKSC 16.* 'Seldon(1)'.

[7] UKEAT/0434/13/RN.

[8] The Forces were enacting cost-cutting measures by choosing officers eligible for pensions under Rule A (19) of Police Regulations. They complained this was unlawful indirect discrimination and the EAT upheld the Forces' appeal against a finding of an employment tribunal in their favour.

[9] *Willey and Sharpe v ECB, White v Ministry of Justice, Engel v Transport and Environment Committee of London Councils.*

[10] http://www.acas.org.uk/media/pdf/e/4/Age-and-the-workplace-guide.pdf [Accessed 18 October 2015].

difficulties. Some advisers are working with individual employers to establish an EJRA, but this work is not widely publicised. From a review of the scanty literature available, there appears also to be widespread misunderstanding about what an EJRA is and how it could be established. There is a prevalent view in business, and in particular in the HR community, that any specified retirement age is now unlawful *per se*, and so there is little discussion of whether, in fact, such a provision could be justified in a particular workplace or in respect of a particular group of employees. Much HR-led comment is ill-informed, with a focus usually on the justification of retirement as the aim itself, rather than as a means of achieving legally a different and objectively justified aim or aims.[11] Perhaps because of this misunderstanding, the impression is that this is a tricky topic to be avoided, if at all possible, especially as most people retire before the age of 65 at present.

The higher education sector, which shares many of the same characteristics as those organisations generally maintaining EJRAs, is an interesting case. Many university employers have simply removed a retirement age and wait for consequential developments, but a few university employers have introduced retirement policies post-2011 enshrining an EJRA for some or all of their staff. In doing so, they have taken account of a context of global competition, recognising inter alia that turnover, especially in the more senior posts, is low, that there is no realistic prospect of expansion and that the lack of a fixed retirement date has the potential to cause a wider and poorly understood detrimental impact on the employment relationship generally. The aims of their retirement policies closely reflect established CJEU jurisprudence on what amount to legitimate aims, and which were echoed by the Supreme Court

---

[11] A fairly typical example, and which demonstrates the lack of understanding of the whole concept, reads: 'As usual there are exceptions to every rule and in some very far and few between cases, employers can still enforce a compulsory retirement age. In order to do that, however, you would need to be able to objectively justify the retirement, therefore, you would need to have addressed the following questions:—Why do you need a compulsory age?—Is your desire for a compulsory age simply based on a preference or assumption about a person's age?—Do you have genuine evidence that can help justify your reasoning for a retirement age? - Are there easier ways of achieving the same results, such as introducing regular employee reviews?' http://www.hr180.co.uk/wp-content/uploads/Retirement-Factsheet.pdf [Accessed 15 October 2015].

in *Seldon (1)*.[12] These universities have also identified that their most senior staff are not at all diverse, and the provision of promotion opportunities for women and minority ethnic staff has also been a motivating element in the introduction of an EJRA. EJRAs, in these higher education institutions, have generally been introduced after extensive consultation and usually include a process echoing the old 'request to remain' procedure that was elaborated in the 2006 regulations.

When an EJRA is implemented, there is clearly a burden on the employer to ensure that its aims remain legitimate, that the means remain proportionate, and that this can be done by periodic reviews. Indeed, ultimately, unless the government changes its mind and reintroduces a general DRA, there must always be some scope for uncertainty. However, the responses to employer consultations, including the widespread approval from younger academic staff encompassing, interestingly, members of the relevant unions where they have been consulted, suggests that there is indeed scope for valid EJRAs in the higher education sector; as does the fact that the aims articulated closely resemble those already found legitimate by the CJEU and the UK Supreme Court. The means chosen must be proportionate, but there is no reason to consider that the age(s) currently chosen are not proportionate. Certainly, the CJEU jurisprudence suggests that an EJRA at or above 65 would currently be held to be proportionate under European law. Two of the universities have an EJRA of 30th September after the person's 67th birthday whilst one tracks the state pension age.

There is a strong case for addressing such issues directly and through the means of a rigorous consideration of the place for a fixed retirement date. If the employer gets it right, and current case law suggests that there is good scope for that, then it is inherently a better, fairer and more dignified approach than a series of *ad personam* decisions, most probably based on invidious considerations of failing performance taken in a relative conceptual void.

---

[12] At the time of writing, Oxford, Cambridge and St Andrews have adopted policies with a fixed retirement age, in the former cases for academic staff only. See generally their policies at http://www.hr.admin.cam.ac.uk/files/retirement_policy2014.pdf (Cambridge) [Accessed 15 October 2015]; http://www.admin.ox.ac.uk/personnel/end/retirement/acrelretire/ejra (Oxford) [Accessed 15 October 2015] and http://www.st-andrews.ac.uk/media/human-resources/new-policy-section-documents/retirement-process/Retirement%20Policy.pdf St Andrews [Accessed 15 October 2015].

15

Extending Working Lives: A Trade Union Perspective

Sally Brett

The trade union perspective on extending working lives can appear to be one of straightforward resistance. The union voice was heard loudest when it opposed increases in the state pension age and resisted changes to occupational pension schemes, such as the recent reforms in the public sector that have raised normal pension ages. But the Trades Union Congress (TUC) and its affiliate unions have also played a key role in campaigning against age discrimination and calling for more support for older workers to access opportunities and remain in work.

The trade union approach to extending working lives is one that is founded on the principle that all deserve fairness throughout their working life and a decent retirement as a reward for a lifetime of work. Trade unions recognise that many individuals now want or need to work for longer. The eventual repeal of the statutory default retirement age was welcomed by the TUC, but there was recognition that removing this method of dismissal alone was insufficient to encourage longevity in the workplace.[1] In the years since the repeal, there has been growing concern that older workers are simply being dismissed by other means. There is a

---

[1] TUC (2010) Response to BIS/DWP Consultation *Phasing out the default retirement age.*

© The Editor(s) (if applicable) and The Author(s) 2016
S. Manfredi, L. Vickers (eds.), *Challenges of Active Ageing,*
DOI 10.1057/978-1-137-53251-0_15

parallel concern that increases in the state pension age are pushing older people to continue in work that is insecure, poorly paid or harmful to their health because they no longer have the option of retirement. The TUC has argued that more needs to be done to improve the opportunities people have for working later in life and to ensure that people have a greater capacity to do so.[2]

There has been a significant rise in the number of people working beyond the age of 65 since the introduction of age discrimination legislation. The number of over 65s in work topped one million for the first time in 2013. However, the increase has been from a very low base and the number staying in work still only represents 1 in 10 of the 65+ population. The majority of men and women stop working by the year before they reach state pension age.[3]

There has been some improvement in recent years in the employment rate for 50–64 year olds, but there are still 2.9 million people in this age group who are out of work. Only 0.7 million see themselves as 'retired', and 1.7 million—over three-quarters of those who are out of work and do not consider themselves retired—think it is unlikely they will ever work again.[4]

It is also worth noting that older workers are much more likely to be self-employed. Two-thirds of workers in the 65+ age group are self-employed, which is a much higher proportion compared to other age groups.[5] For some, self-employment will be a positive choice, but for many, it will be a response to difficulties in finding a job as an employee. For older women, in particular, TUC analysis has shown that since the 2008/9 recession, there has been a substantial rise in self-employment, and this has tended to be in low paid, part-time, 'odd job' work such as cleaning.[6]

---

[2] See TUC (2013) *Life expectancy inequalities and state pension outcomes.*
[3] DWP (2014) *Fuller Working Lives: A Framework for Action.*
[4] DWP (2014) *Fuller Working Lives.*
[5] ONS (2014) Self employed workers in the UK 2014 http://www.ons.gov.uk/ons/publications/re-reference-tables.html?edition=tcm%3A77-371749 (Accessed July 2015).
[6] Touchstone blog, 'What has been happening to self employment lately?': http://touchstoneblog.org.uk/2015/02/what-has-been-happening-to-self-employment-lately/ (Accessed July 2015).

Some of the issues that trade unions see as key to extending working lives and improving opportunities for older people are discussed below: improved choice and flexibility around retirement; positive and early interventions to encourage longevity; better support for carers; and midlife career reviews.

1   Choice and Flexibility Around Retirement

The TUC's response to the consultation on the repeal of the statutory default retirement age (DRA) welcomed the move but warned that: 'Simply removing the default retirement age and the parallel proposal to rapidly increase the state pension age are not going to have the desired effect [of extending working lives].'[7] The TUC supported the repeal of the DRA, and there were many examples of trade unions having negotiated agreements with employers to remove fixed retirement ages. Forcing someone out of their job simply because they had reached a particular age was widely seen as unfair. It was recognised that some individuals were not ready to stop work at a set date and there was also an understanding that some individuals needed to stay in work, perhaps because they still had dependents or mortgages to pay which their expected pension income would not cover.

The government review of the DRA highlighted research that found that while most people were against forced retirement, the majority still expected to retire around the age of 65. However, if people knew they could work on a flexible basis, the proportion of those who would like to work for longer increased to a majority. This suggested that one of the key incentives for working longer is creating more choice and flexibility over how people work in later life and when they retire.[8]

The trade union Prospect cites BAE Systems as an organisation that has taken what they consider to be a positive approach. The company has a longstanding phased retirement policy that allows employees to reduce their working hours two years ahead of their chosen retirement

---

[7]TUC (2010) Response to BIS/DWP Consultation *'Phasing out the default retirement age'*.
[8]BIS/DWP (2010) *Review of the Default Retirement Age: Summary of the stakeholder evidence.*

date (any age after 55), and to adjust their work responsibilities five years ahead of retirement, spending more time in training or mentoring roles. The union reports that not only do individuals make better transitions into retirement, but it has also enabled better workforce planning for the company through early discussions with older workers about their plans and it has ensured that their skills and knowledge are transferred before they exit the workforce.[9]

In more recent years, trade unions have become increasingly concerned by rising pension ages being used as a stick to discourage older workers from retiring whilst, at the same time, employers are using harsh employment practices to push older workers out of the workforce for reasons other than retirement. In 2013, the TUC commissioned research to find out how unions and employers were responding to the repeal of the statutory DRA. Trade unions reported few positive approaches from employers to incentivise and plan for working in later life. Instead, union officers reported increasing caseloads from older workers who were being pushed out of work on performance or ill-health grounds.[10]

One of the sectors where this seemed to be a particular concern was education. At the teaching union NASUWT's annual conference in 2015, delegates expressed concern at growing evidence that older teachers were being singled out for redundancy or were being forced out via abuse of capability procedures. In a press release, the general secretary stated that 'It is disturbing to find, however, that all too often older teachers are being targeted for redundancy, threatened unjustly with capability procedures, denied access to professional development, or subjected to excessive monitoring in an attempt to force them out of the school. They face this harassment and discrimination often for no other reason than they are older and more expensive'.[11]

These studies indicate that while the removal of a DRA may seem to hold the promise of greater choice and flexibility, in reality, that promise has not been fulfilled.

---

[9] M Flynn (2014) *Representing an ageing workforce: challenges and opportunities for trade unions.*

[10] *Representing an ageing workforce.*

[11] NASUWT (press release 6 April 2015) 'Older workers face discrimination' http://www.nasuwt.org.uk/Whatsnew/NASUWTNews/PressReleases/NASUWT_013978 (Accessed July 2015).

2   Positive and Early Interventions by Employers

The acceleration of the increases in the state pension age, the corresponding reforms in public service pension schemes and the repeal of the DRA have been framed by a sense of urgency about the need to respond to an ageing population, but this same sense of urgency does not seem to be there when considering adaptations to the workplace or working practices to encourage longevity.

This issue can be illustrated by the experience of the TUC. Some years ago, shortly after the Age Regulations were implemented, the TUC organised a roundtable with the Employers Forum on Age, which represented good practice employers. A number of employers and union representatives from the finance sector spoke positively about the steps that had been taken in the sector to increase or completely remove fixed retirement ages to enable working into later life. However, part way through the discussion, when asked about the impact of these policies, someone from the trade union side noted that in their experience most workers were still leaving his organisation some years before they reached the old retirement age. On reflection, he put this down to the years of work intensification and aggressive performance management in the sector, which meant that most would still choose to take their pension early if they could rather than stay in work. This was something that was picked up again in TUC research following the repeal of the DRA. Work intensification, such as a pressure to work faster, accept bigger workloads and work additional hours, was mentioned as a trend that pushed older workers out or encouraged them to stop work if they could afford to. This trend was mentioned by union officers in a range of sectors including finance, retail, call centres, education and health.[12]

Another factor that needs to be addressed, if we are to build people's capacity to work for longer, is the physically demanding nature of some jobs and the impact that they can have on health. Older workers are often reluctant to admit to health problems or the strain that the work is placing on

---

[12] M Flynn *Representing an ageing workforce: challenges and opportunities for trade unions.*

them for fear of being pushed out. The shopworkers' union Usdaw reported this from one of their members: 'I'm 62 now and I work in a returns centre. I stand up for seven hours a day and find my job really tiring. I pull heavy cages and get back and shoulder pain. I don't want the company to know I'm struggling though as I need to carry on working. I can't afford to retire. If they find out I'm not coping I might be made to go'.[13]

At TUC Congress in September 2015, delegates debated a motion from one of the health unions which draws attention to the increasing number of older workers who are suffering from repetitive strain injuries, work related upper limb disorders and muscular skeletal disorders. The motion called on the TUC to lead a campaign against 'creeping increases in retirement age' which it stated 'put working people, especially older workers, at an increased risk of being forced to leave work before being eligible to receive a state or workplace pension, which in turn puts them at risk of extreme hardship and poverty in retirement'.[14] The Fire Brigades Union has also been running a high profile campaign against the increase in the normal pension age to 60 for firefighters, pointing out that firefighters will be expected to continue to ride engines, carry heavy equipment and carry people out of burning buildings up until that age. The fact that the objective of these unions' campaigns is to resist requirements to work for longer, must partly reflect the lack of action from employers to adapt jobs to older workers.

One unionised company that has taken positive steps to enable workers to stay in work for longer is BMW (discussed elsewhere in this volume). It has a 'Today for Tomorrow' programme which it says is aimed not just at the ageing worker, but at helping the workforce age better. It is a comprehensive range of interventions including: ergonomic workplace design; job rotation to avoid repetitive stress and strain; a range of health management measures; well-being measures like shorter shifts to reduce daily working hours; flexible working arrangements; and the introduction of processes such as 'reintegration forums' and a 'matching capability' process that facilitates job transfers for workers with medical

---

[13] Usdaw (2015) *The Coalition—Taking Us Backwards on Women's Equality.*
[14] See Congress's CPG Report and Composite Motions 2015 at https://www.tuc.org.uk/sites/default/files/Congress2015GPCReport.pdf (accessed May 2016).

constraints to more suitable roles.[15] This example highlights the scale of action that is needed and which is still lacking in most workplaces if extending working lives is to be a real ambition. It is unsurprising that this example originates from Germany where unions and employers have reached national collective agreements on measures to enable older workers to extend their working lives.

3   Better Support for Carers

Next to poor health, caring is the second most common reason for older people, especially women, to be pushed out of work.[16] The TUC's 'Age Immaterial' campaign in 2013/14 focused on the experiences of women over 50 in the workplace. It identified the lack of support for many older mothers, working grandparents and carers as major barriers to older women continuing to progress or remain in work.[17] For example, polling for the campaign revealed that 41% of grandparents in full-time work, usually grandmothers, provided weekly care for their grandchildren. One in seven grandparents (14%) said they had given up work to care for their grandchildren. Typically, this care-giving was to allow parents to enter paid work. The findings revealed how the shortage of affordable, flexible and good quality childcare can impact on the ability not just of parents, but of older people, to remain in work.

The expectation of a longer working life is also likely to increase the demand for already stretched and underfunded social care services. There would have to be considerable investment in care infrastructure, something that seems unlikely in the current climate of austerity, if the ambition to extend working lives is really going to be fulfilled. The preferences of some older people to take time out of work to become carers themselves should also be recognised. One woman whose partner was diagnosed with an aggressive form of cancer told the TUC's Age Immaterial

---

[15] M Flynn (2014) *Representing an ageing workforce: challenges and opportunities for trade unions.*
[16] G Cory (2012) *Unfinished Business: Barriers and opportunities for older workers* (Resolution Foundation).
[17] TUC (2014) *Age Immaterial: Women over 50 in the workplace.*

campaign that when she was faced with the intense but likely to be short-term responsibility of providing end-of-life care for him, she had asked to reduce her hours or take leave from work. She was refused and so was forced to give up work altogether: 'I tried to juggle work and caring for him, but went off sick with stress. There wasn't sufficient flexibility available with my hours for me to be able to juggle both.' Another older woman explained: 'I'm worried about the impact of the increase in the State Pension Age on my ability to care for elderly parents and a disabled brother who live two and a half hours away. Having the option to retire at 60 would have allowed me to support my daughter back to work and care for my parents and brother but now I am very anxious that we will have to rely on help from outside. I want my parents to be able to stay at home, not go into care because I have to continue to work at a time when they need me most.'[18]

4   Midlife Career Reviews

Older workers need help to build resilience to changes in employment by updating their skills and developing new ones. Workers over 50 years are less likely to take part in workplace training than younger workers. Those who are most likely to participate in training are those who have experienced previous job mobility, and who feel they have the support to continue to learn and progress at work. Older workers in an unsupportive environment may be reluctant to initiate conversations about learning needs, because they fear it might exacerbate people's perceptions of their out-of-date skills or declining ability.[19]

The TUC has shown how effective Union Learning Representatives (ULRs) can be in identifying the training and development needs of workers. Workers are often more willing to reveal skills gaps to ULRs than they are to managers. Between 2013 and 2014, the TUC's Unionlearn was involved in a successful BIS-funded pilot project to develop 'midlife career reviews' which built on ULRs' role as trusted intermediaries.

---

[18] TUC (2014) *Age Immaterial.*

[19] M Flynn (2014) *Representing an ageing workforce: challenges and opportunities for trade unions.*

The project was aimed at helping workers in the middle of their working lives reflect on where they were in their personal and working lives; take stock of their skills, knowledge and experience; and consider their future options including identifying any barriers and opportunities for further progression or a change of direction. It also aimed to signpost individuals to any additional support like financial planning, specialist health and well-being advice or career guidance where necessary. More than 45 ULRs from 15 unions were trained in the initial pilot with the aim of carrying out 360 reviews, but such was the demand for midlife support, 770 individuals were helped.[20]

Having seen the value of this work, especially in supporting midlife workers who are vulnerable to redundancy and may struggle to regain employment, the TUC has called for all workers to have the right to a midlife review at the age of 50. Unionlearn is continuing to develop the 'supporting midlife development' area of its work in its overall strategy for 2014–17 and it intends to engage more employers in this work over the coming years. However, ULRs face increasing barriers to their work as the conservative government seeks to restrict the paid facility time they receive for training and carrying out their duties in the public sector. This is a sector where workers are likely to benefit from the midlife support that trained ULRs can offer, given the expected job losses and the difficult transition that many older public servants will face in finding new work in the private sector.

The ability of older workers to develop new skills and change direction is further undermined by substantial cuts in funding for the further education sector. In February 2015, the coalition government announced a 24% reduction in the further education budget. This came on top of budget cuts of 35% between 2010 and 2015, which resulted in one million fewer adult learners. It is estimated that the next round of budget cuts will cut the numbers accessing adult education by a further 400,000.[21]

---

[20] Unionlearn (2014) *Mid-life career reviews: Helping older workers plan their future.*
[21] Unison (2015) *Briefing on adult education and funding cuts.*

5   Conclusion

Trade unions are supportive of measures that enable people to work for longer, but the extending working lives agenda has been too narrowly focused on measures that push people into work, notably the increase in the state pension age. Not enough has been done to enable or incentivise people to remain productive for longer and to make good use of their skills and experience. The repeal of the statutory DRA removed the main formal barrier to working beyond 65 years of age, but since its repeal, few employers have taken positive and comprehensive steps to build capacity for longer working. At worst, unions report that some employers are using alternative means to drive older workers out of the workforce. Public policy is also failing to address the need for more investment in infrastructure like adult education and care services that facilitate longer working.

16

'Changing Step': The Transition from the Regular Army to Civilian Life and Work

Vincent Connelly

Vincent Connelly gratefully acknowledges the help of the staff of Army Regional Command in the preparation of the chapter, 'Changing Step'. He is also grateful to the staff of the Army Headquarters' Education and Career Development Branch for their comments on an earlier draft of the chapter. The views expressed in this chapter are those of the author alone.

Changing step is an obvious military term to use in this context, and many have used it before. However, it is also a reference to one of the classic in-depth studies on UK Service Leavers in the last 25 years whose qualitative case studies can still enlighten and educate. See R Jolly (1996) Changing Step: From military to civilian life: people in transition, (London Brassey's (UK) Ltd.)

The British Army has always recognized that the majority of their full-time personnel will leave the Army and move into other employment sectors before their formal retirement from the world of work. In fact, the majority of Army personnel will work, on average, longer in other employment sectors than in the Army itself with, for example, about half of personnel serving six years or less in the Army, and with a current mandatory retirement age of 55 for most personnel.¹ Therefore, there has been a long-standing interest in managing the transition from military to civilian life for those leaving the Army. This chapter will deal with the recent history of how the Army prepares its soldiers for leaving the Army, sets the context for why it does this, and describes how individuals are being encouraged to think of a 'through-career' transition to civilian life that emphasizes education, individual development, personal planning and preparation for life beyond the Army. The details of the actual provisions that members of the Army can access in preparation for leaving will also briefly be described along with some of the challenges that may arise in the future.²

The Army is an unusual public sector employer where individuals agree to incur potentially unlimited liability in terms of job location, working hours and their physical and mental well-being. There is often a strong argument put forward that society has an obligation to ensure that those who are prepared to sacrifice their life in the service of the state should not be disadvantaged by their service or when integrating back into civilian life.³ Thus, there can be much public and political debate about the fate of individuals in the Army who have served in such conflicts, which is heavily influenced by the wider attitudes to those conflicts and the changing social

---

¹ The average age of a service leaver is 32, but the distribution is skewed by three significant peaks in the data: those leaving during basic training (17–19 years), those who leave after their initial engagement period of four years (22–23 years), and those who serve a 'full career' of 22 years (40–42 years); only a minority of soldiers and officers serving till the age 55. Under the 'New Employment Model' being discussed, the retirement age may rise to 60, but the three peaks in the number of service leavers will likely remain similar. See the National Audit Office Report (2007) *Leaving the Services,* (HMSO) and also see *Career Transition Partnership quarterly statistics: UK Regular Service Personnel Employment Outcomes 2009/10 to 2013/14* (UK Ministry of Defence 11 June 2015). https://www.gov.uk/government/uploads/system/uploads/attachment_data/file/434406/20150522_CTP_official_statistic_0910_1314Revised.pdf Accessed 21 October 2015.

² In this chapter, we will only deal with the part of the Army in full-time or 'Regular Army' service. Although recent steps have been taken to widen the definition of transition to include the Reservist components of the Army (who are mainly part-time), the Regular Army will continue to provide the bulk of individuals who require transition and resettlement and so is the focus of this chapter. The chapter, due to space constraints, only provides an overview of the transition process. See http://www.army.mod.uk/welfare-support/23590.aspx, Accessed 21 October 2015, for more detail.

³ As detailed in the recent UK Armed Forces Covenant. https://www.gov.uk/government/publications/2010-to-2015-government-policy-armed-forces-covenant/2010-to-2015-government-policy-armed-forces-covenant. Accessed 21 October 2015.

attitudes to 'veterans' in British society.[4] The visibility of the Army in society also interacts closely with media reporting of conflicts which produce a view of the Army that appears to be sympathetic to the individual soldier but not very empathic or understanding of the role of the Army.[5]

The reputation of veterans in British society is complex and has historically not been positive.[6] This has led to the assumption that the Army does not adequately prepare soldiers for the transition to civilian life. For example, a letter from 1881 states '…the nation treats its soldiers like oranges, that having sucked them dry, it throws them aside'.[7] Similar quotes can be found all the way to the present day. Combined with persistent negative beliefs about the impact of military service on the mental health of veterans, it is not surprising that negative beliefs about the employment prospects of veterans still strongly persist.[8]

Yet, Army employment policies related to transition are evident from at least the time of the Napoleonic wars. At the end of the First World War, the Army realized that the masses of citizens who had served in the

---

[4] A UK veteran is officially defined as someone who has served in the military for at least one day. See A Wyatt (March 2002) *Development of the Veterans Initiative by the Ministry of Defence, Case Study* (Sunningdale Park, UK: The International Comparisons in Policy Making Team, International Public Service Group, Cabinet Office's Centre for Management and Policy Studies, the Civil Service College). One of the reasons for this all inclusive definition is that it has been found that 'early service leavers' tend to do worse outside the military than those who leave the military later in life. Thus, this definition allows early service leavers—as veterans— to access external services that can help them with potential transition difficulties. For another perspective on more popular definitions, see C Dandeker et al. (2006) 'What's in a Name? Defining and Caring for "Veterans": The United Kingdom in International Perspective' *Armed Forces and Society* 32, 161.

[5] See for example, Helen B McCartney (2011) 'Hero, victim or villain? The public image of the British soldier and its implications for defense policy', *Defense and Security Analysis*, 27(1).

[6] For example, see P Reese (1992) *Homecoming Heroes: An account of the re-assimilation of British Military personnel into civilian life* (London, Pen & Sword book).

[7] Letter to *Edinburgh Review* dated 1881 cited in D French (2005) *Military Identities: The Regimental System, the British Army, and the British People, 1870—2000* (Oxford, UK, Oxford University Press) 253.

[8] R Gribble, S Wessley, S Klein, D A Alexander, C Dandeker, NT Fear. (3 October 2013) *Are the UK Armed Forces understood and supported by the British Public?* Report for the Public Perceptions Symposium. (Kings College, London). http://www.kcl.ac.uk/kcmhr/research/kcmhr/publicperceptionshandout.pdf. Accessed 21 October 2015.
See also V Connelly& M Burgess (2013) 'Suicide among Falkland war veterans - Understanding why misleading 'sound bites' about veterans are more believable than 'sound statistics', (Rapid Response) *British Medical Journal* http://www.bmj.com/content/346/bmj.f3204/rr/677045. Accessed 21 October 2015.

Army needed a process of education and employment specific training to 'resettle' them back into civilian life. However, the largest leap forward for transition related policies probably happened when the Army moved from being a conscripted force to an 'all-volunteer' body in the early 1960s. There followed a realisation that for an all-volunteer army to succeed in attracting new entrants, it needed to be seen as a 'good employer'.[9] Key to this was amending terms and conditions of service that dealt with out-of-date social assumptions (such as the assumption that officers had a private income they could rely on after service)[10] and enabling a second career through flexible early retirement options (for example, providing an immediate pension from the Army to provide some financial security to offset their late entry into a second career as well as a cash gratuity to help secure a house) as well as options for education and training prior to leaving the Army. Since then, there have been many improvements made to how personnel are prepared for leaving the Army.

Thus, while negative beliefs about poor preparation for transition may have had some validity in the past, more recent longitudinal studies show that military service for most veterans is a positive boost to post-service life.[11] Employment rates for veterans are high, with 84% of leavers in employment within six months, 8% unemployed and 9% economically inactive over the period 2009 to 2014. This compares to the UK Labour Force Survey showing employment rates of 70%, 8% unemployed, and 24% economically inactive over the same period.[12] Further to this, there is evidence that service life acts as a successful form of social mobility for many individuals, through training for personal development, trade qualifications and education for life.[13] The qualities

---

[9] David French (2012) *Army, Empire and Cold War, The British Army and Military Policy, 1945–1971* (Oxford University Press).

[10] Command Paper 545 (October 1958) *Report of the Advisory Committee on Recruiting* (London, HMSO).

[11] A Iversen, V Nikolaou, N Greenberg, C Unwin, L Hull, M Hotopf et al. (2004) 'What happens to British veterans when they leave the armed forces?' *Eur J Public Health* 15, 175–84.

[12] *Career Transition Partnership quarterly statistics: UK Regular Service Personnel Employment Outcomes 2009/10 to 2013/14* (11 June 2015) (UK Ministry of Defence).

[13] 'The Armed Forces Literacy and Numeracy Policy is effective: it provides a statement of high level support for literacy and numeracy improvement and development, an essential element in ensuring a Whole Organisation Approach to literacy and numeracy provision. There is clear evidence of a high record of achievement in literacy and numeracy, a strong culture of training and development,

and level of experience of Army personnel as a result of service, such as a positive attitude, team-work skills, adaptability, commitment, trainability and problem-solving skills all continue to be recognized and valued by many employers.[14]

1   The Move from 'Resettlement' to 'Transition'

While there has always been a message that the professional and personal development aspects of Army life help in the preparation for civilian life, many personnel across the Army have had the perception that the move to civilian life was only to be thought of in terms of the 'end of career' processes offered by the Army, called 'resettlement'. These processes are bounded by either the submission of a notice to leave from an individual, two calendar years before the end of a contract date, or from when the Army has given notice to leave to an individual. Due to this end of career focus, resettlement is primarily concerned with immediate finance, securing housing and providing the knowledge and the capability to compete for employment. Training, education, welfare and health, while present, are seen as more and more peripheral to resettlement.[15] Therefore, the focus on civilian life often came too late for the Army member to take full advantage of the opportunities that existed during service, and some aspects of long-term planning were lacking.

However, since 2012, the Army has taken a more 'whole career' approach that has adopted the term 'transition' wholeheartedly. The support services for those in the Army are grouped under the five "support pillars" comprising Employment, Education, Health, Housing and Welfare (E2H2W). "Transition" uses these familiar pillars for personnel

---

and the Services are strongly committed to supporting personnel with literacy and numeracy needs. Literacy and numeracy policy in the Services thus represents a model of national significance, with lessons and implications for large employers in non-military contexts.' (p. 32) BIS Research Paper Number 78 (June 2012) *Armed Forces Basic Skills Longitudinal Study: Part 1.*

[14] https://www.ctp.org.uk/successstories.

[15] Joint Service Publication (JSP) 534 (2014) *The Tri-Service Resettlement Manual.* (UK, Ministry of Defence).

to provide easier co-ordination and clearer focus "through career" naturally extending them to include preparation for moving to civilian life. It is defined in the following way:

> Transition—Individual Planning and Personal Development (IPPD) is a through-career offer of support, advice and education that supports personal development in order to enable soldiers (and their families) to plan for a successful military career and prepare for their inevitable return to civilian life.[16]

This conceptual change was prompted by the perception that a significant number of individuals left their planning for transition to the few months before leaving the Army,[17] when unsurprisingly, stress can be high, thereby denying themselves the opportunity to progressively develop and plan their futures. Major decisions have to be taken about finance and employment, and the lack of long-term preparation can substantially narrow the options open to the leaver and their family. Those individuals who suddenly find themselves unable to continue in the Army through unexpected circumstances such as injury were also at a disadvantage due to the emphasis on end of career resettlement.[18]

Therefore, transition represents an push towards ensuring that information and support relevant to the pursuit of a successful military career and life post-service should be available at all points in the career of an Army member, and to create an expectation of personal responsibility for post-service life from an early point. This should help ensure that the process of transition is as smooth as possible. Further benefits of a 'through career' transition are thought to come from the greater awareness of education and personal development that will positively impact individuals'

---

[16] See http://www.army.mod.uk/welfare-support/23590.aspx.

[17] Those voluntarily leaving the Army must give at least 12 months' notice to leave if their contract is not yet complete. This elongated notice period is typically longer than the notice periods in civilian life, but gives the Army the chance to adjust their inflows as a consequence. Unlike many other industries or professions, all new starters begin at the bottom of the employment hierarchy and so require extensive periods of training. This does mean that individuals, at least in theory, have a reasonable amount of time to prepare for transition and resettlement.

[18] See the recent review for further examples by Michael Ashcroft (2014). *The Veterans' Transition Review*, (Biteback Publishing).

'personal resilience, independence, confidence and mental robustness',[19] and so will have the double benefit of providing better soldiers in service as well as more successful individuals in civilian life. This increased success is hoped to have a positive impact on the reputation of the Army in society and also enhance the Army's status as a good employer, which in turn will support the recruitment and retention of soldiers in service.

These are ambitious aims, and it has certainly broadened the organisational view of what support should be offered to an individual. Key to this support is the provision of information throughout a career (reinforced with a bank of internet and print resources) that raises the awareness of the benefits of embracing the transition message.[20] It remains to be seen how individual perceptions of transition will evolve within the Army, but an emphasis on transition has highlighted, in particular, the role of education and training throughout a career.

The Army has, in fact, been a provider of educational qualifications from the nineteenth century for the enhancement of both professional and personal development. This continues today, with a large investment in 'through career' education and training for all members of the Army. The different branches, and the many varied occupations or trades, within the Army have educational entry requirements that vary considerably. However, the Army provides professional education and training for all ranks that is appropriate for their military roles throughout their careers. The Army also provides many thousands of apprenticeships each year as a recognized framework for much of this training.

The Army is committed to ensuring individuals achieve government directed targets in functional skills such as English and mathematics and these skills are required for promotion to junior non-commissioned officer rank and advancement to senior non-commissioned officer.[21] This ties education to promotion by ensuring all individuals meet the minimum

---

[19] *Career Transition Partnership quarterly statistics: UK Regular Service Personnel Employment Outcomes 2009/10 to 2013/14* (11 June 2015) (UK Ministry of Defence) https://www.gov.uk/government/uploads/system/uploads/attachment_data/file/434406/20150522_CTP_official_statistic_0910_1314Revised.pdf. Accessed 21 October 2015.

[20] See http://www.army.mod.uk/welfare-support/23590.aspx.

[21] See Ministry of Defence, JSP 898 (2014) *Defence Direction and Guidance on Training, Education and Skills Part 1: Directive*, (London, HMSO).

education standards for their role, and that they have the level of skills and education required to undertake training, be operationally effective, and take advantage of professional and career opportunities. Specialist support to improve literacy and numeracy skills with basic skill development managers is available through a network of Army Education Centres.

Command, leadership and management (CLM) training and education tied to promotions also encompass communication and personal development as core topics. These courses, and many others, can count towards civilian accredited qualifications or membership of memberships to professional bodies. Through their careers, some are selected to attend education courses to access certain job roles, or can pursue education for personal development that, while subsidized, may require out of hours working and some financial contribution (for example, many external undergraduate or postgraduate qualifications). Those who have left the Army can take their first full Level 3 (A Level equivalent) qualification or first HE qualification with full state-paid tuition up to ten years after leaving service.

This is an impressive education offer to the individual over the course of a career and demonstrates the value of education to the organization. However, some have pointed out that, currently, fewer members take up of these education opportunities than might be expected.[22] This will hopefully be addressed by increasing general awareness under the transition initiative.

Financial awareness is another key aspect to successful transition and needs to be developed early. Thus, the Armed Forces have introduced a financial awareness package, 'Moneyforce', available to all its soldiers, their partners and families. This is a joint initiative between Standard Life Charitable Trust, The Royal British Legion and the Ministry of Defence. A mandatory set of briefings are given to soldiers at various stages of their career, including during CLM training. A detailed website and access to bespoke briefings is also available.

Securing housing on leaving the Army can be a concern. The Army provides both, family and single soldier accommodation, during service which makes the mobile nature of service life easier to bear, but which can have the impact of deferring consideration of securing private accommodation until the resettlement phase. Thus, queries about housing and homelessness prior

---

[22] Ashcroft.

to leaving the Army were among the most commonly cited in a recent survey of Army leavers.[23] The UK Government has provided a specific Armed Forces 'Help to Buy' scheme to enable long-term financial planning for a house purchase and assist with a loan for a house deposit. This has proved popular and will help personnel plan for the future more easily.

2 Current Resettlement Provision

Much of current resettlement provision is delivered by a private company, currently Right Management, and is managed through the Career Transition Partnership (CTP) under contract to the MOD.[24] Access to resettlement benefits is based on time served in the Army. Those who have between four and six years' service receive benefits under the Employment Support Programme. Personnel who have served more than six years, or are to be medically discharged, are eligible for the Full Support Programme;[25] whilst the latter are also eligible for the CTP Assist Programme.

The Employment Support Programme provides access to a job finding service, such as those run by the Regular Forces Employment (RFEA) charity or the 'RightJob database' and an employment consultant interview with further consultant support for up to two-years post leaving. Access is also provided (on a standby basis) to Resettlement Training Centre courses and many employment and training fairs. Leavers also receive a 'Housing' brief and a 'Financial Aspects of Resettlement' brief.

The Full Support Programme provides everything above, plus the leaver can access an Individual Resettlement Training Costs (IRTC) grant to spend on training courses as well as resettlement leave of up to a maximum of 35 days. A Career Transition Workshop is also available, with other workshops on topics such as retirement options, future employment option, small business start-ups, etc. Advice on CV writing and interview

---

[23] *Ad-Hoc Statistical Release; Career Transition Partnership: Follow-Up Questionnaires 1 September 2012 to 31 August 2013 (11 February 2014)* (London, Ministry of Defence).

[24] See https://www.ctp.org.uk. Accessed 21 October 2015.

[25] Additionally, the next of kin of those who die or who are incapacitated in service qualify for the Full Support Programme. Those selected for redundancy during periodic force reductions, such as 2011–2014, also qualify for full resettlement no matter their length of service.

skills, access to the career transition interactive website (myPlan), and access to a career consultancy are also provided. In addition, the education benefits specified earlier in the chapter are available.

Contrary to popular belief, those who may have the most difficulty with transition to civilian life are those with the shortest length of service (defined as early service leavers or ESLs), rather than those who have served longest and have often been thought of as 'institutionalized'. ESLs may lack life and employment experience, and may not have benefited from the educational and training opportunities open to those who serve longer. Thus, ESLs (and those who leave for disciplinary reasons) qualify for the CTP Future Horizons Programme prior to leaving. This provides advice and support similar to the Employment Support Programme, through a consultant or adviser, and is designed and delivered by the RFEA and other service charities under contract to the MOD.[26]

3   Conclusions

The transition offer and resettlement package represents a considerable investment in those individuals leaving the Army. This is because it has long been recognized that the transition to civilian life is not necessarily easy, and for a small minority of leavers, is very problematic.[27] Those personnel that fall into hardship or unhappiness can take advantage of the services offered by Veterans UK, part of the Ministry of Defence, or the many government sponsored agencies and other service charities across the UK. It is worth noting that the small proportion of personnel that fall into hardship or unhappiness may have done so for reasons similar to the general population such as relationship breakdown, poor health or well-being issues, employment or business stress, and living in isolation. Planning for the future a bit earlier may help prevent some of these difficulties arising later in life, and there is some evidence that the provision the Army makes available to leavers is positively regarded. For example, the sources of help which leavers found most helpful after service in the

---

[26] https://www.ctp.org.uk/futurehorizons. Accessed 21 October 2015.

[27] See the 'Emotional Pathway' Information sheet at http://www.army.mod.uk/documents/general/Transition_Information_Sheet_2_-_The_Emotional_Pathway.pdf. Accessed 21 October 2015.

Armed Forces during resettlement were: the CTP guidance prior to discharge (71%), employment support (56%), and the overall support from the Armed Forces (51%).[28]

However, the same follow-up questionnaires also elicited the top three challenges facing Army personnel in securing civilian employment, a year after leaving the Armed Forces. These were firstly 'converting military experience into a CV' (47%), then 'converting their experience to provide examples for competence based application forms' (43%), and 'adapting to working within a civilian organization' (29%).[29] This difficulty with converting military to civil experience is not a new issue and has been addressed through recent initiatives to accredit military qualifications with civil equivalents. The Army is considering using a Personal Development Record to assist with this work as part of the 'New Employment Model'. However, accreditation has taken some time to get going, and is not necessarily straightforward for translating some specialist military work.[30]

Fully embracing 'through-life' transition offers rewards for the Army, their personnel and civilian employers if realized. There are challenges to overcome though. For instance, the relatively low take-up of education opportunities, and of public exam qualifications such as GCSEs, in serving Army personnel can potentially lead to difficulty when the attainment of GCSE A*-C in mathematics and English is still seen as fundamental by many employers.[31] The lower take-up may be due to a number of factors relating to a lack of awareness of opportunities and

---

[28] *Ad-Hoc Statistical Release; Career Transition Partnership: Follow-Up Questionnaires 1 September 2012 to 31 August 2013* (11 February 2014) (London, UK, Ministry of Defence). See also the National Audit Office Report (2007) '*Leaving the Services*' (HMSO).

[29] *Leaving the Services.*

[30] See M Ashcroft (2014) *The Veterans' Transition Review.* (Biteback Publishing).

[31] See Ashcroft, page 43 for MOD 2013 TESRR figures, for example, showing an 8% annual take up for Standard Learning Credits for a course of study towards a nationally recognized qualification. See also A Wolf (2011) *Review of Vocational Education—The Wolf Report.* (London: Department for Education) for employer positive attitudes to GCSE's and page 14, Recommendation 9 'Students who are under 19 and do not have GCSE A*-C in English and/or Maths should be required, as part of their programme, to pursue a course which either leads directly to these qualifications, or which provide significant progress towards future GCSE entry and success. The latter should be based around other Maths and English qualifications which have demonstrated substantial content and coverage; and Key Skills should not be considered a suitable qualification in this context. DfE and BIS should consider how best to introduce a comparable requirement into apprenticeship frameworks.'

workplace pressures at that time, or misguidedly focusing on the immediate needs of the job. The move towards through-career transition will
hopefully make more individuals consider education and development
opportunities earlier in their careers. Therefore, further monitoring
is necessary to see if the 'transition' initiative does succeed in helping soldiers plan earlier for the rest of their non-military working life.
However, measuring potential success will not be easy as this will require
the monitoring of civilian life stories across a dispersed population over
a number of years.

Continued work on improving the reputation of the Army so that
employers can recognize and translate the benefits of Army employment
is also required. In the era of the 'strategic corporal',[32] the Army has been
quick to emphasize the development of personal initiative and the ability
to think and plan through complex problems in all ranks. However, societal views on Army personnel as rigid and unthinking persist in many
human resources (HR) departments.[33] There is a marked difference
between employers who can reflect on bringing positive military qualities
into the civilian workplace, and those who may think all service leavers
will continue to behave like a stereotypical soldier in their new workplace. Further work is needed to make this difference clear to employers
so that they may benefit from those who have served in the Army, and
those in the Army can secure fulfilling and worthwhile future employment after experiencing their own transition.

[32] A reference to the modern day fact that a slip in behavior or a wrong decision on the part of a relatively low ranking Army member can find its way into the international media and can have a
decisive impact on the outcome of that conflict. See https://hbr.org/2010/10/the-strategic-corpo-
ral.html. Accessed 21 October 2015.
[33] http://www.newsroom.barclays.com/r/3186/over_half_of_employers_overlook_military_expe-
rience_on_a. Accessed 21 October 2015.

Bibliography

Legislation, Treaties and Charters

European

Charter of Fundamental Rights of the European Union

Decision 940/2011/EU on the European Year for Active Ageing and Solidarity between Generations (2012)

Directive 2000/78/EC of 27 November 2000 establishing a general framework for equal treatment in employment and occupation, (2000) OJ L303/16 ('Directive on Equality in Employment').

Directive 2000/43/EC of 29 June 2000 on Racial Equality

Directive 2006/54/EC Equal Treatment Directive

European Convention on Human Rights

Treaty of the European Union

European Parliament legislative resolution of 2 April 2009 on the proposal for a Council directive on implementing the principle of equal treatment between persons irrespective of religion or belief, disability, age or sexual orientation (COM(2008)426) P6 TA(2009)211

Italian

Law decree 276/300

Law decree no. 61/2000

Law Decree 112/2008

Law Decree 201/2011

© The Editor(s) (if applicable) and The Author(s) 2016   **299**
S. Manfredi, L. Vickers (eds.), *Challenges of Active Ageing*,
DOI 10.1057/978-1-137-53251-0

Law 214/2011
Law Decree 95/2012
Law No 144/2014
Law No 211/2014
Swedish
Discrimination Act (2008:567)
Labour Disputes Act (1974:371)
UK
Children and Family Act 2014
Employment Rights Act 1996
Government Pensions Act 2011

Cases

B F Cadman v Health & Safety Executive CJEU 3 October 2006 C-17/05

Bilka-KaufhausvWeber von Hartz [1986] ECR 1607–1631

Birgit Bartsch v Bosch und Siemens Hausgeräte (BSH) Altersfürsorge GmbH Case C-427/06 [2008]

Susanne Bulicke v Deutsche Büro Service GmbH C-246/09 [2010]

Cadman v Health & Safety Executive [2006] IRLR

Colin Wolf v. Stadt Frankfurt am Main CJEU C-229/08 12 January 2010

Commission v. Hungary CJEU C-286/12 judgment of 6 November 2012

Commission v. Italy CJEU C-46/07 Judgment of 13 November 2008

Court of Appeal of Florence 27.3.2006

Court of Cassation 21.9.2006, no. 20455; 24.4.2007, no. 9866; 26.4.2011, no. 9348

Court of Cassation 18.10.2011, no. 21554

Dansk Jurist- og Økonomforbund, acting on behalf of Erik Toftgaard v Indenrigs-og Sundhedsministeriet CJEU C-546/11 Judgment of the Court 26 September 2013

David Hütter v Technische Universität Graz [2009] C-88/08

Dr. Pamela Mary Enderby v Frenchay Health Authority and Secretary of State for Health C127/92 27 October 1993

Félix Palacios de la Villa v Cortefiel Servicios SA CJEU 16 October 2007

Galina Meister v Speech Design Carrier Systems GmbH CJEU C-415/10 Judgment of the court (second chamber) 19 April 2012

Gerard Fuchs en Peter Köhler v Land Hessen CJEU 21 July 2011, C-159/10 and C-160/10

Gerd Schini v Land Berlin CJEU C-506/12

Handels- og Kontorfunktionærernes Forbund I Danmark v Dansk Arbejdsgiverforening, acting on behalf of Danfoss CJEU C-109/88 17 October 1989

Helga Nimz v Freie und Hansestadt Hamburg CJEU C-184/89 7 February 1991

HK Danmark, acting on behalf of Glennie Kristensen, v. Experian A/S,intervener:Beskæftigelsesministeriet CJEU C-476/11 judgment of 26 September 2013

Ingeniørforeningen i Danmark v Region Syddanmark CJEU C-499/08 judgment 12 October 2010 ('Andersen')

Ingeniørforeningen i Danmark v Tekniq C-515/13 reported 26 February 2015

James v Gina Shoes [2011] UKEAT/0384/11/DM

Johann Odar v Baxter Deutschland GmbH Cases: C-152/11reported 6 December 2012;

Leopold Schmitzer v Bundesministerin für Inneres CJEU C-530/13 judgment of the court 11 November 2014

Mario Vital Pérez v Ayuntamiento de Oviedo CJEU C-416/13 judgment of the court 13 November 2014

ÖBB Personenverkehr AG v Gotthard Starjakob reported 28 January 2015 C-417/13

Paolą Faccini Dori v Recreb Srl, [1994] ECR Case C-91/92

Petersen v Berufsausschuss fur Zahn fur den BezirkWestfalen-Lippe CJEU Case C341/08 Judgment 12 January 2010

R (Reynolds) v Secretary of State for Work and Pensions [2005] UKHL 37.

Ralf Schuster v Bundesrepublik Deutschland (C-541/12) reported 19 June 2014

Reinhard Prigge and Others v Deutsche Lufthansa AG 2011 I-08003 CJEU C-447/09 judgment of 13 September 2011

Rosenbladt v Oellerking Gebäudereinigungsges CJEU 12 October 2010, C-45/09

Sabine Hennigs v Eisenbahn-Bundesamt & Land Berlin v Alexander Mai CJEU 8 September 2011 C-297/10 and 298/10

Swedish Labour Court judgment AD 2004 No 44

Swedish Labour Court judgment AD 2005 No 69

Swedish Labour Court judgment AD 2006 No 126

Swedish Labour Court judgment AD 2010 No 91
Swedish Labour Court judgment AD 2013 No 64
Seda Kücükdeveci v Swedex GmbH & Co. KG CJEU 19 January 2010,
    C-555/07
Seldon v Clarkson Wright and Jakes [2012] UKSC 16
Siegfried Pohl v ÖBB Infrastruktur AG C-429/12 judgment of 16 January 2014
Siegfried Pohl v ÖBB Infrastruktur AG C-529/13 judgment of 21 January 2015
Sindicatul Cadrelor Militare Disponibilizate în rezervă şi în retragere (SCMD)
    v Ministerul Finanţelor Publice C-262/14 judgment of 21 May 2015
The Incorporated Trustees of the National Council on Ageing (Age Concern
    England) v. Secretary of State for Business, Enterprise and Regulatory Reform
    ('Age Concern') CJEU 5 March 2009, C-388/07
Thomas Specht (C-501/12), Jens Schombera (C-502/12), Alexander Wieland
    (C-503/12), Uwe Schönefeld (C-504/12), Antje Wilke (C-505/12), Gerd
    Schini (C-506/12), Rena Schmeel (C-540/12), Ralf Schuster (C-541/12) v
    Land Berlin, Bundesrepublik Deutschland (Joined Cases C-501/12 to
    C-506/12, C-540/12 and C-541/12)
Torsten Hörnfeldt v Posten Meddelande AB CJEU 5 July 2012, C-141/11
Tribunal of Genoa 3 December 2012, no. 1605
Tyrolean Airways Tiroler Luftfahrt Gesellschaft mbH v Betriebsrat Bord der
    Tyrolean Airways Tiroler Luftfahrt Gesellschaft mbH CJEU C-132/11
    Judgment of 7 June 2012
Vasil Ivanov Georgiev v Tehnicheski universitet - Sofia, filial Plovdiv CJEU 18
    November 2010, Joint cases C-250/09 and C-268/09
Werner Mangold v Rüdiger Helm CJEU 22 November 2005, C-144/04

Books, Journals and Conference Papers

Abrams, D., Russell, P. S., Vanclair, C. M., & Swift, H. (2011). *Ageism in Europe: Findings from the European Social Survey.* London: Age UK.
AGE. (2013). Contribution to the European Commission's assessment of the transposition and application of Employment Equality Directive (2000/78/EC).
Age Action Alliance 'Employer toolkit: Guidance for managers of older workers'. (no date). http://ageactionalliance.org/employer-toolkit/. Accessed 1 July 2015.
Ahmedab, A. M., Andersson, L., & Hammarstedt, M. (2012). Does age matter for employability? A field experiment on ageism in the Swedish labour market. *Applied Economics Letters, 19*, 403–406.

Aichholzer, G. (2009). The Delphi method: Eliciting experts' knowledge in technology foresight. In A. Bogner & others (eds.), *Interviewing experts* (Research methods). New York: Palgrave Macmillan.

Alden, E. (2012). Flexible employment: How employment and the use of flexibility policies through the life course can affect later life occupation and financial outcomes. London: Age UK.

Alon-Shenker, P. (2012). The duty to accommodate senior workers: Its nature, scope and limitations. *Queen's Law Journal, 38*(1), 165–208.

Altmann, R. (2015). *A new vision for older workers: Retain, retrain and recruit.* London: DWP.

Alvesson, M., & Willmott, H. (2002). Identity regulation as organizational control: Producing the appropriate individual. *Journal of Management Studies, 39*(5), 619–644.

Andersen, T., Haahr, J. H., Hansen, M. E., & Holm-Pedersen, M. (2008). Job mobility in the European Union: Optimising its social and economic benefits, Final Report, prepared under contract to the European Commission, Directorate General for Employment, Social Affairs and Equal Opportunities, Danish Technological Institute, Centre Policy and Business Analysis.

Anderson, M., Bechhofer, F., McCrone, D., Jamieson, L., Li, Y., & Stewart, R. (2005). Timespans and plans among young adults. *Sociology, 39*(1), 139–155.

Anxo, D., Fagan, C., Cebrian, I., & Moreno, G. (2007). Patterns of labour market integration in Europe – A life course perspective on time policies. *Socio-Economic Review, 5*(2), 233–260.

Armstrong-Stassen, M. (2008). Organisational practices and the postretirement employment experience of older workers. *Human Resource Management Journal, 18*, 36–53.

Armstrong-Stassen, M., & Schlosser, F. (2011). Perceived organizational membership and the retention of older workers. *Journal of Organizational Behavior, 32*, 319–344.

Ashcroft, M. (2014). *The Veterans' transition review.* Biteback Publishing. London

Ashiagbor D (2009) Multiple discrimination in a multicultural Europe: Achieving labour market equality through new governance. *Current Legal Problems, 61*, 265–288.

Atkinson, C., & Hall, L. (2009). The role of gender in varying forms of flexible working. *Gender, Work and Organization, 16*(6), 650–666.

Atkinson, C, & Sandiford, P. (2015). An exploration of older worker flexible working arrangements in smaller firms. *Human Resource Management Journal.* Accessed via Early Online, 26(1), 12–28 (January 2016).

Aversa, M., Checcucci, P., D'Agostino, L., Fefè, R., Marchetti, S., Parente, M, & Scarpetti G for ISFOL in 2014, Il fattore età nelle imprese italiane, Paper for the Espanet Conference "Sfide alla cittadinanza e trasformazione dei corsi di vita: precarietà, invecchiamento e migrazioni" University of Turin, Turin, 18–20 Sept 2014.

Bal, P. M., De Jong, S. B., Jansen, P. G. W., & Bakker, A. B. (2012). Motivating employees to work beyond retirement: A multi-level study of the role of i-deals and unit climate. *Journal of Management Studies, 49*(2), 306–331.

Ball, C. (2007). Defining age management: Information and discussion paper, TAEN - The Age and Employment Network, London.

Ball, C. (2013, March). Age management at work: Adopting a strategic approach, *Employment Relations Comment.*

Barbareschi, B. (2014). Gestire le differenze d'età nel mercato del lavoro e in impresa: il caso francese. Sociologia del lavoro, 134.

Barnard, C. (2012). The financial crisis and the Euro plus pact: A labour lawyer's perspective. *Industrial Law Journal, 41*, 98–114.

Barnes, H., Smeaton, D., & Taylor, R. (2009). The ageing workforce: The employers' perspective, Report 468, Institute for Employment Studies, Brighton.

Barnett, R. C. (2005). Ageism and sexism in the workplace. *Generations, 29*(3), 25.

Barrett, B., & Sargeant, M. (2015). Working in the UK without a default retirement age: health, safety, and the oldest workers. *ILJ, 44*(1), 75–100.

Beale, F. M. (1970). Double jeopardy: To be black and female. In T. Cade (Ed.), *The black woman.* New York: New American Library.

Beck, V., & Williams, G. (2015). The (performance) management of retirement and the limits of individual choice. *Work, Employment and Society, 29*(2), 250–267.

Beecroft, A. (2011). Report on Employment Law, 6. Department of Business Innovation and Skills, London

Beehr, T. A. (1986). The process of retirement: A review and recommendations for future investigation. *Personnel Psychology, 39*, 31–55.

Beehr, T. A., & Nielson, N. L. (1995). Descriptions of job characteristics and retirement activities during the transition to retirement. *Journal of Organizational Behavior, 16*, 681–690.

Belavusau, U. (2013). On age discrimination and beating dead dogs: Commission v. Hungary. *Common Market Law Review, 50*, 1145.

Bell, M. (2002). *Anti-discrimination law and the European Union.* Oxford/New York: Oxford University Press.

Bell, M. (2011). The principle of equal treatment: Widening and deepening. In P. Craig & G. de Búrca (Eds.), *The evolution of EU law.* Oxford: Oxford University Press.

Bell, M., & Waddington, L. (2003). Reflecting on inequalities in European equality law. *European Law Review, 28*(3), 349.

Berta, G. (2014). *Produzione intelligente.* Torino: Einaudi.

BIS. (2011, October). Flexible, effective, fair: Promoting economic growth through a strong and efficient labour market, Department for Business Innovation and Skills, London, 7.

BIS Research Paper Number 78. (2012, June). Armed forces basic skills longitudinal study: Part 1.

Bisom-Rapp, S., & Sargeant, M. (2014). It's complicated: Age, gender, and lifetime discrimination against working women – The United States and the U.K. as examples. *Elder Law Journal, 22*(1), 1.

Blackburn, R. (2002). *Banking on death or investing in life: The history and future of pensions.* London: Verso.

Blackburn, R. (2004). How to rescue a failing pension regime: The British case. *New Political Economy, 9*(4), 559–581.

Blackham, A. (2014). *Extending working life for older workers: An empirical legal analysis of age discrimination laws in the UK,* ch 4. University of Cambridge, Cambridge.

Bonardi, O. (2007). Le discriminazioni basate sull'età. In M. Barbera (Ed.), *Il nuovo diritto antidiscriminatorio. Il quadro comunitario e nazionale* (p. 125). Milano: Giuffrè.

Boudiny, K. (2013). 'Active ageing': From empty rhetoric to effective policy tool. *Ageing & Society, 33*, 1077.

Bown-Wilson, D., & Parry, E. (2013). Career progression in older managers. *Employee Relations, 35*, 309–321.

Boyle, F. (2015, April 7). Nicola Sturgeon is right about retirement you should stop working before you die. *The Guardian.* http://www.theguardian.com/commentisfree/2015/apr/07/nicola-sturgeon-right-about-retirement . Accessed 10 May 2015.

Brannen, J., & Nilsen, A. (2002). Young people's time perspectives: From youth to adulthood. *Sociology, 36*(3), 513–537.

Brown, P., & Vickerstaff, S. (2011). Health Subjectivities and Labour Market Participation: Pessimism and older workers' attitudes and narratives around retirement in the United Kingdom. *Research on Aging, 33*(5), 529–550. for a further discussion of this health pessimism.

Burnay, N. (2011). Ageing at work: Between changing social policy patterns and reorganization of working times. *Population Review, 50*, 150–165.

Burri, S., & Schiek, D. (2009). Multiple discrimination in EU law. Opportunities for legal responses to intersectional gender discrimination? European Commission, Brussels.

Business in the Community. (2015). The mission million. Recommendations for action. *Business in the Community*, 12. http://www.bitc.org.uk/system/files/the_missing_million_-_rec_for_action_23-4-2015.pdf. Accessed 20 July 2015.

Calafà L (2006) 'Licenziamenti collettivi alle Poste e discriminazioni in base all'età: la prima applicazione nazionale della sentenza Mangold', in D&L – Rivista Critica di Diritto del Lavoro 915

Carmel, E., Hamblin, K., & Papadopoulos, T. (2007). Governing the activation of older workers in the European Union. *International Journal of Sociology and Social Policy, 27*(9/10), 387–400.

Carneiro, M. (2015). *Constructing intersectionality in EU anti-discrimination law*. Copenhagen: Copenhagen University.

Casey, B. (2012). The implications of the economic crisis for pensions and pension policy in Europe. *Global Social Policy, 12*, 246–265.

Cebulla, A., & Others. (2007). Working beyond the State Pension Age in the United Kingdom: The role of working time flexibility and the effects on the home. *Ageing & Society 27*, 849–867

Chartered Institute of Personnel and Development/International Longevity Centre (CIPD/ILC. (2015). Avoiding the demographic crunch: Labour supply and the ageing workforce. (CIPD/ILC).

Clarke, A. (2005). *Situational analysis: Grounded theory after the postmodern turn*. Thousand Oaks: Sage.

Clayton, P. (2010). Working on: Choice or necessity?. In Working and ageing: Emerging theories and empirical perspectives. European Centre for the Development of Vocational Training, Luxembourg. 227–252.

Collins, P. H. (2000). *Black feminist thought: knowledge, consciousness, and the politics of empowerment* (2nd ed.). New York: Routledge.

Collinson, P. (2012, July 13). We need to order a Danish Pension. *The Guardian*.

Commission of the European Communities Confronting demographic change: A new solidarity between the generations COM (2005) 94.

Commission of the European Communities Council Resolution 6226/07 Opportunities and challenges of demographic change in Europe; Dealing with the impact of an ageing population in the EU (2009 Ageing Report) COM (2009) 180.

Commission of the European Communities Europe's response to World Ageing COM (2002) 143.

Commission of the European Communities Strategy for Equality between Women and Men 2010–2015, COM (2010) 0491 final.

Commission of the European Communities The demographic future of Europe – From challenge to opportunity, COM (2006) 571.

Commission of the European Communities 'Towards a Europe for All Ages' COM (1999) 221.

Conaghan, J. (2008). Intersectionality and the feminist project in law. In D. Cooper (Ed.), *Law, power and the politics of subjectivity: Intersectionality and beyond.* London: Routledge-Cavendish.

Confindustria 'In Italia più occupati anziani e meno giovani', Commentary Centro Studi Confindustria, no. 1/2015 (see www.confindustria.it). Accessed 30 May 2015.

Connelly, V., & Burgess, M. (2013). Suicide among Falkland war veterans—Understanding why misleading 'sound bites' about veterans are more believable than 'sound statistics', (Rapid Response) *British Medical Journal.* http://www.bmj.com/content/346/bmj.f3204/rr/677045. Accessed 21 Oct 2015

Cooper, D. (2000). A tale of two pension systems. *Employee Relations, 22*(3), 286–292.

Corbin, J. M., & Strauss, A. L. (2008). *Basics of qualitative research: Techniques and procedures for developing grounded theory* (3rd ed.). Thousand Oaks: Sage Publications.

Corti, M. (2013). Active ageing e autonomia collettiva. "Non è un Paese per vecchi", ma dovrà diventarlo presto. *Lavoro e Diritto, 3*, 383.

Cory, G., & Alakeson, V. (2014). The resolution foundation, careers and carers, available at: http://www.resolutionfoundation.org/media/media/downloads/Careers_and_Carers_FINAL.pdf. Accessed 1 Aug 2015

Council of the European Union. (2012). Council declaration on the European year for active ageing and solidarity between generations (2012): The way forward, Council of Europe, Brussels.

Coupland, C., Tempest, S., & Barnatt, C. (2008). What are the implications of the new age discrimination legislation for research and practice? *Human Resource Management Journal, 18*(4), 423–431.

Crenshaw, K., (1989). Demarginalizing the intersection of race and sex: A black feminist critique of antidiscrimination doctrine, feminist theory, and antiracist politics. *University of Chicago Legal Forum, 139*.

Czarniawska, B. (2003). *Narratives in social science research.* London/Thousand Oaks: Sage Publications.

Dalkey, N., & Helmer, O. (1963). An experimental application of the Delphi method to the use of experts. *Management Science, 9*, 458.

Dandeker, C., et al. (2006). What's in a name? Defining and caring for 'Veterans': The United Kingdom in international perspective. *Armed Forces and Society, 32*, 161.

Davies Anne, C. L. (2009). *Perspectives on labour law (Law in context)* (2nd ed.). Cambridge: Cambridge University Press.

Degryse, C., Jepsen, M., & Pochet, P. (2013). The Euro Crisis and its impact on National and European social policies ETUI working paper 2013/05, ETUI aisbl, Brussels.

Deller, J., & Pundt, L. (2014). Flexible transitions from work to retirement in Germany. In C. M. Alcover, G. Topa, E. Parry, F. Fraccaroli, & M. Depolo (Eds.), *Bridge employment: A research handbook*. London: Routledge.

Deller, J., Liedtke, P. M., & Maxin, L. (2009). Old-age security and *Silver Workers*: An empirical investigation identifies challenges for companies, insurers, and society. *Geneva Papers on Risk and Insurance, 34*, 137–157.

Department of Health. (2012). Reforming the NHS pension scheme for England and Wales: Proposed final agreement https://www.gov.uk/government/uploads/system/uploads/attachment_data/file/216219/dh_133003.pdf. Accessed 23 Sept 2015.

Department for Work and Pensions ('DWP'). (2014, June). Fuller working lives: Background evidence, DWP https://www.gov.uk/government/uploads/system/uploads/attachment_data/file/319948/fuller-working-lives-background-evidence.pdf. Accessed 15 July 2015

Dewhurst, E. (2013). Intergenerational balance, mandatory retirement and age discrimination in Europe: How can the ECJ better support national courts in finding a balance between the generations? *Common Market Law Review, 50*(5), 1333–1362.

Dewhurst, E. (2015). Are older workers past their sell-by date? A view from UK age discrimination law. *Modern Law Review, 78*(2), 189–215.

Dickens, L. (2006). Equality and work-life balance: What's happening at the workplace. *Industrial Law Journal, 35*, 445–449.

Dickens, L. (2007). The road is long: Thirty years of equality legislation in Britain. *British Journal of Industrial Relations, 45*, 463–494.

Dickens, L., & Hall, M. (2006). Fairness – up to a point. Assessing the impact of new labour's employment legislation. *Human Resource Management Journal, 16*, 338–356.

Doeringer, P. B. (1990). Economic security, labor market flexibility, and bridges to retirement. In P. B. Doeringer (Ed.), *Bridges to retirement*. Ithaca Press, Garnet Publishing Ltd, Reading (FYI Ithaca Press is an imprint of Garnet Publishing Ltd)

Drevenstedt, J. (1976). Perceptions of onsets of young adulthood, middle age, and old age. *Journal of Gerontology, 31*, 53–57.

Duncan, C., & Loretto, W. (2004). Never the right age? Gender and age-based discrimination in employment. *Gender, Work and Organization, 11*(1), 95–115.

Duvvury, N., & Finn, C. (2014). 'Man-covery': Recession, labour market, and gender relations in Ireland. *Gender, Sexuality & Feminism 1*(2), 59–81.

DWP. (2006). A new deal for welfare: Empowering people to work. Cm 6730. The Stationary Office, London

DWP. (2014). Press release: Pension savings—9 million newly saving or saving more, says Pensions Minister, available at: https://www.gov.uk/government/news/pensions-savings-9-million-newly-saving-or-saving-more-says-pensions-minister. Accessed 1 Aug 2015

Dziurzynski, B. (1996). FDA regulatory review and approval processes: A Delphi inquiry. *Food & Drug Law Journal, 51*, 143–153.

Eagleton, T. (1991). *Ideology: An introduction.* London/New York: Verso.

Eichhorst, W., et al. (2014). How to combine the entry of young people in the labour market with the retention of older workers? *IZA Journal of European Labour Studies, 3*(19), 6.

Eisenhardt, K. M. (2002). Building theories from case study research. In A. M. Huberman & M. Miles (Eds.), *The qualitative researcher's companion* (p. 5–36). Thousand Oaks: Sage Publications, London.

Elliott, Larry. (19 May 2015). Tories Vow to Slash 'Burdensome' Red Tape for Business by £10bn. *The Guardian,* London. http://www.theguardian.com/business/2015/may/18/conservative-party-cut-red-tape-business-sajid-javid. Accessed 1 July 2015.

Ellis, E., & Watson, P. (2002). *EU anti-discrimination law* (2nd ed.). Oxford: Oxford University Press.

EU Commission. (2007). *Tackling multiple discrimination: Practices, policies and laws.* Luxembourg: Publishing Office of the EU.

EU Commission. (2011). *Strategy for equality between women and men 2010–2015.* Luxembourg: Publishing Office of the EU. 32.

EU Commission. (2012). Commission Staff Working Document ex-ante evaluation accompanying document to the decision of the European parliament and the Council on the European Year for Active Ageing SEC (2010) 1002 final.

EU Commission. (2015, April). EU Skills Panorama 2015. Analytical highlight prospects for Germany. Retrieved from http://euskillspanorama.cedefop.europa.eu/AnalyticalHighlights/. Accessed 21 Oct 2015

EU Commission Annex III to the 'Joint Report on the application of the Racial Equality Directive (2000/43/EC) and the Employment Equality Directive (2000/78/EC)' SWD (2014) 5 final

EU Commission 'Confronting demographic change: A new solidarity between the generations', Green Paper, COM (2005) 94 final

EU Commission Green paper – Equality and non-discrimination in an enlarged European Union COM (2004) 379 final

EU Commission Reconciliation of Work and Family Life in the Context of Demographic Change 11841/11 SOC 584 (EPSCO)

EU Commission, White Paper, An Agenda for Adequate, Safe and Sustainable Pensions, 16.2.2012 COM (2012) 55 final.

Eurofound. (2012). Employment trends and policies for older workers in the recession Europe 2020, A Strategy for Smart, Sustainable and Inclusive Growth, COM (2010) 2020 final19.

Eurofound. (2014). *Work preferences after 50*. Dublin: Publications Office of the European Union.

European Parliament Report of 25 June 2013 on the situation of fundamental rights: Standards and practices in Hungary, drafted by Rui Tavares on behalf of the Committee on Civil Liberties, Justice and Home Affairs, doc. ref. PE 508.211v04-00. Accessible at: http://www.europarl.europa.eu/sides/getDoc.do?pubRef=-// EP//NONSGML+REPORT+A7-2013-0229+0+DOC+PDF+V0//EN. Accessed 24 Sept 2015.

European Parliament Resolution of 15 January 2013 concerning Information, consultation of workers, anticipation and management of restructuring. (P7 TA (2013) 0005)

European Union. (2011). *The 2012 Ageing Report: Underlying assumptions and projection methodologies*: Joint report. Publications of the European Union

Eurostat. (2015). Population structure and ageing. Retrieved from http://ec. europa.eu/eurostat/statistics-explained/index.php/Population_structure_ and_ageing. Accessed 21 Oct 2015.

Ezzy, D. (2001). *Narrating unemployment*. Burlington: Ashgate.

Fairclough, N. (2003). *Analysing discourse: Textual analysis for social research*. London: Routledge.

Fasbender, U., Wang, M., Voltmer, J-B. & Deller, J. (2015). The meaning of work for post-retirement employment decisions. *Work, Aging, and Retirement* (Advanced Online Publication) doi:10.1093/workar/wav015. Accessed 21 Oct 2015.

Fasbender, U., Deller, J., Zohr, M., Büsch, V., Schermuly, C., & Mergenthaler, A. (2015b). Absicht zur Erwerbstätigkeit im (zukünftigen) Ruhestand'

[Intentions to work in (future) retirement]. In N. Schneider, A. Mergenthaler, U. Staudinger, & I. Sackreuther (Eds.), *Mittendrin? Lebenspläne und Potenziale älterer Menschen beim Übergang in den Ruhestand*. Opladen/ Barbara: Budrich Publishers.

Federal Statistical Office of Germany. (2015). 13th coordinated population projection for Germany. Retrieved from https://www.destatis.de/bevoelkerungspyramide/. Accessed 21 Oct 2015.

Fejes, A. (2010). Discourses on employability: Constituting the responsible citizen. *Studies in Continuing Education, 32*(2), 89–102.

Feldman, D. C. (1994). The decision to retire early: A review and conceptualization. *Academy of Management Review, 19*, 285–311.

Feldman, D. C., & Kim, S. (2000). Bridge employment during retirement: A field study of individual and organizational experiences with post-retirement employment. *Human Resource Planning, 23*(1), 14–25.

Fenwick, H., & Hervey, T. K. (1995). Sex equality in the single market: New directions for the European Court of Justice. *Common Market Law Review, 32*, 443.

Fischer, R. (2008). Rewarding seniority: Exploring cultural and organisational predictors of seniority allocations. *The Journal of Social Psychology, 148*(2), 167–186.

Fischer, F., & Ury, W. (1985). *L'arte del negoziato*. Milan: Mondadori.

Fleetwood, S. (2005). Ontology in organization and management studies: A critical realist perspective. *Organization, 12*, 200.

Flynn, M. (2011). Ageing populations: Time to get ready. *Training Journal*, 56–59

Flynn, M., & McNair, S. (2013). 'Annex 7' working longer in the NHS, Call for evidence interim findings report http://www.nhsemployers.org/~/media/Employers/Documents/Pay%20and%20reward/WLR%20Prelim%20Report%20-%20Annex%207%20-%20Call%20for%20evidence%20interim%20findings%20report.pdf. Accessed 23 Sept 2015.

Foster, L., & Walker, A. (2013). Gender and active ageing in Europe. *European Journal of Ageing, 10*, 3–10.

Foster, L., & Walker, A. (2015). Active and successful aging: A European policy perspective. *The Gerontologist, 55*(1), 83–90.

Foubert, P. (2002). *The legal protection of the pregnant worker in the European Community: Sex equality, thoughts of social and economic policy and comparative leaps to the United States of America*. The Hague: Kluwer Law International.

Frankl, V. (2004/1946). *Mans search for meaning: The classic tribute to hope from the Holocaust*. London: Rider.

Fredman, S. (2002). *Discrimination law* (Clarendon law series). Oxford/New York: Oxford University Press.

Fredman, S. (2009). Positive rights and duties: Addressing intersectionality. In D. Schiek & V. Chege (Eds.), *European Union non-discrimination law: Comparative perspectives on multidimensional equality law*. London/New York: Routledge-Cavendish.

Fredman, S. (2011). *Discrimination law*. Oxford: Oxford University Press.

Fredman, S. (2012). Breaking the mold: Equality as a proactive duty. *60 American Journal of Comparative Law*, 265–289.

Fredman, S., & Spencer, S. (2003). *Age as an equality issue*. Oxford: Hart Publishing.

Fredman, S., & Spencer, S. (2006, June). Delivering equality: Towards an outcome-focused positive duty—Submission to the Cabinet Office Equality Review and to the Discrimination Law Review

French, D. (2005). *Military identities: The regimental system, the British Army, and the British people, 1870–2000*. Oxford: Oxford University Press.

French, D. (2012). *Army, Empire and Cold War, The British Army and Military Policy, 1945–1971*. Oxford: Oxford University Press.

Frerichs, F., Lindley, R., Aleksandrowicz, P., Baldauf, B., & Galloway, S. (2012). Active ageing in organisations: A case study approach. *International Journal of Manpower, 33*(6), 666–684.

Fudge, J., & Zbyszewska, A. (2015). An intersectional approach to age discrimination in the European Union: Bridging dignity and distribution? In A. Numhauser-Henning & M. Rönnmar (Eds.), *Age discrimination and labour law: Comparative and conceptual perspectives in the EU and beyond*. Alphen aan den Rijn: Kluwer Law Internationa.

Gabriel, Y., Gray, D., & Goregaokar, H. (2010). Temporary derailment or the end of the line? Managers coping with unemployment at 50. *Organization Studies, 31*(12), 1687–1712.

Ganguli, I., Hausmann, R., & Viarengo, M. (2014). Closing the gender gap in education: What is the state of gaps in labour force participation for women, wives and mothers? *International Labour Review, 153*(2), 173–207.

Gijzen, M. H. S. (2006). Selected issues in equal treatment law: A multi-layered comparison of European English and Dutch law. Antwerp: Intersentia.

Glaser, K., Montserrat, E. R., Waginger, U., Price, D., Stuchburg, R., & Tinker, A. (2011). Grandparenting in Europe (Grandparents Plus). Available from: http://www.grandparentsplus.org.uk/wp-content/uploads/2011/03/Grandparenting-in-Europe-Report.pdf. Accessed 15 Oct 2015)

Gosetti, G. (2012). Dalla qualità del lavoro alla qualità della vita lavorativa: persistenze e innovazione nel profilo teorico e nelle modalità di analisi. Sociologia del lavoro 17.

Gough, O., & Hick, R. (2009). Employee evaluations of occupational pensions. *Employee Relations, 31*(2), 158–167.

Grady, J. (2010). From Beveridge to Turner: Laissez-faire to neoliberalism. *Capital and Class, 34*, 163–180.

Grady, J. (2013). Trade unions and the pension crisis: Defending member interests in a neoliberal world. *Employee Relations, 35*(3), 94–308.

Grant, D. (2011). Older women in the workplace. In M. Sargeant (Ed.), *Age discrimination and diversity multiple discrimination from an age perspective.* Cambridge/New York: Cambridge University Press.

Gribble, R., Wessley, S., Klein, S., Alexander, D. A., Dandeker, C., & Fear, N. T. (2013). *Are the UK armed forces understood and supported by the British Public? Report for the public perceptions symposium.* London: Kings College.

Griffin, B., & Hesketh, B. (2008). Post-retirement work. The individual determinants of paid and volunteer work. *Journal of Occupational and Organizational Psychology, 81*, 101–121.

Guaglianone, L., Ravelli, F. (2015). Young and old: Age discrimination in Italian case law. *European Labour Law Journal 2* (forthcoming as at November 2015, 175–182).

Guglyuvatyy, E. (2010). Identifying criteria for climate change policy evaluation in Australia. *Macquarie Journal of Business Law, 7*, 98.

Gullette, M. (2004). *Aged by culture.* Chicago: University of Chicago Press.

Gunderson, M., & Pesando, J. (1988). The case for allowing mandatory retirement. *Canadian Public Policy, XIV*, 32.

Gyulavári, T., & Hős, N. (2013). Retirement of hungarian judges, age discrimination and judicial independence: A tale of two courts. *Industrial Law Journal, 42*(3), 289.

Hacker, J., & Pierson, P. (2010). *Winner-take-all politics.* Simon and Schuster

Hamblin, K. (2010). Changes to policies for work and retirement in EU15 nations (1995–2005): An exploration of policy packages for the 50-plus cohort. *International Journal of Ageing and Later Life, 5*, 13–43.

Hamblin, K. (2013). *Active ageing in the European Union policy convergence and divergence.* Houndmills\New York: Palgrave Macmillan.

Hancock, A.-M. (2013). Empirical intersectionality: A Tale of two approaches. *U.C. Irvine Law Review, 3*, 259.

Harbo, T. I. (2010). The function of the proportionality principle in EU law. *European Law Journal, 16*(2), 185.

Harper, S., Howse, K., & Baxter, S. (2011). *Living longer and prospering? Designing an adequate, sustainable and equitable UK state pension system.* Club Vita LLP and The Oxford Institute of Ageing, University of Oxford, Oxford.

Harvey, D. (2005). *A brief introduction to neoliberalism.* Oxford/New York: Oxford University Press.

Harvey, D. (2010). *The enigma of capital: And the crises of capitalism.* Verso, Oxford.

Hasselhorn, H. M., & Apt, W. (eds) (2015). *Understanding employment participation of older workers creating a knowledge base for future labour market challenges.* Federal Ministry of Labour and Social Affairs, Wilhelmstraße 49 and Federal Institute for Occupational Safety and Health, BAuA Friedrich-Henkel-Weg 1–25.

Hendrickx, F. (2012). Age and European employment discrimination law. In F. Hendrickx (Ed.), *Active ageing and labour law: Contributions in honour of Professor Roger Blanpain in Social Europe Series 31.* Cambridge: Intersentia.

Hepple, B. (2003). Age discrimination in employment: Implementing the framework directive 2000/78/EC. In S. Fredman & S. Spencer (Eds.), *Age as an equality issue: Legal and policy perspectives.* Portland: Hart Publishing.

Hepple, B. (2011). Enforcing equality law: Two steps forward and two steps backwards for reflexive regulation. *Industrial Law Journal, 40*, 315–335.

Hepple, B. (2014). *Equality: The legal framework* (2nd ed., p. 80). Oxford: Hart Publishing.

Hepple, Bob., & Others. (2000). *Equality: A new framework—Report of the independent review of the enforcement of UK anti-discrimination legislation.* Oxford: Hart, 59–65, 69–72

Hertzog, C., Kramer, A. F., Wilson, R. S., & Lindenberger, U. (2008). Enrichment effects on adult cognitive development. Can the functional capacity of older adults be preserved and enhanced? *Psychological Science in the Public Interest, 9*, 1–65.

Hill, E. J., Grzywacz, J. G., Allen, S., Blanchard, V. L., Matz-Cpasta, C., & Shulkin, S. (2008). Defining and conceptualizing workplace flexibility. *Community, Work and Family, 11*(2), 149–163.

HM Treasury. (2011). Independent Public Service Pensions Commission: Final report March 2011 (HM Treasury London public.enquiries@hm-treasury.gsi.gov.uk). Available at: http://webarchive.nationalarchives.gov.uk/20130129110402/http://cdn.hm-treasury.gov.uk/hutton_final_100311.pdf http://cdn.hm-treasury.gov.uk/hutton_final_100311.pdf. Accessed 9 Mar 2013.

Hofacker, D. (2015). *Older workers in a globalizing world. An international comparison of retirement and late-career patterns in Western industrialized countries.* Northampton: Edward Elgar.

Howard, E. (2006). The case for a considered hierarchy of discrimination ground in EU law. *Maastrict Journal, 13*(4), 445–470.

http://www.newsroom.barclays.com/r/3186/over_half_of_employers_overlook_military_experience_on_a. Accessed 21 Oct 2015.

Hudson Margaret, F. (1991). Elder Mistreatment: A Taxonomy with Definitions by Delphi. *Journal of Elder Abuse & Neglect, 3*, 1.

Hummert, M. L., Garstka, T. A., Shaner, J. L., & Stram, S. (1994). Stereotypes of the Elderly Held by Young, Middle-Aged, and Elderly Adults. *Journal of Gerontology, 49*(5), P240.

Ilmakunnas, P., & Ilmakunnas, S. (2011). *Diversity at the workplace. Whom does it benefit?* Berlin: De Economist.

Ilmarinen, J. (2001). Aging workers. *Occupational and Environmental Medicine, 58*, 546–552.

Ilmarinen, J. (2006). *Towards a longer worklife! Ageing and the quality of worklife in the European Union.* Helsinki: Finnish Institute of Occupational Health.

Ilmarinen, J., & Others. (2005). New dimensions of work ability. *International Congress Series, 1280*, 3

Ilmarinen, J., & Rantanen, J. (1999). Promotion of Work Ability during Ageing. *American Journal of Industrial Medicine, 36*, 21–23.

Ilmarinen, J., & Tuomi, K. (1992). Work Ability of Aging Workers. *Scandinavian Journal of Work, Environment & Health, 18*, 8–10.

Italian National Institute of Statistics Report for 2014. www.istat.it. Accessed 30 May 2014.

Itzin, C., & Phillipson, C. (1993) *Age barriers at work: Maximising the potential of mature and older workers.* Metropolitan Authorities Recruitment Agency, London.

Itzin, C., & Phillipson, C. (1995). Gendered ageism: A double jeopardy for women in Organizations. In C. Itzin & J. Newman (Eds.), *Gender, culture and organizational change: Putting theory into practice.* London/New York: Routledge.

Iversen, A., Nikolaou, V., Greenberg, N., Unwin, C., Hull, L., Hotopf, M., et al. (2004). What happens to British veterans when they leave the armed forces? *European Journal of Public Health, 15*, 175–184.

Izzi, D. (2014). Invecchiamento attivo e pensionamenti forzati. *Rivista italiana di diritto del lavoro, 1*, 584.

Jans Jan, H. (2007). The effect in national legal systems of the prohibition of discrimination on grounds of age as a general principle of community law. *Legal Issues of European Integration, 34*(1), 53–66.

Jensen, P. H., & Principi, A. (2014). Introduction: Enhancing volunteering in later life in Europe. In A. Principi, P. H. Jensen, & G. Lamura (Eds.), *Active ageing: Voluntary work by older people in Europe*. Bristol: Policy Press.

Jessop, B. (2010). The cultural political economy of crisis, paper presented at Leicester Business School, De Montfort University Department of Public Policy/Local Governance Research Unit Seminar Series, 2010.

Jolly, R. (1996). *Changing step: From military to civilian life: People in transition*. London: Brassey's.

Jones, D. (2000). *Evaluation of the code of practice on age diversity in employment, Research Brief RBX 6/00*. Nottingham: Department for Education and Employment.

Julén, V. J. (2001). A blessing or a ban? About the discrimination of pregnant job seekers. In A. Numhauser-Henning (Ed.), *Legal perspectives on equal treatment and non-discrimination*. The Hague: Kluwer Law International.

Julén, V. J. (2006). On the gendered norm of standard employment in a changing labour market. In J. Fudge & R. Owens (Eds.), *Precarious work, women and the new economy: The challenge to legal norms*. Oxford: Hart Publishing.

Kantola, J., & Nousiainen, K. (2009). Institutionalising intersectionality in Europe: Introducing the theme. *International Feminist Journal of Politics, 11*, 459.

Kim, S., & Feldman, D. C. (2000). Working in retirement: The antecedents of bridge employment and its consequences for quality of life in retirement. *Academy of Management Journal, 43*, 1195–1210.

Kim, N., & Hall, D. T. (2013). Protean career model and retirement. In M. Wang (Ed.), *The Oxford handbook of retirement* (pp. 102–111). Oxford/New York: OUP.

Kite, M. E., & Johnson, B. T. (1988). Attitudes toward older and younger adults: A meta-analysis. *Psychology and Ageing, 3*(3), 233.

Kondo, D. (1990). *Crafting selves: Power, gender, and discourses of identity in a Japanese workplace*. Chicago: University of Chicago Press.

Koslowski, A. (2009). Grandparents and the care of their grandchildren. In J. Stillwell, E. Coast, & D. Keele (Eds.), *Fertility, living arrangements and care: Understanding population trends and processes*. New York: Springer.

Krekula, C. (2007). The intersection of age and gender – Reworking gender theory and social gerontology. *Current Sociology, 55*, 155.

Krekula, C. (2009). Age coding – On age-based practices of distinction. *International Journal of Ageing and Later Life, 4*, 7.

Krekula, C. (2011). *Åldersdiskriminering i svenskt arbetsliv: om ålderskodningar och myter som skapar ojämlikhet*. Stockholm: The Equality Ombudsman.

Krizsan, A., Skjeie, H., & Squires, J. (Eds.). (2012). *Institutionalizing intersectionality: The changing nature of European equality regimes*. New York: Palgrave Macmillan.

Lain, D. (2012). Working past 65 in the UK and the USA: Segregation into 'Lopaq' occupations? *Work, Employment and Society, 26*(1), 78–94.

Lain, D., & Loretto, W. (2015). Workers over 65 in the UK: The new 'precariat'? Presentation given at British Society of Gerontology conference, Newcastle, 1–3 July 2015.

Lait, A. (2012). *Telling tales: Work, narrative and identity in a market age*. New York: Manchester University Press.

Laulom, S. (2014). Dismissal law under challenge: New risks for workers. *European Labour Law Journal, 5*(3–4), 231.

Laulom, S., Mazuyer, E., & Escande-Varniol, C. (Eds.). (2012). *Quel droit social dans une Europe en crise?* Bruxelles: Larcier.

Leech, J., & Hanton, A. (2015). Intergenerational Foundation Index 2015. http://www.if.org.uk/wp-content/uploads/2015/07/2015-Intergenerational-Fairness-Index.pdf. Accessed 24 July 2015.

Lehr, U., & Kruse, A. (2006). Extending working life—A realistic perspective? *Zeitschrift für Arbeits- und Organisationspsychologie, 50*, 240–247. doi:10.1026/0932.4089.50.4.240. Accessed 21 Oct 2015.

Lenaerts, Koen. (2013). The court's outer and inner selves: Exploring the external and internal legitimacy of the European Court of Justice. In M. Adams, & Others (Eds.), *The legitimacy of the case law of the European Court of Justice*. Oxford: Hart Publishing.

Lewis, J. (2007). Gender, ageing and the 'New Social Settlement': The importance of delivering a holistic approach to care policies. *Current Sociology, 55*, 271–286.

Linstone, H. A., & Turoff, M. (1977). Evaluation—Introduction. In H. A. Linstone & M. Turof (Eds.), *The Delphi method: Techniques and applications*. Reading: Addison-Wesley.

Lombardo, E., & Verloo, M. (2009). Institutionalising intersectionality in the European Union? Policy developments and contestations. *International Feminist Journal of Politics, 11*, 478–495.

Loretto, W. (2010). Work and retirement in an ageing world: The case of older workers in the UK. *21st Century Society: Journal of the Academy of Social Sciences 5*(3), 279–294. Special edition: The Ageing World.

Loretto, W., & Vickerstaff, S. (2013). The domestic and gendered context for retirement. *Human Relations, 66*(1), 65–86.

Loretto, W., & Vickerstaff, S. (2015). Gender, age and flexible working in later life. *Work, Employment and Society, 29*(2), 233–249.

Loretto, W., Duncan, C., & White, P. J. (2000a). Ageism and employment. Controversies, ambiguities and younger people's perceptions. *Ageing and Society, 20*, 279.

Loretto, W., White, P., & Duncan, C. (2000b). Something for nothing?: Employees' views of occupational pension schemes. *Employee Relations, 22*(3), 260–271.

Loretto, W., Vickerstaff, S., & White, P. (2005). Older workers and the options for flexible work. Working Paper Series no. 31. Equal Opportunities Commission, Manchester.

Loretto, W., Vickerstaff, S., & White, P. (2007). Flexible work and older workers. In W. Loretto, S. Vickerstaff, & P. White (Eds.), *The future for older workers: New perspectives*. Bristol: The Policy Press.

Macnicol, J. (1998). *The politics of retirement in Britain 1878–1948*. Cambridge: Cambridge University Press.

Macnicol, J. (2006). *Age discrimination: An historical and contemporary analysis*. Cambridge: Cambridge University Press.

Madvig, T. L., & Shultz, K. S. (2008). Modeling individuals' post-retirement behaviors toward their former organization. *Journal of Workplace Behavioral Health, 23*, 17–49.

Maestas, N. (2010). Back to work expectations and realizations of work after retirement. *Journal of Human Resources, 45*(3), 718–748.

Maitland, A. (2010). *Working better: The over 50s, the new work generation*. London: EHRC.

Mallett, O., & Wapshott, R. (2012). Mediating ambiguity: Narrative identity and knowledge workers. *Scandinavian Journal of Management, 28*, 16–26.

Maltby, Tony. (2009). The employability of older workers: What works?. In Wendy Loretto, & Others (Eds.), *The future for older workers: New perspectives*. Bristol: Policy Press.

Manfredi, S. (2011). Retirement, collective agreement, and age discrimination: Implications for the higher education sector in the UK. *International Journal of Discrimination and the Law 11*(1/2). https://www.gov.uk/government/publications/employment-law-review-report-beecroft. Accessed 1 May 2015.

Manfredi, S., & Vickers, L. (2009). Retirement and age discrimination: Managing retirement in higher education. *Industrial Law Journal, 38*(4), 343–364.

Manfredi, S., & Vickers, L. (2013). Meeting the challenges of active ageing in the workplace: Is the abolition of retirement the answer? *ELLJ, 4*, 251–271.

Mariucci, L. (2013). The real sins of the fathers: Wrong reforms and missed reforms. *Economia e società regionale, XXXI*(3), 84.

Markus, H., & Nurius, P. (1986). Possible selves. *American Psychologist, 41*, 954–969.

Maxin, L., & Deller, J. (2010), Activities in retirement: Individual experience of Silver Work. *Comparative Population Studies, 35*, 801–832. doi:10.4232/10. CPoS-2010-18en. Accessed 21 Oct 2015.

May, T. (1993). *Social research: Issues, methods and process*. Berkshire: Open University Press.

Mazák, Ján., & Moser, Martin. (2013). Adjudication by reference to general principles of EU law: A second look at the Mangold case law. In M. Adams, & Others (Eds.), *The legitimacy of the case law of the European Court of Justice*. Oxford: Hart Publishing.

McCartney, H. B. (2011). Hero, victim or villain? The public image of the British soldier and its implications for defense policy. *Defense and Security Analysis, 27*(1), 43–54.

McDonald, H. G., & Kirsch, C. P. (1978). Use of the Delphi method as a means of assessing judicial manpower needs. *Justice System Journal, 3*, 314.

McGlynn, C. (2001). Reclaiming a feminist vision: The reconciliation of paid work and family life in European Union law and policy. *Columbia Journal of European Law, 7*, 262.

McGovern, P., Smeaton, D., & Hill, S. (2004). Bad jobs in Britain: Nonstandard employment and job quality. *Work and Occupations, 31*(2), 225–249.

McKay, S., Jefferys, S., Paraskevopoulou, A., & Keles, J. (April 2012). Study on precarious work and social rights. Carried out for the European Commission (VT/2010/084). Working Lives Research Institute, London Metropolitan University.

McMullin, J. (1995). Theorizing age and gender relations. In S. Arber & J. Ginn (Eds.), *Connecting gender and ageing: A sociological approach*. Buckingham: Open University Press.

McNair, S. (2006). How different is the older labour market? Attitudes to work and retirement among older people in Britain. *Social Policy & Society, 5*(4), 485–494.

McNamara, T. K., Brown, M., Aumann, K., Pitt-Catsouphes, M., Galinsky, E., & Bond, J. (2013). Working in retirement: A brief report. *Journal of Applied Gerontology 32*(1), 120–132. doi:10.1177/0733464811408085. Accessed 21 Oct 2015.

Meenan, H. (2007). Age discrimination in the EU and the framework directive. In M. Sargeant (Ed.), *The law on age discrimination*. Alphen aan den Rijn: Kluwer Law International.

Meuser, Michael., & Nagel, Ulrike. (2009). The expert interview and changes in knowledge production. In Alexander Bogner, & Others (Eds.), *Interviewing experts* (Research methods). New York: Palgrave Macmillan, 24.

Ministry of Defence. (2014). *Ad-hoc statistical release; career transition partnership: Follow-up questionnaires 1 September 2012 to 31 August 2013*. London: Ministry of Defence.

Ministry of Defence, JSP 898. (2014). *Defence direction and guidance on training, education and skills Part 1: Directive*. London: HMSO.

Minns, R. (2001). *The cold war in welfare: Stock markets versus pensions*. London/New York: Verso.

Moen, P., & Sweet, S. (2004). From "work–family" to "flexible careers". *Community, Work & Family, 7*(2), 209.

Moore, P. (2010) The international political economy of work and employability 32. New York: Palgrave Macmillan.

Morgan, J. (2005). The UK pension system: The betrayal by New Labour in its neoliberal global context. *Research in Political Economy, 23*, 301–347.

Morley, K. (2014, January 23). Rethinking the pension. *Investors Chronicle*, 3.

Morrow-Howell, N. (2010). Volunteering in later life: Research frontiers. *Journals of Gerontology – Series B Psychological Sciences and Social Sciences, 65 B*(4), 461–469.

Morrow-Howell, N., Putnam, M., Lee, Y. S., Greenfield, J. C., Inoue, M., & Chen, H. (2014). An investigation of activity profiles of older adults. *Journal of Gerontology: Social Sciences, 69B*, 809–821. http://doi.org/10.1093/geronb/gbu002. Accessed 21 Oct 2015.

Myles, J. (1984). *Old age in the welfare state: The political economy of public pensions*. Scott Foreseman and Company. Glenview, USA.

National Audit Office Report. (2007). *Leaving the services*. London: HMSO.

Neal, A. (2012). 'Active ageing' and the limits of labour law. In F. Hendrickx (Ed.), *Active ageing and labour law*. Cambridge: Intersentia.

NHS Employers. (2013). Working longer review. Available at: http://www.nhs-employers.org/PayAndContracts/NHSPensionSchemeReview/ImpactofWorkingLongerReview/Pages/NHSWorkingLongerReview.aspx. Accessed 15 June 2013.

NHS Employers. (2015a). Working longer group. http://www.nhsemployers.org/your-workforce/need-to-know/working-longer-group. Accessed 23 Sept 2015.

NHS Employers. (2015b). Working longer group: Preliminary findings and recommendations report. http://www.nhsemployers.org/your-workforce/need-to-know/working-longer-group/preliminary-findings-and-recommendations-report-for-the-health-departments. Accessed 23 Sept 2015.

NHS Employers. (2015c). Working longer group: Steering group meetings—Key messages. http://www.nhsemployers.org/your-workforce/need-to-know/working-longer-group/steering-group-meetings---key-messages. Accessed 23 Sept 2015.

NHS Employers. (2015d). Working longer group: Changing attitudes towards redeployment, task and finish group terms of reference. http://www.nhsemployers.org/-/media/Employers/Documents/Pay%20and%20reward/WLR%20Prelim%20Report%20-%20Annex%207%20-%20Call%20for%20evidence%20interim%20findings%20report.pdf. Accessed 23 Sept 2015.

Nickell, S., & Layard, R. (1999). Labor market institutions and economic performance. In O. Ashenfelter & D. Card (Eds.), *Handbook of labor economics, III*. Amsterdam: Elsevier Science.

Nobles, R. (2000). Access to the law of pensions: The lessons from National Grid v Laws. *Employee Relations, 22*(3), 282–285.

Nolda, C. (2004). Industrial conflict in local government since 1997. *Employee Relations, 26*(4), 377–391.

Nowotny, H. (1994). *Time: The modern and postmodern experience*. Cambridge: Polity Press.

Numhauser-Henning, A. (2013a). Labour law in a greying labour market—In need of a reconceptualisation of work and pension norms. *ELIJ, 4*(94), 84–100.

Numhauser-Henning, A. (2013b). The EU ban on age-discrimination and older workers: Potentials and pitfalls. *The International Journal of Comparative Labour Law and Industrial Relations, 29*(4), 391–414.

O'Cinneide, C. Age discrimination and the European Court of Justice: EU equality law comes of age. *R.A.E. – L.E.A.* 2009–2010/2, 265.

O' Cinneide, C. (2013). The growing importance of age equality. *The Equal Rights Review 11*, 99, according to whom "age [is] used as a 'proxy' for other personal characteristics such as maturity, health or vulnerability".

OECD. (2004). Employment outlook, available at www.oecd.org

OECD. (2011). *Pensions at a glance*. Paris: OECD Publishing.

OECD. (2012). *Live longer, work longer*. Paris: OECD Publishing.

OECD. (2013). *Pensions at a glance 2013: Retirement-income systems in OECD and G20 countries*. Paris: OECD Publishing.

OECD. (2015a). *Silver economy and ageing society: An opportunity for growth and job creation in the G20 countries*. Paris: OECD Publishing.

OECD. (2015). StatExtracts. Dataset: Labour force statistics—Sex and age indicators. Retrieved from http://stats.oecd.org/Index. aspx?DatasetCode=LFS_SEXAGE_I_R#. Accessed 21 Oct 2015.

ONS. (2012). Older workers and the labour market. ONS, London.

ONS. (2013). Pension trends 2013 Edition. ONS.

Osborne, H. (2011, November 29). George Osborne confirms state pension age will rise to 67. *The Guardian*.

Osborne, H. (2012, October 11). Warning over poor performing auto-enrolment pensions. *The Guardian*.

Osbourne, H. (2010, January 27). 2m pensioners live in poverty says ONS. *The Guardian*.

Parry, E., & Harris, Lynette. (2011, December). The employment relations challenges of an ageing workforce (Acas Future of Workplace Relations discussion paper series); CIPD (May 2011) 'Managing Age: New Edition 2011'.

Pengcharoen, C., & Shultz, K. S. (2010). The influences on bridge employment decisions. *International Journal of Manpower, 31*, 322–336.

Piekkola, H. (2008). *Nordic policies on active ageing in the labour market and some European comparisons, in country and regional development*. UNESCO, Paris.

Pierson, P. (1994). *Dismantling the welfare state: Regan, Thatcher and the politics of retrenchment*. Cambridge: Cambridge University Press.

Pleau, R. L. (2010). Gender differences in postretirement employment. *Research on Aging, 32*, 267–303.

Porcellato, L., Carmichael, F., Hulme, C., Ingham, B., & Prashar, A. (2010). Giving older workers a voice: Constraints on the employment of older people in the North West of England. *Work, Employment and Society, 24*(1), 85–103.

PPI. (2013). What level of pension contribution is needed to obtain an adequate retirement income? Available at: http://www.pensionspolicyinstitute.org.uk/publications/reports/what-level-of-pension contribution-is-needed-to-obtain-an-adequate-retirement-income. Accessed 1 Aug 2015.

Prassl, J. (2014). Contingent crises, permanent reforms: Rationalising labour market reforms in the European Union. *European Labour Law Journal, 5*(3–4), 215.

Price, C. (2003). Professional women's retirement adjustment: The experience of re-establishing order. *Journal of Aging Studies, 17*, 341–355.

PWC. (2012). Available at: http://pwc.blogs.com/scotland/2012/09/millennials-pensions-will-fall-short-of-todays-pensioners-despite-auto-enrolment.html. Accessed 1 Aug 2015.

Rau, B. L., & Adams, G. A. (2005). Attracting retirees to apply: Desired organizational characteristics of bridge employment. *Journal of Organizational Behavior, 26*, 649–660.

Rauch, W. (1979). The decision Delphi. *Technological Forecasting and Social Change, 15*, 159.

Ravelli, F. (2015). Alcune questioni in tema di pensioni e turn-over generazionale. Rivista giuridica del lavoro 2.

Rayens, M. K., & Hahn, E. J. (2000). Building consensus using the policy Delphi method. *Policy, Politics, & Nursing Practice, 1*, 308–315.

Rayer, C. W. G. (2010). Note on 'European Court of Justice, 19 January 2010, C-555/07', *ELLJ 1*(2), 264–268.

Rees Jones, I., Leontowitsch, M., & Higgs, P. (2010). The experience of retirement in second modernity: Generational habitus among retired senior managers. *Sociology 44* 0(1), 103–120.

Reese, P. (1992). *Homecoming heroes: An account of the re-assimilation of British military personnel into civilian life*. London: Pen & Sword book.

Regalia, I. (2014). Azione del sindacato nel territorio. Economia e società regionale, 39.

Reich, M., Gordon, D. M., & Edwards, R. C. (1982). Dual labour markets: A theory of labour market segmentation. *The Journal of Human Resources, 17*(3), 359–365.

Riach, K. (2007). Othering' older worker identity in recruitment. *Human Relations, 60*(11), 1719.

Rifkin, J. (2013). La fine del lavoro. Milano: Mondadori.

Roberts, H. (2014a). Available at: http://www.hrmagazine.co.uk/hro/news/1143906/staff-employers-concerned-retirement-savings. Accessed 1 Aug 2015.

Roberts, H. (2014b). http://www.hrmagazine.co.uk/hro/news/1146027/auto-enrolment-doesnt-provide-decent-income-low-paid-workers-tuc. Accessed 1 Aug 2015.

Rodgers, L. (2011). Labour law and the 'public interest': Discrimination and beyond. *ELLJ, 2*(4), 302–322.

Rotondi, A., & Gustafson, D. (1996). Theoretical, methodological and practical issues arising out of the Delphi method. In M. Adler & E. Ziglio (Eds.), *Gazing into the oracle: The Delphi method and its application to social policy and public health* (p. 42). London: Jessica Kingsley.

Saari, M. (2013). Promoting gender equality without a gender perspective: Problem representations of equal pay in Finland. *Gender Work and Organization, 20*(1), 34–54.

Sarfati, H. (2006). Social dialogue: A potential "highroad" to policies addressing ageing in the EU member states. *International Social Security Review, 59,* 49–57.

Sargeant, M. (2006). *Age discrimination in employment.* Aldershot: Gower.

Sargeant, M. (2008). Older workers and the need for reasonable accommodation. *International Journal of Discrimination and the Law, 9*(3), 163–180.

Sargent, L. D., Lee, M. D., Martin, B., & Zikic, J. (2013). Reinventing retirement: New pathways, new arrangements, new meanings. *Human Relations, 66*(1), 3–21.

Saunders, C. (2013, May 1). Pot half full? How women lose out when it comes to pensions. *The Guardian* . Available at: http://www.theguardian.com/women-in-leadership/2013/may/01/women-lose-out-on-pensions. Accessed 1 Aug 2015.

Schiek, D. (2010). Constitutional principles and horizontal effect: Kücükdeveci revisited. *ELLJ, 1*(2), 368–378.

Schiek, D., & Lawson, A. (Eds.). (2011). *European Union non-discrimination law and intersectionality. Investigating the triangle of racial, gender and disability discrimination.* Burlington: Ashgate Publishing.

Schiek, D., & Mulder, J. (2011). 'Intersectionality in EU Law: A critical reappraisal', and 'Organizing EU equality law around the nodes of "race", gender and disability' both in D. Schiek, & A. Lawson, (Eds.), *European Union non-discrimination law and intersectionality. Investigating the triangle of racial, gender and disability discrimination.* Farnham: Ashgate.

Schlachter, M. (2011). Mandatory retirement and age discrimination under EU law. *The International Journal of Comparative Labour Law and Industrial Relations, 27*(3), 287–299.

Schmidt, D. F., & Boland, S. M. (1986). Structure of perceptions of older adults: Evidence for multiple stereotypes. *Psychology and Aging, 1*(3), 255–260.

Schwalbe, M. (2008). *Rigging the game: How inequality is reproduced in everyday life.* New York: Oxford University Press.

Sheppard, H. (1978). The issue of mandatory retirement. *Annals of the American Academy of Political and Social Science, 438,* 40.

Sheppard, H. (1978). The Issue of Mandatory Retirement. *Annals of the American Academy of Political and Social Science. Vol. 438 Planning for the elderly,* 40-49.

Shultz, K. S., & Wang, M. (2011). Psychological perspectives on the changing nature of retirement. *American Psychologist, 66,*170–177. doi:10.1037/a0022411. Accessed 21 Oct 2015

Shultz, K. S., Wang, M., Crimmins, E. M., & Fisher, G. G. (2010). Age differences in the demand-control model of work stress: An examination of data from 15 European countries. *Journal of Applied Gerontology, 29*, 21–47.

Simpson, M., Richardson, M., & Zorn, T. (2012). A job, a dream or a trap? Multiple meanings for encore careers. *Work, Employment and Society, 26*(3), 429–446.

Sinclair, D., Moore, K., & Franklin, B. (2014). Linking state pension age to longevity. Tackling the fairness challenge, International Longevity Centre. http://www.ilcuk.org.uk/index.php/publications/publication_details/ageing_longevity_and_demographic_change_a_factpack_of_statistics_from_the_i. Accessed 20 July 2014.

Skedinger, P. (2010). *Employment protection legislation. Evolution, effects, winners and losers.* Cheltenham: Edward Elgar.

Smeaton, D., & Vegeris, S. (2009). Older people inside and outside the labour market: A review, research report 22, Equality and Human Rights Commission. www.equalityhumanrights.com/en/policyresearch/pages/default.aspx. Accessed 15 Oct. 2015.

Smeaton, D., & White, M. (2015). The growing discontents of older British employees: Extended working life at risk from quality of working life. *Social Policy and Society*, online 1 July 2015.

Spedale, S., Coupland, C., & Tempest, S. (2014). Gendered ageism and organizational routines at work: The case of day-parting in television broadcasting. *Organization Studies, 35*(11), 1585.

Stake, R. (2008). Qualitative case studies. In Y. Lincoln & N. Denzin (Eds.), *Strategies of qualitative inquiry* (3rd ed., p. 130). Sage: Thousand Oaks.

Swinnen, W. (2010). The economic perspective in the reasoning of the ECJ in age discrimination cases. *ELLJ, 1*(2), 261.

Taylor, S. (2000). Occupational pensions and employee retention: Debate and evidence. *Employee Relations, 22*(3), 246–259.

Taylor, M. A., Shultz, K. S., & Doverspike, D. D. (2015). Academic perspectives on recruiting and retaining older workers. In P. T. Beatty & R. M. S. Visser (Eds.), *Thriving on an aging workforce: Strategies for organizational and systemic change.* Malabar: Krieger Publishing Company.

Temming, F. (2007). The Palacios case: Turning point in age discrimination law? *European Law Reporter, 11*, 382.

ten Bokum, N., & Bartelings, P. (Eds.). (2009). *Age discrimination law in Europe.* Alphen aan den Rijn: Kluwer Law International.

The Economist (2014, April 26). A billion shades of grey – An ageing economy will be a slower and more unequal one—Unless policy starts changing now.

The Economist, London: http://www.economist.com/news/leaders/21601253-ageing-economy-will-be-slower-and-more-unequal-oneunless-policy-starts-changing-now. Accessed 21 Oct 2015.

The King's Fund, an independent charity working to improve health care, has pointed to the growing financial pressure in the NHS. http://www.kingsfund.org.uk/projects/funding-and-finances. Accessed 25 Sept 2015.

The Swedish National Audit Office. (2009). Arbetsgivares attityder till äldre yrkesverksamma, Stockholm.

Thomas, A., & Pascal, J. (2010). Default retirement age—Employer qualitative research Research Report 672. DWP, 4.

Thompson, J. B. (1990). *Ideology and modern culture: Critical social theory in the era of mass communication*. Cambridge: Polity Press.

Townson, M. (1994). *The social contract for seniors in Canada: Preparing for the 21st century*. Ottawa: National Advisory Council on Ageing.

Travis, Lawrence F., & Others. (1985). The future of sentencing and parole: A Delphi reassessment of sentencing and parole reforms. *Criminal Justice Review* 10, 45–51.

Tremblay, D.-G., & Genin, É. (2010). Aging, economic insecurity, and employment: Which measures would encourage older workers to stay longer in the labour market? *Studies in Social Justice, 3*, 173.

TUC. (2014). Auto-enrolment pensions must do more for low-paid workers, says TUC, 2014. http://www.tuc.org.uk/economic-issues/pensions-and-retirement/auto-enrolment-pensions-must-do-more-low-paid-workers-says. Accessed 1 Aug 2015.

Tuomi, K., & Others. (1977). Summary of the Finnish research project (1981–1992) to promote the health and work ability of aging workers. *Scandinavian Journal of Work, Environment & Health 23*, 66–71.

Tuomi, K., & Others. (2001). Promotion of work ability, the quality of work and retirement. *Occupational Medicine 51*, 318–324.

Turner, J. A. (2005). *The Pension Commission: Challenges and choices*. London: HMSO.

Turner, J. A. (2006). *The Pension Commission: A new pensions settlement for the twenty-first century*. London: HMSO.

Turoff, M. (1970). The design of a policy Delphi. *Technological Forecasting and Social Change, 2*, 149.

Turoff, M. (1977). The policy Delphi. In H. A. Linstone & M. Turoff (Eds.), *The Delphi method: Techniques and applications*. Reading: Addison-Wesley.

Turoff, M., & Hiltz, S. R. (1996). Computer-based Delphi processes. In M. Adler & E. Ziglio (Eds.), *Gazing into the oracle: The Delphi method and its application to social policy and public health*. London: Jessica Kingsley.

Ugwumadu, J. (2014). Four million now auto-enrolled into workplace pensions. *The Actuary*, available at: http://www.theactuary.com/news/2014/08/four-million-now-auto-enrolled-into-workplace-pensions/2014. Accessed 1 Aug 2015.

UK Cabinet Office 'About Red Tape Challenge' (Red Tape Challenge, no date).

UK Government UK Armed Forces Covenant. https://www.gov.uk/government/publications/2010-to-2015-government-policy-armed-forces-covenant/2010-to-2015-government-policy-armed-forces-covenant. Accessed 21 Oct 2015.

UK Ministry of Defence Career Transition Partnership quarterly statistics: UK Regular Service Personnel Employment Outcomes 2009/10 to 2013/14 (UK Ministry of Defence 11 June 2015). https://www.gov.uk/government/uploads/system/uploads/attachment_data/file/434406/20150522_CTP_official_statistic_0910_1314Revised.pdf. Accessed 21 Oct 2015.

UK Ministry of Defence 'Emotional Pathway' Information sheet at http://www.army.mod.uk/documents/general/Transition_Information_Sheet_2_-_The_Emotional_Pathway.pdf. Accessed 21 Oct 2015.

UK Ministry of Defence Joint Service Publication (JSP) 534. (2014). The tri-service resettlement manual, Ministry of Defence, London.

UNECE Active Ageing Index Concepts. (2013). *Methodology and final results.* Vienna.

Uren, A. (2013). The 12m workers who risk retiring on inadequate incomes with middle earners hit hardest by a pensions shock. Available at: http://www.thisismoney.co.uk/money/pensions/article-2418601/12m-working-adults-face-retiring-inadequate-incomes.html. Accessed 1 Aug 2015.

Van Dalen, H. P., Henkens, K., & Schippers, J. (2009). Dealing with older workers in Europe: A comparative survey of employers' attitudes and actions. *Journal of European Social Policy, 19*, 47.

Van Dalen, H. P., Henkens, K., & Schippers, J. (2012). Productivity of older workers: Perceptions of employers and employees. *Population and Development Review, 36*, 309.

van Gigch, J. P., & Hommes, R. (1973). A study of how correctional counsellors and psychologists agree upon pre-sentence recommendations. *Canadian Journal of Criminology & Corrections, 15*, 93.

Verloo, M. (2006). Multiple inequalities, intersectionality and the European Union. *European Journal of Women's Studies, 13*, 211.

Verloo, M., & Walby, S. (2012). Introduction: The implications for theory and practice of comparing the treatment of intersectionality in the equality architecture of Europe. *Social Politics, 19*, 433.

Vickers, L., & Manfredi, S. (2013). Age equality and retirement: Squaring the circle. *Industrial Law Journal, 42*(1), 61.

Vickerstaff, S. (2010). Older workers: The unavoidable obligation of extending our working lives? *Sociology Compass, 4*(10), 869.

Vickerstaff, S., Loretto, W., & White, P. (2007). The future for older workers: Opportunities and constraints. In W. Loretto, S. Vickerstaff, & P. White (Eds.), *The future for older workers: New perspectives* (pp. 203–226). Bristol: Polity Press.

Vickerstaff, S., Loretto, W., Billings, J., Brown, P., Mitton, L., Parkin, T., & White. P. (2008). Encouraging labour market activity among 60–64 year olds DWP Research Report No. 531, DWP. Available from: http://www.dwp.gov.uk/asd/asd5/rrs-index.asp. Accessed 15 Oct 2015.

Vickerstaff, S., Loretto, W., Milne, A., Alden, E., Billings, J., & White, P. (2009). The employment support needs of carers, DWP Research Report No. 597, DWP. Available from: http://research.dwp.gov.uk/asd/asd5/rports2009-2010/rrep597.pdf. Accessed 15 Oct 2015.

Von Bonsdorff, M. E., Shultz, K. S., Leskinen, E., & Tansky, J. (2009). The choice between retirement and bridge employment: A continuity theory and life course perspective. *International Journal of Aging and Human Development, 69*, 79–100.

Votinius, J. J. (2012). Having the right attitude: Cooperation skills and labour law. *The International Journal of Comparative Labour Law and Industrial Relations, 28*(2), 223–248.

Vough, H., Bataille, C., Noh, S., & Lee, M. (2015). Going off script: How managers make sense of the ending of their careers. *Journal of Management Studies, 52*(3), 414–440.

Walker, A. (2001, November 29–30). Towards active ageing in the European Union. Paper prepared for the Millennium Project workshop—Towards active ageing in the 21st Century. Tokyo: The Japan Institute of Labour.

Walker, A. (2002). Ageing in Europe: Policies in harmony or discord? *International Journal of Epidemiology 31*, 758, 760.

Walker, A. (2008). Commentary: The emergence and application of active aging in Europe. *Journal of Aging & Social Policy, 21*, 75–93.

Walker, A., & Maltby, T. (2012). Active ageing: A strategic policy solution to demographic ageing in the European Union. *International Journal of Social Welfare, 21*, S117–S130.

Walsh, D. C., & Gordon, N. P. (1986). Legal approaches to smoking deterrence. *Annual Review of Public Health, 7*, 127.

Wang, M. (2007). Profiling retirees in the retirement transition and adjustment process: Examining the longitudinal change patterns of retirees' psychological well-being. *Journal of Applied Psychology, 92*, 455–474. http://dx.doi.org/10.1037/0021-9010.92.2.455. Accessed 21 Oct 2015.

Wang, M. & Shi, J. (2014). Psychological research on retirement. *Annual Review of Psychology, 65*, 209–233. http://doi.org/10.1146/annurev-psych-010213-115131. Accessed 21 Oct 2015.

Wang, M., & Shultz, K. S. (2010). Employee retirement: A review and recommendations for future investigation. *Journal of Management, 36*, 72–206.

Wang, M., Zhan, Y. J., Liu, S. Q., & Shultz, K. S. (2008). Antecedents of bridge employment: A longitudinal investigation. *Journal of Applied Psychology, 93*(4), 818–830.

Warburton, J., Paynter, J., & Petriwskyj, A. (2007). Volunteering as a productive aging activity: Incentives and barriers to volunteering by Australian seniors. *Journal of Applied Gerontology, 26*(4), 333–354.

Warhurst, C., Eikhof, D. R., & Haunschild, A. (2008). Out of balance or just out of bounds? Analyzing the relationship between work and life. In C. Warhurst, D. R. Eikhof, & A. Haunschild (Eds.), *Work less, live more? Critical analysis of the work-life boundary*. New York: Palgrave Macmillan.

Warr, P., Butcher, V., Robertson, I., & Callinan, M. (2004). Older people's well-being as a function of employment, retirement, environmental characteristics and role preference. *British Journal of Psychology, 95*, 297–324.

Warren, T. (2003). A privileged pole? Diversity in women's pay, pensions and wealth in Britain. *Gender Work and Organization, 10*(5), 605–628.

Webb, S. (2013). Pensions Minister Steve Webb on welfare reforms—Video The Guardian, available at: http://www.theguardian.com/politics/video/2013/apr/01/pensions-minister-steve-webb-welfare-reforms-video. Accessed 1 Aug 2015.

Webley, L. (2010). Qualitative approaches to empirical legal research. In P. Cane & H. M. Kritzer (Eds.), *The Oxford handbook of empirical legal research*. Oxford/New York: Oxford University Press.

Weckerle, J. R., & Shultz, K. S. (1999). Influences on the bridge employment decision among older USA workers. *Journal of Occupational and Organizational Psychology, 72*, 317–329.

Williams, J. C. (2001). *Unbending gender: Why family and work conflict and what to do about it*. Oxford/New York: Oxford University Press.

Williamson, J., & Williams, M. (2005). Notional defined contribution account neoliberal ideology and the political economy of pension reform. *American Journal of Economics and Sociology, 64*(2), 485–506.

Winklemann-Gleed, A. (2011). Retirement or committed to work? Conceptualising prolonged labour market participation through organisational commitment. *Employee Relations, 34*(1), 80–90.

Wöhrmann, A. M., Deller, J., & Wang, M. (2013). Outcome expectations and work design characteristics in post-retirement work planning. *Journal of Vocational Behavior, 83*, 219–228. doi:10.1016/j.jvb.2013.05.003. Accessed 21 Oct 2015.

Wöhrmann, A. M., Fasbender, U., & Deller, J. (2016). Using work values to predict post-retirement work intentions. *Career Development Quarterly*, 64, 98–113.

Wolf, A. (2011). *Review of vocational education – The Wolf report*. London: Department for Education. https://hbr.org/2010/10/the-strategic-corporal. html. Accessed 21 October 2015.

World Health Organization. (April 2002). Active ageing: A policy framework, A contribution of the World Health Organization to the Second United Nations World Assembly on Ageing, Madrid, Spain.

WRC 'Women's equality in the UK – A health check', CEDAW. (2013). Shadow report 2013. Women's Resource Centre, London.

Wright, K. N. (1982). A Delphi assessment of the effects of a declining economy on crime and the criminal justice system. *Fed Probation, 46*, 36–40.

Wyatt, A. (March 2002). Development of the Veterans Initiative by the Ministry of Defence, Case study. Sunningdale Park, UK: The international comparisons in Policy Making Team, International Public Service Group, Cabinet Office's Centre for Management and Policy Studies, the Civil Service College.

Young, S. J., & Jamieson, L. M. (1999). Perceived liability and risk management trends impacting recreational sports into the 21st century. *Aging and Retirement, 9*, 151.

Young, S. J, & Others. (2004). Best case scenario: The development of a teaching tool for sport law. *Journal of Legal Aspects of Sport 14*, 1.

Zacher, H. (2015). Successful aging at work. *Work, Aging and Retirement, 1*(1), 4–25.

Zaniboni, S., Sarchielli, G., & Fraccaroli, F. (2010). How are psychosocial factors related to retirement intentions? *International Journal of Manpower, 31*(3), 271–285.

Zanoni, P. (2010). Diversity in the lean automobile factory: Doing class through gender, disability and age. Organization org.sagepub.com. Accessed 22 Oct 2015.

Zepelin, H., Sills, R. A., & Heath, M. W. (1986). Is age becoming irrelevant? An exploratory study of perceived age norms. *International Journal of Aging and Human Development, 24*(4), 241.

Zhan, Y., Wang, M., Liu, S., & Shultz, K. S. (2009). Bridge employment and retirees' health: A longitudinal investigation. *Journal of Occupational Health Psychology, 14*, 374–389.

Ziglio, E. (1996). The Delphi method and its contribution to decision-making. In M. Adler & E. Ziglio (Eds.), *Gazing into the oracle: The Delphi method and its application to social policy and public health*. London: Jessica Kingsley.

Index

A

Advisory Conciliation and
    Arbitration Service (ACAS),
    273–4
Age Action Alliance, 182
Age Action Alliance Employer
    Toolkit, 171
age discrimination law, CJEU
    'active ageing' agenda, 5
    anti-discrimination law, 17
    collective and interest-based
        approach, 4, 22–3
    collective nature, 23–4
    dilemmatic nature, 23
    economic paradigm, 24–6
    employment policy, 18
    European Union, 18
    interdisciplinarity of, 21–2
    internal labour market
        justifications, 20

labour market and employment
    policy, 4
subsidiarity and proportionality,
    18–20
'Age Immaterial' campaign in
    2013/14, 283
age management approach, 168–9,
    177–9, 180
2006 Age Regulations, 78, 270
auto-enrolment pensions, 63–8
automatic retirement or default
    retirement schemes, 11, 13,
    15, 24, 36, 42, 123–5

B

BAE Systems, 279–80
Bartlett's test of sphericity, 246
Basic State Pension, 64, 67
'biological age,' concept of, 259

BMW group case study
  concept of 'biological age', 259
  ergonomically friendly working
    environment, 258–9
  'Fit for Work Index', 260
  pre-retirement seminars, 262
  skills of older workers, 261–2
  'Today for Tomorrow'
    programme, 257–8, 262
  working patterns, 260–261
BMW Plant Hams Hall, 257
Bosch Management Support GmbH,
  253
British Airways (BA), 59–60
British State Pension (BSP), 57,
  60–61

C
Cadman approach, 16
career renewal, pathway of, 229
Career Transition Partnership (CTP),
  295, 297
Career Transition Workshop, 296
case-by-case approach, 26
case law, CJEU
  age-related pay structures ('wage
    classifications'), 15
  case of Fuchs, 14
  case of Georgiev, 13–14
  case of Hennigs, 16, 22
  case of Hörnfeldt, 4, 14–15
  case of Kücükdeveci, 16
  case of Mangold, 9–10, 16–17, 22
  case of Palacios de la Villa, 11–12,
    17, 22, 23
  case of Rosenbladt, 12–13, 17, 22
  seniority-related pay amounts,
    15–16

CBI. See Confederation of British
    Industry (CBI)
Chartered Institute of Personnel and
    Development (CIPD), 169,
    182
CJEU. See Court of Justice of the
    European Union (CJEU)
'cliff-edge' retirement, 205–6
command, leadership and
    management (CLM), 294
Commission's 2010–2015 action
    plan, 1076
Community Action Programmes,
    102
company-level contracts, Italy
  national trade unions, 131–2
  production activities,
    reorganisation of, 132
  voluntary retirement agreements,
    131
  working environment,
    reorganisation of, 132
compulsory retirement
  age, 29–30, 33, 187, 199
  in Palacios, 11–12, 23
  rule, 25, 26
  and seniority pay, 25
Confederation of British Industry
    (CBI), 76, 270
content analysis, 242, 250–251
'contribution holidays', 58
corporate social responsibility (CSR),
    134
Court of Justice of the European
    Union (CJEU), 90, 270. See
    also age discrimination law,
    CJEU
CSR. See corporate social
    responsibility (CSR)

CTP. *See* Career Transition Partnership (CTP)
CTP Future Horizons Programme, 296

D

DB schemes. *See* defined benefit (DB) pension schemes
DC schemes. *See* defined contribution (DC) schemes
default retirement age (DRA), 76, 269–271, 279
defined benefit (DB) pension schemes, 57–8, 59, 61–3
defined contribution (DC) schemes, 57, 62–3
Delphi method
  analysis, 180–183
  challenges, 183
  consensus around policy options, 183
  description, 161
  inter-quartile range, 166
  percentage of respondents, 166
  policy Delphi (*see* (policy Delphi method))
  RAND Corporation, 160
  scenarios and results (*see* (scenarios, Delphi method))
Department of Work and Pensions (DWP), 50, 65, 182
dignity or collegiality, 80, 82
Discrimination Act of 2008, 110
dividend tax credit (DTC), 60
DRA. *See* default retirement age (DRA)
DTC. *See* dividend tax credit (DTC)

DWP. *See* Department of Work and Pensions (DWP)

E

'Early Retirement Reduction Buy out Assessment Framework' (ERRBO), 146
early service leavers (ESLs), 296
employer's justified retirement age (EJRA), 78, 269, 273–4
Employers Network for Equality & Inclusion (enei), 182
employment contract, Italy
  age and termination of, 120–121
  anti-discrimination law tools, 126–7
  automatic termination, 124–5
  dismissal of redundant employees, 125–6
  mandatory retirement, 121–4
Employment, Education, Health, Housing and Welfare (E2H2W), 292
Employment Equality Directive 2000/78, 103–4
Employment Equality (Age) Regulations 2006, 270
employment patterns, UK
  legislation prohibiting discrimination, 189
  population ageing, 188–9
  'signs of flexibilisation of work patterns', 190
  UK official labour market statistics, 189–90, 191
  workplace policy and practices, role of, 190

Employment (Age) Regulations
    2006, 77
Employment Support Programme,
    296
Enterprise and Regulation Reform
    Act 2013, 84
Equality Act 2010, 79
Equal Opportunities Ombudsman,
    111
Equal Treatment Directive 2006/54,
    103, 111
EU court and mandatory
    retirement age
  external factors, 43–4
  judgments (see (judgments on
    mandatory retirement age))
  provisions of Directive 2000/78,
    30–31
  social and employment policy, 30
EU Employment Equality Directive
    2000/78, 110
EU employment policies
  active ageing policy, 100–101
  European Employment Strategy,
    101–2
  prohibition on age discrimination,
    99
  on work life discrimination,
    102–7
European age discrimination
    legislation
  direct and indirect discrimination,
    7–9
  occupational social security
    schemes, 7–9
  preamble, 6–7
European Employment
    Strategy, 102

extended working lives, UK
  active ageing, notion of,
    206–7
  'cliff-edge' retirement, 205–6
  Delphi study (see (Delphi
    method))
  employment patterns, 188–91
  and flexible work, 197–205
  i-deals, concept of, 207–8
  paid work, 206
  policy implications, 205–8
  reinvention in retirement,
    192–7
  trade union perspective (see
    (Trades Union Congress
    (TUC)))
extending working life, Italy
  job-on-call contracts, 128–30
  legal and contractual rules, 130
  legal bases for policies in favour
    of older workers, 129
  legal perspective, 128–30
  violation of prohibition of age
    discrimination, 129
extending working lives, NHS
  data challenge, 145
  employees and managers, 147
  ERRBO, 146
  HR departments, 146
  issue of redeployment, 147
  NPA, 144–5
  occupational health, safety and
    wellbeing, 146
  pension options and retirement
    decision-making, 145
  WLG, 145
  working arrangements and
    environment, 146

F

1986 Finance Act, 59
'Financial Aspects of Resettlement'
    brief, 295
'financial security', 50
Fire Brigades Union, 282
'Fit for Work Index' (FWI), 260
flexible working
    nurses and midwives, 155–6
    retaining older workers, 154–5
    retirement and pension crisis, 49–51
    scenarios, Delphi method, 169–70
flexible working and extending
        working lives
    health reasons, 198–9
    mismatch between employers and
        employees, 202–3
    and older workers, debates, 143
    opportunities, 201–2
    poorest respondents, 204
    prevalence of, 198
    quality of, 200–201
    retaining older workers, 154–5
    socio-economic characteristics,
        197–8
    women in sample, 204–5
formal retirement, 287
'Fornero Reform', 127–8
FWI. *See* 'Fit for Work Index' (FWI)

G

GCSEs, 297
general or individual justification
    age discriminatory measure, 83–4
    EJRA, 84
    intergenerational fairness, 83
    proportionality in retirement
        cases, 82–3

worker's pension provision, 83
workforce planning, 84
German active retirees, 231–2

H

Hobson's choice, 70
'Housing' brief, 295
HR. *See* human resources (HR)
    departments
human resources (HR) departments,
    146, 298

I

i-deals, concept of, 207–8
implementation scenarios
    age management, 177–9
    information and guidance,
        179–80, 181
Independent Public Service Pensions
    Commission, 139
Individual Planning and Personal
    Development (IPPD), 292
Individual Resettlement Training
    Costs (IRTC), 296
'intergenerational fairness' argument,
    73–7, 80, 81, 83
inter-quartile range (IQR), 166
intersectionality
    age and gender in labour law, 96–7
    EU employment policies, 99–102
    EU law on work life
        discrimination, 102–7
intersectionality (*cont.*)older women's
        position in labour market,
        98–9
    working life and labour law,
        108–14

introduction of FRS17 (financial
    reporting standard 17)
    accounting procedures, 62
Investors in People Gold and
    Champion accreditations,
    263
IRTC. *See* Individual Resettlement
    Training Costs (IRTC)
Italy, labour market perspectives
    active ageing policies, 118
    anti-discrimination law, 138
    contractual perspective, 130–133
    corporate governance, trade
        unions, 133–4
    early retirement schemes and exit
        pathways, 127–8
    employment contract, age and
        termination of, 120–127
    employment rate, older workers,
        117–18
    European Parliament Resolution,
        136
    inclusion measures, extending
        working life, 128–30
    individual and collective interests,
        134–5, 137
    issue of age, 134–5
    local/regional level, 136
    retirement age, 119–20
    retirement policies, 118
    'Senior @ Work', 135–6
    trade union representation, 135

J
job-on-call contracts, 128–30
job-sharing contracts, 129–30
judgments on mandatory
        retirement age

accepting national provisions, 36–43
internal and external to Court, 32
national provisions, 31, 45
rejecting national measures, 33–5
justification of retirement
    compulsory retirement, 81
    dignity or collegiality, 82
    EU law, 79–80
    general or individual justification,
        82–4
    reinstating retirement, 84–6

K
Kaiser-Meyer-Olkin measure, 246
Kaiser normalization, 246

L
labour law
    age and gender, 96–7
    intersectional effects, 95–6
    older women's position, 98–9
    and working life, 108–14
labour market, older women's
        position
    'age and gender factor', 115
    care responsibilities, 98
    demographic developments, 98–9
    taxpayers and providers, 98
Lawson's law, 60
leadership scenarios, 171, 181
LGPS. *See* local government pension
        scheme (LGPS)
Lisbon Treaty, 103
Live Longer, Work Longer, 187
local government pension scheme
        (LGPS), 58, 264, 265
'low cost' Stakeholder Pension, 63

M

mandatory retirement
abolition of, 80, 90–91
age discriminatory practice, 90
direct services workforce, 265
EU court (*see* (EU court and
mandatory retirement age))
LGPS, 264, 265
office-based workforce, 264–5
productivity, pay linked to, 266
second jobs, 266
Man's Search for Meaning, 230
'master narrative of decline', 229
'matching capability' process, 282–3
MAXQDA, 213
Member States' labour market
policies, 19
MINI Plant Oxford, 257
MINI Plant Swindon, 257
'Moneyforce', 294
Monti Pension Reform of 2011, 119,
127
myPlan, 296

N

narrative research
choosers, survivors and jugglers,
212
debates on older workers,
limitations, 212–13
identities and decision-making,
210–211
periods of transition, individuals'
experiences, 211–12
socialisation processes, 211
NASUWT's annual conference, 280
national contract, Italy
ageing to social partners, 137
awareness campaigns, 131
collective bargaining agreements,
131
contract of credit, 131–2
defensive policies, 130–131
European Community policy, 131
National Employment Agency, 111
National Health Service (NHS)
Pension Scheme, 140–141, 148,
150, 156
trade unions, 141
National Insurance (NI)
contributions or credits, 67
national measures, rejecting
case *Commission v. Hungary*, 33–4
case *Prigge*, 34–5
national provisions
Age Concern, 39–40
Fuchs, 42
in *Georgiev*, 41–2
Hörnfeldt, 42–3
Palacios de la Villa, 36–8
Petersen, 40–41
in *Rosenbladt*, 41
neoliberal ideology and discourse,
pension crisis. *See also*
pension crisis
contemporary capitalism, 53
conventional and hegemonic
account, 55
current pension provision in UK,
56–8
dominant social groups or classes,
52–3
potential cause of social action, 55
power and domination, 54
stage of naturalisation, 54
NESTs—National Employment
Savings Trusts, 58

New Auto-Enrolment pension, 51
'New Employment Model', 297
New Flat Rate State Pension, 67
new scenarios, 164, 176–7
NHS. *See* National Health Service
(NHS)
NHS Working Longer Review, 140
non-discrimination, principle of, 3
non-discrimination provisions,
role of, 27
non-exit solutions, 133, 137
normal pension age (NPA), 144–5
nursing and midwifery profession,
older workers
employers and trade unions of
working, 158
and extending working lives,
debates, 141–4
increased life expectancy, 139–40
NHS, extending working lives,
144–7
NHS Pension Scheme, 148–50
pension arrangements, 139
reforms of public sector pensions,
139
to remove mandatory retirement,
139, 147–8
retaining older workers and
flexible working, 154–5
senior clinical managers'
perceptions, 150–154

O
OECD, 21, 73–4, 187
older workers, 75
age-related needs, 91
employers' stereotypical views,
87–8

flexible working opportunities, 88
healthy life and disability-free life
expectancy, 89
in nursing and midwifery
profession (*see* (nursing and
midwifery profession, older
workers))
older workers and extending working
lives, debates
choosers, survivors and jugglers, 142
flexible working, 143
job satisfaction, 142
redesigning jobs and working
patterns, 143–4
'work ability,' concept of, 144
old 'seniority retirement', 127
Oxford City Council, case of
Council's Direct Services
workforce, 264
gender and role composition, 268
job, physical demands, 267
Living Wage Employer, 263
mandatory retirement, workplace
management, 265–6
part-time employment, 266–7
performance management, 267

P
paid work, 142, 149–50, 157, 187,
190, 193–6, 206–8, 230
low, 51, 68, 70
unpaid, 108, 204, 206, 208, 230,
234, 237, 242, 245, 252
participants' narratives
complexity of career trajectories,
214
contribution to society, 220
dominant narratives, 216–18, 219

participants' narratives (*cont.*)
  'employee mentality', 221
  first jobs as accidents, 214
  new initiatives and technologies, 220
  'not a career' labelling, 214–15
  participants' assessment, 219
  potential, 225–7
  project management education, 221
  reassessment of value of different types of work, 219–20
  of renewal, 222–3
  of reorientation of sense of self, 224–5
  of seeking progression, 223
  sense of planning, 215
  systemic perspective on social change, 220–221
  of winding down, 223–4
  work flexibly, 215–16
part-time employment, 266–7
pension crisis
  1986 Act, 59
  contribution holidays, 60
  DB pension schemes, 59, 61–3
  DC schemes, 62–3
  dividend tax credit, 60
  final salary schemes, 58–9
  FRS17 accounting procedures, 62
  Lawson's tax cap, 60–61
  nature of artificial crisis, 59–60
  and retirement (*see* (retirement and pension crisis))
pension provision, UK
  BSP, 57
  conventional crisis, 57
  DB scheme, 57–8
  DC schemes, 57

employee retention rates, 56
  process of neoliberalisation, 56–7
  three tiered pension system, 64
performance-related pay, 25
Personal Development Record, 297
policy Delphi method
  face-to-face interviews, 162
  implementation scenarios, 164, 177–80
  new scenarios, 164, 176–7
  online surveys, 162–3
  repetition of scenarios, 164, 176
  response rate, 165
  reworded scenarios, 164, 174–6
  scenarios as 'straw models', 163–4
post-retirement activities
  adequate transition plans, 231
  career-oriented activities, 238–9
  concept of 'active aging', 251–2
  conceptualization of, 236–8
  context of self-employment, 237
  developed countries' pension systems, 232
  healthy life expectancy, 252
  high labor demand, 238
  individual level factors, 239–40
  job characteristics, 241
  non-career-oriented activities, 239
  organizational level factors, 240–241
  paid or unpaid work activities report, 234, 237
  qualitative-quantitative approach, 235–6, 250–251
  rate of work satisfaction, 234–5
  retirees' former professional jobs, 250

post-retirement activities (*cont.*)
  retirement eligibility age, 233
  shortage of skilled workers, 233
  silver work, 237
  traditional retirement age, 233–4
  value of working retirees, 252–3
  work-related activities, 236
public sector pensions, 139–40

Q

qualitative approach
  allocation of time, 242–3
  comparability, 243
  content of task and demands, 243–4
  extent of freedom, 242
  perceived responsibility, 244
quantitative approach
  correlation of results, 247, 248
  factor analysis, 245–6, 248, 249
  former professional job and post-retirement activity, comparison, 244
  item statistics comparison, 245
  job-related factor scores, 247, 249
  person-related variables, 245–6, 249
  Senior Experts Service, 245

R

Regular Forces Employment (RFEA), 295
'reintegration forums', 282
reinvention in retirement
  activities, 193–4
  barriers, 196–7
  reasons, 194–6
  respondents' expectations, 192

repetition of scenarios, 176
resettlement to transition
  CLM, 294
  'end of career', 291
  finance and employment, 292
  financial awareness, 294
  functional skills, 293–4
  'Help to Buy' scheme, 295
  long-term planning, 291
  military career and life post-service, 292–3
  'through career' transition, 293
  value of education, 294
  'whole career' approach, 292
retirement age, Italy
  active ageing policies, 119
  Commission v. Italy, CJEU, 119–20
  EU Employment Guidelines, 120
  financial sustainability of pension system, 119
retirement age, UK
  ACAS, 273
  age discrimination, 86–7
  2006 AGE Regulations, 270
  CJEU and UK Supreme Court, 275
  DRA, 269, 270
  EJRA, 269, 273–4
  fixed-term contracts, 272
  informal and formal processes, 85
  legally mandated general fixed retirement age, 271
  mandatory retirement rules, 87
  protected conversations, 85
  'request to remain' procedure, 275
  retirement policies post-2011, 274
  service-related benefits, 272

retirement age, UK (*cont.*)
  State Pension Age, 271
  termination of employment, 85
  use of performance management
      practices, 86
retirement and pension crisis
  dominance of neoliberal ideology,
      52
  economic compulsion, 68
  financial security, 50
  flexible working practices, 49–51
  labour market past traditional
      retirement ages, 52
  longer working lives, 68–9
  neoliberal ideology and discourse,
      53–63
  new policy changes, 63–8
reworded scenarios
  national dialogue, 175–6
  positive duty, 174–5
'RightJob database', 295
Rolls Royce Plant in Goodwood, 257

S

'Save Italy Decree', 119
scenarios, Delphi method
  ageing for labour law, 170–171,
      182
  age management approach,
      168–9, 177–9, 180
  decision-making on equality
      matters, 173
  employment equality, 172–3
  flexible working arrangements,
      169–70
  implementation (*see*
      (implementation scenarios))
  leadership, 171, 181

national dialogue, 171, 175–6
new (*see* (new scenarios))
repetition (*see* (repetition of
      scenarios))
results, 173–4, 181
reworded (*see* (reworded
      scenarios))
work ability strategy, by individual
      workplaces, 167–8
senior clinical managers' perceptions
  childcare commitments, 153
  employment, advantages and
      disadvantages, 151–3
  McNair's choosers, survivors and
      jugglers, 156–7
  nurses and midwives, 150, 151,
      156
  resurgence, 151
  technology in workplace, 154
Senior Experts Service, 245, 253
seniority pay schemes, 24–5
'Senior @ Work', 135–6
settlement agreements and
      performance management,
      use of, 71–2
social security schemes, 232
'socioemotional skills', 26
state pension age (SPA), 49, 51, 73,
      140, 141
Swedish Labour Court, 111
Swedish labour law, 110–111, 114

T

TAEN. *See* The Age and
      Employment Network
      (TAEN)
The Age and Employment Network
      (TAEN), 169, 182

'through career' transition, 293, 298
'through-life' transition, 297
'Today for Tomorrow' programme,
    257–8, 262, 282
Trades Union Congress (TUC)
    age discrimination legislation, 278
    Age Immaterial campaign, 283–4
    Age Regulations, 281
    campaigning against age
        discrimination, 277
    demand of jobs, 281–2
    employment rate, 278
    Fire Brigades Union, 282
    longer working life, expectation
        of, 283
    midlife career reviews, 284–5
    performance management, 281
    public policy, 284
    public service pension schemes,
        281
    removing method of dismissal,
        277–8
    rise in self-employment, 278
    'Today for Tomorrow'
        programme, 282
    ULRs, 283–4
transition, army to civilian life
    'all-volunteer' body, 290
    current resettlement provision,
        295–6
    employment policies, 290
    follow-up questionnaires, 297
    formal retirement, 287
    reputation of veterans in British
        society, 288–9
    resettlement to transition, 291–5
    'through-career' transition, 288
    UK Labour Force Survey,
        290–291

Treaty of Amsterdam, 103
Treaty of Rome, 102
TUC. *See* Trades Union Congress
    (TUC)

U

UK, challenges of active ageing
    'age/employment' paradox, 72–3
    forced retirement, 81
    intergenerational fairness, 73–5,
        76–7, 81
    justification of retirement, 79–7
    needs of older workers, 75, 87–9
    pension sustainability, 73
    removal of default retirement,
        80–81
    workplace and employers, 75–6,
        77
UK government's Department for
    Work and Pensions (DWP),
    197
UK legal framework
    2006 Age Regulations, 78
    employer's justified retirement
        age, 78
    Employment (Age) Regulations
        2006, 77
    justification of retirement,
        79–80
    non-enforceable Code of Practice
        on Age Diversity in
        Employment, 77
    workforce planning, 78
Union Learning Representatives
    (ULRs), 283–4
UNISON and Unite, 264
University Superannuation
    Scheme, 58

V

Value Added Production System
    (VPS), 257–8
'value for money' for
    taxpayers, 140

W

work and careers
    differences between participants'
        narratives, 221–5
    field research, 213–14
    narrative approaches, 210–213
    'older worker' category, 210
    participants' narratives, 214–19
    potential, 225–7
    retirement, 227–9
    socio-demographic characteristics,
        209–10, 213–14
workforce planning, 78, 92
working life and labour law
    ageist attitudes and presumptions,
        113

'double jeopardy', 109–10
employers' perceptions of older
    workers, 109
gendered ageism, 114
gender inequalities, 108
intersectionality, 113–14
prohibition against
    discrimination, 111–12
sex discrimination, 108
Swedish labour law, 110–111
Working Longer Group (WLG),
    141, 157
work life discrimination, EU law
    CJEU case law, 107
    direct and indirect discrimination,
        103–4
    employment policies, 107
    lack of intersectional perspective,
        105–6
    multiple discrimination, 104–5
    non-discrimination law, 106–7
    promotion of gender equality, 102
    sex discrimination, 103

Printed by Books on Demand, Germany